CRITIQUE OF LATIN AMERICAN REASON

CRITIQUE OF LATIN AMERICAN REASON

SANTIAGO CASTRO-GÓMEZ

TRANSLATED BY ANDREW ASCHERL

FOREWORD BY LINDA MARTÍN ALCOFF

INTRODUCTION BY EDUARDO MENDIETA

Columbia University Press

New York

Published through a grant from the Andrew W. Mellon Foundation

Columbia University Press
Publishers Since 1893
New York Chichester, West Sussex
cup.columbia.edu

Library of Congress Cataloging-in-Publication Data
Names: Castro-Gómez, Santiago, 1958– author. | Ascherl, Andrew, translator.
Title: Critique of Latin American reason / Santiago Castro-Gómez ;
translated by Andrew Ascherl.
Other titles: Crítica de la razón latinoamericana. English
Description: [New York] : [Columbia University Press], [2021] |
Includes bibliographical references and index.
Identifiers: LCCN 2020052130 (print) | LCCN 2020052131 (ebook) |
ISBN 9780231200066 (hardback) | ISBN 9780231200073 (trade paperback) |
ISBN 9780231553414 (ebook)
Subjects: LCSH: Philosophy, Latin American.
Classification: LCC B1001 .C3813 2021 (print) | LCC B1001 (ebook) |
DDC 199/.8—dc23
LC record available at https://lccn.loc.gov/2020052130
LC ebook record available at https://lccn.loc.gov/2020052131

Cover design: Lisa Hamm
Cover image: Shutterstock

CONTENTS

FOREWORD

A Principled Pessimist of the Left—Castro-Gómez's *Critique of Latin American Reason*

LINDA MARTÍN ALCOFF

Providing rich opportunities for transnational conversation, Santiago Castro-Gómez's *Critique of Latin American Reason* has finally, very belatedly, been translated for English speaking audiences. For anyone addressing the very general questions of critical theory, of liberation, and of philosophy's relation to history and its social context, this text is irreplaceable. The current discussions about the relationship between colonialism, Eurocentrism, and the European critical theory tradition cannot be advanced without attention to Castro-Gómez's capacious analysis and original critical interventions. This engagement is long overdue.

The challenge of Castro-Gómez's work for the Anglo-European philosophical community lies in its thorough embeddedness within Latin American philosophy. He does not, as Walter Mignolo does in the main, write books intended to provide strategic interventions in North American or European debates. For those unfamiliar with Latin American philosophy, this will be a challenge. It is also the book's strength—given Castro-Gómez's extensive and insightful summaries of the traditions and debates in Latin America, new readers to this tradition will learn a tremendous amount from reading just this single book. This is what makes the English translation all the more of an important intervention. Since Castro-Gómez's interventions are centrally aimed at the Latin American critical intellectual scene, this book operates to shift the center and to realign the central topics of debate, a much more effective way to defeat Eurocentrism than simply turning away from or vilifying all European texts, which Castro-Gómez rightfully refuses to do.

When it was published in 1995, the *Critique of Latin American Reason*'s central intervention in Latin America was to create a left pole or a new kind of left position that articulated a certain pessimism (or skepticism) toward the dominant anticolonial left. His was the most well worked through and thoroughly argued version of this left pole. Since 1995, a larger grouping has emerged that includes left critics of Hugo Chávez in Venezuela such as Fernando Coronil, left critiques of Evo Morales in Bolivia in the work of Silvia Rivera Cusicanqui and Catherine Walsh, left critics of Lula da Silva in Brazil, and others. Their many differences notwithstanding, this group have shared a worry about re-creations of old forms of socialism based on unreconstructed and overly unified ideas about "the poor" or "the people" that legitimate exclusionary binaries and authoritarian practices. This clearly was a motivation for Santiago's critique as well, given his championing of the concept of dissensus and rejection of all metanarratives within which social movements could be judged, as if from above. Equally anti-imperialist and decolonial, this group of critics—or left pessimists—offer different notions of liberation or of the way forward. Mignolo and Román de la Campa's own criticisms of Latin Americanism would belong to this camp as well.

So although this book must be understood in relation to a very different time and place, its relevance has if anything increased as we try to navigate new political formations in the twenty-first century. It should be stressed that the book's contextualization to Latin American philosophical debates does not restrict its relevance to the continent. It is also essential reading for revised understandings of Anglo-European critical philosophy. Castro-Gómez engages fraught debates concerning how to understand the situatedness of philosophy (a debate that has lasted centuries) and real battles about how to conceptualize liberation. Going far beyond either Marxism or liberalism, these Latin American debates should, in their nonuniversal register, be instructive of the limitations of the Anglo-European intellectual horizon. In my historical metanarrative, Latin America is way ahead in offering positional understandings of philosophy and shares this with African theorists such as Kwame

Nkrumah, Amílcar Cabral, Frantz Fanon, and others. Castro-Gómez's critical analysis of the various arguments within this trend does not return philosophy to its transcendental space. This 1995 book contests the way in which contextualization was itself understood in relation to its site of enunciation, rendering Latin American thought an object of knowledge. In this, his work is an invaluable push for all of us on the left to think more deeply.

This is not to say, of course, that the analysis can be accepted as is. As we know, the Santiago of 2020 is not the Santiago of 1995, as new translations in the works (including *Zero-Point Hubris*) will reveal. Critical questions have been posed to *Critique of Latin American Reason* by an array of brilliant young thinkers on the question of identity in general and of race in particular. (Santiago has to be happy with the quality and the amount of dissensus his book has already generated.) Barnor Hesse, for example, has observed that the extensive debates over populism summarized in this book entirely neglect the crucial issue of the racialized basis of such popular appeals. I share these concerns, but I would encourage readers to read this text in the context of its locus of enunciation, its time and space. So often we pore through works exhibiting similar lacunae for some glimmer of relevant analysis, straining to find something in work by Michel Foucault or Gilles Deleuze (or, for that matter, Judith Butler or Wendy Brown) more adequate to a thinking of race or analogous to race. In this effort, we often sidestep missteps, reading generously, concentrating on what is useful.

Like more recent decolonial theorists, Castro-Gómez warns us to be wary of metanarratives that can—unwittingly in some cases, purposefully in others—derail dialogue, condemn dissensus, and obscure certain kinds of voices. Importantly, many of the most marginalized voices speak a more local tongue, rejecting the need to situate their claims within a legitimated meta-account that espouses mastery over the whole. Herein lies, I suggest, the key to Castro-Gómez's politics, a pessimism toward projects of mastery, an optimism toward the many forms of resistance that continue to exceed the predictions of the mapmakers.

TRANSLATOR'S NOTE

A number of the citations in the original Spanish edition of this book refer to texts originally published in languages other than Spanish. I have endeavored in all of these instances to use published English translations (or the original English text as the case may be). All translations of Spanish language sources for which no published English translation is available are my own. Any explanatory endnotes that I have added to this translation are signed "—TRANS."

PREFACE

Critique of Latin American Reason is a book I wrote twenty-five years ago that reflects my impressions of and experiences in a world very different from the one we live in today. A world in which the Internet, where social networks as we know them did not yet exist, had just started to take shape. A world in which the two great geopolitical blocks associated with the Soviet Union and the United States struggled for global hegemony. Latin America was a crucial zone of that struggle, and a broad segment of the left hoped that the region would become a stronghold for socialism and a bulwark against capitalism. It was a world full of "morbid symptoms," as Antonio Gramsci said, in which the new was visible on the horizon, but the old refused to die. Protest music and Cuban nueva trova coexisted with Rock en español. Dependency theory and liberation theology coexisted with cultural studies and debates on postmodernity. And the impoverished masses coexisted with an emerging urban middle class symbolically connected to a world that became increasingly globalized by mass media. I spent my adolescence in this zombie world, into which my country was rapidly transforming. I was introduced to television when I was twelve years old, on the occasion of the moon landing in 1969, and from that point on I was a fan of North American canned goods and science programs. In the 1970s I studied with Spanish priests at a small school in the Bogotá neighborhood of Chapinero, and several of my teachers sympathized with liberation theology. Some of the older kids in the neighborhood joined the urban guerrilla movement M-19, believing that socialism was just around the corner. But the truth is that almost all of my friends were afraid, because Colombia was becoming more and more besieged by the drug-trafficking mafias that, in alliance with sections of the political right, terrorized the country with bombs and wanted nothing to do with socialism. I wasn't able to understand it at the time, but a new country was being born, one that was completely unknown up to that point in time.

It was in the midst of all this that I began my studies in philosophy at the Universidad Santo Tomás in the early 1980s. The Dominican priests who were the regents of the university had made political commitment to Latin American reality their official aim. Along with seminars on Immanuel Kant, Aristotle, and G. W. F. Hegel, I attended seminars dedicated to the work of unknown thinkers like Arturo Andrés Roig, Enrique Dussel, and Leopoldo Zea. The Bogotá Group, a name given to the professors I studied with at Santo Tomás, enthusiastically welcomed the project of Latin American philosophy. However, at that time no distinction was made between the two primary tendencies of this project, historicism and liberationism, which were instead seen as complementary or even identical to one another. I became enthusiastic about the history of ideas and the possibility of philosophically re-creating Latin America's intellectual past, but I had many problems with the philosophy of liberation, with its heavy messianic and populist influences. I did not identify with the idea that Latin America was a "cultural unity" that must be understood as existing outside the parameters developed by modern philosophy. Perhaps it was due to my rebellion against this that I decided to write my thesis on the epistemology of John Locke. Moreover, my comrades from the university and I were beginning to discover the debate on postmodernity, which at that time was most famously connected to the work of Jean-François Lyotard, Jürgen Habermas, and Gianni Vattimo. One of the central professors of the Bogotá Group, Roberto Salazar Ramos (who would eventually direct my thesis), understood that this debate could shed some light on how we might rethink the project of Latin American philosophy, as, at the time, he was involved in a crisis within the group. Thus it was with Roberto, and against the backdrop of a crisis threatening to dissolve the Bogotá Group, that I first read some of Michel Foucault's writings.

In the midst of all this, having recently completed my bachelor's thesis, I decided to apply to study in Germany. It was 1986, and my prospects of finding work with a bachelor's degree in philosophy were very slim. But the truth is that I wanted to escape from the onerous atmosphere in Colombia and see the world—I wanted to open myself to new experiences, learn another language, and continue to study philosophy. I was interested in the Frankfurt School because while at university I read several works by Herbert Marcuse, but I was also eager to deepen the discussion of postmodernity that was at that time being led by Habermas. Germany seemed to be the best place to go. I wrote to a professor at the University of Tübingen to express my interest in pursuing this line of study there and, to my surprise, just a short while later I received an affirmative response. The process for obtaining a student visa was easy enough; a few months later, in April 1987, I boarded an airplane headed for Germany. I could never have imagined that while I was there I would witness the fall of the Berlin Wall, an experience that made clear to me what I had not understood back in Colombia: an old world was collapsing and another new one was emerging in its place. From that moment on, I was no longer afraid of monsters and I became interested in a series of theoretical debates that were virtually unknown in Colombia: cultural studies, postcolonial theory, deconstruction, contemporary political philosophy. Specifically, in the field of philosophy, I was drawn to authors like Friedrich Nietzsche and Foucault, but I also began to acquire a familiarity with the theory of reason developed by Habermas.

I believe that everything I have just written constitutes the ingredients that would come together to make up the book you have before you: *Critique of Latin American Reason*. The uncertainty I felt in Colombia, the seminars on Latin American philosophy I attended at Santo Tomás, the fall of the Berlin Wall, the debate between Habermas and the postmodernists, the emergence of postcolonial theory, and my readings of Foucault—all these things were swimming around together in my head without ever synthesizing. The opportunity to reflect on them arrived when, one morning in the library at the University of Tübingen, I saw an announcement that the Barcelona-based publishing house Editorial Puvill was sponsoring a contest for essays about Latin America. Although I had not even finished my master's degree in philosophy, I figured I had nothing to lose, so for three months (the summer of 1995) I diligently sat down and wrote the five chapters that originally made up the book.

The first surprise was that my book was selected for publication. The second was that, once the first edition was published in 1996, criticism of it began to appear. I wasn't really expecting this, since I figured the book would hardly be noticed, given all the other academic texts being published. Despite what I expected, several reviews of the book emerged in various countries, and the majority of them expressed discomfort about "mixing" Latin America into the debate on postmodernity, which, I suppose, was for them a "European" debate that had absolutely nothing to do with "we Latin Americans." But that was precisely the point of the book! What I sought to do with it was "disrupt" that sector of the philosophical left in Latin America that was entrenched behind the region's supposed "exteriority" to the modern Western world. This was an intellectual tendency that continued to insist on ideas such as a romanticized notion of the people, the moral perfection of the Indigenous world, and the "telluric" and "Dionysian" condition of popular culture, all of which were diametrically opposed to the odious European world governed by reason and science. I was left with the impression that such a representational strategy was nothing other than a colonial discourse that was paradoxically uttered by intellectuals who claimed to want to defend the interests of the oppressed—in whom they had entrusted their hopes for "redemption." Ever since my days at Universidad Santo Tomás, I had been mistrustful of this literary exaltation of the people as the "subject of philosophy," endowed with a special kind of "wisdom" based solely in the fact that they are poor. This was the moralist discourse of the philosophy and theology of liberation, which saw "Christ's image" in the poor, interpellating us and moving us to transformative action.

As you can imagine, my criticisms of this discourse were not well received. The book was dismissed as "Eurocentric" for making use of the debate on postmodernity in a discussion of Latin America. It was also derided as "reactionary" for daring to criticize figures who were considered irreproachable by the Latin American philosophical left. However, what was not properly recognized at the time was that I did not make my criticisms simply by invoking the authority of European philosophers but rather by entering into a dialogue with new Latin American cultural theory. Authors like Nelly Richard, Néstor García Canclini, José Joaquín Brunner, Renato Ortiz, and Jesús Martín Barbero were reassessing some of the assumptions that had been used for decades to think Latin

America, especially those of Marxist sociology. The postmodernity debate had given them plenty of ammunition for a similar critique. In the same way, postcolonial theories destabilized the old assumptions of the critique of imperialism and introduced new elements beyond strictly economic and sociological variables. It is true that the book makes frequent use of Foucault's theory of power (which I was reproached for right away), but it does so in dialogue with readings of Foucault by two non-European theorists: the Uruguayan Ángel Rama (in his book *The Lettered City*) and the Egyptian Edward Said (in his book *Orientalism*). Both proved to be central to my argument, as they allowed me to understand how to "use" Foucault beyond Foucault himself.

Curiously, and in spite of the bitter criticisms I received at the time, the book became for me a central element that ended up defining my entire professional life. The publication of *Critique of Latin American Reason* and the much-talked-about debate it gave rise to in different intellectual circles led the Universidad Javeriana in Bogotá to take an interest in my work. On my return to Colombia after having completed my master's work in Germany, the university hired me to develop the research program set out in the book. At the Instituto Pensar at Javeriana, I attempted to fulfill this program, which was given the title "Genealogies of Colombianness." The conceptual horizon opened up by *Critique of Latin American Reason* allowed me to write my books *La hybris del punto cero* (2005; *Zero-Point Hubris: Science, Race, and Enlightenment in New Granada (1750–1816)*, forthcoming) and *Tejidos oníricos* (2009). Today I see these three books as a "trilogy" that makes use of Foucauldian genealogy to rethink the colonial inheritances of Latin America, especially those of my country, Colombia. In short, *Critique of Latin American Reason* was a true event in my life; it was the book that changed everything.

I have had to take this detour in order to explain why *Critique of Latin American Reason* should be understood as a "book of its time." This era in which it was first published was, as I am sure you can understand, very different (both geopolitically and philosophically) from our contemporary era, nearly three decades later. But it must also be understood as a "youthful" book written by a thirty-five-year-old philosophy student who suddenly had the opportunity to write an untimely text. However, I am not interested in providing a retrospective reading of the book;

rather, I would like to go over some of the central themes that run through it. The first and undoubtedly most important is the critique of Latin Americanism. With this notion I am referring to all those discourses or families of discourses that create an object of knowledge called "Latin America" and generate a "truth" about this object. Of course, I am not saying that Latin America "does not exist," or that it is an "illusion." What I am doing is questioning a certain mode of the narrative existence of Latin America as a cultural unity located outside of and antagonistic to modernity, with this latter understood as a geopolitical and cultural unity marked by technological and scientific rationality, colonialism, and the will to power. The construction of Latin America as a unitary, collective "We" therefore entails the construction of an "Other," also unitary, who is seen as an obstacle to achieving "liberation."

The book attempts to trace the genealogy of this kind of identitarian discourse and explores this genealogy in different registers: the Catholic sociology of culture in chapter 2, the history of ideas in chapter 3, literary modernism in chapter 5, postcolonial semiotics in chapter 6, and Latin American philosophy in chapter 7. My thesis is that this kind of narrative construction exemplifies the colonial motif of Othering, in which the Indigenous world, savage nature, impoverished peoples, *mestizaje,* or popular religiosity appear as radical alternatives to a modern, capitalist, imperial Europe that encroaches from outside. In short, the book argues that, just as Orientalism constructs the "Orient" as an exotic object that is external to Europe, Latin Americanism constructs "Latin America" in the same way. Except in this case the exoticizing discourses are not propagated by nineteenth-century European travelers, but rather by twentieth-century Latin American intellectuals. Latin America is nostalgically represented as a world outside the globalizing reach of technology, global symbolic markets, and deterritorialized mass culture, none of which reflect the "soul of the people" but are instead seen as simple expressions of "cultural colonialism." This hypothesis was already being challenged at the time, empirically by communication studies (Martín-Barbero) and by the new cultural studies (García Canclini, Brunner, Ortiz). *Critique of Latin American Reason* criticizes the construction of a "Latin American identity" that ignores the creative appropriation of (now outdated) technologies by broad segments of the population that destabilized the borders between high culture and popular culture. While one group of intellectuals continued to see modernity as the expression of a "reifying rationality," many people took advantage of the new market for symbolic goods that emerged in the 1980s in order to both "enter and exit modernity."

From a methodological point of view, the book takes on the mode of "critique" developed by Foucault, for whom critique must be above all else genealogical; it must show the historicity of the forms of power, denaturalize their absolute pretensions, and expose their techniques and their complicity with the production of certain "truth effects." All of this was extremely useful for me in my efforts to show how Latin America (or at least a specific narrative about it) was the product of the intersections between certain mechanisms of power and certain academic discourses. The purpose of the book was to trace the genealogy of these intersections, to examine how a supposed "Latin American reason" is produced out of and against a homogeneous and totalizing entity called "modernity." This should be the critical gesture of philosophy. Instead of presupposing a transcendental entity called "Latin America" and on that basis constructing a series of categories appropriate to that entity, philosophy should begin by doing away with this presupposition. Is this not precisely the inaugural gesture of *Kritik?* This book attempts to show that when we speak philosophically of Latin America we are not referring to a "thing in itself" but rather to a historically constructed meaning. The central purpose of the book is to reconstruct this construction through genealogical critique.

I would like to conclude this brief "author's note" by reflecting on what elements of this book written twenty-five years ago still remain with me today. Twenty-five years really is a long time, and philosophical reflection (at least as I understand it) is always changing and exploring new paths. It is true that one book leads to another, but new problems always appear, as do new theoretical challenges. I do not understand philosophy as the construction of a "system," or as the elaboration of a "conceptual architectonic," but rather as a practice of permanent experimentation. *Critique of Latin American Reason* is the beginning of a long philosophical road on which many of the problems that preoccupied me at the time were slowly losing their grip on my attention. However, at the same time, some of the problems I addressed in the book are still present today. One of these is the issue of politics. Although *Critique of Latin American Reason* does take up the question of democracy at certain points (let us recall that at the time the Southern Cone was just emerging out of a series of ferocious military dictatorships), the book does not offer any kind of systematic reflection on the matter. Very much in line with Foucault, the book focuses on exploring the mutual relations between power and truth, but it does not ask whether democratic politics contains an internal "excess" with regard to the exercise of power—which is to say, whether or not there are any normative criteria we can refer to in order to justify this exercise of power. My book *Revoluciones sin sujeto* (2015) reflects on this complicated problem by entering into dialogue with political philosophers like Enrique Dussel and Ernesto Laclau. Another line of thought opened up by *Critique of Latin American Reason* that remains a central focus of my work is the attempt to rethink the historicist tradition of Ortega, Gaos, and Zea—the so-called history of ideas. Only now I do not use the genealogy of power as a method; rather I have come closer to the approach of intellectual history developed in Latin America by thinkers like Elías Palti. I am interested in knowing how certain "conceptual regimes" emerged at specific moments in history and how they operated as an "epochal condition of thought." This is the task I have set out to accomplish in the book I am currently completing on the political thought of Left Hegelianism in Germany between 1835 and 1846. It is not a "history of ideas" of the young Marx, but rather a conceptual genealogy that examines the discursive universe of the Young Hegelians.

Nevertheless, in spite of it having been published twenty-five years ago, *Critique of Latin American Reason* continues to be a contemporary work, particularly because of the antimodern turn that certain currents of decolonial thought have taken. There are more than a few decolonial thinkers who see modernity as identical to capitalism and colonialism, assigning to it responsibility for all the misfortunes suffered by the Indigenous and Afro-descendant populations of the Americas—populations that these thinkers in turn situate in a kind of "epistemic exteriority" with regard to modernity. It appears that some decolonial theorists are repeating the same gesture toward radical exteriority that I criticized in my book in 1995. This gesture has motivated me once again to offer a critique of it in my most recent book, *El tonto y los canallas* (2018).

ACKNOWLEDGMENTS

Santiago Castro-Gómez thanks colleagues of the Critical Theory Cluster at Northwestern University and its Critical Theory in the Global South programming (supported through funding from the Andrew W. Mellon Foundation to the International Consortium of Critical Theory Programs in the form of generous grants to University of California, Berkeley, and to Northwestern University) for their enthusiastic cooperation in realizing this translation. The Northwestern group was grateful for the opportunity to work again with translator Andrew Ascherl. He has realized a superb translation of *Crítica de la razón Latinoamericana*. The translation along with the prepublication forum were funded by the Andrew W. Mellon Foundation. We thank Judith Butler, without whom this funding and the extraordinary breadth of ventures funded by the ICCTP through her continuing initiatives would not have been possible. We thank Breana George for her solidarity, tireless contributions, and cooperative spirit. This publication was also made possible through the vigorous support of Wendy Lochner at Columbia University Press. Rocío Zambrana (Emory University) and María del Rosario Acosta Lopez (University of California, Riverside) were invaluable to its realization and an ongoing source of advice and suggestions about important interlocutors. We are particularly grateful for the willingness of all those who have worked on this initiative to accommodate its tight timeframe. We have greatly valued Tristan Bradshaw's impeccable attention to detail and his assistance with project management. We have welcomed this opportunity to work with him, along with Lowell Frye at Columbia University Press and Cintia Martínez Velasco (whose role in this project was made possible by the Andrew W. Mellon Foundation as part of a postdoctoral fellowship), who also provided linkage and a considerable intellectual contribution. Santiago Castro-Gómez thanks Penelope Deutscher and Siobhan LaGro for their organization of this translation, its publication and prepublication forum, all the latter's speakers and contributors (including graduate student leaders of cross-university discussion groups), and Columbia University Press for their support and interest.

PROLOGUE TO THE SECOND EDITION

Critique of Latin American Reason was written in Germany in the summer of 1995 and published the following year in Barcelona by Puvill. The contract stipulated that the book consist of a single edition that would exhaust its print run over the next couple of years. Since then, many people asked me to arrange for the book to be republished, but I wasn't sure I wanted to for a number of reasons. When I returned to Colombia in 1998, I lost interest in the topic of Latin American philosophy and began to work on issues related to postcolonial theory and cultural studies. I didn't see any need to republish a text written several years ago and at theoretical and personal junctures that I no longer felt were my own. This is not to mention the distance I had since taken from the avant-garde language I used in the book.

However, a couple of years ago I began to realize that my genealogical works on the history of Colombia covered some of the same themes already addressed in Latin American philosophy and that it might not be a bad idea to consider publishing a new edition of the book. The idea was fully embraced by the director of the Instituto Pensar and by Universidad Javeriana Press, and I began to work on the project in January of this year. In any event, as I began to reread these old lines, I felt the uncontrollable urge to "correct" my own arguments and eventually to rewrite the book entirely. It is not an easy thing to reissue a fifteen-year-old text. One feels the sensation of being estranged from oneself, of an almost instinctive rejection of the way things were said back then—things that today we would say in other ways.

I finally arrived at a sort of compromise: I would leave the structure of the book intact, as it appeared in its original version, and preserve its postmodern language. I would limit myself to correcting basic issues of style and spelling and introducing some citations and notes, but I also revised a few arguments that simply could not be left as they were written. This was the case particularly in chapters 5 and 6 as well as in some sections of chapter 4. I also wanted to include in this new edition a text written in 1999 that, although it is in a different tone, complements some of the arguments presented in the original six chapters of the book. Last, I decided to include as an appendix an extensive interview from 2011 in which I discuss in depth some of the topics that led me to write the book.

In the prologue to the 1996 edition I explained that the first time I heard of a "critique of Latin American reason" was when I was a philosophy student at the Universidad Santo Tomás de Bogotá in the early 1980s. It was Daniel Herrera Restrepo who, arguing from the perspective of phenomenology, stated that it was necessary to determine what constitutes the "specificity of reason" in Latin America without undermining the "universal" character that philosophy should have. What must be clarified, according to Herrera, is how the concept of reason can be "expanded" through a phenomenological analysis that demonstrates the peculiarities of our "lifeworld." The philosophical task of a critique of Latin American reason would therefore be "to elaborate the categories proper to this reason, understanding by categories those principles that make our being and our world intelligible and which at the same time express the ultimate constituents of that being and that world" (Herrera, "El futuro de la filosofía en Colombia" 457). Even so, the program formulated by Herrera was critiqued in the same era by Roberto Salazar Ramos, a member of the Bogotá Group, who, via Foucault, reformulates it as follows: the romantic project of a "phenomenology of Latin American reason" should be abandoned and replaced by an alternative project, that of an "archaeology of Latin American reason." It was no longer a matter of conceptualizing the "deep structures" in the world of an authentically Latin American life, but rather of demonstrating the practices and apparatuses through which a series of discourses on Latin America and the Latin American has been constructed (Salazar Ramos, "Los grandes metarrelatos en la interpretación de la historia latinoamericana" 92). The critique of Latin American reason thus becomes an archaeology of Latin Americanism.

My purpose in the book was therefore to follow that path indicated by Roberto Salazar Ramos's work. Using Foucault's archaeological and genealogical methods, I critically examined the family of discourses that made it possible to create an entity called "Latin America," endowed with an ethos and a cultural identity that supposedly distinguish it from modern European rationality. In this sense, the book bears a certain similarity to Edward Said's famous *Orientalism*. In the same way that the Palestinian theorist examines the way in which knowledges like Egyptology and linguistics produce a colonial image of the Orient, I was also interested in the way in which a particular knowledge—philosophy—constructs a colonial image of Latin America, with one noticeable difference: while Said sketches out his genealogy of orientalism with an eye toward exogenous practices (constructed and based in imperial metropoles), I wanted to delineate the genealogy of Latin Americanism through endogenous practices. I was no longer interested in "external colonialism," that is to say, the way Europeans have represented the inhabitants of their colonies, but rather the way in which Latin American intellectuals themselves have represented life on this continent through a kind of "colonial gesture": exoticism. I'm referring here to the postulation of Latin America as "the other of modernity."

Like Said with regard to Orientalism, I believe that Latin Americanism does not consist only of inoffensive discourses whose circulation is limited to intellectual elites, but that it is also a political praxis whose consequences the book analyzes through a consideration of two registers in particular: nationalism and populism. It seems that Latin Americanism has always been the perfect fit for those political proposals that focus on the demand for the "proper," the identification of the will of the people with justice and morality, the tendency to blame imperialism for all our ills, the portrayal of the caudillo as the leader of the masses, etc.—political tendencies we hoped were left behind in the era when the book was written that have tragically returned to Latin America in recent years. Perhaps this is also a good reason for it to be republished.

The new edition of this book coincides with a renewal of my interest in the tradition of "Latin American philosophy" that I so vehemently criticized fifteen years ago. This does not signify a reversal of my criticisms, but rather a clarification of them, separating them from the postmodern language that it was necessary to take up at that time and place. My impression is that the members of the Bogotá Group did not distinguish clearly enough between the two traditions of Latin American philosophy that developed in the last century: historicism and liberationism.[1] Historicism, which can be traced back to José Ortega y Gasset through the influence of José Gaos in Mexico in the 1940s, leads finally to the project of the "history of ideas" disseminated by Leopoldo Zea between the 1950s and 1970s. Liberationism, in contrast, is a current that emerged alongside Marxism in the 1960s with the critical writings of Augusto Salazar Bondy and which found in Argentina its point of convergence with the writings of Enrique Dussel, Juan Carlos Scannone, Mario Casalla, Oswaldo Ardiles, Horacio Cerutti, and others. Of course, there were intersections between the two traditions (the "Declaration of Morelia" and the famous debate between Zea and Salazar Bondy), but the Bogotá Group tended to subsume the two under a single label: "Latin American philosophy of liberation."

My work during these last several years has consisted of clearly separating these two lines and trying to connect the tradition of historicism with the archaeological and genealogical thought of Michel Foucault, which of course presupposes a profound rearticulation of the history of ideas. Looking at things in retrospect, I would say that the movement from a "history of ideas" to a "localized history of practices" as an expression of critical thought in Colombia is the line of work I have followed in my two books *La hybris del punto cero* (The hubris of the zero point [2005]) and *Tejidos oníricos* (Oneiric constitutions [2009]), and it is also the perspective of the research group I am currently part of, Philosophical Histories and Historiographies in Colombia.

Bogotá, May 16, 2011

INTRODUCTION

The Othering of Latin America and the Critique of the Critique of Colonial Reason

EDUARDO MENDIETA

Great philosophy books are like time machines, timely and timeless. They teleport us to a space-time in which history was caught in thought, briefly. They allow us to zoom out and in, to see their context from still further space-times, including our own. Santiago Castro-Gomez's *Critique of Latin American Reason* time-travels 120 years of ideas, debates, currents, and great thinkers who shaped the development of Latin American thinking. It is also one of the most subtle, deep, suggestive, and challenging analyses of the discourses of alterity and difference that have been articulated from and about Latin America. Marked by, but transcending, the period of its writing, this book is a classic of Latin American thinking. Scrutinizing a series of intense debates from the early part of the century, then turning to the decades of the sixties, seventies, eighties, and nineties, it maintains its gaze on the longue durée of Latin American thinking. This expanded and revised edition, wonderfully translated by Andrew Ascherl, now strikes me as more than a masterful study of the debates and transformation of philosophy and theory in Latin America. It is also a fascinating look at thinking done in Spanish in the twentieth century. The last chapter extends the scope of this book from Latin America to the Spanish and Portuguese speaking worlds. It is thus a cosmopolitan and ecumenical history that reveals the earliest developments of what became the influential philosophical movements of the twentieth century:

phenomenology, existentialism, ontological hermeneutics, poststructuralism, deconstruction, psychoanalysis, and postcolonial theory.

Critique of Latin American Reason masterfully combines methods and approaches: it is in part a history of ideas; it is also the exemplification of what can be called "immanent critique"; it is a polemic; above all, it is a "genealogy" of the discursive practices around "Latin America" in Latin America itself. Indeed, Castro-Gómez's *Critique* is both an archeology and a genealogy, or, better yet, an archeological genealogy. More than that, using Colin Koopman's useful typology of genealogies (subversive, vindicatory, and problematizing), we can see how the *Critique of Latin American Reason* is at the same time a subversive, vindicatory, and problematizing archeological genealogy of the discourses of altericization or othering that have undergirded those regarding the difference and alterity of Latin America, what Rodolfo Kusch calls "América Profunda." To the processes of making "Other" of the "other" there belongs a certain logic, a certain reason, in fact.

One of the accomplishments of this book is to have developed a critique of this logic, of this reason, of its ratio, as it has been articulated in Latin America over the last century. Its unity is held together by the term *critique* in the title, which is meant in a triple sense: Kantian, Dilthenian, and Foucauldian. As he makes explicit in the informative interview with Hernán Cortes included as an appendix, Castro-Gómez is interested in the "rational" conditions of possibility of an array of pronouncements by Latin American philosophers about the epistemic and hermeneutic privilege of the poor, the historical priority of the *pueblo,* the sui generis and singular character of the Latin American historical experience, and so on. At the same time, Castro-Gómez is clearly interested in the historical evolution of these theoretical pronouncements because, although some were formulated as ontological claims, or affirmations about the historicity of reason itself, a historiography that makes their evolution evident corresponds to them. The seventh chapter is a fascinating account of this historiography.

The convergence of these two approaches results in the Foucauldian-flavored "critique" in the title. This critique asks how Latin American and Latin Americans were constituted in their historicity by these discourses. Critique, in this Foucauldian sense, is the archeological excavation of the discursive, historical, and institutional conditions of possibility of the discourses about the nature of the historical experience and alleged identity of Latin America. It concerns the historical ontology woven by "philosophical Latin Americanism." Here, the problematizing and subversive character of Castro-Gómez's archeological genealogy becomes most explicit. Therein also lies its highly charged polemical character. But, as an "archeological genealogy," this critique cannot but be undisciplined, undisciplining, and transdisciplinary. The debates and discourses engaged by *Critique of Latin American Reason* jump between different disciplines: sociology, political theory, cultural studies, literary studies, the multidisciplinary debate about modernity/postmodernity, and, of course, the philosophical debates about whether there is or can be a distinct and authentic Latin American philosophy. I would claim that this book is, in fact, a metaphilosophical reflection about philosophy in general and philosophy in Latin America more specifically. Thus it should be compared to Edward Said's *Orientalism* (1978), an inspiration averred by the author. It should also be compared to Gayatri Chakravorty Spivak's *A Critique of Postcolonial Reason* (1999), already anticipated in her paradigm-shifting "Can the Subaltern Speak?" (1994), a text that haunts Castro-Gómez's own book as much as Michel Foucault's *The Order of Things: An Archeology of the Human Sciences* (1970) haunts it. Another text to keep in mind when reading Castro-Gómez's book, while not evident at first blush, is Jürgen Habermas's *Philosophical Discourse of Modernity: Twelve Lectures* (1985), one that is for European philosophy what Castro-Gómez's is for the Latin American Philosophical Discourses on Coloniality/Modernity/Decoloniality. Since we are plunged in *medias res*, I first offer a synopsis of the chapters, then conclude with questions and critical observations concerning the book's argumentative reach and what I will call, appealing to Habermas's critique of Foucault, Castro-Gómez's crypto-normativism.

I

Critique of Latin American Reason opens with what has become the de rigueur point of reference for the debates about postmodernity and Latin America. While much has now been written about this debate within and outside Latin America, very few texts are as systematic and synoptic as this chapter. "Postmodernity's Challenges to Latin American Philosophy" begins with a discussion of thinkers within Latin America who rejected the movement and the designation of postmodernity, especially Franz Hinkelammert and Adolfo Sánchez Vásquez, who from Marxist positions challenged postmodernity's alleged ideological and practical consequences. The chapter then considers those who embraced the term *postmodern* as a way to make sense of Latin American reality. Those discussed include Néstor García Canclini, José Joaquín Brunner, Jesús Martín-Barbero, Beatriz Sarlo, Jean Franco, and Nelly Richard. These thinkers became part of the Latin American cultural studies movement, which can be characterized as a "left postmodernism" (of the type associated in the United States with journals such as *Social Text, Diacritics,* and *Critical Inquiry*). The chapter concludes with what can be called an exorcism and dissolution of four misrepresentations, misunderstandings, or clichés about postmodernity: that modernity has come to an end, that history has also come to an end, that the modern subject is dead, and that utopia has been totally exhausted. With respect to the first cliché, Castro-Gómez argues that postmodernity is the realization of, because it is part and parcel of, modernity, not a rupture with it. Postmodernity is but modernity's fulfillment. Castro-Gómez makes use of arguments from Zygmunt Bauman similar to those also found in Anthony Giddens, Christopher Lash, and Ulrich Beck, namely that modernity is above all the imperative of self-reflexivity, where postmodernity is merely the name for an exacerbated form of modern societies' self-reflexivity. The argument is that postmodernity is modernity raised to the second power.

With respect to the cliché that we have entered a posthistorical epoch (that history has come to an end), Castro-Gómez affirms against Francis Fukuyama, the name most immediately associated with this oxymoronic claim, that postmodernity is in fact the rediscovery and reappropriation of history through the very historicization of quotidian experience, what Henri Lefebvre called the critique of everyday life. (Incidentally, Fredric Jameson also makes this claim in his ruminations on social life during late capitalism and postmodernity.) In this way, Castro-Gómez argues that one can be a Marxist without rejecting postmodernity and postmodernism. Here, he takes recourse to microhistories to illustrate this rehistoricization of our social optics, which have been bewitched by the ideology of social progress. With respect to the cliché of the death of the subject, Castro-Gómez shows that the postmodern dismantling of the Cartesian-Kantian-Lockean subject does not leave us bereft of either a moral anchor or a moral compass. If we see postmodernity as a turn toward the economics of micropowers, we can recognize its ethical valences. In fact, whether against the absolutism of Western humanism or the ethical Manichaeism of some philosophies of liberation (and Castro-Gómez takes particular aim at Enrique Dussel's ethics of liberation), he identifies in the postmodern celebration of the decentered and dethroned ethical subject the possibility for new moral attitudes and ethical practices. Finally, with regard to the cliché that postmodernity signals the exhaustion of utopian thinking, the Colombian philosopher notes that postmodernity and postmodernism (as new forms of aesthetic practices and production) enabled new forms of sober utopian critiques grounded neither in the impossible eradication of alterity nor in the dogmatic affirmation of radical otherness. Postmodernism is a potentiation of what Ernst Bloch called the spirit of utopia. Whether its projections are utopian or dystopian, this spirit aims to open the future to our agency. Which differences are tolerable and necessary (or abhorrent and dehumanizing) is, in the end, the crux of the matter. Here, Castro-Gómez echoes Jean-François Lyotard's arguments in *The Postmodern Condition* (1984) and *Au Juste* (1979).

Chapter 2, "Modernity, Rationalization, and Cultural Identity in Latin America" focuses on the different ways in which theories of social and cultural modernization, as forms of social rationalization, have been both assimilated and rejected in Latin America. Here Castro-Gómez focuses on social theorists Pedro Morandé and Cristián Parker as exemplifying the kind of social discourse that conflates the affirmation of identity, de facto and de jure, with an antagonistic attitude toward modernity/postmodernity. Castro-Gómez makes explicit the dissolution of cultural identities that is endorsed by the authors he criticizes. For Morandé and Parker, the appropriate resources for countering and confronting modernity/postmodernity can only be identified by discerning the cultural unity and stability of Latin America as a lifeworld (*Lebenswelt*) and social unity.

But two philosophical sins are committed when a Latin American cultural unity is attributed with the resources to nourish communitarian values, socialization through rituals, face-to-face encounters, and the sense of a Latin American transcendental ethos. First, this retroactively reconstructs a homogeneous, alterity-excluding unified, cultural identity. Second, Max Weber, Talcott Parsons, and Jürgen Habermas are caricatured by Latin American thinkers, becoming straw men. These are sins of falsification and disfiguration. Pace Theodor Adorno and Max Horkheimer, it is simply not the case that modernization requires all human relations to be instrumentalized, all social interactions to be standardized, all religious values to be secularized, all ethics to dissolved into legality. Nor has modernization entailed a comprehensive colonization of the lifeworld by commodifying the mundane and existential. In fact, modernization has taken multiple routes. Plural modernities obey different imperatives and logics. Not all of them culminate in humanity's complete imprisonment in the iron prison of rationality bemoaned by Weber. Modernity has opened up different horizons of humanization, brought forth new values and new forms of enchantment and sacralization (such as the sacralization of human life and the sacredness of nature itself, evident in human rights discourses and the ecological movements of the last half-century). By the same token, Castro-Gómez also demonstrates that Latin American societies can be studied with the categories used to analyze semi-industrialized and semimodernized societies. Comparison with the previous century shows how Latin American societies have become urbanized, modernized, diversified, and highly literate. In fact, Castro-Gómez surveys debates from a period in which Latin America was undergoing an accelerated urbanization, proletarization, modernization, and cultural heterogenization. Latin America has ceased to be Macondoamerica and has instead turned into a Babelamerica, a land of cultural polyglotism and layered temporalities. To invoke any telluric and putatively autochthonous cultural identity is an anachronism, he argues, highly suspect and politically regressive.

Chapter 3, "Populism and Philosophy" (which can also be read as an *avant la lettre* commentary on our most recent decade), takes up these themes through the lens of its investigation into the philosopher's role in Latin American thought and societies. It stands in contrast to the dual role of the European philosopher (both public intellectual and *Wissenschaftler* or scientist) and also in contrast to the U.S. professional philosopher sequestered in the ivory tower. Latin American philosophers and intellectuals have tended to align themselves with political projects, to embody an assigned role of social conscience and critical voice. As Castro-Gómez underscores, the role of the philosopher and the intellectual in Latin America has followed closely the role of the caudillo in Latin American history. Where the caudillo was the people's voice and conscience, the philosopher and intellectual have assumed the roles of savior and messiah who dispense the gospel to *el pueblo*. Without pulling punches, he criticizes their having become the curators of museums of alterity, adjudicators or authenticators of alterity and difference. They have become what Kwame Anthony Appiah has named "otherness machines," whose principal role is the "manufacture of alterity."[1] When Castro-Gómez addresses the main points of reference in this manufacture of "otherness"—the concepts of *pueblo* (people) and *nación* (nation)—he engages in an acute and perspicacious juxtaposition of Carlos Cullen and Dussel, both seen as paradigmatic of the machinations and manufacture of otherness. Nonetheless, we also find excellent discussions of works by Ezequiel Martínez Estrada, Rodolfo Kusch, Vicente Ferreira da Silva, Antenor Orrego, Rafael Rojas, Cintio Vittier, Juan Carlos Scannone, Augusto Salazar Bondy, José Vasconcelos, and Samuel Ramos (these last two reappear in chapter 7), among others, a veritable who's who of the Latin American discourses about people and nation. What Castro-Gómez diagnoses as unifying this cacophonous debate about the subject of Latin American history has been the attempt to pinpoint the causes of Latin America's malaise by searching for the origins of a cultural difference distinguishing Latin America from Europe or the so-called West. He concludes an unquestionable tour de force by rejecting the view of the philosopher and intellectual in Latin American society as standing against and apart from the state. In fact, they have been its witting and unwitting functionaries. The philosopher, the *letrado*, the lettered one (we could also say the *Aufklärer*), the intellectual who "examines the truth of culture and discursively assigns to people a specific identity (whether authentic or inauthentic), is a form of observation present in normative societies where individuals are surveilled and regulated by the centralizing activity of the state" (78).

Playing a different note within the same key, chapter 4, "Latin America Beyond the Philosophy of History," criticizes the idea of the philosopher as arbiter of difference and catalyst of a fictitious identity whose task is to think the temporality of Latin American historicity. After interrogating, in the prior chapter, the "agent" of history, now Castro-Gómez asks how "history" constitutes a collective Latin American suprasubject. The history, historicity, and historiography of Latin American philosophy have unquestionably been the identifying brand of Latinamericanism in their Zeaian and Roigian versions. Eloquently and lucidly, Castro-Gómez shows how they advanced the early twentieth-century initiatives of José Ortega y Gasset and his foremost student José Gaos, the construction of a "transcendental subject" a priori to making sense of the historical experience of Latin America.

Castro-Gómez is offering (we could interject) an archaeology of the ontologies of people and nation just surveyed in the previous chapter. In this chapter he draws on Ángel Rama and Foucault to articulate a critique of the "historicism" of the great Latinamericanists, who in the name of an allegedly unique historical experience claim the authority to arbitrate the moral character, the moral ethos, of a discovered (but in fact invented) cultural and historical unity: *lo latinoamericano* and, as its germinal, *lo hispano.* The two chapters level a combined accusation against the role played by philosophers and intellectuals in Latin American history. As disguised agents of the normalizing and administering state, they have contributed to the domestication and docility of Latin American peoples through their alterization of both Europe and Latin America. This is a fascinating account of how the philosophy of history, in its ontological and phenomenological versions, is a key gear in the "otherness machine" at which Appiah points an accusatory finger. Notably, as the caudillo's shadow, archiver of the people's true history, and letrado of the Latin American city, the regimenting "Latin American" has surveyed, unseen, from the panopticizing tower of "historical reason."

In chapter 5, "The Aesthetics of the Beautiful in Spanish American Modernism"—one of the chapters most substantively revised from the first edition, Castro-Gómez turns to literature and literary criticism, close allies of the disciplines of philosophy in Latin America, while still continuing the paths laid out in the prior chapters. This chapter's problematic is what, on the one hand, Iris M. Zavala calls Hispanic modernism, and the philosophical-sociological postulate of modernity, and, on the other, high modernism and modernity. Ultimately, the issue is whether and to what extent Hispanic modernism can be decoupled in any meaningful sense from modernism as such. Castro-Gómez frontally attacks Zavala's division, or juxtaposition, according to which Hispanic modernism was an anarchic poetics that departed from an aesthetics of the beautiful in what was, allegedly, the Latin American response to modernity. He responds that Hispanic modernism was an aesthetic movement synergized by an aesthetic of the beautiful, but with a resulting alignment of the totalizing and homogenizing imperative that animated modernity itself. Thus the idea is that Hispanic modernism was intrinsic to the aesthetic of the beautiful of modernity itself. Both Zavala and Castro-Gómez's contentions have as their background, of course, Kant's distinction between the beautiful and the sublime, as painstakingly interpreted by both Wolfgang Welsch and Lyotard (frequent voices from the sidelines in this book, along with Foucault, Gianni Vattimo, and other postmodern thinkers). In contrast to the European experience of modernity—not *an* experience, but a plurality of experiences—the Hispanic experience was putatively determined by the experience of underdevelopment, poverty, marginalization, and the critique of North American imperialism and its legitimating ideology of pragmatism. Underscoring Castro-Gómez's critique of the invidious distinction, there is no document of European modernism that is not branded by the same concerns. Nonetheless, common to both alleged forms of modernism are the leveling and evisceration of quotidian experience resulting from capitalism's mutations and the material and symbolic order in which everything is reduced to quantitative equivalents. The Hispanic reaction to modernity was expressed as a celebration of Hispanic culture, a bulwark against capitalist modernity's leveling and homogenizing effects (as is evident in José Enrique Rodó, Rubén Darío, Leopoldo Lugones, and other great Latin American modernists discussed by Castro-Gómez), that took the form of *el Arielismo* (Arielism), as a counter to the crass, mediocre, materialist consumerism of Anglo-American culture, the North's gigantic mechanism, and human deracination. This Arielismo harkened back to exalting the aristocracy of mundane existence and to yearning for a "golden age" of authentic culture now banalized by capitalist commodification. As a romantic response to the alleged hegemony of instrumental reason, however, this response continued to negotiate a trajectory through an aesthetic of the beautiful. Its logic harmonizes, synthesizes, sublimates, and assimilates into a totality all that is heterogeneous, dissenting, and dissonant. As he writes: "Modernism was consequently the response to the spiritual void that positivism created in the traditional elite classes of Latin America. As Paz remarks, it was our true Romanticism. Hence the modernists desire to seek reconciliation and harmony, just as the German Romantics had in their day" (115). The romantic reaction of Hispanic modernism, which harkens back to the utopian discourse of the late nineteenth century, did not constitute an alternative project of emancipation that would have enabled Latin Americans to weigh against the hegemony of instrumental reason that accompanied modernity as its shadow. These discourses constituted merely modernity's counterpart.

"Postcolonial Reason and Latin American Philosophy," the final chapter of the first edition, is now the sixth and penultimate. In the mid-nineties, it aimed to offer the most up-to-date overview of important developments in Latin American philosophy and social theory. But Castro-Gómez's approach and critiques have remained relevant and prescient through the many subsequent developments in postcolonial theory and Latin American philosophy. This includes his interrogation of whether there could be a critique of the West from a perspective and with a point of departure other than that available in the West. As the Argentine-born semiotician and literary and cultural critic Walter Mignolo argued in the early nineties, while postmodern critique was enunciated from the ex-colonies of the imperial West, postcolonial critique was enunciated from the deep settler colonies that were conquered through enduring processes of cultural and racial destruction and imposition. The long-term consequences of this original "encounter" with Europe are still suffered in Latin America, where *mestizaje* and syncretism were processes of assimilation and/or exclusion. Mignolo seeks to make explicit the plural loci of enunciation from whence different theories seek to analyze and criticize historical reality and social imaginaries. This "plurotopic hermeneutics" was developed by the philosophers who, *avant la lettre*, developed a distinct Latin American postcolonial critique, namely Kusch, Leopoldo Zea, and Dussel. While Castro-Gómez does not aim to challenge Mignolo's incisive and suggestive readings of these three thinkers, he disagrees that they already offered "postcolonial" critiques of modernity and the West. He sees them as having offered countermodern critiques. To the extent that they remained within the epistemological horizon of modernity, their critiques were neither postcolonial nor an exercise of the "postcolonial reason" proclaimed and defended by Mignolo. Instead, and making a creative use of Niklas Luhmann's systems theory, Castro-Gómez shows how these Latin American thinkers are examples of "second-order" reflections, which still operate within the autopoietic discourse of the West and modernity. Such second-order reflections, which are undoubtedly important and certainly illuminating, are still enunciated in the language of Prospero, that is, the transcendental language of historical thinking, the philosophy of origins (*Ursprüngsphilosophie*) and primordial sources. Instead, in a departure from the aftermath of Foucault's critique of the modern episteme, Castro-Gómez shows how these Latin American discourses are not external but absolutely internal to the self-observation of the "West" and modernity. Against Mignolo, the "locus of enunciation" is not, he argues, geoculturally determined. Clinging to this spatialization of a theoretical practice has its dangers: "It is dangerous because it could lead us to the legitimization of any kind of political or moral authoritarianism, simply because it is rooted in non-Western traditions and 'other knowledges.'" Furthermore, not only is it morally and politically dangerous, it is also philosophically mistaken and incorrect because, to claim epistemic privilege for a distinct geocultural location leads to "the theorization of an *epistemic alterity* that is nonexistent in Latin American discourses. . . . An epistemic break is not produced when the universal pretensions of philosophy are criticized in the philosophical register, in imitation of Caliban's gesture. As long as Caliban continues to speak in the same philosophical register as his modern master, there will be no dissolution, only displacement, and always within the *same* episteme" (162).

The last chapter, "The Birth of Latin America as a Philosophical Problem in Mexico" was written more recently. Again, Castro-Gómez exhibits a honed skill for incisive and synoptic readings of different philosophers in his fascinating archeology of the origin of what he calls "philosophical Latin Americanism," a philosophical discourse about Latin America and its differences from Europe and the United States. In its far-reaching overview, Castro-Gómez's archeological genealogy takes us back to the powerful influence of, on the one hand, Vasconcelos and Ramos and, on the other, the Spanish exiles and refugees Ortega y

Gasset and his student Gaos. The continuing reverberations of their influence still frame contemporary debates in and about Latin America. The focus in this chapter is Mexico, historically the heavyweight in Latin American philosophy, if only as the Latin American country with the longest and most stable academic institutions supporting the professional study of philosophy. It was in Mexico that philosophy became academicized and professionalized. Here, we are introduced to the members of the Ateneo, one of the most impactful cohorts of philosophers, and their progeny, the Hyperión group. For the English-speaking world, this chapter will be an unexpected, illuminating study of early twentieth-century developments in phenomenology, existentialism, historicism, and phenomenological and ontological hermeneutics, predating the introduction of some of those philosophical currents in the United States and the Anglo world in general. This final chapter is in many ways the point of departure for the whole book. We are returned to the sources of its trajectory: the genealogy of a "Latin American" reason and historical being that would be distinct from Europe and the Giant in the North.

II

This book of rich, expansive, and synthesizing analyses and critiques is a tour de force that manages to give us approximately one hundred years not of solitude but of cacophonous and intense debates that shaped how Latin Americans have thought about themselves and their efforts to grapple with their histories and challenges. It will be evident that I share Castro-Gómez's critique of the metaphysics of alterity that has influenced a significant sector of Latin America, especially what developed in the late sixties and early seventies. The discourses of difference and otherness that frame the philosophical Latin Americanism profiled in this book are no less and not more than discourses of identity in reverse. Most important, and as Castro-Gómez eloquently shows, they remain entangled within the discursive practices of the "West" and "modernity." I agree with the book's impetus to develop a sociology of culture and a critical theory of Latin American societies that combine self-reflection (with respect to its own acts of self-reflection) with a mix of economics, political theory, sociology, and literary theory. While Castro-Gómez engages Latin American critiques of European sociology, he resists the neocolonialist models that seek to impose on Latin America a one-size-fits-all model of modernization and rationalization. For this reason, Castro-Gómez is also skeptical of Habermas's universal pragmatics and theory of communicative rationality, which he resists through his Foucauldian-inspired relentless historicization. Castro-Gómez shows us how all theory is the product of given conditions of possibility, particular social imaginaries, and certain national projects that weave discursive and social practices.

Mine are not so much critiques or objections as a series of questions that foreground what is clarified in the appendix's interview as well as in Castro-Gómez's subsequent works. In this book Castro-Gómez could have differentiated more clearly and explicitly between identity and identification. This is the difference between the logic of individuation by means of subjection, which characterizes modernity and the logic of individuation through agency, which is a form of socially enabled subjectification. This is the difference established by Foucault between subjection and subjectification. In the former, one is an object of social control. In the latter, one is a subject of one's actions and sense of self. To affirm an identity is different from constructing a discourse about identification. In the former case, as Castro-Gómez notes correctly, identity assumes a homogeneous unity that is retroactively constructed, which turns out to be fictitious and imposed. In the latter, the process of identification is a claim, a position-taking that announces and denounces a form of social power. It results in defetishization, the unmasking of an absent source of legitimacy to grant recognition. In the process of identification resides the heart of the problem of a differential and social topography of social agents, namely the problem of who has the power and authority to allow or disallow certain voices to speak or be silenced. In fact, discourses about identification thematize our own representation (*darstellen*) and deconstruct and challenge those who clandestinely and stealthily want to represent (*vertreten*) others and speak for them—to use Spivak's generative reading of Marx's distinction. If we do not dwell long enough on this differentiation, we may neglect the power that discourses of self-identification can have and deploy. Would it even be possible to celebrate plurality without a plurality of agents who had affirmed their own identification? My claim is that *Zero-Point Hubris* and

Castro-Gómez's two volumes on the history of governmentality redress the *Critique*'s ambiguity concerning what Foucault called "practices" and "technologies of the self."

A second question for this book concerns the extent to which the philosophical and sociological critiques of modernity by some Latin American thinkers, particularly Dussel, Morande, Parker, and later Mignolo, are also religious-theological critiques. They point out that modernity qua result of secularization and disenchantment was not just the modern world's turning Protestant. For these thinkers, the doors of the church at Wittenberg are not the only entry into modernity. Their critique of "imperial" and "colonial" reason is also a critique of a putative "secular reason," which turns out to be a form of "Protestant" reason. To this extent, these thinkers were already arguing for something that has been given the name of *postsecularism*. It thus seems that the project of a *Critique of Latin American Reason* should be accompanied by a critique of secular reason, as I think is developed by Castro-Gómez in his two volumes on the history of governmentality, especially in volume 2.

This leads to a third question concerning how "race" was constituted at the same time that "America" was invented. The colonization of the Americas was originally a project of evangelization or at least a project of conquest imbricated with religious imperatives. Among the earliest institutions prefiguring the social hierarchies that would become distinctive of the Americas were the *encomiendas* and the *repartimientos*. They prefigured the slave plantations that would mark so profoundly and indelibly the geography of the Americas. In at least two chapters, Castro-Gómez engages the role of mestizaje in the archeology of philosophical Latin Americanism, but the focus is predominantly on continental Latin America, to the occlusion of the Caribbean, whether Spanish, French, or Anglo-Saxon. In many discourses about *América profunda*, mestizaje displaces and occludes the role of "Blacks" or "Afro-Latin Americans" in the constitution of Latin America. Indeed, "philosophical Latin Americanism" eclipses the traditions of *négritude, negrismo, antillanité*—what Edouard Glissant called Caribbean discourses. América profunda was also "América negra," Black America. Here, it is important to point in the direction of Castro-Gómez's *Zero-Point Hubris*, in particular chapter 2, "Purus ab omnia macula sanguinis," which deals with the racial-colonial imaginary of Nueva Granada. There we discover the constitutive role of "race" in the construction of a Latin America for which an interminable project was the purification of blood.

A fourth question concerns the relationship between cosmopolitanism and provincialization. It was placed in a global context as a result of all the discourses about the historical, cultural, social, and philosophical uniqueness of Latin America, whose Janus face was the provincialization of Europe. Inchoate in Castro-Gómez's archeological genealogy of the discourses about Latin America is the idea of "Latinamericanization" as a counterpart to Edward Said's "Orientalism" and the discourses of "Orientalization." But as Fernando Coronil eloquently showed, Orientalism is Occidentalism's shadow. We can thus read Castro-Gómez's *Critique* of Latinamericanization doubly. The othering of Latin America and of Europe results in a dual "provincializing" of both. This dual provincializing potentiates a "rooted cosmopolitanism," to use Appiah's terms, or a cosmopolitanism of the subaltern, as I would call it.

The fifth and final leading question concerns Castro-Gómez's crypto-normativism. From what authorial and philosophical location does he criticize philosophical Latin Americanism? Just as Foucault sought to disappear as a gay Frenchman writing in the shadow of Jean-Paul Sartre, Claude Lévi-Strauss, Louis Althusser, Roland Barthes, Georges Canguilhem, Gaston Bachelard, and Alexandre Koyré, Castro-Gómez seems to want to anonymously disappear behind the sediments of his archeology. And yet the author's preface and concluding material added to this new edition make clear that this book has its own archeology in an important moment in Colombian philosophy, and also in European, specifically German, philosophy. It is thus the more noteworthy that Castro-Gómez takes off his Ring of Gyges and the Invisibility Cloak of discourse analysis and declares, in the excellent interview providing biographical context: "Let's be clear. The book is not a crusade against the legitimate aspirations to decolonization and the overcoming of cultural and economic dependency in our countries. Not in any way. What it is fighting against is rather the language in which such aspirations were formulated in Latin American philosophy. . . . The book resonates with the kind of politics that some Southern Cone cultural theorists (Martin Hopenhayn, Beatriz Sarlo, Carlos Altamirano, Nelly Richard, et al.) defended in the 1990s, right when those countries were coming out of the military dictatorships and transitioning to democracy." To this extent, the book aligns itself with the process of democratization in Latin America that took off during the nineties, which came to Colombia after long decades of a peace process that is still underway. The question, then, is how Castro-Gómez's postmodern historicism and archeological genealogy contribute to the project of democracy? It seems to me that he takes up this question in *Revoluciones sin sujetos: Slavoj Žižek y la crítica del historicismo posmoderno* (2015). It is extremely important that *Critique of Latin American Reason* has finally been made available in English in a faithful and fluid translation. It registers more than a century of thinking in an unparalleled feat of synthesis and critique.

CRITIQUE OF LATIN AMERICAN REASON

1

POSTMODERNITY'S CHALLENGES TO LATIN AMERICAN PHILOSOPHY

In 1979, Horacio Cerutti gave a presentation at the Ninth Inter-American Congress of Philosophy in Caracas titled "Posibilidades y límites de una filosofía latinoamericana 'después' de la filosofía de la liberación" (The possibilities and limits of a Latin American philosophy "after" the philosophy of liberation). In this presentation, Cerutti recognized the intention of the philosophy of liberation to address Latin American reality as a philosophical problem, thus renewing the concern for meaning and the need for thought that is committed to the reality of our peoples, such as what Juan Bautista Alberdi and the founding fathers of the "mental emancipation" of Hispanic America drew up in the nineteenth century. He also acknowledged the great effort of this movement to adopt the philosophical contributions of the other two intellectual currents that appeared in the first and second halves of the 1960s: dependency theory and liberation theology. However, in spite of all these achievements, Cerutti saw that the productivity of these three liberationist discourses had become sterilized during that era ("Posibilidades y límites").[1] As proof of this decline, Cerutti pointed to how both philosophy and theology distort dependency theory by separating it from the core of theoretical reflection that sustains and constitutes it, as well as to the expiration of a certain "Christian" thought in which faith appears as a prerequisite for engaging in liberatory philosophizing.

Several years after these reflections, it is still worth addressing the questions Cerutti posed and reformulating them in the following way: What kind of socio-structural transformations have accelerated the decline of the philosophical, sociological, and theological categories of liberationist discourses? What contributions from these discourses are still available to us for making a contemporary diagnosis of Latin American societies? And what categories must be readjusted to consolidate a new type of *critical discourse* in Latin America?

I strongly doubt that there is any Latin American thinker still affiliated with the philosophy or theology of liberation who does not wonder about the inevitable reconfiguration of categories that resulted from the recent collapse of socialist regimes in Eastern Europe. Even taking into account the differences that existed among them, almost all liberationist discourses were strongly influenced by the same rhetoric that inspired the ideological consolidation of socialism. The liberation of the oppressed, the thesis that imperialism is solely to blame for the poverty and misery of Latin American nations, faith in the moral and revolutionary resources of the people, the establishment of a society in which class antagonisms do not exist: these were all central themes of philosophical and theological reflection in Latin America in the 1960s and 1970s. This was the era of the Cold War and the consequent ideological polarization that existed throughout the entire continent; of the fear of nuclear threat that hovered over humanity; of the emancipatory processes in Asia and Africa; of student movements and the apex of guerrilla wars of national liberation; of the Cuban Revolution and the bravery of Fidel Castro in the Sierra Maestra and the Bay of Pigs; of the sacrifices of Che Guevara and Camilo Torres in South America; of the extraordinary return of Juan Domingo Perón in Argentina; of the martyrdom of Monsignor Romero and many other committed Christians in Central America; of the triumph of Unidad Popular in Chile and the Sandinista movement in Nicaragua, as well as of the popular resistance to the brutal dictatorships that stained the continent with blood. In many places there was an atmosphere of hope that the real revolution would soon arrive and that bourgeois capitalist power would finally be defeated, thus eradicating poverty and underdevelopment from our nations.

However, the 1980s came and went without the long-awaited revolution appearing, and wherever its presence drew near it was ruthlessly crushed by the powerful forces of the establishment which thereby demonstrated its immunity to any "qualitative leaps" in the structural order. Quite to the contrary, poverty, foreign debt, and rampant population growth in large cities increased to such an extent that those years went down in history with the dishonorable name of "the lost decade." But what was lost in Latin America is not measurable in quantitative terms alone (decreases in per capita rent, gross social product, exports, etc.) but also includes a *disenchantment of the world* that is felt throughout vast segments of our societies.[2]

How should we interpret phenomena like the failure of socialism and the change of sensibility that one observes today in almost all Western nations, including of course, Latin America? I maintain that a dialogue with the theorists of postmodernity will help shed light on the situation. However, a dialogue like this would first of all require us to confront the enormous avalanche of criticisms from certain sectors in Latin American philosophy that are determined to judge postmodernity from a *modern image of thought.*[3] We will therefore concern ourselves with examining the content of these criticisms so that we may then begin a dialogue with Latin American cultural studies, focusing on its diagnosis of the "disenchantment of the world." Finally, we will examine some postmodern theoretical proposals, emphasizing those elements that can assist us in reformulating a critical discourse in Latin America.

1. LATIN AMERICAN PHILOSOPHY'S CRITIQUE OF POSTMODERNITY

In Gabriel Vargas Lozano's view, the debate over postmodernity centers on the new phenomena that are appearing in the current phase of capitalist development. Following Fredric Jameson's Marxist analysis, Vargas Lozano argues that postmodernity is nothing other than the "cultural logic of late capitalism" ("Reflexiones críticas sobre modernidad y postmodernidad"). The emergence in industrial societies of new features like the popularization of mass culture, the deregulation of labor, and the growing technologization of everyday life has caused the capitalist system to develop an "ideology" that allows it to compensate for the imbalances resulting from new tendencies in the world of labor and in conceptions of individual or collective life. In order to confront these imbalances, the capitalist system must release itself from its own past, that is to say, from the emancipatory ideal of modernity and announce the coming of a postmodern era in which reality is transformed into images and time becomes the repetition of an eternal present. According to Vargas Lozano, we are confronted with an "ideological legitimation of the system" in line with the current orientation of computerized and consumerist capitalism.

Adolfo Sánchez Vázquez, also following Jameson, writes that postmodernity is an "ideology" of the "third phase of the expansion of capitalism" that began after World War II ("Posmodernidad, posmodernismo y socialismo"). In contrast to the first two, this third phase no longer recognizes any kind of borders and has inserted itself into the realms of art, nature, and the collective unconscious. In order to achieve its objectives, "late capitalism" engenders an "ideology" that completely immobilizes any attempt to change society. According to Sánchez Vázquez, postmodern thought does away with the very idea of a "foundation," thereby ruining any attempt to morally legitimize projects of social transformation. By negating the emancipatory potential of modernity, postmodernity discredits political action and shifts attention toward the contemplative world of aesthetics.[4] Furthermore, by announcing the "death of the subject" and the "end of history," postmodern philosophers have freed the artist from the responsibility to protest that modern aesthetics had granted to it. Likewise, the vindication of the fragmentary and the eclectic eliminates any type of resistance and unites humanity in resignedly waiting for the end.

The economist and philosopher Franz Hinkelammert sees in postmodernity a dangerous return to the sources of Nazism ("Frente a la cultura de la postmodernidad" 135–37). The influence of Nietzsche on postmodern philosophers is not surprising, as what they seek is to corrode the very foundations of rationality. Like Nietzsche, postmodern authors identify God with the "grand narrative" of universal ethics and announce his death from the rooftops. And just as Nietzsche legitimized the power of the strongest by declaring that universal ethics is the crutch of the poor, the enslaved, and the weak, postmodernity sides with the wealthy and the powerful by undermining the foundations of a universal ethics of human rights based on reason. In this way, postmodernity shows itself to be an ally of contemporary neoliberal tendencies oriented toward the expulsion of ethical universalism from the realm of the economy.[5] Hinkelammert also believes that postmodernity's "antirationalism" is in line with an anarchist tradition that spans from the workers' movements of the nineteenth century to the student protests of the 1970s. It is a kind of antisystem protest that clashes with all types of institutionality and whose final objective is to construct an ideal society without a state. However, he cautions, the anti-institutionalism of anarchist movements always prevents them from proposing any kind of political project, which leads them to look for extremist solutions. Such is the case with terrorist and guerrilla organizations that, unable to find a way to abolish the state from the left, have turned toward the direction indicated by Mikhail Bakunin: destruction as creative passion.

The neoliberalism of today, Hinkelammert continues, offers anarchists a new perspective on abolition. It is not surprising that a good number of hippies, Maoists, and other militants of the old protest movements have ended up as neoliberals. Out of this encounter we see the emergence of "anarchocapitalism," the new market religion founded by Milton Friedman, among whose exegetes include Robert Nozick, André Glucksman, Friedrich Hayek, Francis Fukuyama, Mario Vargas Llosa, and Octavio Paz—all of whom follow the old dream of the abolition of the state, but this time on the realist basis of a radical capitalism rather than on the basis of Bakunin's romantic ideas. However, the end result is the same: abolishing the state through the totalization of the market, without worrying about the amount of human sacrifice that it will cost. The postmodern battle to eradicate rationality is, for Hinkelammert, a mechanism for the definitive elimination of the enemies of the "system": no more utopias, no more theories capable of thinking reality as a whole, no universal ethics ("Frente a la cultura de la postmodernidad" 130–35).

For his part, the Cuban Marxist philosopher Pablo Guadarrama warns of the grave danger represented by the negation of two basic concepts for Latin America: social progress and a linear sense of history ("La malograda modernidad latinoamericana"). In his view, the postmodern critique of teleology does not acknowledge one "undeniable fact": there has never been a historical process that is not built on lower or less advanced stages of society. Another point is that some peoples "advance" at a more accelerated pace than others or attain higher or lower standards of living in the economic or cultural order. What is certain, however, as Guadarrama argues, is that there are in fact "moments of advancement of the humanization of humanity" (47), and Latin America is no exception but rather the confirmation of this rule. In some areas of the continent one can observe the persistence of precapitalist forms of production, while in others there exist very advanced processes of industrialization. Guadarrama is convinced that capitalism entails an "evolutionary advance" over the feudal and colonial structures of Latin American society, and for precisely this reason one cannot speak of the "entrance" of Latin America into postmodernity: as long as they are still settling their accounts with modernity, that is, as long as they have not had a complete experience of capitalism and eradicated feudal relations of production, it is useless and futile to think of a postmodern experience for Latin American countries. "The Habermasian view that modernity is an incomplete project," Guadarrama writes, "has understandably found sympathizers in Latin America, where it is easy to see the fragility of the majority of the paradigms of equality, freedom, brotherhood, secularization, humanism, enlightenment, and so on that so inspired our eminent thinkers in past centuries. It is common knowledge that we have not finished being modern, and yet now we are told we must be postmodern" (52).

Another critique comes from Argentine philosopher Arturo Andrés Roig, for whom postmodernity, in addition to being a discourse that is alienated from our social reality, is also alienating because it invalidates the highest achievements of Latin American thought and philosophy (*Historia de las ideas* 118–22). Declaring the exhaustion of modernity would mean giving up a powerful tool used in the struggles of all liberatory tendencies in Latin America: the critical narrative. Roig argues that modernity was not only violence and irrationality but also an opening to the critical role of thought. The so-called hermeneutics of suspicion (Friedrich Nietzsche, Karl Marx, and Sigmund Freud) taught us that "behind" the immediate reading of a text there is another hidden level of meaning that, to be read, must be mediated by criticism. It is precisely this idea of "unmasking" that has given Latin American philosophy meaning, interested as it is in laying bare the "ideological mechanisms of the oppressor's discourse." To renounce suspicion, as the postmodernists attempt to do, is equivalent to giving up criticism itself and falling into the trap of the "justifying discourse" of the large centers of global power.

Roig writes that this "justifying discourse," which tries to convince us that we exist in a sort of "epistemological orphanhood," declares that all utopias have been definitively discredited and that history has come to an end. However, in his opinion, Latin American philosophy has been characterized as a sort of "morning" philosophy whose symbol is not the Hegelian owl but rather the Argentine mockingbird. That is to say, it is not a discourse that looks backward to justify its past (as in the case of Hegel) but rather always looks forward, firmly rooted in the utopian function of thought. Therefore, renouncing this "discourse of the future" would be to deny the desire for a better life held by the oppressed of Latin America. Falling into postmodern nihilism is equivalent to renouncing politics in favor of a "laissez-faire" approach to economics, "incorporating a weak and self-satisfying will through cassette players and stereos" (Roig, *Historia de las ideas* 126–29).

2. POSTMODERNITY AS A "CONDITION" IN LATIN AMERICA

Perhaps the best way to begin to respond to these criticisms is to show that what has been called "postmodernity" is not an *ideological phenomenon*, that is to say, it is not something that occurs only in the "consciousness" of certain philosophers alienated from their own Latin American world, but rather is above all an *ontological phenomenon* that entails a transformation of *practices* on the level of everyday life. Moreover, this is not only the case in the countries of the center but also in peripheral nations, particularly during these final decades of the twentieth century. Postmodernity, as Jean-François Lyotard explained so well, is a *condition* and not an *ideology* one can dispense with through argument. Nor is it an issue of *consciousness* but rather of *experience*, which has consolidated in the majority of Latin American nations with the help of capitalist globalization.[6] Gianni Vattimo put it well: postmodernity is not a reference to the "overcoming" (*Überwindung*) of modernity, as if we had entered into an era that comes "after" the modern, but rather to the planetwide spread and "culmination" (*Verwindung*) of modernity itself, which entails putting its metaphysical legitimacy into question (*The End of Modernity* 20–21).

I propose to show, therefore, that postmodernity is not a simple "ideological trap" that has ensnared certain intellectuals who insist on examining our reality with concepts that do not correspond to it, but rather that it is a *stage of culture* that is *also* present in Latin America. It is a condition that otherwise (as we will see later) corresponds to a new "image of thought." To take this proposal further, I will refer to the recent diagnoses of so-called Latin American cultural studies, which includes the work of José Joaquín Brunner, Beatriz Sarlo, Néstor García Canclini, Jesús Martín-Barbero, George Yúdice, Renato Ortiz, Jean Franco, Martin Hopenhayn, and Nelly Richard, among many others. These approaches go beyond what we might call the "open veins syndrome," insofar as the emphasis is no longer on the investigation of the structural causes of underdevelopment in the field of international economic relations, that is to say, on privileging the *exogenous factors*, but rather on the way in which the processes of modernization and capitalization are assimilated and transformed in what Norbert Lechner has called the "inner sanctums" of culture.[7] Rather than macrostructural factors (the inheritance of the nineteenth-century languages of social sciences), these authors emphasize the *practices of everyday life* and the multiple rationales that exist within them.

I will begin by responding to the question of the need for and/or the relevance of a discussion about postmodernity in Latin America. Almost all the previously discussed authors insist that a Latin American debate on this topic either follows the foreign interests of the alienated elites, who seek to be "fashionable," or that it is the ideological expression of "late capitalism" in its current phase of global expansion. In both cases the criticism is based on the same presupposition: the socioeconomic imbalance that can be observed between the Global North, where the hyperconsumerism of goods prevails, and Latin American societies, which are marked by poverty and violence, makes any transfer of theoretical and critical content to the discussion either impossible or at least suspect.[8] However, Chilean thinker Nelly Richard has pointed out that this argument remains within a typical Marxist framework that subordinates cultural processes to socioeconomic developments ("Latinoamérica y la postmodernidad" 210–22). If, in contrast, we begin from an analytical framework in which both culture and economics do not operate on the basis of the same "logic" but rather are in an asymmetrical relation to one another, we will then see that the structural fulfillment of postmodernism in First World societies would not necessarily have to be reproduced in Latin America in order for its *cultural registers* to appear. Instead, these latter would enter onto the Latin American stage due to reasons and circumstances that are very different from those that can be observed in the countries of the "center," since they refer to a *peripheral experience of modernity*. Therefore, taking the socioeconomic model of development of the First World as a referential guarantee through which a discussion of postmodernity in Latin America would make sense or not means remaining trapped in a discourse that reduces culture to a simple "ideological reflection" of economic processes. Modern societies are not based on a single rationality but rather on many, and the task is to analyze the kind of relations and antagonisms that are established between them.[9]

Richard highlights two factors that, in her view, would explain the reticence a certain part of the Latin American intellectual milieu has toward the debate on postmodernity. The first is the trauma of the colonizing mark, which causes many Latin American intellectuals to look with suspicion on anything that comes from "abroad" and creates a division between what belongs and what is alien, between the foreign and the national. The second factor has to do with postmodern discourse's implicit critique of the heroic ideals of the generation of Latin Americans who put their faith in revolution and the "new man" ("Latinoamérica y la postmodernidad" 212). It is not surprising that, instead of taking advantage of postmodern critique and resemanticizing it through a diagnosis of Latin American reality, a large number of our intellectuals have chosen to see this critique as a new "imperialist ideology." Fortunately, several authors have argued in favor of promoting Latin American interest in the debate on postmodernity, thus acknowledging that this debate addresses important questions about diagnosing the ambiguity of the experience of modernity in Latin America.

We will first examine Argentine political theorist Daniel García Delgado's assessment, according to which Latin America is experiencing a transition from "holist culture"—spanning from the end of the 1970s—toward "neoindividualist culture," which emerged in the 1960s but had its strongest impact during the 1990s ("Modernidad y posmodernidad en América Latina"). *Holist culture* encompasses "broad identities" based in belonging to collectives and the experiences of union and class solidarity, within a community politics that emphasizes the integrative role of the nation, the foundational role of popular and working-class culture, as well as the imperative of redistributive justice assured by the state. This phenomenon was strongest in countries that had managed to industrialize and construct a state more rapidly, such as Mexico or Argentina, but in general it can be said that it is rooted in the colonial inheritance shared by all Latin American countries. *Neo-individualist culture*, in contrast, is characterized by a tendency toward forming "restricted identities" in which microgroup and private experiences are valued. Identifying with the "national," which previously served as an integrating element of recognition, is diminished before the force of a transnational culture staked out by mass media and culture industries. This weakening of traditional solidarities causes personal identities to stop revolving around the nation, the family, and work, and instead to form micrological and often depoliticized spheres of activity. Traditional "holistic culture" still persists, although it is increasingly pushed toward the margins (particularly the rural and generational margins) due to the growth of the urban and globalized youth population that no longer defines itself in relation to broad group belonging as their parents did (Catholics, proletarians, liberals, conservatives, and socialists) but rather on the basis of restricted belonging (urban tribes and cultural consumers).

García Delgado claims that this loss of traditional certainties is not produced only by the breaking of the national state before the "economic imperialism" of transnational powers but that it also has *endogenous* causes. In many Latin American countries this situation follows the dissolution of the ideological antagonisms that existed during the nineteenth century and part of the twentieth century, which formed the basis for civil wars and which were retroactively reinforced during the Cold War. If the previous processes of integration positioned individuals and collectives with respect to their "common enemies"—whether conservatives, liberals, the oligarchy, imperialism, or communism—which brought together and gave meaning to mass politics, this modality has been weakened insofar as the ideological blocs have disappeared and the logic of power has become increasingly complex and diffuse.[10] "Heavy ideologies" stop functioning as elements of integration and give way to a culture that is skeptical of "grand narratives." Social integration shifts to the realm of "light ideologies" that offer individuals the opportunity to become the protagonists of their own lives. The cult of the body mediated by the practice of sports, the intense enjoyment of moments and sensation associated with rock music or drug consumption, ecological culture, the private religiosity of evangelical sects, or the growing popularity of "new age" culture could be counted as this sort of micropractice.

Seeking the endogenous causes of this change of sensibility in Latin America, Argentine sociologist Roberto Follari points to two factors: firstly, the unusual brutality with which the dictatorships of the Southern Cone eliminated or weakened leftist political organizing, sowing an inescapable sensation of fear among the population (*Modernidad y posmodernidad* 146). This led to the spread of a heightened skepticism about the possibilities of structural change in society, as the high social cost that any attempt at such change would entail was now known in advance. From this perspective, the "softening" of political opinions, as well as adherence to any project of "integral liberation," seems inevitable. The other factor Follari mentions is the lack of social alternatives (145). The misery of large segments of the population, the increasingly restricted income of the middle classes, the corruption of the political class—all these factors lead to a *culture of immediacy* in which what is most important is to learn to survive for today, and we will see what happens tomorrow. In recent years, broad segments of the population have been forced to turn to the informal economy to survive, without either protection or social representation, left entirely to their own luck. The *present* is the only horizon of meaning, for lack of a future project.

Under these conditions, it is not surprising that an immediatist sensibility has spread throughout Latin America, mistrustful of the "grand projects" of social engineering. Nor is it surprising that this sensibility does not come from "outside" like a product imported by intellectual elites, but rather emerges *from within*, as the result of a long, historical process: the experience of five hundred years of socioeconomic underdevelopment, authoritarianism, and inequality on all levels of daily life, without any political project having successfully prevented it. The promises of economic reform and social justice, exalted by political parties since independence, have resoundingly failed in Latin America, and this failure makes up part of the *collective memory* in such a way that the great majority of the population is indifferent to any political attempt to make these promises into reality. Thus there is a growing loss of confidence in political institutions and in the efficacy of participation in the *public* space, which, as we have already pointed out, leads to the search for personal realization in the *private* sphere.

An example of this skepticism of grand narratives is the intense opposition to revolutionary messianism that exists in most Latin American countries. If the revolutionary left of the 1960s and 1970s was oriented around identifying the utopia of equality with the possible future, the tendency today, as Chilean sociologist Norbert Lechner has shown, is to "discharge" from politics all reductionist elements in order to strip it of any religious motivations ("La democratización en el contexto de una cultura posmoderna"). Instead of a heroic vision of politics and a messianic focus on the future, politics is now reestablished in a pragmatic form as the "art of the possible." The result is a *disenchantment of politics* in the sense that its primary objective is not to erase the traces of power and exclusion from the foundations of grand revolutionary ideologies but rather to make visible their designs and conflicts and to try to manage them through negotiation. Instead of establishing a social situation of unity and harmony, the politics that has slowly been emerging in Latin America since the 1980s is oriented toward the recognition of dissensus as a central element of democracy. What is important now is not to "break with the system" but rather to try to reform it from within, understanding that in every case there are no *metaphysical guarantees* for such reform. The fact that broad segments of society recognize that the purpose of politics is not one of eliminating either contradictions or indeterminacies seems to Lechner to be one of the clearest signs of postmodernity in Latin America.

Even so, this *defoundation* of politics also brings with it an enormous susceptibility to the influence of institutions like the market and mass media. If politics is no longer understood as an activity oriented around metaphysical certainties, it could dangerously become a performative spectacle engineered by market forces. The decisive factor for which candidate or party will take office is no longer the rationality of their political ideals but rather the ability to create an artificial "world" with which voters can identify. The style, body language, tone of voice—in a word, the "charisma"—of a presidential candidate are produced and administered according to aesthetic advertising criteria in such a way that they can be successfully sold in the market of images. Argentine critic Beatriz Sarlo mentions the case of the 1990 elections in Peru, in which both Fujimori and Vargas Llosa presented themselves to the public using carefully designed images ("Basuras culturales, simulacros políticos" 223–32). The former appeared on billboards dressed as a karate expert, in a white *gi* tied at the waist with a belt, in the act of breaking a brick with the edge of his right hand. The latter visited a poor neighborhood, enthusiastically greeting poorly dressed and Indigenous residents. Both cases substituted rational discourse for scenes that were constructed for the mass media in which the candidates sought to influence not voters' consciousness but rather their *affects*. Fujimori did not want to be associated with the traditional Peruvian oligarchy, and thus, in order to avoid appearing like a politician, he dressed up as a karate expert. Vargas Llosa wanted to be seen as an intellectual whose moral principles compelled him to identify with the suffering of the poor. In this way, political discourse remains part of a *symbolic hyperreality* in which the image no longer refers to reality but is rather a commodifiable product with a self-referential character.[11] Politics becomes a *simulacrum*, an image of images whose only reality is that of a world occupied by the rhetoric of the media. It is not discourse but rather the image that has the most impact on the Latin American masses, who experience modernity under the influence of movies and television.

The influence mass media have on the Latin American social imaginary is one of the most common themes addressed by contemporary cultural studies. Certainly, it is not an unwarranted interest: if up until the 1950s personal and collective identities in Latin America were still formed according to traditional models of socialization, with the popularization of mass media this situation has radically changed. Television, cinema, radio, and video lead to the discovery of other social realities, of numerous language games, and the revitalization of culture itself.

Spanish-Colombian communication theorist Jesús Martín-Barbero criticizes the view that postulates *European* modernity as "original" and immutable, in the face of which successive modernizations in Latin America have been merely copies or "deformations" ("Modernidad y posmodernidad en la periferia" 283–85). This sacralization of the model of European modernity makes it difficult to see that the Latin American masses have not assimilated modernity through the discourses of Enlightenment and political rights but rather through culture industries starting in the 1960s. More than as an *intellectual experience* connected to Enlightenment principles or the ideological agendas of political parties, Latin Americans have "lived" modernity as an *affective and emotional experience* through cinema and television. The "secularization" that brings about modernity has not necessarily meant the abandonment of traditional lifestyles (as occurred in Europe) but rather its assimilation to new forms of cultural consumption mediated by the globalization of symbolic universes. As Martín-Barbero writes, "It appears that cultural politics have taken neither interest in nor responsibility for this modernity, occupied as they are by the search for roots and the conservation of authenticities or in denouncing the decline of art and cultural confusion" (*De los medios a las mediaciones* 93). The *heterogeneity* present in Latin American societies makes possible the *simultaneous* assimilation of both modernity and its postmodern crisis.

In much the same way, Chilean sociologist José Joaquín Brunner remarks that, in Latin America, mass media have constructed a sui generis experience of modernity in which signifiers no longer refer to territorial meanings but rather to deterritorialized signifieds (*América Latina* 15–72). This means that, along with the media, the socialization of the individual is related to transnational criteria and guidelines of behavior, all at the expense of taking distance from the traditional forms of cultural transmission. *Mass culture* promotes the dissolution of traditional certainties that used to function as guarantees of social integration (the "holistic culture" mentioned by García Delgado) and gives shape to a complex scene in which the national and the transnational coexist. It is a culture that no longer refers to a specific territory but rather to a culture created by, and for that very reason globalized by, the market. Global mass culture has nothing to do with the purity of folklore and popular traditions but with the way in which people independently appropriate the territory-less signs disseminated by the media. The majority of cultural commodities that circulate in Latin American cities today are not produced manually or artisanally, nor are they transmitted from person to person via an oral tradition; rather they are produced, as

Giddens would say, by "abstract systems" like the telecommunications industry, schools, and museums.

With regard to the *disenchantment of tradition*, Brunner points to a consequence of modernization that dependency theorists had not considered: the paradoxical effects of the massive increase in education in Latin America. Beginning with the modernization of the educational system, subaltern segments of society were subject to a new dynamic, one that uprooted them from their traditional environment and submitted them to an intensive and systematic socialization through schooling. The primary realm of socialization shifted from the family to the educational institution, which was now responsible for imposing or promoting a bodily and mental discipline that would enable individuals to take on specific roles in society. Schools transmit a *modern* conceptualization of the world based on Western humanist traditions (reading, writing, calculating) and on the scientific model of comprehending natural processes. According to Brunner, all this indicates that Latin America has blurred the aristocratic and colonial distinction between "high" culture and "popular" culture. Popular culture, understood as a symbolic universe that transmits the religious, moral, and cognitive heritage of the people, can no longer resist the advance of the educational system, the culture industry, and mass media. The forms of popular culture that do offer some resistance are increasingly restricted to the residual modality of "folklore," which has not remained uncontaminated but instead has been modified by the international market of images and symbols. In addition, "formal education" is considered a source of social prestige insofar as learning the official language and knowledge taught in schools increases the likelihood of both stability and social mobility for Indigenous and peasant populations (Brunner, *América Latina* 135–61).

This brief survey of some of the most recent work in Latin American cultural studies allows us to conclude the following: first, postmodernity is a form of being-in-the-world (a "condition") that is also prevalent in Latin America, although for reasons that *differ* from the way in which this phenomenon exists in Western nations. This sufficiently addresses the thesis according to which postmodernity is an "ideology of advanced capitalism" that has been adopted in Latin America by intellectuals who are alienated from their own cultural reality. The second conclusion is a corollary of the first: postmodernity cannot be reduced to a simple, secondary effect of neoliberalism. It is true that the latter has favored the "devaluation of supreme values" insofar as it entails an extension of exchange value to areas that do not belong to the world of economics, for example, subjectivity, affects, and desires. These are areas in which "use value" was once prevalent but which now have begun to be commodified, thus deepening the "disenchantment of the world" mentioned earlier. However, it would be incorrect to reduce this phenomenon to a simple matter of "false consciousness" that emerges as a byproduct of the withdrawal of the state and the expansion of the market. Brunner, Martín-Barbero, and Follari have clearly demonstrated that, long before the advent of neoliberalism, at least since the developmentalist period of the 1960s, Latin Americans have experienced in their own way the "flight of the gods" that ushered in modernity. Postmodern disenchantment is not the ideological correlate of a technocratic and neoliberal offensive but rather the result of a transformation *of the lifeworld* across vast segments of Latin American societies, the result of the asymmetries unleashed by the very processes of modernization. The third conclusion, finally, is that cultural studies properly speaking now operate with a new "image of thought" that breaks with the parameters of the discourse of modernity and that, as we will see shortly, cannot help but astonish the defenders of philosophical Latin Americanism.

3. LATIN AMERICA AND THE "CLICHÉS" OF POSTMODERNITY

Having seen that the debate on postmodernity in Latin America is not simply an intellectual fad but rather is founded on a particular "mode of being" in both discourses and everyday practices, I will examine more closely some of the critiques sketched out previously and seek to respond to them in the form of an "internal dialogue" with certain postmodern philosophers. I say "internal dialogue" because I am convinced that the majority of these critiques are based on "clichés" popularized by philosophers who, clinging to the old nostalgic ideal of "Latin American identity," are stunned by thought that is so radically different from their own, such as that of philosophers like Jean-François Lyotard, Jacques Derrida, Gianni Vattimo, Michel Foucault, Jean Baudrillard, Gilles Deleuze, or Félix

Guattari.[12] Unfortunately, what usually happens is that philosophical polemics generate personal alliances and outright rejections instead of profound reflections. Convinced that they are therefore insufficient, I will present my argument by discussing four of the most common clichés on which these critiques are based: 1. the "end of modernity," 2. the "end of history," 3. the "death of the subject," and 4. the "end of utopias."

1. Perhaps the most well-known of these clichés is that of presenting postmodernity as the "end of modernity." It is true that the prefix *post* suggests some sort of periodization and that Vattimo's most well-known book is titled *The End of Modernity*. However, there is nothing more inaccurate than understanding this "end" as the conclusion of one era and the beginning of another. Postmodernity is not that which comes *after* modernity, but rather is the acknowledgment of the crisis unleashed by modernity itself. It is a matter of accepting responsibility for what modernity has always entailed since its inception, namely the disenchantment of the world, without trying to conceal this phenomenon behind legitimizing metanarratives like those that were disseminated between the eighteenth and twentieth centuries.

It is no secret that modernity brings with it a series of transformations and ruptures whose end result is a crisis of the human experience on five levels: cognitive, economic, political, ethical, and cultural. On the first level there is the possibility of knowing the natural and social world without relying on theological or cosmological legitimation but rather on an immanent analysis of phenomena that operates on the basis of constant experimentation and self-correction. The idea of a revealed and/or metaphysical knowledge enters into crisis. In the field of economics, we talk about the emergence of capitalism, which connects wealth with wage labor, the world of business, and personal effort. The idea that the accumulation of wealth is sinful and that material abundance is a prerogative associated with noble birth is brought into question. In the political sphere, modernity entails the emergence of the state as an agent capable of centralizing power and exercising military and political sovereignty through laws. The concept of the divine right of kings and personal justice ("an eye for an eye, a tooth for a tooth") collapses. In the realm of ethics, we see the emergence of the notion that the achievement of the "good life" is not a question of adjusting existence to moral norms dictated by external elements like tradition and the Church. Finally, the cultural horizon of modernity brings about the birth of the school and mass media as elements that can "socialize" individuals, and this causes a crisis for the primacy of family authority and the oral transmission of knowledge.

Nevertheless, when philosophers like Vattimo refer to the "end of modernity," they are not saying that these five transformations of human experience have been "left behind" and that we are beginning a new era, but rather that the time has come to fully *accept* these transformations and to abandon the *metaphysical legitimation* that tries to see these processes as phenomena related to the rational order of "progress." We are talking about a crisis of legitimation, namely the Enlightenment narrative that assumes a kind of "preestablished harmony" between the scientific, economic, political, ethical, and cultural development of humanity. This unitary conceptualization of progress is based on the mode of being of thought predominant in the West from the middle of the eighteenth century to the middle of the twentieth century.[13] Such was the conviction of the liberal bourgeoisie in Europe and Latin America during the nineteenth century: the ideal of a *synthesis* between the accumulation of capital, technological advancement, and the ethical and artistic needs of culture. It was believed that *behind* all these processes existed a "rational order" that would guarantee the indissoluble unity between the true, the good, and the beautiful.[14]

Near the end of the nineteenth century, there emerged a growing awareness of the essentially antagonistic and divided character of modernity. G. W. F. Hegel, Karl Marx, Henri Bergson, Wilhelm Dilthey, Edmund Husserl, György Lukács, and José Ortega y Gasset in Europe, as well as the modernist writers in Latin America, all realized that modernity generated the unfolding of *multiple rationalities*. Yet, still clinging to the modern image of thought, they always sought in different ways to recover the loss of unity and to "reconcile" all these rationalities in a single common project.[15] It was necessary to go through the experience of two world wars in Europe and the ideological conflict that resulted from it in order to become conscious of the fact that any attempt at "reconciliation" almost always ends up in state bureaucracy, broader social controls, technologization of daily life, and political intolerance.

Postmodern philosophers teach us that the unitary ideal of modernity cannot continue functioning as a legitimizing "metanarrative" of political praxis. The expression "end of modernity" therefore refers to *this* kind of narrative's loss of credibility and not the cancellation of modernity as a historical era. The goal is to "incorporate" (*einverleiben*) modernity into our lives instead of the disenchantment generated by the explosion of multiple rationalities. What is abandoned is not the "ideals of modernity," as Hinkelammert and Sánchez Vázquez argue, but rather the attempt to base these ideals in a supposed "human nature" that has been "alienated" by modern rationality (Vattimo, *The End of Modernity* 27). Today, freedom resides precisely in extinguishing the modern project of the unification of rationalities in order to progress toward the creation of immanent mechanisms that allow for transversality and the political wager of dissensus. To assume modern disenchantment in all its radicality: this is what postmodern emancipation consists of.

2. When we use the expression "end of history," we need to make a similar distinction to the previous one, because this "end" has little to do with postmodernity. This thesis has two variants: one is the theory of "posthistory," outlined in the 1950s by the German sociologist Arnold Gehlen as a critique of the lack of innovation in advanced industrial societies where a high degree of material sophistication has paralyzed the emergence of new energies and values ("Ende der Geschichte?"). Human history has "ended" in this case because the only thing that advances is the technological machinery that guarantees perpetual satisfaction to the masses, who are incapable of creating something new. The other variant was presented by the North American political theorist Francis Fukuyama: human history "ends" with the emergence of a global culture of consumerism mediated by liberal democracy and market economics (*The End of History*). Fukuyama's argument is based on Hegel (read through Alexandre Kojève) and claims that the psychological need for recognition is the meaning and motor of history. The desire of some people to be recognized by "others" has been the impulse behind passions like religious fanaticism, war, nationalism, and hate. However, toward the end of the twentieth century, with the globalization of mass culture, people began to no longer need the gaze of an external "other" in order to feel accepted. Nationalisms and fanaticisms pale before the triumph of mass democracy, which is able to offer citizens the full satisfaction of their psychological need to be accepted without having to look for "external enemies." For Fukuyama, history has come to an end because

the desire to be recognized is satisfied by the mass consumerism that guarantees the market economy.

The thesis of the "end of history," in either of its two variants, points to the crisis of the philosophical vision that attributes a "finality" (*telos, Zweck*), an *eschaton* to human history. Nietzsche, Ortega y Gasset, and Foucault emphasized the *radical historicity* of humanity, which means that what we have become can only be understood according to the contingency of our historical practices, without recurring to metaphysical criteria of any kind. "The human has no nature, only history," Ortega y Gasset used to say. The immediate consequence of this assertion, as Foucault shows, is that it is not possible to think history in terms of continuities, regularities, or incremental processes (*The Archaeology of Knowledge*). History is not the "unfolding" of an originary essence (human nature) but rather the result of a multiplicity of competing interpretative and evaluative practices. However, behind this competition there is no originary "psychology" (the need for recognition), as Fukuyama claims, nor is there a reason that directs human events, nor is there a natural morality that loses or finds its way, nor are there any subjects constituted prior to their experiences. For Foucault, history is the permanent emergence of difference. Therefore, the task of the genealogist is to recognize the multiplicity of the "small histories" that coexist, are articulated together, or are in conflict among themselves, but without resorting to a transcendental criterion that would allow for a hierarchical organization of these histories.[16]

Foucault's critique—which is also asserted by Vattimo, Lyotard, and Derrida—allows us to see that human societies are not the result of a quantitatively progressing historical process that necessarily leads to modernity or tradition, civilization or barbarism, development or underdevelopment. This was exactly what Latin American liberal elites believed during the nineteenth and twentieth centuries, convinced as they were that the programs of modernization would be enough to move beyond all the "irrationality" inherent to the ethos of colonial Hispanic society. Dependency theory critically reacted to this claim only to fall victim to an equally totalizing reading of history. The development-underdevelopment dialectic has now become the "inherent logic" that explains not only the wealth and poverty of nations but also all the artistic, philosophical, and cultural expressions of a given society.

However, by showing that different human societies cannot be thought as embedded in a single current of history, postmodern criticism eradicates any pretensions of elevating European history to the paradigmatic category of "universal History." This has been the case with the grand historical narratives of Hegel and Marx, who sought to explain human development in its totality without realizing that what they considered "universal" was in reality determined by particular historical circumstances. Certainly twentieth-century Latin American philosophy, in its historicist and liberationist version, produced a formidable and well-deserved critique of Marx and Hegel's Eurocentrism. However, blinded by a romantic Third Worldism, some philosophers of liberation simply chose to invert the roles: instead of looking at all of human achievement from the point of view of the conquerors, they decided to look at things from what they called "the other side of history," which is to say, from the point of view of the conquered and oppressed. Here again we see, albeit in an inverted form, the enlightened purpose of the "subject of history," except that this honor no longer corresponds to the oppressors but rather to the oppressed.

Our intention is to show that dependency theory and liberation philosophy remain trapped in an enlightened *pathos* that postmodernity seeks to leave behind, since the postmodern perspective seeks to examine the past without looking for a fixed Archimedean point and to avoid universalizing any particularity.[17] However, wouldn't this mean denying the historiographical work to which twentieth-century Latin American philosophy was so committed, as Arturo Andrés Roig suggests? What would happen to the "history of ideas," which we see today as the foundation of an "authentically Latin American" philosophy? I would say that the history of ideas must experience a profound methodological and conceptual transformation that would allow it to seek out and dust off the "small histories" Foucault mentions, but without integrating them into comprehensive discourses. This would mean not subsuming them in abstract categories like "people," "nation," or "economic dependence," or to read them according to binary interpretative frameworks: oppressor versus oppressed, center versus periphery, instrumental reason versus popular reason. We believe that such models and categories obscure the multiplicity of historical *practices* that explain why we have come to be who we are. It is now time that we understand that the development of

Latin American societies cannot be comprehended from elite intellectuals' "logic of ideas" but rather from the study of multiple and irreducible rationalities and practices that should be appreciated in their *singularity.*

3. At the end of *The Order of Things*, when Foucault says that man is a recent invention that is about to be erased "like a face drawn in sand at the edge of the sea," he is not referring to the empirical subject but rather to the discourse that claims that man is the source and origin of language and meaning, as early human science explained it in the late eighteenth century. This is the *humanism* of Sartre, which establishes the possibility that man can be free from all external determinations beyond his control thanks to the knowledge he has or could have of himself: Man as subject of his own freedom and his own existence through an act of reflexive consciousness ("Foucault Responds to Sartre" 36). However, Foucault writes, twentieth-century human science discovered that "human nature," which is capable of being reflexively known, is nothing other than a fiction. Psychoanalysis, for example, has shown that the thinking subject is not the *center* of human activity; rather, reason interacts with unconscious forces that determine our behavior to a large extent. Linguistics proves that the difference between object and subject is a contingent effect of the combination between determinate language games. Foucault himself maintains that the relation between power and truth is much more complex than one might believe, as science itself is based on relations of power. Medicine, psychiatry, and pedagogy are disciplinary systems that make up the fields of knowledge, investigative techniques, and collection of data on which the epistemological status of the object is "created." The natural sciences do not operate on the basis of a speculative concept of truth, but instead acknowledge that our theoretical edifices are subject to chance and contingency.

Does this lead us into the kind of anarchist irrationalism that so many Latin American philosophers fear? We do not think so, because postmodern criticism does not seek to annihilate the subject but rather to *decenter it.* If the Enlightenment subject, either in the solipsistic form of the Cartesian cogito or in the Marxist guise of the "collective subject," used to function as the foundation of cognitive, political, and moral power, now it tries to open the field to a plurality of subjects who, instead of some kind of foundation, demand *participation* in public life in a society that is increasingly multipolar and interactive, such as that which awaits us in the twenty-first century. The democratic pluralism needed in Latin America necessarily requires abandoning humanism as a *foundational* resource. For democracy to exist, no single agent can make claim to any kind of centrality (whether cognitive, aesthetic, or moral) in society. Neither the state nor the Church, the market, political parties, intellectuals, science, social movements, or any other group or institution can demand the right to represent the totality in the name of humanism. Ernesto Laclau and Chantal Mouffe have shown that democratic politics cannot be instituted in the name of a "disalienation" that attempts to overcome social antagonisms, for its objective is not to recuperate the essence of the human but rather to constitute forms of power that allow for dissensus and a plurality of values (*Hegemony and Socialist Strategy*). Unburdening ourselves of humanism thus does not mean leaving open the path to anarchist irrationality; it means favoring a broader vision of sociocultural, politico-ideological, and economic-productive heterogeneity as well as an expanded understanding of all kinds of differences.

Therefore, it is necessary to recognize that Latin American philosophy—particularly the philosophy of liberation—very appropriately took critical distance from the Enlightenment subject of European modernity. Before Lyotard, Vattimo, and Derrida in Europe, Argentine philosopher Enrique Dussel drew from the consequences of Heidegger's critique of Western metaphysics and identified the inherent relation between the Enlightenment subject of modernity and European colonial power. Behind the Cartesian *ego cogito*, out of which modernity originated, there is a hidden logocentrism through which the Enlightenment subject is deified and made into a sort of demiurge capable of constructing and dominating the world of objects. The modern ego cogito thus becomes a will to power: "I think" is equivalent to "I conquer," the epistemic foundation on which European domination has rested since the sixteenth century. For this reason, Dussel tells us, it is necessary to advance toward the construction of a new type of society that escapes the metaphysics of modern subjectivity. It will be a "postmodern" society that has as its fundamental characteristic what Emmanuel Levinas calls "the humanism of the Other."[18]

We could initially critique Dussel for reducing modernity to a totalizing version that does not recognize the array of alternative rationalities that are not purely instrumental and colonial. However, this problem becomes more acute when he expands his analysis of *alterity* through dependency theory and liberation theology. The *other* of modern "sameness" is the poor and the oppressed of peripheral Latin America, Asia, and Africa. This other, located "outside" the modern colonial system, becomes the only source of renewal for the entire planet, since the *ethos* of oppressed peoples contains values that are very different from the instrumentalism that reigns in the "center": love, communion, solidarity, face-to-face relations, a sense of social justice. In this way, Dussel commits a further reduction, that of making the poor into a kind of *transcendental subject* through which the history of humanity acquires an emancipatory consciousness. Here we find ourselves at the antipodes of postmodern criticism, as Dussel does not seek to decentralize the Enlightenment subject but rather to replace it with another absolute subject. In my opinion, the relation of the "same" to the "other," as Dussel consistently calls it, functions as a form of control over the *event*. In place of the "other"—a discourse that reproduces the modern code of "identity"—it is preferable to speak of the *outside* as the space from which the event irrupts and destabilizes both the "same" and the "other."

It is precisely this conflation of the "outside" with the "other" that causes Dussel to contrast a "good power" and a "bad power" in a Manichaean fashion, with the former coming "from below," from the world of the poor, and the latter originating "from above," from the selfish interests of imperialism. This is an extremely problematic contrast, because power, as Foucault clearly demonstrated, is not an *attribute* linked to the colonial state or to an oppressor class or a specific "mode of production," but rather is a relation of forces that inheres within both the dominator and the dominated. Domination is not something that can be reversed simply by changing "the place of the king," so that the dominated would occupy it, precisely because the latter have been *constituted* by the very power they seek to overcome. Thus, Dussel's critique of modernity is not capable of cutting off the king's head, only of changing its location, of inverting it. Additionally, as a consequence, Dussel places the oppressed "outside" modern relations of power, which leads him to reproduce the typical paternalistic gesture of Christianity. In fact, the philosophy of liberation affirms that the mission of intellectuals is "to give voice to those who have none." Its moral duty is *to speak for* the poor and the meek, for those who have been battered by life, believing that they represent the outside of modernity. However, as we have seen, thinkers like Martín-Barbero, Brunner, and García Canclini have convincingly shown that the poor in Latin America do not dwell in an exterior relation (whether technological, economic, or moral) to the "cultural logic" of modernity. To the contrary, culture industries have resignified the world of the subaltern classes in Latin America, which allows us to see that it is not possible to nostalgically turn our view back to "popular culture," as if it resided in a relation of "exteriority" to the modern world, since identifying with the *signs* of capital is an aspiration held by people in all segments of society, including the poorest.[19] It seems to us, therefore, that the philosophy of liberation is nothing other than a romanticization of the poor that strips them of the possibility of speaking for themselves or of strategically *entering and exiting* modernity, as García Canclini has so astutely argued (*Hybrid Cultures*).[20]

What still remains is to resolve the question posed by Arturo Andrés Roig about whether the crisis of the Enlightenment subject also signifies the neutralization of critical rationality. To this question, we can simultaneously reply both yes and no. "Yes" when by "critical rationality" we mean the philosophical tradition of *Ideologiekritik*—that is, a practice of reason that can reveal the ultimate causes and mechanisms of all human alienation. "No" when "critical rationality" is seen as the possibility of creatively taking responsibility for our own present, *with and against modernity*, without following romantic illusions like those proposed by the philosophy of liberation. In the first case, the practice of the critique of ideology presupposes the figure of a *transcendental subject* that is "external" to all alienation and has guaranteed access to an unadulterated truth. In the second case, it is, in contrast, accepted that there is a multiplicity of *historical subjects*, struggling from different *perspectives* to reconfigure existing power relations, but without making absolute cognitive, ethical, or aesthetic claims—for example, *democratic struggles* that have no transcendental guarantee.[21] For this same reason, criticism does not attempt to reach a point where we can avoid the opacities, contradictions, and instabilities of modern life, but rather aims at a place where we can accept "paralogy" (Lyotard) itself as part of the rules of the game. The objective is not to achieve consensus (Habermas) with regard to the ultimate values that should govern public life, but rather to prepare ourselves for the *agonistic confrontation* of values through politics.[22] It is in this sense that we can, along with Wolfgang Welsch, speak of a *transversal critique* that does not aim to deideologize perspectives but rather to multiply them (*Unsere postmoderne Moderne* 295–318).

4. Finally, I will address one of the most common rejections of postmodernity to have come out of Latin American philosophy: the so-called end of utopias. Once again, we must ask first what kind of utopia we are talking about. We will examine the specific case of Lyotard, as he is one of the most controversial authors on the topic. The French philosopher argues that, beginning with Wittgenstein's analyses, language games are structured in such a way that it is impossible to use them to conceive of a human community where conflict, and therefore injustice, do not exist. Games such as "a question," "a description," or "a narrative" are constructed on a basis of very complex chains of enunciation where there are different possibilities for connecting some propositions with others. If there is no linguistic metacriterion that allows us to know which connections we *should* make, choosing one or more possibilities always comes at the cost of others. The result is the unavoidable conflict between different language games or, what amounts to the same thing, among different *forms of life*. The heteromorphism of language games means that dissension, incommensurability, dissonance, and paradox cannot be eliminated from social life without recurring to a political metalanguage: fascist violence. According to Lyotard, any attempt to "reconcile" the differences between these language games and between the forms of life shaped by them almost always ends in dictatorship and terror (*The Postmodern Condition* 63–67).[23]

However, almost all the "future utopias" that were developed between the sixteenth and nineteenth centuries conceived of the ideal society as that in which unity and harmony reign, class struggle no longer exists, and interpersonal communication is transparent and unmediated by power relations. Happiness in such a society would be the experience of the *absolute absence of differends.* Harmony and hegemony are characteristics of a community in which there is no longer any place for the polytheism of values. But if, as Lyotard shows, heterogeneity and difference are inherent in all human communication, it is then clear that this kind of utopia would be likely to degenerate into authoritarian models of social existence in which homogeneity and consensus could only be guaranteed through the despotic practice of a religious, economic, political, or social metacriterion.

What does the end of *this kind* of totalizing utopia mean for Latin American philosophy? Is it perhaps the negation of the "discourse of the future" as an essential form of narrative about what organizes a large portion of our thought, just as Roig fears? Does it mean we must ruthlessly drown the morning song of the Argentine mockingbird? The answer is surely yes if this "discourse of the future" is simply identified with what has been called the "Latin American utopia," whose origins the Uruguayan essayist Fernando Aínsa has studied. In elaborating on this narrative form, Aínsa distinguishes four levels: 1. transposing to the New World topics and classical myths like the biblical paradise, the golden age, the primitive Christian community, and the bucolic Arcadia where the human being lived in absolute reconciliation with himself and with nature; 2. the notion of *alterity*, which is to say, the conception of Latin America as a totally different world that has consequently been transformed into the repository of all the dreams of perfection that were not achieved in Europe; 3. the millenarian visions of religious orders that sought to test a theocratic model of society in Latin America; and 4. the dream of improving the individual and collective situation of Indigenous populations by converting them to Christianity—that is, under their assimilation to forms of life dictated by a higher authority (*De la Edad de Oro a El Dorado* 131). Unfortunately, this foundational discourse of the "Latin American utopia," which is characterized by its *comprehensive and totalizing* pretensions, has been reproduced since then by a great number of our intellectuals as the socialist utopia par excellence in which Latin America is seen as the "absolute other" of European rationality, the continent of grand synthesis, the spiritual reserve of humanity, the future of the Church, or the land of mystery, magic, and poetry. If this is the "discourse of the future" to which Roig refers, then we welcome its departure, as this discourse consists of the same rhetoric that has been used to legitimize authoritarian and populist regimes of all kinds in this region.

However, by proclaiming the end of unitary and totalizing utopias, are we not also undermining an inalienable concept in Latin America, that of "social justice?" Of course, the answer is yes when this "justice" is equipped with the myth of a *transparent society.* I think that this concept of justice as an "absence of all evil" is a legacy of Judeo-Christian eschatology, which must be eradicated from Latin American politics (the belief in a reconciliation between man and nature and in the appearance of a redeemed man),[24] and I think, along with Lyotard, that any attempt to transpose this myth onto social reality almost always degenerates into its opposite: some of the most notorious authoritarian regimes of our time have been established in the name of "social justice." Therefore, it is now time to recognize that we cannot go beyond ourselves and understand that justice can be nothing other than the (not always successful) attempt at democratically regulating *dissension.* In sum, we must understand that, in a democratic society, the fight against injustice necessarily generates new forms of injustice.[25] The question is therefore: What injustices are more or less *tolerable* for society as a whole? However, this is a question that can no longer be decided a priori, without a universal metalanguage, but rather must always be the provisional and contingent result of "democratic struggles."

Ortega y Gasset saw that utopian politics are one of the typical features of modern rationalism, with its attempt to see the world *sub specie aeternitatis,* from the point of view of eternity. "The concept of utopia is created out of nowhere and yet, nevertheless, claims to be valid for all" ("History as a System" 191). However, wanting to see the world not as it is and has been but rather as it *should be* is equivalent to imposing moral and political ways of thinking that do violence to the multiplicity of dynamics and forms of life in society. The problem of utopianism is not so much that it offers false solutions to our social problems, but its inability to accept that life does not allow itself to be shaped by our rational and moral plans. This is why we must oppose *utopianism* with the notion of *perspectivism.* This means that, instead of imagining the future from the basis of values like unity, consensus, harmony, homogeneity, transparency, and reconciliation, we must now imagine it as the alignment negotiated between different forms of knowledge and different moral criteria for action. Because it does not have messianic and rationalist pretensions, perspectivism could be an excellent legitimation narrative for democratically inclined politics. Thus, abandoning utopianism does not mean no longer imagining the future from an emancipatory perspective, as Roig argues; rather, it means no longer supplanting the multiplicity of points of view with a homogeneous and normative vision. Daring to imagine a future continues to be a regulating statute of change and the struggle for change; however, after Auschwitz, Hiroshima, and Ayacucho we can only understand this change under the paradigm of difference and heterogeneity.[26]

We conclude this chapter with four commentaries by way of synthesis. First, discussing postmodernity in Latin America is not the product of an ideological deception or of a theoretical mode or of a Eurocentric atavism that has infected our intellectuals. Rather, it follows a *condition* that affects both the mode of being of discourses and the mode of being of daily practices. Second, this epistemic and social change maintains a direct relation to the globalization of a capitalist system of signs that began to take shape during the second half of the twentieth century, which has extended "exchange value" to areas that were previously untouched by the economy in Third World countries. Third, postmodernity puts us face-to-face with the challenge of *assuming* the disenchantment of the world as the ultimate horizon of politics in Latin America, thus freeing us from the metaphysical temptations of populism.[27] Fourth, Latin American philosophers, inhabitants of a modern order of knowledge, behave like Foucault's portrayal of Don Quixote in *The Order of Things*. That is to say, they behave like intellectuals who live and think in a world they do not understand and who inhabit a discursive order that is disconnected from the present era. For postmodernists do not criticize "error" in the name of "truth," we do not want to "humanize ourselves" or look for the origin of our cultural identity, nor are we moved by continuity and unity but rather by multiplicity and the event.

2

MODERNITY, RATIONALIZATION, AND CULTURAL IDENTITY IN LATIN AMERICA

If there is one distinguishing feature of the twentieth century, it is the globalization of interdependent economic, social, and political processes. This is a heterogeneous globalization that, driven by the processes of structural transformation in Western societies, directly affects the lives of all human beings wherever it manifests. The borders that for thousands of years separated some cultures from others have vanished because of the transnational regulation of activity. The development of high-speed transportation systems, the endless supply of images distributed all over the world by the culture industry, the continuous flow of immigrants, tourists, or refugees, and the globalization of the market economy are factors that have contributed to the elimination of *radical alterity* between cultures. At the end of the twentieth century, a heightened sensitivity emerged around problems that affect the international community as a whole: the destruction of the environment, the indebtedness of the Third World, the proliferation of nuclear weapons, the uncontrolled growth of the global population, the propagation of diseases like AIDS, the globalization of drug trafficking and organized crime. These are all phenomena that, because they are incorporated into a very complex network of causes and effects that ignores all borders, have become immune to every attempt to control them.

However, these global transformations have also provoked defensive reactions, particularly in those regions that have directly suffered the experience of European colonialism, where one finds the extremes of nationalist and fundamentalist tendencies. Deep anti-Western sentiment in Islamic countries, wars in the former Soviet republics and in ex-Yugoslavian countries, ethnic conflicts in sub-Saharan Africa, the Catholic Church's "evangelization of culture" programs, certain Latin American intellectuals and activists' exaltation of the material world, as well as the rebirth of xenophobia and racism in Europe—these are all examples of the fractured and heterogeneous spaces of the world we inhabit, where identities, whether individual or collective, frequently oscillate between the global and the regional, between the national and the postnational. How this conflict between the deterritorialization and the reterritorialization of identities will be resolved depends on whether the twenty-first century yields a more tolerant and peaceful world or whether we fall back into the despotism and barbarism that was all too common in the twentieth century.

The present chapter is a reflection on how social sciences and Latin American cultural studies at the end of the century have focused on the problem of collective identity. I will therefore analyze the theoretical proposals of the Catholic sociologists Pedro Morandé and Cristián Parker and I will then engage in a dialogue with the arguments elaborated by Jesús Martín-Barbero, Néstor García Canclini, and José Joaquín Brunner. My purpose is to show how the relation between modernity, rationalization, and culture has been thought in Latin America at the end of the twentieth century.

1. MORANDÉ, PARKER, AND THE EXTERIORITY OF THE POPULAR ETHOS

In his book *Cultura y modernización en América Latina* (Culture and modernization in Latin America), Morandé sets out to analyze the crisis of developmentalism and find an alternative solution rooted in Spanish American "cultural identity." He begins from the presupposition that modernity is a process that breaks with the specific cultural and political formations, which, until the decline of Spanish hegemony in Europe in the eighteenth century, were common in Latin America for three hundred years. With their ties to Spain broken, the young Latin American nations had to readjust their identities to the new global balance of power, adopting values that were completely foreign to their Hispanic and Lusophone cultural inheritance (*Cultura y modernización en América Latina* 16). According to Morandé, by trying to imitate the models offered by England and France, the political orientation taken by local elites entailed denying the "cultural synthesis" that emerged in Latin America during the sixteenth century, when Indigenous populations began to mix with Iberian populations. One immediate consequence of this denial was the profound distance that developed between the educated criollo oligarchies (who engaged in mutually destructive ideological quarrels) and the bulk of the mestizo population (who kept their traditional forms of generating and transmitting knowledge through popular Catholicism).

However, we will proceed step by step, first looking at how Morandé characterizes this new modern rationality that originated in Protestant European nations. Closely following Max Weber, the Chilean sociologist knows that the Protestant ethic has resulted in a type of person that is unknown in the Catholic world: a disciplined, austere worker thrown into the dominion of the world. This is the educated, critical individual who rises up against dogmas and religion and who, assisted by new advances in science, sets out to conquer the world while trusting in the autonomy of reason. This unleashes the modern process of secularization that, according to Morandé, originates in the "functionalization of ethics." Interpersonal relationships lose their connection to a transcendent order and turn into "social functions" with the sole objective of assuring the equilibrium of a system dominated by the self-regulating laws of the market (107).

Based in a reading of Weber mediated by the Frankfurt School, Morandé argues that in Western modernity the "system" domesticates the individual absolutely. Modern society is organized as an immense bureaucratic machinery that assigns all of its members to determined functional roles. Behind all this is the system's logic of self-preservation: individuals learn to be disciplined and to puritanically renounce all extravagance in order to save and invest in businesses that generate wealth and wellbeing for all, which is precisely how the system as a whole can guarantee its own existence. Any other type of behavior is considered immoral and must be scrupulously punished, since it can lead to the structural disequilibrium of the "totality" (109). This functionalist logic, which Morandé calls the "introjection of sacrifice," results in the absolute bureaucratization of European societies.

By way of contrast, Morandé introduces a Latin American cultural ethos that is based in the encounter between Hispanic, African, and Indigenous traditions and is diametrically opposed to modern rationality. His thesis is that, starting in the sixteenth century, a pre-Enlightenment, baroque cultural identity that was essentially different from Western rationality began to take shape in Latin America: "Our hypothesis is that the rationality of our ethos is not the same as the rationality of European Enlightenment. . . . The advent of the formal rationality of the modern world was produced at a time when Latin America had already formed and consolidated a cultural *ethos*" (140; 145).

We have before us a "genuinely Latin American" rationality that is not derived from Western modernity but rather existed *before* it, or to be more precise, existed *under* it. It is a rationality that is not premodern but rather *submodern*, as it is not based on a synthesis on the level of language and discourse but rather on the level of religious ritual. In effect, the essential difference between the pathos of modernity and the Latin American ethos is, according to Morandé, that, wheras the former's synthesis is founded in logos, the latter's is based on ritual ("Grupos sociales y en conflicto" 278). Modernity is a phenomenon that is generated in textual cultures that do not require the presence of more than one person to initiate communication. It is a monological and individualist culture that is transmitted through written language. In contrast, Latin American countries belong to cultures that are orally constituted and transmitted. Oral culture, contrary to written culture, emerges from the experience of the encounter of a plurality of people who share values present in the same lifeworld. There is no such thing as a private subject who, due to some kind of social pact, later becomes a public subject. To the contrary, public space is constitutive of oral culture and in no way defined by the state or by a form of economic organization but rather by religious festivals that bring everyone together around the historical memory and traditions of the people. In Latin America, this oral and ritual tradition has been significantly marked by the Catholic Church. The arrival of Catholicism does not represent for Indigenous peoples a rupture in their world of meaning since, as a result of the Counter-Reformation, baroque Hispanic Catholicism favored the complete sacramentalization of worship. Hence, to this day, the mythico-religious values of this lifeworld retain the roots of their religious practices and oppose the imposition of modern rationality in Latin America.

In Morandé's opinion, the historical subject of "cultural synthesis" between the Indigenous, the European, and the African was not the criollo but the mestizo. To be sure, while undoubtedly a product of a cultural intersection, the criollo could never recognize his own mestizaje. Instead, the criollo idealizes both the Indigenous and the European in order to affirm his own position as the synthesis of the best of both worlds, thereby disdaining both the Indigenous and the European for "whitening" his own mestizo status on the basis of an imaginary notion of "blood purity." According to Morandé, here we are confronted with a synthesis that takes place on the abstract level of discourse, because true cultural synthesis exists in ritual praxis, the subject of which is the mestizo, the result of the carnal encounter between the Indigenous mother and the European conquistador, and not the criollo. Therefore, modernity in Latin America is a process that directly affects not the mestizo—who retains the cultural identity inherited from colonialism—but solely the criollo. The Latin American criollo oligarchy in the nineteenth century saw in the project of modernity a useful tool for camouflaging the reality of its own mestizaje, which explains its virulent contempt for Indigenous populations and its determination to Europeanize Latin American societies. Dressed in modernizing clothing, the criollo devalued the "cultural synthesis" of the Latin American ethos and regarded it as an "obstacle to development" (*Cultura y modernización en América Latina* 158). Based on the juxtaposition between society and community (taken from the sociological models of Émile Durkheim and Ferdinand Tönnies), Morandé constructs a cultural foundation for Latin America located in its *external* relation to Western modernity: a "baroque ethos" consolidated in the sixteenth century through the synthesis of three cultures fundamentally expressed in the ritual practices of "popular religiosity" ("La síntesis cultural hispánica-indígena").

However, Morandé is not the only Latin American sociologist who has studied the underlying rationality of popular sites of worship, pilgrimages, and processions. His colleague and fellow Chilean Cristián Parker also works along similar lines, although Parker notably broadens the concept of popular religiosity to include religious expressions connected to Catholicism as well as urban phenomena like Pentecostalism, Afro-descendant cults, spiritualism, and evangelical sects. Like Morandé, he seeks to overcome the developmentalist Enlightenment paradigm, showing that Latin American popular culture operates under "another logic" that is not merely different from but also *opposed to* Western modernity.

To carry out this task, Parker bases his analysis on the reflections of the Argentine school of the philosophy of liberation (Rodolfo Kusch, Carlos Cullen, Enrique Dussel, and Juan Carlos Scannone), which since the 1970s has developed and promoted a hermeneutics of Latin American popular culture.[1] In my view, up to the present, this is the most serious effort to comprehend structures of thought that differ from those of the dominant intellectual and "learned" culture of Latin American criolloism:

> We maintain that, at the base of the syncretic religious mentality of the Latin American structure, in the structuring code of that mentality's multiform plurality, lies a sort of vitalistic anthropology, alternative to the Promethean anthropology of Western modernity. It is a chthonic, maternal anthropology, derived from the great telluric intuitions of the pre-Columbian cultures, as over against a dualistic, pantocratic, patriarchal anthropology derived from the Western Greco-Roman worldview. . . . It is a question no longer of primitive human beings immersed in nature (without having yet developed their cultural rationality), nor of Western, modern human beings suffocating in their instrumental, private rationality. It is a question of the "Latin" human being, neither pre- nor postmodern.
>
> We have found a hemidernal anthropology, not antagonistic but cooperative and, under many aspects, alternative to Western modernity. We have found a different human conception, multiple and holistic, the human being who harmonizes, from amidst an ancestral wisdom, feeling and reasoning, thinking and acting, seeking and hoping, rejoicing and mourning.
>
> (PARKER, *POPULAR RELIGION AND MODERNIZATION IN LATIN AMERICA* 261–62)

Following the line of thought developed by Morandé, Parker goes even further: he no longer relates this "other logic" of popular culture to the "baroque ethos" resulting from the synthesis resulting from the conquest, but rather to the "telluric intuitions of the pre-Columbian cultures" that have survived in spite of the "cultural synthesis" Morandé discusses.[2] On this basis, he argues that in Latin America there is a predominant sui generis rationality that is not modern, premodern, or postmodern but rather the synthesis of all three, capable of "phagocytozing" (as Kusch might say) modern logics and symbolically transforming them, pulling them out of their Cartesian roots. This rationality is primarily expressed through symbols and oral discourse, not through texts and abstract discourse.[3] Like Morandé, Parker is convinced that the telluric world of Latin American popular culture can "engulf" the modernizing attacks that come from Europe and translate them into "other logics."

The project of a sociology of Latin American popular culture conceived of by Parker and Morandé is based on two problematic conceptions: the first is a substantialist and unitary conception of popular culture as a "ground" (*Grund*) that can subsume all external rationalities to its own basic logic; the second is a narrow reading of Weber's elaboration of the concept of *rationalization*. The combination of these two conceptions results in an idealized and romantic representation of "Latin American popular culture" that is presented as both "external" to modern rationality and the alternative that will save it. We will analyze this problem in the following section.

2. MAX WEBER AND THE NARRATIVE OF RATIONALIZATION

I want to focus my critique on the way in which Parker and Morandé use the Weberian thesis of rationalization, for it is precisely Weber's tendentious reading that allows the two Chilean sociologists to construct a field of "Latin American exteriority" in relation to modernity. The instrumentalization of human relations is set in opposition to socialization by language, and the disenchantment of the world is contrasted with face-to-face experience and the sense of transcendence proper to the "Latin American ethos."

As is well known, beginning in the 1940s, the Frankfurt School popularized a "tragic vision" of the process of rationalization described by Weber. According to this interpretation, rationalization is a homogeneous and progressive process of demystification that is present in all intellectual, artistic, and institutional activities in the Western world. "Images of the world" (*Weltbilder*) were no longer necessary to legitimate the threads that hold society together, since it is differentiated into compartmentalizations that each follow their own logic. If, during the Middle Ages in Europe, science, art, and morality were legitimized through reference to the cosmovision of Christianity, with the advent of modernity these spheres have become independent and claim their own right to exist. Science no longer requires metaphysical foundations but is instead based on mathematical formalization and experimentation; morality is no longer based on the authority of the Church but rather on an ethics of responsibility that develops within individual consciousness. Religion thus recedes into the private sphere and becomes a matter of personal choice. The disenchantment (*Entzauberung*) of the world and the absolute bureaucratization of society has taken place. The economy and the state take on the form of an autonomous machinery that subdues and determines individuals, thus advancing toward an "administered society" in which life is entirely governed by self-regulating laws that are void of moral content. For the first generation of Frankfurt School thinkers, particularly for Horkheimer and Adorno, the rationalization of the West necessarily entails the *totalization of irrationality*.[4]

According to Habermas, this fatalistic interpretation of Weber is based on a philosophy of history that resonates with "instrumental reason."[5] Along with Lukács, and negatively influenced by their experiences with mass culture in the United States, Horkheimer and Adorno identify the totality of the Western civilizing process with the evolution of a historical logic guided by the domination of nature. This same dynamic ends up establishing increasingly hierarchical relations of domination in areas such as economics, legislation, culture, and state administration. The advance of irrationality one finds at the core of the process of rationalization in modern societies is so powerful that it seems there is no longer any aspect of human subjectivity that is protected from objectifying reason. These are the roots of the triumphant impersonal forces that govern individual psychology, which ultimately lead to concentration camps and a society gone mad.

The question is whether this ominous reading by the Frankfurt School philosophers corresponds to what Weber actually understood "rationalization" to mean. It seems clear that for him rationalization is not a "constant anthropology" that belongs to *all* human cultures, and it is much less a teleological process that could be understood as the "unfolding of reason."[6] There is no "evolutionary process" in Weber that culminates in Western modernity, as Habermas would have it. To the contrary, if we examine Weber's *empirical* analysis of the social dynamic put into motion by the Protestant ethic in certain European countries, we can see that this phenomenon follows particular circumstances that *in themselves* have no universal significance. His theory of rationalization is in fact opposed to the Enlightenment philosophy of history and nineteenth-century theories of evolution. In Europe, the rational-capitalist development of labor, the training of technicians and specialists as those who hold the most important positions in social life, the systematic cultivation of scientific specializations, and the strengthening of the machinery of the state are all *contingent products* that emerged under very specific historical circumstances.

Now, in his genealogy of modernity, Weber recognizes that "inner-worldly asceticism," the breeding ground of rationalization, was a phenomenon that was produced by Protestant churches as well as in Roman Catholicism, particularly in religious orders like the Jesuits:

> Without doubt Christian asceticism, both outwardly and in its inner meaning, contains many different things. But it has had a definitely rational character in its highest Occidental forms as early as the Middle Ages, and in several forms even in antiquity. The great historical significance of Western monasticism, as contrasted with that of the Orient, is based on this fact, not in all cases, but in its general type. In the rules of St. Benedict, still more with the monks of Cluny, again with the Cistercians, and most strongly the Jesuits, it has become emancipated from planless otherworldliness and irrational self-torture. It had developed a systematic method of rational conduct with the purpose of overcoming the *status naturæ*, to free man from the power of irrational impulses and his dependence on the world and on nature. . . . This active

> self-control, which formed the end of the *exercitia* of St. Ignatius and of the rational monastic virtues everywhere, was also the most important practical ideal of Puritanism.
>
> (*THE PROTESTANT ETHIC AND THE SPIRIT OF CAPITALISM* 118–19)

According to Weber, if we understand *rationalization* to be the methodical organization of life and the submission of human behavior to a specific group of rules with the goal of achieving certain results, then it is clear that it came from Catholicism and that it therefore arrived in the Americas in the sixteenth century along with the enterprises of conquest and colonization. Morandé's thesis that the "baroque *ethos*" of Latin America, formed between the sixteenth and seventeenth centuries, is *opposed* to the "modern pathos" is nothing more than a nostalgic mythology. The religious orders that took as their task the evangelization of Indigenous and Black populations in the Americas were rationalized and furthermore *rationalizing* efforts.[7] It is sufficient to recall the rational organization of labor that the Jesuits instituted at their own haciendas and in their "reductions" (in Paraguay, for example), as well as in their schools and pedagogical methods (the famous *Ratio Studiorum*) to show us that the mestizo population was never "external" to the processes of rationalization.[8] In fact, and as dependency theory itself demonstrated, the conquest and evangelization of the Americas was the foundation for the rational and international division of labor that would drive the expansion of capitalism to cover the entire planet.

This is all to point to the fact that both Parker and Morandé use Weber's theory of rationalization, but they ignore his genealogy (the originary relation between inner-worldly asceticism and the Protestant work ethic) and subsume it to the Frankfurt School philosophers' unilateral and "tragic reading." Based on this interpretation, they argue in favor of a supposed "Latin American identity" that remains untouched by the processes of rationalization between the eighteenth and twentieth centuries in Europe, which are seen as a "totalization" of instrumental reason. The rereading of Weber we have proposed here shows us that Latin America never existed "externally" to Western modernity. However, this does not mean arguing that the processes of rationalization emerged in Latin America *in the same way* as they did in Europe. In fact, the purpose of the following section is to investigate this differentiality.

3. IDENTITIES AND RATIONALITIES IN LATIN AMERICA

The fact that modern rationalization cannot be reduced to a unique and teleological process (seen as a kind of "ontological decline"), as well as the fact that Latin America has not remained untouched by such rationalizing processes since the very beginning, are two of the central ideas that have defined cultural studies in recent years. The point of departure here is radically different from that adopted by Parker and Morandé, because, instead of discursively creating a "Latin American authenticity" that confronts the processes of modernization, it seeks to question how these processes have been culturally assimilated in our society as well as what type of hybrid identities are thereby generated. This reflection was undoubtedly triggered by the favorable reception of French poststructuralism toward the end of the 1980s, particularly in Brazil and in other countries of the Southern Cone (see Rincón "Die neue Kulturtheorien" and *La no simultaneidad de lo simultáneo*). Critiques of teleology and humanism by Foucault, Deleuze, and Derrida opened up the path for distancing oneself from those models of social analysis that attempted to evaluate the development of Latin American societies on the basis of binary, universalist, and exclusive categories (modern vs. traditional, civilization vs. barbarism, oppressor vs. oppressed, development vs. underdevelopment, and center vs. periphery). In contrast to classical sociology, which established the problem of modernity in terms of an irreconcilable opposition between the old and the new, cultural studies show that the different levels of a society (e.g., economic, political, social, and cultural) cannot be connected to a unitary framework of development. Rather, rationalization takes on different intensities on each level without inhibiting the mutually dependent coexistence of tradition and modernity. In Latin America, the modern has never replaced the traditional; they are so closely linked to one another that it is impossible to know where one ends and the other begins. In a word, cultural studies in the 1990s demonstrate that the relation between modernity and culture cannot be understood according to models that dissociate logos from mythos, the popular from the cultured, the authentic from the foreign, and the public from the private, as Parker and Morandé assert. Modernity does not conform to a unitary and homogeneous setting that would make it possible to imagine an "authentically Latin American" ethos; rather, it generates a complex network of ordering, reappropriation, and interpretation of *different kinds of rationality.*

Let us take the case of the Spanish-Colombian thinker Jesús Martín-Barbero and his polemic with the Adornian concept of the cultural industry in his book *De los medios a las mediaciones* (translated into English as *Communication, Culture, and Hegemony: From the Media to Mediations*). We have already seen how, by reading Weber in a tragic register, the Frankfurt School argued that Western rationalization necessarily leads to an irrationality articulated by political totalitarianism and mass culture. Referring to the latter, Adorno writes that all products of the culture industry (movies, jazz, pop music, etc.) are pervaded by "instrumental reason" and therefore represent the absolute triumph of barbarism and decline. The culture industry, with its repetitive rhythms and always predictable settings, reproduces the working logic of the Taylorist factory. However, supporting his argument through reference to Walter Benjamin's study of the technological reproducibility of art, Martín-Barbero writes that this pessimistic vision is nothing more than an aristocratic and callous response to how the masses have taken advantage of the possibilities opened up by technologies of reproduction. Far from instigating an "atrophy of consciousness," these new cultural practices make it possible to enrich perceptual experience, which is not reserved for the elites but is accessible to all: "Before, for the majority of people, things—and not only art, as close as the two may be—were always far away because a mode of social relations made them *feel far away.* Now the masses, with the help of technology, feel close to the furthest and most sacred things. And this 'feeling,' this experience, engenders egalitarian demands that make up the energy of the masses" (*De los medios a las mediaciones* 58). What Martín-Barbero means is that the Latin American masses are able to creatively assimilate the experience of modernity, with all its powers of rationalization. Modern technologies and media are not the catastrophic tools of a totalitarian alienation—as Morandé and the philosophers of liberation would have it[9]—since the consumption of modern symbols does not necessarily signify acritical passivity but rather the creation of meaning.[10] It is not so much the *media* as the symbolic *mediations* that allows the masses to recodify the messages they receive. According to Martín-Barbero, the predominance of the verbal in Latin American televisual discourse (primarily in *telenovelas*) is inscribed in the need to subordinate visual logic to the logic of contact, thereby producing a sensation of *immediacy*. The faces and characters from telenovelas become familiar and close because they are integrated into the intimate space of everyday life. Through melodramatic kitsch, which portrays the struggle for social recognition (the child abandoned by his parents, the poor but honorable young woman who falls in love with a wealthy young man, etc.), viewers internalize *strategies* that are intended to micrologically reconfigure power relations. In this way, television becomes an indispensable factor in the formation of personal and collective identities in Latin America.[11] Refusing to reckon with this—under the guise of wanting to defend "cultural authenticity"—is equivalent to remaining trapped in the romantic myth of the people as a pristine source of collective identity or supporting a paternalistic and despotic regime that snatches away from people what they require and need (Martín-Barbero, *De los medios a las mediaciones* 100).

It is clear that Martín-Barbero's reading of popular culture is far from the substantialist vision that Parker and Morandé defend. For these latter two popular culture is a substratum, while for Martín-Barbero it is the *result* of the asymmetrical interaction between multiple rationalities. In fact, the "popular" is largely an effect created by mass media. His analysis shows that the processes of rationalization in Latin America completely exceeded the Frankfurt School model of "instrumental reason" and that the discourses of the "people" and "cultural identity" acquired *meaning* in the region through the influence of mass media on the formation of so-called national cultures.[12] This took place primarily between 1930 and 1960, when, along with populism and against the backdrop of the incipient processes of modernization, the media began to symbolically construct the idea of the "people-nation." Regarding the case of Colombia, Martín-Barbero writes that, before the advent of broadcast radio, the country was a jigsaw puzzle of highly isolated regions, but after 1940, when radio spread to the furthest corners of the country, a national identity "appeared" that was supposedly shared by people from all over Colombia, including the Caribbean coast, Pasto, Bogotá, Antioquia, and Santander (*De los medios a las mediaciones* 79). This also occurred in Mexico, where cinema was the backbone of the idea of the popular well into the 1950s. Mexican films did not reflect a homogeneous cultural ethos that existed prior to its portrayal in the movies but rather one that was symbolically *created*, as moviegoers learned codes of conduct, ways of speaking, seeing, and feeling that later became associated with "Mexican identity." This means that "discourses of identity" do not refer to a preconfigured cultural unity, but rather to symbolic productions connected to rationalized practices that, as Foucault shows quite clearly, are inscribed in apparatuses of power that operate on the basis of exclusion and inclusion. Some elements of culture (fashion, humor, accent, idiomatic expressions, and macho attitudes) are selected to become narrativized stereotypes that are *later* projected onto the entire nation, while other elements are marginalized or remain in the shadows.

If Martín-Barbero focuses his analysis on how the culture industry has generated new identities and subjectivities in Latin America, Néstor García Canclini's thesis proceeds in a parallel direction, but also shows the form taken by the processes of rationalization that impact artistic production throughout Latin America. The central theme of his work is "hybrid cultures." This term itself already announces a methodological and investigative program, since it is nothing less than a rupture with Enlightenment epistemology and its conception of culture as based on such dualist oppositions as myth vs. logos, tradition vs. modernity, and civilization vs. barbarism. García Canclini wants to escape the false choice between *entering* modernity under the model of capitalist rationalization (as aspired to by neoliberal political elites) and *exiting* modernity in an attempt to safeguard the purity of popular culture (as in the example of the Catholic Church and intellectuals like Parker and Morandé). He knows that this escape will require destroying three myths that are deeply rooted in Latin American intellectual culture: the first is the idealization of modernity as the solution that would guarantee well-being and development for all; the second, in contrast, identifies modernity with colonialism, alienation, and the will to power; and the third, constructed in response to the second, portrays popular culture as a sacred and valuable domain that must be protected from modern rationalization. García Canclini is aware that escaping the first myth could lead to the impasses of the other two, so he seeks an alternative solution.

The first path he explores is to show that Latin American art, both in its content and its form, constitutes an example of rupture with these romantic Enlightenment myths (García Canclini, "Memory and

Innovation in the Theory of Art"). Modernist painting in Latin America in the 1930s (Diego Rivera in Mexico, Tarsila do Amaral and Emiliano Di Cavalcanti in Brazil, and Antonio Berni in Argentina) is in itself a hybrid formation that combines modern formal elements (cubism, impressionism, and expressionism) with traditional local motifs (landscapes, street scenes, and familiar personalities). Mexican muralism does not represent a choice between the traditional and the modern but is rather a synthesis between avant-garde art and the recuperation of historical memory. The affirmation of new aesthetic tendencies from Europe was not at all in conflict with the pre-Columbian setting of Mexico, nor with peasant life, the revolution, or political and union activity. Even the avant-garde artists, who from the 1950s to the 1970s began to experiment with new materials and techniques (plastic, acrylic, polyester, installations), incorporated traditional elements (pyramids and pre-Columbian figures) in a geometric discourse. In the same way, postmodernist art of the 1980s and 1990s often refers to social contradictions in an antievolutionist language that combines styles and movements from different eras. Here, García Canclini remarks, we find the difference between the postmodernist discourse of the "center," with its tendency to dissolve the past in a nihilistic presentism, and the postmodernism of "peripheral" authors like Nahum Zenil, Felipe Ehrenberg, Gerardo Sutier, and Alejandro Corujeira, with their interest in *rewriting* Latin America's past.

However, it would be a mistake to think that this multitemporal heterogeneity is only at work in the art of elite intellectuals who have had the opportunity to study in Europe or the United States. Like Martín-Barbero, García Canclini is convinced that popular culture is the best venue for observing the phenomenon of the hybridization between tradition and modernity. In Latin America, artisans, peasants, and Indigenous peoples have more than made use of the capitalist market's need to include traditional goods among its increasingly transnationalized array of symbolic offerings. The creative ways in which these groups have incorporated themselves into the demands of the international market undermines the idea that socioeconomic modernization and consumer mentality inevitably destroy Indigenous cultures. The same thing has happened with the transformations of popular music due to processes of cultural modernization. New popular forms, such as ballads, reggae, rock, or salsa are born out of the symbiosis between traditional rhythms and electronic media. All these artistic expressions entail what García Canclini calls the *deterritorialization* of popular culture (*Hybrid Cultures* 263). The dynamic brought about by the processes of rationalization and new communication technologies disconnects the popular from any kind of territorial or substantialist bond. Symbols of national identity, which populism had elevated to the category of an "essential patrimony" and exhibited publicly in museums,[13] have been separated from their primary referents and turned into transnational goods.

The second analytical path García Canclini explores consists of demonstrating how the globalization and transnationalization of culture has changed the configuration of personal and collective identities in Latin America (*Hybrid Cultures* 107). His starting point is a thesis that also appears in Martín-Barbero's work: national or continental identity is a discursive construction connected to institutional mechanisms. During the nineteenth century and into the beginning of the twentieth, identity was produced through disciplinary educational technologies such as schools, civic rituals, and museum collections, which discursively created a series of foundational events (battles for independence, the martyrdom of the founding fathers, the signing of the constitution, etc.). One's "own" culture is defined in relation to a given territory and is discursively organized on the basis of texts, objects, and *ahistorical* rituals that represent the "roots" of nationality. These apparatuses are later reinforced in the cinematic staging of common habits, tastes, and manners of speaking and dressing that significantly differentiate one specific community from another. Films and radio popularized the idea that the inhabitants of a certain geographical space have a homogeneous and coherent identity. Later, in the 1960s and 1970s, television supplanted cinema as the primary means for the construction of "national identity." As media outlets were predominantly based in national capitals and adhered to a developmentalist ideology, they were interested in spreading cultural knowledge in order to stimulate the consumption of local and Indigenous products. Thus broadcasts of locally focused series, full-coverage newscasts, and the national soccer team's games created the illusion of an identity shared by everyone in the country, in spite of all the regional differences.

According to García Canclini, this illusion began to disappear in the 1980s. The opening of national economies to global markets, the transnationalization of technologies, and the global circulation of symbolic goods diminished the importance of traditional referents of identity. With the advent of the increasingly free and common circulation of people, capital, and information, identity is no longer defined by exclusive belonging to a national community (*Hybrid Cultures* 109). At the end of the twentieth century, when 70 percent of Latin Americans live in cities and are symbiotically connected with the global culture industry, it is necessary to examine personal and collective identities in terms of their heterogeneity, their diverse symbolic codes, and how they are continuously negotiated. However, García Canclini writes, our politicians and intellectuals remain trapped in a folkloric and chauvinist conception of cultural identity (*Hybrid Cultures* 94). Politicians still believe that culture is formed in the traditional space of fine arts, artisanal craft, and popular music and ignore the reality of their mass mediated resemanticization. The so-called critical intellectuals continue to be tied to the magical realist fundamentalism that has frozen Latin Americanness in a surrealist universe of violent passions, indomitable nature, and the boundless nobility of its "other-rationality"—a discourse that, as José Joaquín Brunner notes, constitutes the last *aristocratic gesture* of a continent that refuses to recognize itself *in* and *with* modernity.[14]

The conclusions Brunner reaches in his investigations of Latin America's "peripheral modernity" are very similar to those of Martín-Barbero and García Canclini. For the Chilean sociologist, Latin America at the end of the twentieth century has become a kind of city-labyrinth (Tamaramerica) where all possible symbolic experiences come together in a vertiginous dance of signs,[15] which range from the most archaic forms of sociopolitical experience to familiarity with the latest communication technologies (Brunner, *América Latina* 37–72). The difference between high culture and popular culture, associated with Macondoamerica, has been overrun by the staggering force of a mass culture offering such a vast array of signs that it becomes impossible to define it under any kind of fixed "national identity." Deterritorialized and no longer controllable from any center, mass culture does not reflect the "soul of the people" but rather the sensibility of symbolic producers and mediators, as well as the practices of millions of consumers who, each in their own way, process, interpret, and experience this flow of transmitted messages (64). Thus we face a mazelike web made of signs that no longer reflect a primary reality (the "Latin American ethos") but instead are interpretations of other signs and interpretations of other interpretations of signs. In this context, it is impossible to accept a basic reality that would offer us the truth of our "Latin American being." The old and mythical Macondoamerica, where broad and powerful identities were defined, where the world was the community and what was "external" to it, is losing its position to the symbolic, differentiated, and international space of Tamaramerica, where identities are continuously made and unmade, just like the symbolic goods they produce.

What then remains of "Latin American identity" once the borders between high culture and popular culture have been dissolved? It is evident that it is no longer possible to imagine Latin America as a mythical space that is somehow "outside" of modern rationality, as Parker and Morandé would have it. On the contrary, what recent cultural studies have shown us is that personal and collective identities are shaped through mutual symbolic influences, violent conflicts, and continuous metamorphoses that resist all "cultural synthesis." Models that insist on portraying modernity as the triumphant unfolding of an objectifying rationalization cannot explain the multitemporal and radically heterogeneous experience of living in Latin America during the second half of the twentieth century. Given this modernity, in which narco-democracy and consumerism, advanced technology and absolute poverty, institutional modernization and *caudillismo* all coexist, it is clear that such totalizing models had to be destroyed.

At the dawn of the twenty-first century, cultural identity in Latin America must be thought as a constant process of *negotiation*. This means, first of all, accepting that referents of identity are no longer found only in religious rituals, oral culture, and folklore. Instead, they are primarily to be found in the symbolic goods that circulate through electronic media, the globalization of urban life, and the transnationalization of the economy. Thus deterritorialized, identity is no longer defined by exclusive belonging to a material community but rather, as García Canclini demonstrates, by belonging to a *community of consumers*, that is to say, to a heterogeneous group of subjects that does not necessarily share a language, religion, or territory but rather tastes, desires, and aesthetic commitments regarding certain symbolic goods (*Hybrid Cultures* 196). Second, accepting this entails understanding that modern rationalization does not generate a cultural homogenization similar to the proverbial dark in which "all cats are gray," but rather sets off the explosion of multiple rationalities that can articulate, disassociate, or fight amongst themselves without any historical teleology existing to guide the process. The problem, therefore, does not stem from mass media networks and their flow of information (as if the use of modern technologies necessarily led to the destruction of tradition) but instead from the institutional mechanisms that exclude a large part of the population from access to these media, preventing them from renewing, enriching, or transforming their identity.[16]

To summarize: "popular culture" in Latin America is not only rural and premodern. Rock music, cinema, telenovelas, and international television series also form part of the popular, the production of which no longer refers to the sentiments of subaltern groups but to the activity of what Anthony Giddens called "abstract systems" (media, state agencies, private foundations, etc.). The popular has been deterritorialized, which means that it is no longer possible to consider the old problem of Latin American identity in terms of *alterity*. The latter entails the narrative production of monolithic identities (a homogeneous "us" and a homogeneous "them") that, as we will see in the next chapter, legitimizes the exclusion of transversal identities and "small histories." The idea, however, is to move toward thinking identity in terms of *articulation and difference*, such that personal or collective identity is no longer thought of as derived from an ethos located outside of modern rationality but rather as a product of symbolic intersections, discursive relocations, and cultural hybridizations.

3

POPULISM AND PHILOSOPHY

One of the defining features of twentieth-century Latin American thought is its close connection to political life and its preference for themes related to the analysis of society. Unlike in Europe, where intellectual life enjoys a relative degree of independence from inopportune changes in the social environment (which allows scientific disciplines to develop on the basis of the internal logic of their own paradigms), in Latin America there has always been a strong kinship between thought and politics. This is because, since the mid-nineteenth century, the categories of sociocultural analysis have been constructed at the intersection of the reception of European ideas and the political participation of intellectuals.[1] Thus there has been no success in establishing an autonomous intellectual field where different disciplines can re-elaborate the material inherent to their own analytical models. Quite to the contrary, transformative political change conditions the topics of interest and orientation of each discipline. Hence, in spite of the increasing modernization of university degrees and the consequent specialization of knowledges, in Latin America the relationship between intellectuals and politics continues to function as a layer of *topsoil* out of which all disciplines grow.

During the twentieth century, the political phenomenon that had the greatest influence on the task of the intellectual in Latin America was undoubtedly populism. The Bolivian sociologist Fernando Calderón describes it as follows:

> Even with all its incoherencies, populism was the most genuine social and cultural creation of Latin America in the twentieth century. Populism changed even those who were opposed to it. It modified the culture of our peoples, their sexuality, their ways of loving, of thinking, and even of dancing and walking: in short, all of daily life. Only under populism, with the integration of the masses into the market, import substitution, urbanization, and other social changes of different degrees of intensity and rhythm, was modernity finally imposed in Latin America, with a Latin American style.... Populism was the instrument of our fuller integration into the universal and paradoxical experience of modernity.
>
> ("LATIN AMERICAN IDENTITY AND MIXED TEMPORALITIES, 58)

Taking advantage of the conjuncture that arose out of the European economic crisis of the 1920s, a large number of Latin American countries began the process of industrialization based on import substitutions and the configuration of domestic markets. This process was driven by bourgeois nationalists who wanted to control the world of trade and politics and saw the need to incorporate the modern life of North Atlantic countries into Latin American nations. As Jesús Martín-Barbero points out, these new bourgeoisie resumed the old "civilizing project," designed by criollo elites in the middle of the nineteenth century, that had as its sole and indisputable aim the construction of nations (*De los medios a las mediaciones* 166). In the twentieth century, particularly during the interwar period, this project shifted its focus toward the formation of a state capable of incorporating different cultures into a single "national sentiment" that would be reflected in all areas of social life: politics, economics, art, literature, and, of, course philosophy. The problem was not, as in the nineteenth century, that of constructing the nation but rather that of ensuring a *spiritual unity* that would be a platform for modernizing projects. The unity of the nation should be guaranteed by the state, which would assume the task of building a repertoire of representative symbols and stereotypes of national identity.[2] Populism thus revealed itself as the agent that realized the dream of nineteenth-century liberals and positivists: the definitive entrance of Latin America into cultural modernity (Paris Pombo, *Crisis e identidades colectivas en América Latina* 58–60).

How can we describe populism *politically*? According to Calderón, we could say that populism is a Latin American version of modern politics and not simply a phenomenon of societies in transition, as Gino Germani has proposed (*Política y sociedad en una época de transición*). It is not U.S. or European liberal democracy that guarantees civil liberties and pluralism but a *substantialist* vision of democracy that would allow us to imagine a singular identity of the people embodied in the figure of the supreme leader. This figure, as Ernesto Laclau puts it, *permanently* occupies the empty place of power and presents itself as the very *foundation* of national unity. In reality, it is a vision that is very close to Carl Schmitt's theory, in which the democratic ideal seeks to establish an *unmediated* identity between the government and the governed, which means that parliament and any other instance of mediation (including an independent press, public opinion, the judicial system, etc.) are seen as undesirable. That is to say, while the liberal democratic ideal favors a virtual multiplication of mediating instances, the populist ideal entails its reduction or even elimination. In other words, it is *mediation* itself that conspires against the process of national identity formation.

From this perspective, populism can be seen as a form of *mass democracy*. The primary referent for populism is neither citizens nor civil society but rather "the people," which is considered to be a homogeneous and substantive mass (O'Donnel, *El Estado burocrático-autoritario*)[3]—the people, as given beforehand, not as a *previous* referent to politics itself, as the "thing-in-itself" that expresses the identity of the nation. Popular will is not formed on the basis of the pluralist constitution of political subjects but is rather an act generated from above that fundamentally depends on the leader's charisma. This top-down approach to the political mobilization of the masses (through political meetings, the media portrayal of stereotypes, or the repetition of slogans) is the basic component of populist politics. Hence the role of the people is not deliberation but rather *enthusiasm*.

The first of the *four links* in the populist chain that most influenced Latin American thought in the twentieth century was the Mexican Revolution of 1910, with its strong antioligarchic sentiment (agrarian reform, redistribution of land, nationalization of industry, and a planned economy) and its rejection of all foreign influence. Second, in Peru in 1931, the Alianza Popular Revolucionaria para América (APRA) was formed, hoisting the flag of Latin American unity as a tool for political struggle against U.S. imperialism, just as the Arielist generation had used it at the beginning of the century. Its goal was the creation of a "new" Latin America that would be capable of fully assuming its Indigenous and Spanish legacies. The integration of Indigenous peoples into the progress of the nation, that is, as productive forces, represented for APRA the movement toward a true synthesis of two traditionally overlapping cultures in Latin American societies. Third, in 1945, Peronism emerged in Argentina in an attempt to break the country's economic dependence on the interests of foreign capital. For Peronism, traditional oligarchies were no longer the central focus of the nation and the state but rather the common people, the dispossessed masses, the *descamisados*[4]—those who should be the recipients of social justice administered by a strong state and could ensure the nation's independence in relation to both individualist capitalism and totalitarian communism. And finally, in 1959, the Cuban Revolution triumphed and sparked in Latin America the process of translating Marxism to the language of populist movements, which found its fullest expression in dependency theory.[5]

These four political developments have several elements in common that, as I hope to show in this chapter, later reappear in the discourses of identity developed by twentieth-century Latin American philosophy. These elements include, among others, the critique of universalist solutions, the idea that "evil" is found *outside* the nation, the postulation of a Latin American cultural specificity, the recourse to the popular as a legitimizing instance of truth, the invocation of religious sentiment and political messianism, the promotion of state paternalism and charismatic leadership, the cult of heroes, the radical opposition between the authentic and the foreign, the attempt to reconcile all social oppositions, the romanticization of mestizaje, and the *ex negativo* definition of the self. My thesis here is that such figures operate within Latin American philosophical discourse as mechanisms that tend to *homogenize differences* and thus serve as the perfect correlates to the authoritarian and exclusionary practices of populism. I am not referring to these discursive figures as an ideological reflection of some fundamental social instance (politics or the economy); rather, I am highlighting the aforementioned role of intellectuals as *interpreters and legislators* of "continental identity." Nor am I interested in the connections or critical distance authors may or may not maintain with regard to these political developments. Instead, I want to situate my argument on the ground of *regimes of truth* in order to show how certain characteristic figures of populism enter and exit philosophical discourses on identity. My thesis is that, as a political phenomenon, populism opened up the spaces that were necessary for understanding Latin American philosophy as a reflection on the self, an attitude that generated a series of works that have given a very fitting personality to the task of Latin American philosophy in the twentieth century.[6]

1. THE PEOPLE AND THE NATION AS PHILOSOPHICAL CATEGORIES

Perhaps the best way to begin our analysis is to show how continental identity has been thought in terms of the people and the nation by Latin American philosophical discourse, particularly by the Argentine current that emerged in the 1970s known as the *philosophy of liberation*.[7] The origins of this philosophy's categories can be traced back to the German Romanticism of the nineteenth century; however, in the twentieth-century Latin American context, they take on a particular significance as a result of Juan Domingo Perón's role in Argentine history.[8] Although there were many philosophers of liberation who reflected on the categories we focus on here, I will center my analysis on two specific texts: Carlos Cullen's *Fenomenología de la crisis moral* (Phenomenology of moral crisis) and Enrique Dussel's *Filosofía de la liberación* (*Philosophy of Liberation*).

The purpose of Cullen's text is to recuperate the figures presented by Hegel in the *Phenomenology of Spirit* in order to describe the ascendant itinerary followed by "Latin American popular consciousness." Just as Hegel described the three moments that consciousness goes through in its long journey toward self-consciousness, from its most primitive and immediate form toward absolute knowledge, Cullen proposes to investigate how the consciousness of the people arrives at consciousness of the universal. The first moment of this journey is the experience of knowing that one is "rooted to the earth" (13–18). The most immediate experience of consciousness that a people has is that of recognizing itself as a "we-are-here," that is to say, as a subject vitally placed in a geographical landscape from which it derives its existence. This first form of a people's knowledge, which is objectified in myths like that of the Pachamama, lends a sacred character to geographical surroundings. However, in such an experience of immediacy, the people remains an undifferentiated "we" that feels a commitment to the telluric but still cannot recognize what characterizes it as such. It becomes necessary to move on to a second moment—which Cullen identifies, like Hegel, with "self-consciousness"—in which the people understands itself as a community with its own traditions, that is, as the *subject* of a symbolic code manifesting in religious ceremonies, social institutions, and political practices (*Fenomenología de la crisis moral* 19–20). Here, in this second moment, Cullen introduces the concept of the nation. Knowing itself as the subject of its own tradition, the people divides in order to understand itself as political consciousness; it becomes the nation, and the latter appears as its self-consciousness, that is, as the political expression of its *cultural identity*.

More than a form of political organization, the nation is a form of consciousness directly linked to the cultural identity of the people, because it is equivalent to the political self-knowledge of the members of what Hegel called the *Volksgeist*, the organic principle that forms the "substance" of a people and determines art, philosophy, religion, and morality as they correspond to a determinate moment. And just as for Hegel the means and tools of the "spirit of the people" are political individualities like Napoleon, Julius Caesar, and Alexander the Great, in Cullen this role is played by caudillos, those charismatic figures who know how to incarnate the desires and symbols of the people:

> It is the masses' confidence in the country's leadership that allows it to develop as self-consciousness. The masses situate themselves by adopting and doing the will of the leadership, and then they know *self-leadership*: because what was another's will has become one's own will reflected in the development of the country as a nation. The people now reflexively know themselves as sovereign because they are self-led.
>
> (*FENOMENOLOGÍA DE LA CRISIS MORAL* 24)

However, the possibility always remains that the caudillo might distance himself from Mother Earth and exercise his leadership through violence, or that institutions are transformed into a legality external to the people and thus require ideologies (progress, development, and modernization) to justify the caudillo's violence. Therefore, it becomes necessary to move to a third moment (reason) in which the people is thought to be absolutely free (Cullen, *Fenomenología de la crisis moral* 24). This is the moment of "civilization" where the law of the nation becomes a *universal law*, that is to say, an expression of the sovereignty of the people as a human community (*Fenomenología de la crisis moral* 36–42). Again, as in Hegel, for Cullen reason is fully objectified in the state, the only instance capable of reconciling the general will and the subjective will, as well as of expressing the ethical life (*Sittlichkeit*) of the people.

The nation and the state appear in Cullen's philosophical discourse as moments of an organic and homogeneous whole that does not tolerate difference or which resolves it in a teleological dialectical movement. This tells us nothing about which social actors are included in the category of the people, nor does it say anything about which stages of Latin American history correspond to different moments of the unfolding of its consciousness. However, if in Cullen the categories of the people and the nation are permanently indeterminate, philosopher Enrique Dussel tries to give them a *geopolitical* connotation and relate them to concrete social subjects: he identifies the people with the peasants, Indigenous populations, and workers who share the same project of liberation, while the nation is the geographical, cultural, and religious horizon of the people's telluric roots (*Philosophy of Liberation* 70–71). For Dussel, both the nation and the people are oppressed by the global system of capitalism and imperialism based in industrialized countries; furthermore, they live in a situation that is in fact politically, economically, and, above all, ethically external to this system: "The oppressed or popular classes of dependent nations are those that are maximally external to the current global system; only they can present a real, new alternative to future humanity, given their *metaphysical alterity*" (88). This means that the people has another sense of life, another ethos that is very different from, and even diametrically opposed to, that of the dominant global system. For while the nation is experienced in the center of the world-system as *imperio*, in the periphery it is an essentially telluric experience, firmly anchored in the "ethico-mythical core" that defines the identity of the people.

By trying to negatively define the categories of the people and the nation (the "other" of totality, the oppressed periphery), Dussel's discourse is unable to overcome the difficulties that we saw in Cullen's project. There are certainly some determinations (peasants, workers, marginalized classes, etc.), but these are quickly integrated into a totalizing and homogeneous identity (the *ethos* of liberation) in which there is no place for differences. For Dussel, the war in Angola, the Cuban Revolution, and Palestinian guerrillas are *the same*; Indigenous Mexicans, Vietnamese peasants, and Saharan Bedouins are *the same*, because they are all manifestations of a geopolitically constituted subject (the "peripheral other") and they all share the same struggle against *one* single common enemy.[9] This struggle is for the "liberation of the periphery," for the establishment of a new world order in which it is no longer the *ethos* of the dominator that reigns but rather solidarity, love, and face-to-face relations. The assumption of state power by popular groups therefore represents a radical inversion of values: the possibility that humanity might make a qualitative leap toward real humanization (Dussel, *Philosophy of Liberation* 74–75). Along with Cullen, Dussel also addresses the religious and messianic glorification of those telluric men, the caudillos: "The liberating politician is the prototype of the statesman. . . . I am referring to Joan of Arc, Washington, Bolívar, San Martín, Agostinho Neto, Castro, Mao, and those who give up their lives for the oppressed. . . . They are like Moses or Muhammad, symbols of a people that is born, that grows, that lives. They are prophets of life, not of death; founders of freedom, not its assassins" (*Philosophy of Liberation* 76–77).

2. IN SEARCH OF "DEEP AMERICA"

We have already seen how in the Argentine version of the philosophy of liberation, the concept of the nation is embedded within strong telluric elements. Of course, this is not an uncommon figure in Latin American philosophy. On the contrary, referring to the influences of the earth, the landscape, and nature on cultural forms is one of the most widely used motifs in philosophical discourses on identity. In its background one can detect the voices of Martin Heidegger, Oswald Spengler, and Hermann von Keyserling, who, in the 1930s gained both prestige and popularity across the entire continent (Roig, *Teoría y crítica del pensamiento latino-americano* 138–69; Biagini, *Filosofía americana e identidad* 187).

We will first examine one of the texts that most clearly addresses this problem: Ezequiel Martínez Estrada's essay *Radiografía de la pampa* (1933) (*X-Ray of the Pampa*, [1971]). His central thesis is that the immense power of the *land*—and, in the case of Argentina, of the pampa—has determined the entire historical development of Latin America. Martínez Estrada sees in the symbolic action of taking possession of the land, dramatized by the Spanish conquistadors in the sixteenth century, the beginning of a ritual that was repeated over and over: the American man claiming as his own something that in reality completely exceeds him and that remains only as the false hope of possession, if only through language and discourse. For, in reality, the land has always possessed him (*X-Ray of the Pampa* 11–12). The conquistadors could not help but capitulate to the overwhelming immensity of the mountain ranges, plains, rivers, and valleys of the New World. Therefore, instead of staying there to build and work, the Spanish set about living off the work of others; to take what they could from the land without dominating it. Fearful of the threatening chaos of the telluric, the conquistador sought refuge in an inverted scale of values in which labor appeared as a form of self-barbarism and as yielding to the imperatives of nature (11). In order to defend himself from it, the conquistador fabricated the idea that everything he saw was his solely due to the fact that he had planted a flag; he invented laws to legitimize that possession and built cities to govern his territories. However, the cities were simply refuges where the governors imagined they had control over a land that was always external in its telluric virginity. The forces of the earth and the atmosphere conducted their slow and secret work on the invaders and forced them to respect what never was nor could be theirs. The heavy stupor, routine, sloth, ignorance—in a word, *barbarism*—triumphed over the Spanish and their descendants, obligating them to prostrate themselves before the superiority of the earth (*X-Ray of the Pampa* 84–85).

We are thus dealing with an identity that is essentially determined by the monotony of the valleys, the vastness of the land, and the primitiveness of the forests. Passivity, apathy, sudden explosions of violence and euphoria, solitude, unbounded eroticism, and legalism: these are all characteristics of the Latin American man that are related to the domination to which he is subjected by the telluric forces of nature. As in the case of Dussel and Cullen, Martínez Estrada discursively generates an all-encompassing identity that includes all social subjects without establishing differences of any kind. At best, and as can be seen in liberationist discourses, he constructs binary oppositions that affirm or deny the inherent truth of Latin American identity. Thus, for example, in Cullen there is the figure of the state that is divorced from the land, while in Dussel it is the empire's "will to power" that alienates the people from its culture. In Martínez Estrada, this alienating role is occupied by the *founding fathers* (particularly liberals) who ineffectively sought to construct rationalist utopias in the Americas without taking into account the radical incompatibility of de jure law and de facto law, between European civilization and the barbarism of Latin America (*X-Ray of the Pampa* 376).[10] On the contrary—and here we find an unsurprising coincidence with the philosophy of liberation—Martínez Estrada identifies the figure of the caudillo as the genuine representative of the *telluric ethos* of Latin America. Guided by the imperatives of the land, the caudillo knows that the laws of the state are chimerical structures and that they therefore embody a rebellion against the civilizing project of the founding fathers of the nineteenth century; he comes from the countryside—the site of barbarism—and rises up against the fictitious system of values coming from the cities. He is not necessarily antisocial, but rather, as Martínez Estrada puts it,

> [the caudillo] believes himself divinely ordained to punish with fire and sword a society bereft of its principles of justice. . . . In [Latin] America, which lacked a society, he was the embryo of one. He could say: I am the state—because there was no state. He was Power and Law in the dominions of chaos, a Messiah whose tragic destiny was to bear the burden for his people's sins, to be sacrificed, and in the course of time to be disbelieved.
>
> (*X-RAY OF THE PAMPA* 49)

However, not all valorizations of the telluric take on the dark character Martínez Estrada gives it. The Latin American man's barbaric and primitive identity can also be interpreted as a form of creative energy and an inexhaustible source of spiritual renewal. This is what Rodolfo Kusch, a relentless scholar of Quechua and Aymara cultures, shows us in his book *América Profunda* (Deep America [1962]), in which Latin America is a place where two opposed cultures coexist: one visible on the surface, the product of European civilization, and the other deep in the unconscious, popular and Amerindian. Kusch categorizes the difference between these two cultures through a distinctive linguistic feature of Spanish: the separation and difference between two verbs, *ser* and *estar*. Modern European culture presupposes the existence of a type of man who is practical, shrewd, and confident in the possibilities of reason to bring reality in line with his project of *ser-alguien* ["being-someone"] in life. This is the culture of *ser*, which is present in large cities in Latin America (Kusch, *América Profunda* 124). Alternatively, there is the culture of *estar*, which is typical of the countryside and suburbs and represents passivity, the vegetality of life, and the spiritual apathy that is expressed as *dejarse-estar* ("letting-be") in the world. It is a culture rooted to the land, firmly committed to the here and now (*América Profunda* 89). Based on the distinction between these two cultural identities, Kusch argues that Latin America is irremediably split between modern European rationality and its own inherent earthly and violent rationality. Latin Americans are obliged to live two irreconcilable truths: one that comes from below, from the very soil of Latin America, and the other from above, from Western civilization. One depends on the leadership of the criollo bourgeoisie and the other on the "authentic" and pure instincts of the people. The world of *ser*, represented by the Europeanized elites, has always denied Latin America's telluric nature and considers it barbaric, disgusting, and inauthentic (*América Profunda* 9–15). However, Kusch prophetically claims that this artificial, urban world will be absorbed by the telluric world of *estar* in a cultural process of "phagocytosis" that will ultimately encompass the entire continent.

We see how the same discursive figures utilized by Martínez Estrada appear in Kusch's work, but in opposite roles. Kusch presents a narrative in which two conflicting identities fiercely struggle to take control of the Latin American soul. However, if in Martínez Estrada the telluric appears as the negative pole, responsible for the resentment and solitude of the Latin American man, in Kusch it represents the authentic, the holy, and the true. The world of *estar* is the sign of the positive pole, the root source that will subsume the Westernized world of *ser*, which comes from an exhausted Europe without any vital energy. The absolute superiority of the telluric, which is also evident to Martínez Estrada, is for Kusch like the triumph of a popular ethos that originates in Indigenous populations (telluric beings par excellence) and is slowly transmitted to peasants in small rural communities, immigrants in large cities, and even the petit bourgeois middle classes. Phagocytosis is the (irreversible) incorporation of a series of social actors into a *previously constituted* identity that has as its only subject the Indigenous peasant population.[11]

3. MESTIZAJE AS AN EXPRESSION OF IDENTITY

In its optimistic version, this philosophical tellurism has many similarities to Spenglerian discourses that, between the 1920s and 1940s, constructed an opposition between the "spiritual fatigue" of an aging, decrepit, and war-torn Europe and the brilliant future of Latin America, young and revitalized by mestizaje. Kusch interprets Kafka's literature and Freudian psychoanalysis as unequivocal signs of the exhaustion of the telluric in the Western world. In his opinion, Europe is practically devoid of telluric spaces, which were all destroyed by modern rationalization—in contrast to the great presence of the Indigenous legacy in Latin America (Kusch, *América Profunda* 180). As we will see, this contrast was also noted by other Latin American philosophers, including Vicente Ferreira da Silva, Antenor Orrego, and José Vasconcelos.

Based in a peculiar reading of Nietzsche, Brazilian philosopher Ferreira da Silva argues that Western reason is characterized by a deep hatred of all that is natural and vital,[12] which is rooted in Orphism and Judeo-Christian religion, with its categorical separation of the spiritual world—to which belong God, the soul, and reason—and the profane world of corporeality and the senses. This separation ultimately leads to the objectification of nature by scientific-technical rationality as well as to the negation of what, according to Ferreira da Silva, constitutes the vital foundation of all culture: the *orgy*. For this reason, the West is a decadent and antilife culture that is slowly dying under the imperatives of industrialization, technology, and capitalism. In Brazil, in contrast, things are very different. There, Western reason has been absorbed in a syncretic and orgiastic world. European Christianity has been reconverted into the festive and animist language of Afro-Brazilian religions in which man is not seen as an autonomous subject confronting nature but rather as an integral part of it. Candomblé, the rhythms of bossa nova, Carnival, the colors of dwellings, the forms of new architecture—everything in Brazil is proof that the Christian hatred of nature has been transformed here into a Dionysian pagan celebration in which man completely identifies with the vital foundation of culture.

For his part, Peruvian philosopher Antenor Orrego, one of the founders of APRA, was convinced that every human culture has a basic core that generates its most authentic vital energies. It is on the basis of this *intrahistory*, and not culturally foreign experiences, that Latin America should construct its political institutions. The question is: what is this "vital and organic zone" that shapes the deep history of the Americas? It does not, as Martínez Estrada argues, come from the wild power of the earth, but nor does it come from our inherited Amerindian roots, as Kusch would maintain. For Orrego, Latin American intrahistory is based on the *experience of mestizaje*. Latin America has been from the very beginning the place where all races and cultures come together. However, this mestizaje cannot be reduced to two or three peoples, as has always occurred in human history, but rather, for the first time, all groups come together in one place to bring forth a new universal culture:

> We do not believe that another land exists that could muster the extraordinary, irresistible, absorbing, and transformative power of Latin America. Neither ancient Greece or Rome, those powerful distillations of the Western world, nor contemporary India or China can offer us anything similar in terms of either volume or monumental proportions. Those places were or are partial fusions, combinations of *some* segments of humanity. Latin America is the complete fusion, the ecumenical absorption, the summation of all disconnected human labor throughout innumerable millennia.
>
> (ORREGO, *HACIA UN HUMANISMO AMERICANO* 48)

Due to migratory cross-pollination, all human cultures converge in Latin America, which points to the completion of one human evolutionary cycle and the beginning of another. All living cultures around the globe come to die in Latin America, if only to regenerate, to leave rejuvenated as a new, universal, more human, vital force. "The continent is thus becoming an enormous crucifixion and a prolific cradle, in the agonic matrix of a new and unheard-of human transfiguration" (Orrego, "La configuración histórica de la circunstancia americana" 1397). Just as in Dussel we find the idea of Latin America as a continent destined to complete a global *redemptive mission*, we also encounter the same image in Orrego: Latin America is tasked with advancing the world toward a unitary and integrated culture. "Latin America received this message of unity as a *Vox Dei*, as a metaphysical grasping of its soul, at the beginning of the nineteenth century and has been propagating it all over the world since then" ("La configuración histórica de la circunstancia americana" 1404). The recipient of this extraordinary revelation, the *prophet* who knew how to interpret the intrahistory of the Americas like no one else, was naturally Simón Bolívar. At this point in the narrative, the Venezuelan leader enters into Orrego's discourse in order to take on the same role that Dussel attributes in his work to figures such as Fidel Castro, Mao Zedong, Yasser Arafat, and other Third World leaders.[13]

Latin America is a continent destined to complete a mission. Ferreira da Silva argues that Brazil is preparing for the emergence of a revolutionary and ecstatic culture in which man orgiastically identifies with nature. Orrego thinks instead in terms of a planetwide humanization that would be the result of mestizaje. However, both philosophers' messianisms are derived from an organicist and *substantialist* conception of culture, and both argue that a people's identity depends on factors that are *prior* to their political practices. There is an intrahistory that, although it is not immediately accessible to the individual consciousness (since it is invisible and subterranean), permeates all of a people's cultural activities and therefore *unifies* them. Thus the role of the state should be precisely to reflect in an organic way this popular, unitary intrahistory. Therefore, Orrego will say that all attempts to politically organize the peoples of Latin America through Old World institutions are destined to fail:

> Democracy should come from the heart, from the *internal* reality of Latin American peoples; from their particular conditions and circumstances, whether economic, social, political, cultural, or historical, if it aspires to a permanent and organic stability. Any political theory

> designed to channel the thought and immediate action of the masses toward the organization of the state and the government should come from the people itself, that is to say, from the *intrahistory*, that internal, underground, and invisible richness that simultaneously expresses and impresses itself on the spirit and most private realities of nations.
>
> (ORREGO, *HACIA UN HUMANISMO AMERICANO* 24)

However, the intrahistory Orrego discusses here should not be confused with the geographical peculiarities of Latin American countries, and much less with the predominant races in each of them, but rather with the profound identity of what he calls a *people-continent*. This is also emphasized by another founder of APRA, Victor Raúl Haya de la Torre, according to whom the basic characteristic of a people-continent is not geographical borders but rather a specific "historical space-time." He thus maintains that what identifies these grand cultural unities (which are not the same as countries) is their psychological capacity to evaluate and interpret their own histories. A human conglomerate becomes a people-continent when the people acquire the maturity that allows them to take charge of and interpret their own history. Influenced by Spengler, Haya de la Torre says that there is no one single universal history, nor is there a sole technological path that all peoples should follow, but rather there are as many histories as there are people-continents:

> There are many peoples in the world that can offer a relative simultaneity or similarity of degrees or temporary stages of economic, political, or cultural development—in Asia, Oceania, Amerindia, perhaps the Balkans—but this similarity is modified by the historical space that is not *simply one* geographical continent but rather the content of human consciousness, the relation between man and the earth, inseparable from its specific Time.[14]
>
> (*ESPACIO-TIEMPO-HISTÓRICO* 24–25)

Latin America as a *cultural unity* (and not just Argentina, Chile, Colombia, or any other specific Latin American country) has finally arrived at the category of "people-continent" and is politically ready to direct its own history. This populist message is also the starting point taken by Mexican thinker José Vasconcelos, for whom the basic principle that governs the development of civilizations and the world as a whole is a "vital impulse" that is transmitted from the level of organic material throughout developed organisms and produces all their variations. Like Bergson, Vasconcelos insists on the *unity* of this impulse, which runs through all forms of life and gives strength to and pushes the movement of universal evolution. In cultural forms, the vital impulse follows a teleological movement oriented toward the *unification of humanity*. The different races and human civilizations fulfill (without knowing it) a specific role in this universal plan, which will ultimately lead to unity, freedom, and harmony for humanity. Each one of these races and civilizations lives only in order to fulfill this mission and later disappears when it has fully realized its labor: "There is no going back in history, for all transformation and novelty. No race returns; each one states its mission, accomplishes it, and passes away" (Vasconcelos, *The Cosmic Race* 16).

However, in this grand conjuncture of civilizations, Vasconcelos assigns a special role to the two "races" that, in his judgment, will contribute most to the formation of a genuine universality: Anglo-Saxons and "Latin peoples." Inheritors of Greco-Roman civilization, Anglo-Saxons represent the importance of science and technology for achieving mastery over nature, which previously overwhelmed humans and prevented them from being free. However, as humanity's primary achievement, this mastery becomes its own most absolute limitation. Anglo-Saxon ideals have brought with them a form of ethnic barricading that prevents any assimilation of contributions from other cultures. Instead of mixing with the people they dominated, the Anglo-Saxons preferred to destroy them outright or to subjugate them by force. Thus their historical mission was fully accomplished. Given the advantages of dominating the material world, the white man's civilization slowly proceeds toward its natural death (*The Cosmic Race* 20–21).

In Vasconcelos's opinion, the historical destiny of humanity will not be achieved by the Anglo-Saxons but rather by the "Latin peoples." This latter is a new race, a product of the mixture between Iberian (Spanish and Portuguese) and Indigenous populations (who, according to Vasconcelos, are descended from the ancient civilization of Atlantis), to which African cultures would later be added. The definitive advance toward the unification of the human race began with the Conquest of the Americas, when the Spanish and Portuguese mixed with Indigenous peoples and broke with the dominant racial prejudices of Europe. However, in Vasconcelos, Ferreira da Silva's disdain for Christianity is transformed into glorious exaltation:

> This mandate from History is first noticed in that abundance of love that allowed the Spaniard to create a new race with the Indian and the Black, profusely spreading white ancestry through the soldier who begat a native family, and Occidental culture through the doctrine and example of the [Christian] missionaries who placed the Indians in condition to enter into the new stage, the stage of world One.
>
> (*THE COSMIC RACE* 17)

In Latin America, the Christian message of love of one's neighbor produced the best result, as in this spirit a true "synthetic race" could be formed, made out of the disposition and blood of all people (Vasconcelos, *The Cosmic Race* 18). No other civilization will be able to displace Latin America in its mission of revealing the principles that govern the "universal era of humanity"—principles that are no longer based in the cold logic of science but rather in the ideals of love, contemplation, and beauty. As with almost all discourses on identity, the prophetic intention here is difficult to miss: Vasconcelos proclaims that in the tropics of Latin America—the Amazon region, to be precise—an unprecedented civilization will flourish, where the laws of morality, harmony, and love will reign. However, the birth of this civilization will be preceded by a great battle between the Anglo-Saxons and the Latin peoples, which, like the biblical Armageddon, will prepare the way for the globalization of knowledge and beauty (*The Cosmic Race* 24–25).

If we look carefully, we will see that Vasconcelos's argumentative strategy is very similar to almost every discourse on identity we have examined up to this point: the creation of two homogeneous identities (Latin peoples and Anglo-Saxons) is only one way to affirm the existence of a "we" located *outside* European modernity, which is dogmatically considered to be an expression of a "will to power." The real Latin American identity would therefore be a space of *counterlight* and *alterity* in the face of a "them" that Vasconcelos identifies as the white race, Dussel refers to as the nations of the global center, and Kusch calls the culture of *ser.* This discursive turn represents, at bottom, the (colonial) proclamation of European modernity as the *original* of Latin American identity, which is by definition its opposite. Once these two *substantialized entities* are constructed, identity can no longer be thought as anything but that which uncompromisingly belongs to one or the other. In this construction there is no place to think hybrid spaces, intermingling, or epistemic multiplicity. On the contrary, identity discourses, with their *passion for unity*, fetishize both Europe and Latin America insofar as both appear as homogeneous entities that obscure the multiple power relations they contain.

4. THE IDEALIZATION OF LATIN AMERICAN ETHICS

As we have seen, Vasconcelos's Latin American messianism leads to the idealist postulation of a Latin American ethos located outside egoism, the will to power, the love of money, and everything that supposedly belongs to the pathos of modernity. This *topos* is closely associated with the early twentieth-century Arielist generation (José Enrique Rodó, Francisco García Calderón, and Manuel Ugarte), but it was also widely accepted by many leftist intellectuals—for example, José Carlos Mariátegui, who in spite of having denied any kind of aggrandizement of Latin America, argues that one finds in Indigenous communities a living ethos of solidarity that remains uncontaminated by modern rationality and could serve as a basis for the construction of an "Amerindian socialism" ("El problema de las razas en América Latina").

In Cuba, socialist thinkers like Rafael Rojas and Cintio Vitier sought (in a project similar to that of Carlos Cullen) to reconstruct the historical development of what they called "Cuban ethics." However, their point of departure is not Hegelian phenomenology but rather the critiques of the Frankfurt School insofar as they see the development of modern culture as the result of the tension between an emancipatory ethical rationality and an oppressive instrumental rationality (Rojas, "La otra moral de la teleología cubana" 85). In his book *Ese sol del mundo moral* (That sun of the moral world), which bears the subtitle *Para una historia de la eticidad cubana* (Toward a history of Cuban ethics), the poet Vitier promotes the thesis that in Cuba ethical rationality has always prevailed over instrumental reason. Cuban history can be read, according to Vitier, as the teleological development of an emancipatory morality embodied in social institutions and public life, which ranges from the Enlightenment bourgeoisie's opposition to Spanish domination at the dawn of the nineteenth century to the triumph of the socialist revolution in 1959. In the sphere of thought, Cuban ethical rationality is a *constant* that has its origins in the writings of Félix Varela, runs through the work of José de la Luz y Caballero, Enrique José Varona, and José Antonio Saco, finds its maximal expression in the work of José Martí, and triumphantly culminates with the political thought of Fidel Castro and Ernesto "Che" Guevara:

> Those bearded men, like patriarchs or wild pages from a mythical American kingdom, had [no] other motivation than the need, generously heard by all the humble poor, to water the earth with innocent blood so as to fertilize history and to ignite its Sun. And then, on that glorious day, the first of January, the confrontation of the fragments of reality appeared, broken and dispersed, and a ray of justice fell on us all and stripped us bare, in order *to put everyone in a precise moral location*. . . . In the blink of an eye, the truth, which had been broken in agony or buried, was remade. The truth, the poetic reality, the overabundance of *ethos* overflowing from the nightmarish gates of hell.
>
> (VITIER, *ESE SOL DEL MUNDO MORAL* 177)

The basic feature of this "insular teleology" is the conception of the nation and the state as institutions that are antagonistic to the market, the city, money, property, and capitalism, which reflect a morality opposed to love, solidarity, and patriotism that benefits the individual and the will to power. This insular ethical teleology, as Rafael Rojas writes, functions as a resistance to the prerevolutionary elites' entrenched understanding of modernity and capitalism. "The beginning of desire is opposed to the reality principle, and this confrontation results in the predominance and enshrinement of emancipatory morality in 1959" (Rojas, "La otra moral de la teleología cubana" 88).

However, some intellectual circles within the Catholic Church also produced a significant romanticization of the Latin American ethos toward the end of the twentieth century. Vasconcelos argued that the

Christianization of Indigenous populations was the seed of love, planted in preparation for the advent of the "cosmic race." Vitier himself is convinced that the root of Cuban ethics is fundamentally Christian. During the 1970s, *liberation theology* proposed to discover in the popular religion of marginalized groups an inexhaustible source for the material and spiritual renewal of society. The Argentine philosopher Juan Carlos Scannone, a major representative of this tendency, holds that the foundation of Latin American peoples' historical and cultural experiences is the source of a profound ethical (human-human) and religious (human-God) relationship. Based in the philosophical theses of Rodolfo Kusch and Carlos Cullen, he argues that the underlying instrumental reason of both capitalist and Marxist projects has been ethically transformed in Latin America by a symbolic-religious rationality. Rootedness to the land, which for these thinkers represents the most basic characteristic of Latin American ethos, is for Scannone a fundamentally "chthonic and numinous" experience. The Argentine Jesuit reads Kusch's *estar* as a sphere of symbolic mediation that ontologically preexists and functions as the *foundation* of predicative *logos* (*Nuevo punto de partida de la filosofía latinoamericana* 43). All the values that came from Europe, whether expressions of power or merely discursive enunciations, are seen or analyzed in Latin America (especially by the poorest) from an "ethico-mythical center" that gives it new meaning. Thus, while the criollo aristocrats assume in an unmediated way modern values like emancipation, written constitutions, public education, universal suffrage, or labor organizing, the consciousness of simple people immediately translates these values into demands for *justice* (147). In this way, Scannone understands his philosophy as the attempt to respond to one of the fundamental questions posed by the Episcopal conference of Puebla in 1978:

> Whence the emergence of *structures* of scientific thought, of economic production, and of social and political coexistence that correspond to the ethico-religious core of Latin American culture and which are not structures of oppression but rather of liberation? In Kusch's language, it is a matter of reconciling the structure of *ser* in Latin America with its profound *estar,* such that its "way" of *estar-siendo* will come out of the rootedness of its *estar.*
>
> (35)

Once again, we find here the problem of binary oppositions (instrumental reason versus ethical rationality), in which the instrumental is attributed to a phenomenon from "outside" (European modernity), while the ethical emerges from "within," from the very heart of the Latin American people. Outside and inside both correspond to virtues (egoism/justice), expressions (the discursive/the symbolic), and subjects (criollos/the poor). The problem is reduced to preserving what belongs to each through an inculturation of the instrumental in the ethical, even if this does not apparently give rise to serious difficulties. At least, this is how it is presented by Vitier and Rojas, for whom Cuban ethics always behaves like a kind of King Midas, turning everything it touches into gold. While in Europe, instrumental reason colonizes the space of the ethical, in Cuba the exact opposite is true. Scannone adopts a similar, although slightly different, position because, although he recognizes that the criollo elites were always dominated by the logocentric world of *ser*, he ends up constructing an invincible ethico-symbolic core in the face of all colonizing acts of instrumental reason. Confronted by this profound core of religious and popular feeling, modernity has given in and bent its knee. Therefore, while Vitier and Rojas extol the space of the *institutional* by posing the Cuban nation and state as the standard bearers of ethics, Scannone understands that this area is dominated by the antipopular interests of the criollo elites and prefers to safeguard the treasure of ethics in popular religiosity. However, in both cases, Latin America continues to be thought from within the paradigm of alterity, as the "other" of Western modernity.

5. LATIN AMERICA AND CULTURAL MALAISE

This ethical and telluric optimism contrasts with the position of those philosophers who see in Latin America the presence of *defective* forms of civilization. According to them, an exploration of "deep America" would show that Latin American messianism is a dangerous mechanism of self-deception that covers over the sad reality of a morally and materially backward continent, corrupted by ignorance and authoritarianism.

In his book *El perfil del hombre y la cultura en México* (1934) (*Profile of Man and Culture in Mexico* [1962]), Samuel Ramos suggested combatting Vasconcelos's philosophy through a disembodied analysis of Mexican reality. Far from being the successor to the spiritual leadership of Europe (as the members of the Ateneo de la Juventud had optimistically proclaimed), Latin America, and specifically Mexico, continues to be a subsidiary of European culture. But it is a subsidiary so inauthentic that all its spiritual products are marked by the presence of an *inferiority complex*. Inspired by the cultural psychology of Adler and Jung, Ramos claims psychoanalysis allows one to discover obscure forces in the Mexican soul, disguised as aspirations toward elevated ends, concealing the feeling of having failed to create its own culture:

> It is my thesis that some expressions of the Mexican character are ways of compensating for an unconscious sense of inferiority. . . . Mexicans have been imitating for a long time without actually realizing that they were imitating. They have always sincerely believed they were bringing civilization into national existence. Mimesis is an unconscious phenomenon that reveals a peculiar characteristic of mestizo psychology. . . . The unconscious tendency has been rather to conceal the absence of culture not only from foreign eyes but also from our own. . . . Imitation looms forth as a psychological defense and, upon assuming a cultural appearance, it frees us from that depressing sentiment.
>
> (RAMOS, "EL PERFIL DEL HOMBRE Y LA CULTURA EN MÉXICO" 92; 98)

Imitation is thus a pathology that comes from the kind of infantile relationship that exists between Mexico and its mother culture in Europe.[15] This pathology consists in the imitator feeling inferior to what he copies because he sees himself in relation to a scale of *external* values that prevents him from recognizing that his situation is different. Foreign models have often been adopted throughout Mexican history not only because they seemed better but, what is worse, because they were seen as suitable for Mexican reality. There has been a consistent effort to adopt the most lauded values of Western culture, in the naive belief that Mexican reality is the same as French, English, or U.S. reality. In a word, Mexican culture (and Latin American culture in general) has always experienced a constant *schizophrenia*. Political institutions, art, literature, and thought have all actually been disguises intended to distort our own idea of ourselves. Psychologically speaking, this distortion is a defense mechanism, a *sublimation* that frees individuals from the uncomfortable feeling of knowing we are incapable of producing something similar to or better than what is made in Europe. The trauma of colonization causes our countries to abandon the terrain of reality and take refuge in fiction. Unconsciously, Mexico and all the other countries of Latin America have substituted their authentic being for that of fictitious characters, believing them to be real. We have always lived a lie, but this was the price of freeing our consciousness from the painful idea of our own inferiority.

The philosophical critique of culture initiated by Samuel Ramos and continued in Mexico by thinkers like Octavio Paz was taken up again later in other Latin American countries. Toward the end of the 1960s, the disavowal of telluric propositions was led in Peru by Augusto Salazar Bondy. Like Ramos, Salazar Bondy makes use of the strategy of "unmasking," confident that this methodology is capable of revealing the *ultimate causes* of Latin American alienation. The first step toward achieving this objective is to determine the inexistence of an authentic philosophy in Latin America:

> [In Latin America] one thinks in accordance with theoretical templates that were previously shaped by the models of Western, primarily European, thought imported in the form of ideas, schools, systems completely defined in their content and intention. To philosophize in Latin America is to adopt a foreign *ism*, to subscribe to certain preestablished theses, adopted with regard to a more or less faithful reading of the most significant figures of the era. . . . There is no Latin American philosophical system, no doctrine of meaning with influence on the conjuncture of universal thought, nor are there any polemical responses on the global level to the arguments our thinkers make. . . . Unsatisfied and insecure, Latin Americans have felt like they are in a foreign land when crossing onto the terrain of philosophy, the result of a strong awareness of their lack of speculative originality.
>
> (SALAZAR BONDY, *¿EXISTE UNA FILOSOFÍA DE NUESTRA AMÉRICA?* 20; 30)

But if philosophy as a conceptual expression of a culture lacks authenticity in Latin America, if our main concern is the nonexistence of a Latin American thought capable of making itself heard in the conjuncture of universal thought, this—Salazar Bondy reasons—must point to a serious *cultural defect*. Here we will take up once more the motives proposed by Samuel Ramos: philosophy in Latin America has been an illusory image of reality itself; a mystified representation that has projected as its own the ideas and solutions of *other* men. Instead of generating its own interpretative categories, Latin Americans have adopted foreign ideas and values, believing that they see themselves in these ways of acting. This illusory attitude reflects, in Salazar Bondy's opinion, the state of colonial prostration in which Latin American culture is mired. The illusory representations lie about the being that they take on, yet in doing so they express the true defect of being. They fail to offer a profound image of reality, but they are correct (without intending to be) as expressions of the absence of a full and original being (81–82). Therefore, the mystified philosophical consciousness of Latin America reflects the social situation of an alienated and culturally disintegrated community: "In the final instance, we live *on the level of consciousness* according to cultural models that have no foundation in our conditions of existence. . . . These models function as a myth that prevents us from recognizing the real situation of our community to establish the basis of a genuine edification of our historical essence, our own proper being" (84). However, what are the ultimate causes of this cultural alienation? In contrast to Ramos, Salazar Bondy argues that the cultural schizophrenia of Latin America is merely the expression of an *economic alienation*. Like all Third World countries, Latin America also suffers the consequences of imperialism, dependence, and domination. Firstly, being subject to the dominion of Spanish power and later becoming supply markets for England and the United States, Latin American countries have always lacked their own economic lives. And the depressed conditions of production explain why they have not been able to articulate cultural and social expressions that are capable of neutralizing the impact of the foreign and the temptation of imitation (Salazar Bondy, *¿Existe una filosofía de nuestra América?* 87). Mired in the reality of underdevelopment, the cultures of these nations have been and will continue to be incapable of producing an authentic philosophy until the day when this reality is definitively canceled. Therefore, Salazar Bondy writes, without the triumph of a *social revolution* that would free Latin America from economic imperialism, it will be impossible to consider the creation of its own culture (*¿Existe una filosofía de nuestra América?* 88). Nevertheless, philosophy has the opportunity to be authentic in the middle of the inauthenticity surrounding it, insofar as it serves as a "lucid consciousness" of the process of national and continental liberation.

Both Salazar Bondy and Ramos agree that the traumatic historical experience of Latin America has impeded the creation of an authentic cultural identity, and the consequences of this *lack* are manifest on all levels of social life. Both philosophers ignore the multiplicity out of which a unitary paradigm in which *all* social subjects, regardless of age, sex, race, or social condition, emerge as epiphenomena of the same collective pathology. This pathology is for Ramos inherent to the psychology of Latin American peoples (the result of the colonial legacy), and for Salazar Bondy, it is a fundamentally economic problem determined by the unfortunate position of the subcontinent in the global economic system. In this sense he can be somewhat more optimistic than Ramos: at the moment when the obstacle that determines the cultural alienation of these peoples is canceled, individuals will be conscious of themselves and their own value as people. This is a simple formula: if the economic infrastructure changes, then its "ideological reflection"—culture—will also change. For Salazar Bondy, all the psychological problems diagnosed by Ramos will disappear in a matter of years when socialism finally arrives.

An intermediary (but not alternative) path between these two positions is proposed by Hugo Felipe Mansilla in his book *La cultura del autoritarismo ante los desafíos del presente* (The culture of authoritarianism facing the challenges of the present [1991]). Mansilla directs his attention to the internal and external factors of the "Latin American failure," but he tries to explain them through a critique of instrumental reason from a Freudian-Marxist perspective, much like the proposals of Theodor Adorno, Erich Fromm, and Herbert Marcuse. From this position, the Bolivian sociologist argues that the problem of authoritarianism in Latin America is not to be found in rationally developed criteria and values of orientation—and expressed, for example, in institutions or in critical thought—but rather in supra-individual desires and prescriptions within the "collective preconscious." Like Freud, Mansilla holds that the individual superego is shaped by patterns of behavior and normative ideals that are externally imposed on the subject and then internalized in the process of socialization: "It is not a matter of paradigms or criteria produced by the rational activity of consciousness through critically weighing different alternatives . . . but rather models of development, collective desires, and criteria for judging history that originated in the culture and tradition of metropolitan centers" (190).

We can see how Mansilla's thesis combines the arguments of Salazar Bondy with those of Samuel Ramos. Because of the length of time for which peripheral nations have had to suffer the effects of a violent and expansionist European civilization, they have internalized a series of beliefs and paradigms of development within the "collective psyche" that up to the present still operate as *regulative ideals* in Latin America. However, this is not about representations that hide or deform a supposed cultural identity,[16] as Ramos and Salazar Bondy presume, but rather models of progress assumed to be true for a relatively large part of the population (Mansilla, *La cultura del autoritarismo ante los desafíos del presente* 194–95). Among these *collective myths*, Mansilla includes blind faith in the good intentions of science and in the perfectibility of humans, the idea that nature has the sole purpose of being intensely exploited by human activity, the insistence on economic growth as connected to overcoming misery, the confidence in the regulative role of the state, the need for a "strong man" who would be able to show the people the path of liberation, and the belief in the advent of a society in which class contradictions no longer exist (196–97).[17] Located in the "collective preconscious," these ideas remain alien to rational questioning and are protected from it by mechanisms of control and censorship. These mechanisms, as Freud demonstrated, punish and repress attempts to bring to the level of consciousness what is taken by the collective as a self-evident truth. Discrimination, accusations of irrationalism and retrograde spirit, as well as the loss of social status are some of the ways those who refuse to recognize the liminal, benign nature of modernity in Latin America are punished. However, as Mansilla ironically points out, "the relevance of this mechanism is sufficiently diminished, as the number of individuals who expose themselves to being called enemies of progress and are also reactionaries is insignificant" (96).

It is necessary to remark that Mansilla's use of the argument of the "collective psyche" has the serious flaw of thinking subjectivities as *constituted beforehand*, with complete independence from the political practices of empirical subjects. Instead, he assumes a transcendental subject that functions as the a priori of all individual assessments. However, as in the case of Ramos and Salazar Bondy, he also naively trusts in the power of rational critique as a mechanism that can illuminate or "bring to consciousness" the pathological elements that remain hidden to the great majority of the population, which brings us once again to the *heroic role of the intellectual*, a figure exalted by nearly all discourses of identity. This figure operates as a kind of therapist or "doctor of culture" with the expertise to show the patient the ultimate causes of neurosis. The critical practice of rationality is therefore able not only to diagnose the pathologies and alienation that affect Latin American culture but also *to heal it*. It is not in vain that Ramos and Salazar Bondy's discourses are respectively inspired by the desire to "salvage" the circumstances in Mexico and to "liberate" Latin America from imperialism.

However, is *this* really what the "hermeneutics of suspicion" teach us? Perhaps the arguments of Marx, Freud, and Nietzsche do not actually show us the road to a *decentering of subjectivity*, as Foucault has posited? Marxist analysis of the relations of production and the class struggle demonstrates the impossibility of seeking a global history in which all societal differences would be reduced to a single form of consciousness and a unification of values. Nietzschean genealogy demystified the search for an originary foundation and pointed out the fallacy of trying to convert reason into the telos of humanity. Freudian psychoanalysis also decentered the subject in relation to the laws of desire and the forms of language, demonstrating that human reason has no control over the forces of the unconscious. Nevertheless, Mansilla, Ramos, and Salazar Bondy insist on protecting the centrality of a unique subject that is the *origin* of truth, meaning, and language. As we will see shortly, this is precisely the axis around which all discourses of identity circulate.

6. FROM THE NOSTALGIA FOR *ORIGINS* TO THE GENEALOGY OF *EMERGENCE*

In his famous essay "Nietzsche, Genealogy, History," Michel Foucault refers to the uses of the word *origin* in the heart of a historical narrative. If we understand origin as *Ursprung*, we are referring to discourses that are committed to looking behind all masks for the very secret of a primal identity. The search for a genesis demands a top-down movement of the intellect toward the ultimate depths where one will find buried an identity that is completely adequate to itself. This is an investigation that takes on religious characteristics, because finding identity means going back to a state of things that preexisted the fall in which humans were still on the side of the gods, listening to the true word (Foucault, "Nietzsche, Genealogy, History" 142). Therefore, nostalgia for origins is directly associated with the question of the *foundation*. In order to know identity, it is necessary to have a metaphysical guarantee that what one finds will correspond to the truth of what is being explored. To reveal the truth of an identity therefore means showing the proof of ownership that authorizes it as a permanent resident in the neighborhood of being.[18]

What Foucault's text teaches us is that the philosophical search for a Latin American identity leads to a denial of the historicity of practices and therefore *depoliticizes them*. At the moment when one explains (and evaluates) historical practices through a transcendental instance that acts as a *foundation*, one loses the possibility of analyzing its *singularity* and of understanding the kind of *local* relationships of power that frame it. The "will to truth" expressed in discourses of identity wants Latin Americans to recognize themselves in a primary instance that serves as a marker of the authenticity or inauthenticity of their historical practices: mestizaje, popular religion, and an inferiority complex.[19] In this way, local histories drown in the sea of identitarian metanarratives that actually explain nothing.

This philosophical search for the origin has three consequences: first, *salvationist messianism*. The consciousness of the Latin American identity entails the moral responsibility of disseminating, teaching, and institutionalizing it. Making this truth known to the ignorant masses is a task of absolute *political* priority, given that such knowledge is key to overcoming the flaws that have prevented Latin America from being conscious of its historical mission. Caudillos, those representatives of *Volksgeist*, whose language will be heard and understood by all, play a very important role here. The second consequence is the *exclusion of differences*. Latin American identity is a space shared by everyone, and it transcends all differences of sex, race, age, and sexual orientation. In this identity we recognize ourselves as homogeneous and without differences, only variations or moments of a single true essence. Third, discourses of identity entail the postulation of an *alterity with respect to modernity.* Once the foundation of "we, the Latin Americans" is uncovered, it is possible to delimit its borders with "them, the Europeans," the representatives of the modern "will to power." In this way, Latin America becomes the "absolute other" of the West, and modernity becomes a foreign body that is placed in opposition to the foundations of "our culture."

Avoiding these consequences necessarily requires changing the order of the questions. It entails moving toward a type of reflection that does not revolve around the search for identities but instead concentrates on how these identities are historically produced. Instead of looking for the truth of Latin American identity, we should ask about the *history of the production of that truth*, that is, we should want to know how the rules of the game that shape the truth of these discourses were constructed and under what conditions they appeared. This is not the game of *analogy*, in which the signs of Latin American culture faithfully correspond to the discourses they express, but rather the game of *discontinuity*, in which words and things are related in historically diverse ways according to how they are positioned within certain apparatuses of power/knowledge. That is to say, if in the game of analogy it was necessary to presuppose a subject that could decipher the codes of connection between the discourses of identity and identitarian referents, then in the game of discontinuity such assistance is not required, since what it seeks is not the sources of the truth of Latin America but rather the *apparatuses* that produce that truth and make it sayable. In a word, avoiding the consequences described here is equivalent to substituting the philosophical search for the *Ursprung* with the genealogy of the *Entstehung*, thereby addressing the second of the uses Foucault mentions.

The genealogical method Foucault proposes does not concern itself with origin but rather with emergence (*Entstehung*), which is to say, the appearance of certain regimes of action and enunciation that make possible both discursive and nondiscursive practices ("Nietzsche, Genealogy, History" 148–49). Discourses of identity, like all discourses, are inscribed in historical regimes of power that order the relation between signifiers and signifieds. From this point of view, the genealogical question to which I have attempted to respond in this chapter is the following: out of what type of historical and political regime did the discourses of identity in twentieth-century Latin American philosophy *emerge*? The answer is already to be found at the very point at which I began this reflection: discourses of identity emerged from within a *populist order* that for much of the twentieth century guaranteed the production, circulation, and distribution of "self-knowledge." As we saw at the beginning of this chapter, the identification of the charismatic leader with the "deep identity" of the people, the substantialist conception of politics, the emphasis on national unity, the identification of "external enemies," and the messianic role of intellectuals are all very familiar to Latin American populisms. This disciplinary order produces figures, signs, codes, and signals designed to establish the symbolic empire of identities. We have seen how some of these figures appear over and over again in the discourses elaborated by philosophers, sociologists, anthropologists, and economists. These intellectuals and scholars fulfill the role of discursively sanctioning a truth put into circulation by the same regimes of power/knowledge in which they are participants. The system of rules on which their words and actions are established authorizes them to interpret the signs of "Latin American identity" and thus tell people who they are, how they feel, and what they want as well as clarify for them who their friends and enemies are.

To summarize, the figure of the intellectual who examines the truth of culture and discursively assigns to people a specific identity (whether authentic or inauthentic), is a form of observation present in *normative societies* where individuals are surveilled and regulated by the centralizing activity of the state. This kind of society, which flourished in certain Latin American countries between the 1930s and the 1960s, is an appropriate framework for the emergence of the truth of our society. The paternalistic actions of the national populist state are reproduced by discourses oriented toward ensuring the *symbolic continuity* between people, nation, and culture. It was necessary for these people to feel protected in a world without rupture or uncertainty. Everyone should feel proud of belonging to a culture with a historical mission and to be represented by a state that faithfully represents this mission—a culture in which all signs have referents and all words denote things consistently, where discourses of identity can faithfully contribute to this objective.

4

LATIN AMERICA BEYOND THE PHILOSOPHY OF HISTORY

The purpose of history, guided by genealogy, is not to discover the roots of our identity but to commit itself to its dissipation.

—MICHEL FOUCAULT, "NIETZSCHE, GENEALOGY, HISTORY"

In a recent study, the philosopher and historian of ideas José Luis Gómez-Martínez highlighted the critical importance of José Ortega y Gasset in the development of twentieth-century Latin American philosophy. In Gómez-Martínez's opinion, two of Ortega y Gasset's theses constitute fundamental bulwarks for Latin American thought: first, *circumstantialism* or the theory of circumstances, which asserts the need to come to terms with the sociocultural context itself as a philosophical problem; second, *generationalism* or the theory of generations, which tries to offer an analytical model that can explain the historical evolution of ideas in Latin America. These two theories were taken up by Ortega's students, José Gaos and Leopoldo Zea, and subjected to a creative development through reinterpreting the history of Latin American philosophy, which laid the foundations for the construction of the philosophy of liberation today (Gómez-Martínez, *Pensamiento de la liberación* 9–18).

In what follows, I would like to explore the connection that Gómez-Martínez makes between the concepts of circumstance, generation, and liberation. I will show how these concepts are inscribed in Ortega's narrative and the way in which they were resemanticized in the work of José Gaos. I will also examine the way they move toward the register of the philosophy of history in Leopoldo Zea's and Arturo Roig's thought. Finally, taking advantage of the heuristic possibilities offered by Foucault's notion of episteme, I will attempt to show what kind of regime of truth these three concepts generate and identify the mechanisms of exclusion that are connected to them. My purpose is to investigate the content of the "epistemic violence" (Spivak, "Can the Subaltern Speak?" 280) that is produced by the metanarrative of a philosophy of history in the Latin American context.

1. "HISTORICAL REASON" IN ORTEGA Y GASSET AND GAOS

The basis of Ortega y Gasset's historicism is his opposition to the faith in objective reason that dominated the European intellectual field since the seventeenth century. Starting with Descartes, European philosophy believed it had discovered that the world possesses a rational structure coinciding with the purest form of human intellect, which is mathematical reason. Proud of this discovery, rationalism proclaimed the beginning of an era in which nothing would be hidden from human knowledge. Not allowing the mind to be clouded by passions and serenely exercising the universal faculty of thought would suffice for the thinking subject, *independently of their historical circumstances*, to be able to peacefully immerse themselves in the abyssal depths of the universe, certain that they will extract the ultimate essence of the truth (Ortega y Gasset, "History as a System" 169–71).[1] However, according to Ortega, this rationalist vision ultimately implied a total rejection of the dynamics of life. By placing its confidence in the abilities of an abstract subject to be sufficient to itself, rationalism turned into an ahistorical vision, opposed to all that is natural and spontaneous. Behind the mask of objectivity and truth, rationalism left human life itself without any "foundations [or] any profound implications in the scheme of things." Faced with the most urgent and subjective problems of humanity, "pure reason," oriented toward the analysis of objective structures, "did not know what to say" (182). In its concept, "radical reality," to which all other realities necessarily refer, is not the Cartesian cogito but rather human life (198–99, 223).[2]

In fact, for Ortega y Gasset, human reason is always practical reason, as it is oriented toward solving problems that directly affect the life of the thinking subject. To live fundamentally consists in having to deal with the world around us, with our *circumstances*. As life is not already made but rather yet to be made, humans must constantly choose from among the possibilities offered by the world. However, to choose means to think, and to think, in turn, is the ability to invent *projects* that respond to the difficulties imposed by circumstances (202). Thought functions as an organ of the *practical* comprehension of reality that allows humans to be aware of the most appropriate possibilities for action, as well as of the projects they must invent in order to preserve and perpetuate their lives. These projects are articulated around fundamental beliefs that form the repertory of basic ideas on which the individual and society base their existence (166–68). However, beliefs are not simple, abstract ideas: they possess a *practical dimension* and are a combination of technical, moral, or political representations that are not derived a priori from a metahistorical reason but rather emerge a posteriori as the result of the dynamic relationship between the subject and their circumstances (210).[3] Ortega therefore speaks of a vital and historical reason that serves to show man to be a product of himself, of his own past actions, and that comprehending this past is the key to projecting his future actions:

> The only element of being, of "nature," in man is what he has been. The past is man's moment of identity, his only element of the thing: nothing besides is inexorable and fatal. . . . Man is what has happened to him, what he has done. Other things might have happened to him or have been done by him, but what did in fact happen to him and was done by him, this constitutes a relentless trajectory of experiences that he carries on his back as the vagabond his bundle of all he possesses. . . . *Man, in a word, has no nature; what he has is . . . history.* Expressed differently: what nature is to things, history, *res gestae*, is to man.
>
> ("HISTORY AS A SYSTEM," 213, 216–17)

Understanding the past is the key to saving the present. It is no longer possible to make use of a priori ideals that tell humans what they should or should not do (as rationalism attempted to do). Instead, we should look to the only thing we have, our own history, in order to learn how to orient ourselves in the present. It is necessary to see what kind of fundamental beliefs we constructed in the past and to understand what their essential function has been. The origin of the role of historical reason is here, in the clarification of the *pragmatic function of thought*. This is because ideas have no other meaning than being in the service of life, that is to say, being a *mode of acting* in response to circumstance: "I invent projects of being and of doing in light of circumstance. This alone I come upon, and this alone is given me: circumstance" (202–3).

With this thesis, Ortega shows that historical changes obey the weakening or intensification of a society's fundamental beliefs. If social life is supported by a repertoire of beliefs, then it is clear that historical changes are directly influenced by that group of people concerned with developing and redefining these ideas: elite intellectuals. They are the true motor of history, they generate the ideas that replace current practices, which have weakened with the passing of years, through the practice of thought and philosophical meditation. In this way, intellectuals enact a *rescue mission* in the heart of society. In his 1922 book *España invertebrada* (*Invertebrate Spain* [1974]), Ortega writes:

> A nation is a human mass which is organized and given structure by a minority of chosen individuals. . . . In a nation, when the mass refuses to be a mass—that is to say, when it refuses to follow the directing minority—the nation goes to pieces, society is dismembered, and social chaos results. The people as a people are disarticulated and become invertebrate. . . . History shows a perpetual swinging back and forth between two kinds of epochs—periods in which aristocracies and therewith society are being formed, and periods in which those same aristocracies are decaying and society is dissolving along with them.
>
> (62–63, 68–69)

Thus, we come to the second of Ortega's doctrines, which, according to Gómez-Martínez, exercised a decisive influence on the project of a Latin American philosophy: *generationalism* or the theory of generations. This doctrine—formulated in the first chapter of *El tema de nuestro tiempo* (*The Modern Theme*)—asserts that generations are the result of the dynamic relationship between a select minority and the masses, in such a way that the latter's incorporation of ideas created by the ruling elite amounts to what philosophy calls the "fundamental beliefs" that constitute the sensibility held in common by an entire epoch (Ortega y Gasset, *The Modern Theme* 78).[4] Therefore, each generation has a different sensibility than the previous one, which manifests as rupture (the creation of a new common sensibility) or decadence (the exhaustion of the "fundamental beliefs" that structured society in the past). This now gives us the full scope of Ortega's philosophy: the fundamental beliefs that gave life to rationalism for more than two centuries have declined and are no longer relevant. Therefore, he calls for the emergence of a new intellectual elite able to generate ideas that, with time, will become *uses*—namely beliefs—for the masses. The time has come to create new ideas and to mark out a new direction for history. The "modern theme" consists of submitting pure abstract reason to vital, practical reason—that is, showing that reason is essentially *historical.*

Ortega y Gasset's ideas were well received in Latin America during the 1920s and 1930s, particularly in the work of thinkers like Haya de la Torre, Orrego, and Ramos (Medin, *Ortega y Gasset en la cultura hispanoamericana* 46–72). However, it was undoubtedly José Gaos who, from the time of his arrival in Mexico in 1939, definitively consolidated Ortega's reception in Latin America and sketched out the path that Leopoldo Zea's historicist work would take. In fact, Gaos's primary merit is to have "Latin Americanized" Ortega's philosophy, particularly his thesis that historical change follows the way that intellectual elites at a given moment generate ideas that can account for the present reality. This opened the doors to understanding philosophy as the philosophy of circumstances and, consequently, to the possibility of an *authentic* Latin American philosophy. This invitation to recuperate circumstance was quite welcome at a time when there was a strong effort to reclaim Indigenousness in Mexico, where the creation of a national culture was high on the list of political priorities.[5]

According to the program outlined by Gaos, philosophically recuperating circumstance means examining how *ideas* are transformed in sociopolitical agents of change in Latin American history. Using Ortega's terminology, such a program could be understood as an attempt to clarify why some ideas formulated by the intellectual minority in the past were able to impose themselves as fundamental beliefs of the masses and subsequently change how society as a whole reacts to determinate circumstances. It necessarily presupposed the development of a *history of ideas* that could show how intellectuals came up with creative responses to the demands of their time. Its goal was to leap onto the stage of history to see how Latin American thinkers accounted for their own circumstances during their lifetimes (Gómez-Martínez, "Una influencia decisiva"). The program of any Spanish American philosophy, therefore, had to be responsible for the patient historical reconstruction of each country's intellectual traditions,[6] a program that must in turn reflect a particular common sensibility.[7] This represented a rupture with the universalist paradigm that conceived of the philosopher as the representative of a thought that is always equal to itself and of philosophy as an unrooted knowledge that had nothing to do with the ethos of any particular society. What Gaos was able to show is that philosophy is not only articulated *in* certain circumstances, but that it is always the philosophy *of* those circumstances. The historical reality in which philosophy takes place conditions not only the *form* of thought but also its *contents*. As we can see, Gaos puts Ortega's philosophical historicism to work through the project of a "history of ideas":

> The repeated efforts to philosophize about our life have revealed it to be ultimately and decisively characterized by its "historicism." We have a historical knowledge, a knowledge of our history.... This knowledge has given us a new historical consciousness. The men of earlier eras lived and even considered truth, values, and principles as "in themselves," objective and as such ubiquitous, eternal, and universally valid for any possible subject.... These philosophies seem to us to be fundamentally, and even exclusively, effects and expressions of *their* time, that is to say, from the men of a certain time, from a human group of a certain time, and even from certain human individuals: that is, relative to those collective or individual subjects belonging to and valid only to them.
>
> (GAOS, *PENSAMIENTO DE LENGUA ESPAÑOLA* 32)

With these arguments, Gaos believed he had cleared the path for elaborating a "characterology" of Spanish American thought, a program he began in 1945 with the publication of his book *Pensamiento de lengua española* (Spanish-language thought). In this text he expressed his conviction that the specific disposition of Spanish American thought was organically linked to the historical processes of the formation of national states in both Spain and Latin America. Here the Enlightenment plays a special role—again, both in Spain and in its colonies—as it presupposed a rupture with Scholastic metaphysics and an orientation of thought toward *this* world, toward *this* life in particular, toward *this* historical circumstance. The Bourbon Reforms resulted in the conundrum of *historical identity* in both the metropolis and the colonies: what is Spain? what are the Spanish colonies? (Gaos, *Pensamiento de lengua española* 77–78). Gaos is not interested in Enlightenment *practices,* but rather Enlightenment *thought,* as he is convinced that these "lights" give rise to the question of the historicity of the Spanish American circumstance and the restlessness of the present through an interrogation of the past. Those who pursue these questions are Enlightenment *intellectuals*: Pablo de Olavide, Gaspar Melchor de Jovellanos, and Pedro Rodríguez, Count of Campomanes in Spain; José de la Luz y Caballero, Juan Montalvo, and Francisco Javier Clavijero in Latin America. With them, Spanish American thought was properly born. It was the eighteenth century that yielded all the elements that would characterize this thought during the nineteenth and twentieth centuries. What are these elements?

Regarding its *contents,* it is a thought that prioritizes sociopolitical themes, which can be explained by the fact that the historical moment of its emergence was marked by the problem of political independence from the metropolis (Gaos, *Pensamiento de lengua española* 77–78). It is not surprising that Latin American thinkers have adopted an immanentist position, completely foreign to the concerns of the metaphysical order, and oriented instead toward a critical meditation on circumstance itself. As for its *form,* it is an asystematic thought that prefers the essay, the article, the conference, and the talk as its vehicles of expression, which is related to special characteristics of the Spanish language that make it favorable to the poetic and literary registers.[8] All of this would give *unity* to Spanish American thought, which Gaos defines as follows:

> Among all these themes and forms a unity appears, which comes to be *the* radical characteristic of Spanish American thought, around which its greatest significance gravitates. It can be formulated like this: a political pedagogy for ethics and even more for aesthetics; an educational or, more broadly and deeply, "formative" undertaking—whether creative or reformist, "constituent" or "constitutional," a matter of "independence," "reconstruction," "generation," or "renewal"—by Spanish

> American peoples through the operative minority's "formation" and direct education of the people. . . . It is possible that any endeavor of this nature must be (by its very nature and in its object and purpose) a labor of thought "applied" to "this world," this life," "the here and now," with the correlative feigning of ignorance of—or playing dumb about—any "other world," "other life," or "beyond."
>
> (*PENSAMIENTO DE LENGUA ESPAÑOLA* 87–88)

Defined in these terms, Spanish American thought is precisely that which Ortega y Gasset himself claimed in the name of historical reason, but which, blinded by his fixation on Europe, he never was able to catch a glimpse of.[9] This thought, like no other, proposed to take "radical reality" as the point of departure for philosophy, and it would take place through the activity of elite intellectuals capable of saving their circumstances and giving structure to the historic destiny of nations. Hence the program of the history of ideas Gaos formulated in Mexico toward the beginning of the 1940s proposed to reconstruct this historical wealth of fundamental beliefs as the basis for creating an authentically Spanish American philosophy. As we will see, this conception of a thought of salvation developed by lettered elites and the history of ideas as a prerequisite for the creation of an authentically Latin American philosophy found itself at the center of the reflections developed by Leopoldo Zea in Mexico and Arturo Andrés Roig in Argentina.

2. ZEA, ROIG, AND THE PHILOSOPHY OF LATIN AMERICAN HISTORY

The Latin Americanization of Ortega y Gasset's philosophy, begun by José Gaos in Mexico, sparked great enthusiasm in many countries of the region. In particular, the thesis that the recuperation of the fundamental beliefs of the past is the key to recognizing national identity and saving the present circumstances resounded with significant force in the populist milieu that had been consolidating since the 1930s. The discovery of cultural identity explains the warm reception of Ortega and Gaos's historicism in Latin America during the 1950s. For, what attracted thinkers like Zea, Ramos, Roig, Arturo Ardao, and so many others, was the way the two Spanish philosophers demystified universality by connecting it to concrete circumstances. Philosophy appeared as a *historical* knowledge and not as the product of a pure reason that transcends the coordinates of time and space, which promoted overcoming the acritical servility that Latin American philosophers always seemed to have with regard to European thought. Thus the door remained open for a philosophical reflection on our own history and consequently for the elaboration of our own philosophy. The mission of this philosophy would be to show that what makes the Latin American different from the European is the specificity of historical circumstance and, therefore, of the creative responses (on the level of thought) to the challenges posed by that circumstance.[10] First, we will examine these motifs in the thought of Leopoldo Zea.

In the spirit of Ortega y Gasset, as well as of Gaos, who was his professor at UNAM and the Colegio de México, Zea argues that ideas are not derivations of a universal metahistorical reason, but rather they are accretions of a situated reason with the purpose of solving the practical problems imposed by circumstance. The role of these ideas is to elaborate projects around which the life of a society is structured during a specific era. Therefore, Zea's objective is to figure out the structuring projects of Latin American history and the fundamental beliefs that constituted the common sensibility of a historical era. Based on this and inspired by Hegel, he proposes to move toward a *Latin American philosophy of history* that is capable of revealing the logic that unites all these historical projects. Analogous to Hegel's project in the *Phenomenology of Spirit*, Zea seeks to show the torturous path followed by Latin American thought on the way to becoming conscious of its own universality.

The origins of this path go back to the eighteenth century, with the emergence of the first of the grand historical projects that managed to structure life in the Spanish colonies at that time. Enlightenment ideals served as tools for the "coming to consciousness" of circumstance itself and were implemented by specific subjects: criollos. This awakening from the long colonial dream taught them to know and to love their own circumstance and to feel deeply connected to it. In this generation of Enlightenment criollos, Zea recognizes the emergence of the first moment of Latin American consciousness.

> The coming to consciousness of Spanish Americans about their own reality was achieved in a series of stages whose origins go back to the conquistadors themselves. However, it was in the middle of the eighteenth century when, due to a series of historical and cultural circumstances, this coming to consciousness became clearer. Theoretical support for this knowledge came from the philosophical ideas in vogue at that time, which were grouped under the name of the Enlightenment. . . . Armed with the experimental method of the new science, [the Spanish American] began this difficult task. The flora, fauna, land, and sky of Latin America were the objects of his knowledge. It would not take long for him to realize what it was to experience this reality. Latin America had its own personality; it possessed a rich individuality in all areas. The Spanish American men of science taught how to know and love this reality.
>
> (*DIALÉCTICA DE LA CONCIENCIA AMERICANA* 65–66)

Closely following Ortega y Gasset, Zea shows that coming to consciousness is not an abstract affair but rather is necessarily translated into *action*, into the transformation of circumstances. This is why the *subjects* of this process, the criollo men of science, were great contributors to the libertarian project that ultimately led to movements for independence. Men of action like Simón Bolívar, Francisco de Miranda, and Simón Rodríguez formulated the utopia of the Latin American nation, Gran Colombia, which would reunite all peoples of Hispanic origin in a community of free men (Zea, *Filosofía de la historia americana* 188). However, once independence was achieved, the inherent limitations of this "first dialectical moment of the Latin American consciousness" became evident. The Enlightenment criollos naively believed that imitating existing constitutions in Europe and the United States would be enough for Spanish American nations to miraculously achieve freedom. However, the freedom promised by revolutionary exhortations did not correspond to the reality of the young republics, which were now immersed in bloody and painful civil wars. The optimism that preceded the independence movement quickly turned into a deep pessimism. In the middle of the nineteenth century, the time had come for Latin American thought to advance toward a second moment of self-consciousness.

According to Zea's narrative, the generation that came after the wars of independence set out to discover the obstacle that prevented Spanish America from entering onto the path of freedom. Liberal criollo thinkers like José Victorino Lastarria, Domingo Faustino Sarmiento, Juan Bautista Alberdi, Esteban Echeverría, José María Samper, and Francisco Bilbao realized that political freedom had not brought about an emancipation from the *mental habits* inherited from the colonial past (Zea, *El pensamiento latinoamericano* 78). Without having achieved intellectual autonomy, the Latin American man could not shake the colonial legacy, no matter how rational and enlightened his political constitutions were. Thus it was a matter of forming a "new man," like the kind that had made possible the cultures of Europe and the United States. The complete "de-Hispanicization of culture" had to be achieved through a reformation of educational institutions. It was necessary for Spanish America to liberate itself from customs and habits of Spanish origin in order to be inscribed in the movement of universal history, the rising tide of all nations toward freedom. It was therefore also necessary to create, as if out of thin air, a national grammar, literature, and philosophy (Zea, *El pensamiento latinoamericano* 70). And the fundamental belief that was finally able to make society cohere around this emancipatory purpose was *positivism*. This was the perspective of the generation that assumed the spiritual leadership of Spanish America in the second half of the nineteenth century:

> Positive philosophy tried to be, in our independent America, what Scholasticism had been in the colonial era: an instrument for mental order. Those who championed this doctrine attempted to achieve something that had not been possible until then, in spite of political emancipation: mental emancipation. . . . Spanish Americans saw in positivism the philosophical doctrine that would save them. It was presented to them as the most suitable tool for achieving their complete mental emancipation, and thus, a new order that was to have repercussions in the social and political arena. Positivism was presented to them as the most adequate philosophy for imposing a new mental order that would replace the one that had been destroyed, thereby ending a long period of violence and political and social anarchy.
>
> (ZEA, *EL PENSAMIENTO LATINOAMERICANO* 78)

Zea sees in positivism the "second dialectical moment of Latin American consciousness," which results in a grand project of social transformation called the "civilizing project." The generation of Latin American intellectuals that sketched out this project (Sarmiento, Alberdi, Echeverría, Justo Sierra, Mario Augusto Bunge et al.) and was able to implement it as public policy sought to establish order by reforming colonial customs and habits. However, the promises of mental, political, and social change heralded by positivism were not completely fulfilled, and the vast majority of the population found itself in a situation that differed little, if at all, from that of colonialism. Conversely, the emergent bourgeoisie became conscious of their economic subordination to the United States, a new imperialist power that embodied the values praised by positivism. The civilizing project failed, in Zea's opinion, for the same reasons the emancipatory project had failed: both insisted on preserving circumstances, but without daring to come to terms dialectically with the legacy of the past. Seeking to approximate the achievements of European modernity, nineteenth-century Latin Americans wanted to emulate England, France, and the United States. Paradoxically, they wanted to be others so they could be themselves.[11] However, at the beginning of the twentieth century, the generation that was beginning to take over from the previous one became conscious of this paradox. By observing that the entrance to modernity necessarily happened through a recuperation of history itself, that generation set in motion the "third moment of Latin American consciousness" in its long journey toward itself.

This third moment, which Zea calls the "assumptive project"—which corresponds to the final figure of the triad defined by Hegel in the *Phenomenology of Spirit*—is in reality the joint work of three generations. The first generation was represented by thinkers like José Martí, José Enrique Rodó, Manuel Ugarte, Carlos Arturo Torres, José Vasconcelos, and Francisco García Calderón, who fought against the positivism of the previous generations, taking as their starting point the *Latin spirit* of "Our America" (Zea, *El pensamiento latinoamericano* 424). For all these thinkers, Latin America had to look back at itself in order to seek the elements that would allow it to become part of an effort with a truly universal scope. This is the program of *Aufhebung* created by the following generation, including thinkers like Germán Arciniegas, Ramos, Orrego, Octavio Paz, Guillermo Francovich, Ezequiel Martínez Estrada,

Alfonso Reyes, Ardao, Francisco Romero, and Sérgio Buarque de Holanda, which, in the 1940s, gave itself over to the task of saving not only the Latin American circumstance in particular but that of the West as a whole, threatened as it was by the onslaught of fascism in Europe.[12] According to Zea's interpretation, a truly universal humanism began to take shape in the Latin American philosophical consciousness. This was not the Enlightenment humanism that turned a concrete manifestation of the human, European culture, into a universal archetype by virtue of which all the peoples of the Earth had to justify themselves. The truth that was so painfully attained by Latin American consciousness is that one is a man only in determinate historical circumstances and only insofar as the possibilities offered by those circumstances are freely chosen. Moreover, this truth is Latin American thought's most genuine contribution to universal culture. This is how the thinkers of the generation that began to emerge in the middle of the 1960s understood it. Figures like Frantz Fanon, Aimé Césaire, João Ubaldo Ribeiro, Sebastián Salazar Bondy, Fernando Enrique Cardoso, Paulo Freire, Enrique Dussel, Roig, Francisco Miró Quesada, and many others argued that *freedom* necessarily entails *liberation*. That is to say, humanism does not only spread through proclaiming a selective and abstract freedom that is valid for some but not for others; rather, it necessarily demands the creation of humane living conditions for *all* people. With this third generation, the generation of the philosophy of liberation, Latin American thought finally was able to elevate itself after having traveled down a long road before it arrived at a truly universal humanism:

> Europe produced human recognition but has been unable to recognize this in other humans. This recognition should be universalized. . . . By discovering the inauthenticity of the West, Latin Americans discovered themselves as men. This is why Latin Americans and other men who were haggling over human quality can now accomplish what Western culture kept at the borders of its limited interests, and with greater results. . . . The framing of the struggle for human liberation as the source of meaning and the goal of history is a connection to the West, along with which it enters into the orbit of a common destiny, each with its own circumstance: the West tending toward a process of decolonization and material and human reparations toward the peoples it

> subjugated and whose destiny it denied; and Latin America, struggling against underdevelopment, against the archaic economic and social structures of the colonial era, vindicating the vast majorities that have suffered contempt and neglect for centuries, each with its own path converging toward the new history, toward the history that must begin when the process of human recognition that constitutes the definitive reconciliation between the West and Latin America has ended.
>
> (ZEA, *EL PENSAMIENTO LATINOAMERICANO* 537–38)

As we can see, the reception of Ortega y Gasset's circumstantialism is mediated in Zea's work by Hegel's philosophy of history, through which Zea seeks to discover the path by which Latin American consciousness travels toward universality. This path paradoxically recognizes that the humanist ideals forged in Europe were ideals that Europeans were unable to implement because of their colonial pretensions. They saw themselves as humans but saw non-Europeans as subhumans. Nevertheless, in Latin America (and in the Third World in general), these values, created and denied by Europe, are reclaimed as the inheritance of *all* humanity thanks to the processes of decolonization. With this, Zea arrives at one of the central motifs of Eurocentrism: the myth of the inherent universality of European thought and of the Third World as the focus of the application or implementation of this universality. According to this myth, humanism is valid for all peoples not because it was initially thought of as by and for Europeans, but because with it humanity itself (as a species) makes a qualitative leap. That is to say, the humanist thought developed in Europe between the sixteenth and twentieth centuries updated the "originary dispositions of the species." The ideas that emerged in modern Europe are thus posited as an "original" against which the path taken by Latin American history ought to be judged.[13]

The Argentine philosopher Roig noticed this paradox and attempted to resolve it, first through a Marxist critique of circumstantialism, in which he asserts that even if the Mexican school proved to be fruitful in its promotion of a recuperation of the history of ideas in Latin America, it failed to understand that ideas are immersed in relations of power. Complete comprehension of this was finally achieved toward the end of the 1960s, when dependency theory and the philosophy of liberation demonstrated that the question of the authenticity of Latin American thought first requires an analysis of how *ideologies* operate in economically dependent countries. It is necessary to then move from a phenomenological history to a *social* history of ideas that is aware of the role ideologies play (Roig, "La historia de las ideas y la historia de nuestra cultura" 87).[14] Within this history, circumstantialism functioned as an alienating discourse that tended to see in the exogenous the causes of any inauthenticity in the endogenous:

> This is how "circumstantialism" and the concept of "adjusting to circumstance" (in this case, European ideas) emerged as a way to consider something like this as the lifeline of our authenticity and therefore of our "cultural identity." Needless to say, we must pause to point out the extreme poverty of this circumstantialism, which in our opinion does not reflect so much the poverty of our ideas but rather of our historiographers. This method, which in its time was widely practiced among us, also entailed a logical interest in the determination of *influences*. In any case, this question of influences . . . suffers from a primary defect that we could express as the problematic of the *exogenous* and the *endogenous*. The starting point was that which accepted as an indisputable principle, in spite of our minority, the permanently exogenous origin of anything that could be creative . . . This exogenism was born from a desperate search for models that generally never arose from our own reality, which in fact couldn't offer us anything because it was seen precisely as an *antimodel*. This exogenism—which has prolonged the old system of "civilization and barbarism"—has been the general tendency and has even given rise to undoubtedly deplorable cases of intellectual pathology.
>
> (ROIG, "LA HISTORIA DE LAS IDEAS Y LA HISTORIA DE NUESTRA CULTURA" 85–86)

The question, therefore, is not one of examining how European ideas have been applied in the Americas, and then from there inquiring about the identity of Latin American thought; rather, the point is to interrogate the social role of the *subjects* behind these ideas (58). Roig is not referring to the individual biographies of men like Alberdi, Sarmiento, Andrés Bello, Martí, and Rodó (among others) but to the axiological positioning these men drew up in the nineteenth century that corresponds to what we call today "the intellectual." More than the influences and appropriateness of ideas in the Latin American circumstance, the question is about the vital commitment of intellectuals in a class-stratified society, particularly societies that have formulated the question of Latin American identity for the first time. However, the analysis of this question should follow a paradigm that goes beyond the philosophy of knowledge, in which the circumstantialism of Ortega y Gasset, Gaos, and Zea was trapped—namely, the *linguistic paradigm*.

In effect, Roig tries to go beyond idealist notions like those of consciousness and *Weltanschauung* to understand the position of intellectuals who, since the nineteenth century, have posed the question of identity. Therefore, he starts from the assumption that language is both a historical fact and a reflection of the inherent conflict of society itself (Roig, "¿Cómo leer un texto?" 108). He attempts to show that commitment to Latin American reality should not be sought in the consciousness of intellectuals (their biographies, their intellectual influences, the creative adaptations they made of certain European ideas) but rather in their *discursive forms*.[15] The objective of the *social history* of ideas is to map the discursive universe of a specific era in order to uncover how some intellectuals in this universe were discursively positioned in relation to others (Roig, "La radical historicidad de todo discurso" 130–33). In other words, the objective is to draw up a map of the important discursive moments in Latin American history in order to show how the different discursive forms are a consequence of different *axiological positionings* in relation to reality.

Roig develops this philosophical program in his most important book, *Teoría y crítica del pensamiento latinoamericano* (Theory and criticism of Latin American thought). There he concentrates on the period between 1837 and 1845 in the Southern Cone, since he considers this era as marking the great discursive moment from which a very particular register emerged, "Latin American philosophy."[16] The discursive world of this era is marked by a heterogeneity of forms that confront one another, from Antoine de Stutt de Tracy's idealism, passing through Jeremy Bentham's utilitarianism, through French romanticism—at the moment when the old feudal structures of colonialism come into conflict with the emergent bourgeoisie and the figure of the caudillo who will lead the masses consequently appears. This is when intellectuals such as Sarmiento, Alberdi, Bilbao, Andrés Lamas, and Echeverría—all of whom were part of the Rio de la Plata region's bourgeoisie—adopted a socialist, nationalist, and Latin Americanist option in the pursuit of what Roig calls a liberatory discourse that advocates for specifically *Latin American* forms of literature and philosophy:

> "Latin American" philosophy and "literary Latin Americanism" arose with a young group made up of a cultured elite that had been influenced by European romantic historicism in the formulations of it generated by the 1830 Revolution in France. Its ideology was initially "socialist," within frameworks that approached a certain kind of utopian socialism that was at the same time nationalist, with an understanding of "nation" that was apparently not incompatible with the pursuit of continental Latin American unity. . . . In the initial programmatic documents written by Alberdi and Lamas (both in 1838), the formulation of "Latin American" literature and philosophy was considered to be a "second emancipation," which Lamas called an "intelligent independence" and Alberdi named the "conquest of Latin American intelligence." This demand was undoubtedly not exclusive to the romantics of the Río de la Plata region and can be noted in other Spanish American writers of the era.
>
> (*TEORÍA Y CRÍTICA DEL PENSAMIENTO LATINOAMERICANO* 286–87)

Roig constructs a kind of genealogy of Latin American philosophy, demonstrating its inscription in a radically historical discursive universe (that of Río de la Plata between 1837 and 1845), but also making evident that this was a liberating discourse in relation to other discourses that were circulating at the same time and place, for instance, the science of ideas (Destutt de Tracy) and utilitarianism (Bentham).[17] It is a discourse that, unlike the latter, arises from a specific axiological position: one in which a group of intellectuals from the Río de la Plata region makes a *vital commitment* to the reality in which they think. We can see this as an instance of the formation of what Gramsci called the "organic intellectual," directly expressed here as a reencounter with the roots of the nation, with the constituent elements of the Great Latin American Nation, which had remained obscure in the discourses of other intellectuals of the era (Roig, "El siglo XIX latinoamericano" 148). The oppressive (and ideological) discourse of these other, foreign intellectuals is opposed to the liberating discourse of the young *rioplatense* romantics. In the historical analysis Roig proposes, all discursive universes are characterized by a *constituent duality*. There is no liberatory discourse without an oppressive discourse, and vice versa. All discourse always presupposes and contains its own opposite discourse (Roig, "¿Cómo leer un texto?" 110).

Roig proposes the project of a Latin American philosophy—no longer the philosophy of circumstances (as in Ortega and Gaos), nor the dialectic of the Latin American consciousness (as in Zea), but rather the analysis of the historical forms of Latin Americanist discourse that determine an axiological position. However, this proposal seems to fall back onto that binary language so common in modern Marxism: the oppressor/oppressed dichotomy, as if all social formations in an era can be reduced to such an antagonism, and as if the axiological position of subjects were the privileged locus for investigating the logic that has moved Latin American intellectual history. In the end, Roig surreptitiously introduces the "philosophy of history," but in a Kantian rather than Hegelian register.[18] Ultimately, and in spite of the linguistic turn with which he believes he has surpassed the philosophy of consciousness, Roig is not far from neo-Kantian thinkers like Wilhelm Dilthey and Ernst Cassirer, for whom history can be judged entirely on the forms of objectification of *practical reason* in which man "establishes himself as valuable."[19] The logic of Latin American history can be reconstructed on the basis of an imperative of practical reason that Roig calls the anthropological a priori:

> It has not been observed, for example, to what extent criticism assumes a regulative function in Kant and turns philosophy into a normative knowledge in which the norm is not something external to philosophy but rather something derived from its own structure. . . . Philosophy thus appears as a normative knowledge that is aware not only of the nature of reason but also of the man who uses that reason. . . . The fact that philosophical knowledge is a practice clearly emerges from the presence of the anthropological a priori, whose point of view restores to philosophy the value of the knowledge of life, more than its pretensions to scientific knowledge. . . . In relation to this programmatic value of the normative, which allows us to discover the value of the guidelines of

> any norm which functions as an anthropological a priori, one undoubtedly finds a view of philosophy as a morning knowledge and not an evening knowledge. . . . It is from this perspective that we speak of *historicism*, understanding that its roots lie in the recognition of man as actor and author of his own history. . . . This is a historicism that, as a regulating idea, indicates to us an ought-to-be, a goal, which is not foreign to the attitude that mobilizes utopian thought.
>
> (*TEORÍA Y CRÍTICA DEL PENSAMIENTO LATINOAMERICANO* 9, 11, 13, 15)

There will be Latin American philosophy when historical subjects arise that, on the basis of an a priori *ideal normativity*, see themselves as valuable, as subjects committed to their own historical reality and to the need to transform it. Reaching the age of majority, which Kant understood as the subject's capacity to make their own law, to be *autonomous*, to act independently of external authorities, is the common thread that allows the historian of ideas to recognize the logic that has made Latin American philosophy possible. It is only with this historical affirmation of the subject, understood as a fundamental anthropological demand, that philosophy ceases to be a knowledge of abstract things and becomes a knowledge oriented toward praxis. The question—no longer about the possibility but rather the *necessity* of Latin American philosophy—is resolved for Roig in this process of the constitution of subjects who declare themselves to be *free*, builders of their own history, like the young *rioplatenses* of the Generation of 1838 did. Hence the social history of ideas must be oriented toward keeping track of how, out of different, historically localized discursive universes, subjectivities have emerged that position themselves as "we Latin Americans."

3. TOWARD A GENEALOGY OF LATIN AMERICANISM

It is easy to see that Zea and Roig's philosophical historicism is a legitimate expression of the discontent in Latin American culture generated by the peripheral experience of Westernization. For Ortega y Gasset, historical reason is primarily an alarm that signals the crisis of European modernity. He was conscious of the fact that he was living in a historical moment (the beginning of the twentieth century, the First World War) when the common sensibility took a radical turn with regard to the rationalist ideals on which the West had supported itself for over four centuries. In this regard, the Spanish philosopher is in accord with Nietzsche, Dilthey, Georg Simmel, Weber, and Heidegger, who saw rationalism as the source of a technological and bureaucratic machinery that threatened to completely suffocate individual and communitarian life.

For his part, Gaos understood that this historical turn represented the definitive crisis of a philosophical discourse that, although it was vitally connected to specific circumstances, insisted on presenting itself as the bearer of a universal and necessary knowledge. Consistent with this reaction, Zea and Roig set out to develop a philosophical critique of European modernity through a Latin Americanization of its normative contents. As in Shakespeare's *The Tempest*, in which the slave Caliban uses his master Prospero's own language to condemn him, the two philosophers articulate their critiques *in the philosophical language* of modernity—and concretely, through the register of the philosophy of history—in order to criticize modernity itself and overcome its pathological manifestations. However, what would happen if the pathologies they see in modernity were connected with precisely *the same* language they use? What would happen if colonialism, rationalization, authoritarianism, the technologization of everyday life—in sum, all the dehumanizing elements of modernity—were directly related to humanist discourses? Where would Zea's and Roig's critiques be if what was considered the remedy for the illness was actually connected to the illness itself?

Ortega y Gasset, Gaos, Roig, and Zea construct their philosophies on the same basis upon which all modern European thought is supported: the idea of Man as a being endowed with abilities that can be rationally directed in the cultural, political, and social realms; Man as the absolute master of his own history and as a subject, namely as a fundamental reality that underlies and guarantees the unity of all processes of change; the subject as conceived of by humanism, as self-consciousness, the *center and origin* of language and meaning. Thus Ortega y Gasset, for example, was convinced that economic and political changes are surface phenomena that actually depend on the aesthetic ideas and preferences of the intellectual elite. This led him to the thesis that history is a process anchored in the experiences of generationally grouped subjects. It is no longer Hegel's Absolute Spirit or Carlyle's solitary hero who act as subjects of history; rather it is the "we" that belongs to a tradition and acquires self-consciousness by means of its own historicity. As Ortega himself says, the *letrados and intellectuals* become "the pivot responsible for the movements of historical evolution." They have the mission—and the moral responsibility—of saving their circumstance through ideas and by elaborating common projects designed to humanize their own world.

Nevertheless, toward the end of the twentieth century, intellectuals have begun to develop other readings of Latin American history that, instead of seeing discourses as the positions of an autonomous or heteronomous subject (Roig), understand them as historical phenomena without any relation to human nature. Theorists like Ángel Rama, to give just one example, have created narratives in which discourses appear as reverberations that are not formed in either subjective consciousness or choice, but rather in anonymous regimes of signs and relations of forces that generate their own norms of truth. In this way, a scenario is created in which *writing* is stripped of its mission of salvation and in which there is no longer any place for a philosophy of history like that developed by Zea and Roig.

Let us consider Rama's sober *genealogical* approach to Latin American letrados. The Uruguayan critic takes up Foucault's thesis that discourses do not directly obey the intentions of human consciousness but rather follow an order of signs that operates in relative independence from the people who use it, inscribed in social relations of power. From this point of view, Rama's emphasis is not on the subject who writes but rather on *writing* as such, on the act of writing itself. The lettered city is not the set of intellectuals who act as writers in a given time and place and give society a common sensibility (Ortega y Gasset); neither is it the generation of thinkers who have taken on the task of giving meaning to Latin American history and public life (Gaos and Zea). On the contrary, it is a society of discourse that operates through an autonomous rationality and whose history is not suppressed by the biographies, works, and intentions of its inhabitants. According to Rama, the lettered city is

> an abstract, rationalized system, able to articulate its component parts without any appeal to anything outside it, drawing only on internal

> logic of the universe of signs. . . . The evolution of [this] symbolic system did not lose momentum with the passage of time, and it seems to have reached its apotheosis in our own era, replete with schemes of signals, indices, acronyms, diagrams, logotypes, and conventional images so many of which imitate, or even aspire to replace, language. The component symbols in each of these systems respond only vaguely to particular, concrete facts of daily life. They respond, instead, to the needs of the symbolic system wherein they were originally conceived, the choice of signifiers being something of an afterthought, indispensable to expression but not essential to their genesis. Their function—founded on reason and instituted through legal mechanisms—is to prescribe an order for the physical world, to construct norms for community life, to limit the development of spontaneous social innovations, and to prevent them from spreading in the body politic. Their profusion in contemporary Latin America lends enduring testimony to the work of the lettered city.
>
> (*THE LETTERED CITY* 24–25)

The *history* of the lettered city—which is not the same thing as the history of letrados—begins in the colonial era with the foundation of cities based on abstract designs, but it becomes relevant with the advent of the processes of mass urbanization at the end of the nineteenth century that set in motion a social dynamic in which symbolic languages, and particularly *writing*, attained supremacy. An urban elite of letrados formed that was closely connected to political power and whose role was to safeguard the preservation, production, and circulation of discourses, distributing them according to strict rules in the midst of an illiterate society. Lawyers, clerks, bureaucrats, and intellectuals took control of that repertory of signs, which legitimized the institutionality of power (documents, laws, edicts, constitutions, and books). A conflict gradually emerged between the real city, where the indeterminacy of meanings (connected to oral communication) predominates, and the lettered city, where the only thing that matters is the field of meanings Foucault called the *order of discourse*. Nevertheless, and even though they were operating under different logics, the real city and the lettered city could not exist independently (*The Lettered City* 70). Letrados assumed the role of serving as mediators between the two cities and operated out of institutions of writing like universities, high schools, seminaries, newspapers, and language manuals and schools, seeking to place all possible *writing* in the frame of a single regime of truth. In this way, control over the production and circulation of statements has been their primary mission in Latin America.

We can now see how Rama's reading of Latin American intellectuals clashes directly with the metanarratives created by Roig and Zea. Let us take, for example, the case of the nineteenth century, specifically the period of so-called mental emancipation when, in both philosophers' opinion, thinkers like Alberdi, Sarmiento, Bello, Echeverría, Bilbao, and Lastarria inaugurated the "for-itself" of Latin American consciousness. If we follow Rama's interpretation, what these letrados accomplished was nothing other than the consolidation of a regime of truth intended to unify and humanize the fabric of society through writing. The nation had to be constructed and endowed with a perfectly defined identity. For this reason it was necessary to produce through narrative an idiosyncrasy that would be faithfully reflected in language, history, and literature. This gave rise to projects intent on reforming the way Spanish grammar (Bello) and national historiography—with its cult of heroes and patriotic actions—are institutionalized in schools. And, of course, Alberdi's famous manifesto gave expression to a project of a Latin American philosophy that did not adhere to any need to salvage circumstances (Gaos, Zea), nor did it enshrine the Latin American subject as inherently valuable (Roig), but instead envisioned a *disciplinary society* in which the letrados themselves would actively participate as teachers, lawyers, writers, philologists, and even presidents.[20] This would be a society organized around the modern idea of the nation, where there is no place for the "outside," that is, for those small histories that interrupt from the margins. The epistemic and linguistic multiplicity present in nineteenth-century Latin American societies should be integrated into the totality of grammars created by letrados and taught in schools:

> The great Latin American educators of the period—Andrés Bello, Simón Rodríguez, and later, Sarmiento—all understood this, and it animated their almost obsessive concern with the problem of spelling reform. Facilitating access to writing was a central purpose, but so was creating a system that functioned consistently according to the most rational

> possible norms. . . . The spelling reformers of nineteenth-century Spanish America, on the other hand, were altering that previous norm to close the gap between everyday American speech and the ossified written language assiduously preserved by generations of letrados. That gap presented a pedagogical problem, since it made writing more difficult to learn for speakers of the ordinary American idiom, but there was also a higher theoretical purpose for undertaking orthographic reform. Independence in matters of writing would complement the political independence already achieved and lead to the creation of a *national literature.*
>
> (*THE LETTERED CITY* 43–44)

Rama's interpretation does not support the idea of a Latin American consciousness that would be free from the violent dispossession, deception, and trickery of power. What he shows is that knowledge of the self is always connected to the letrados' passion, to their reciprocal hatreds, their fanatical arguments, and their political ambitions. Based on his reflections, we can say that it is not the *history of Latin American ideas* that interests us but rather the *genealogy of Latin Americanism.* We are referring here to a kind of discourse that, analogous to what Edward Said demonstrated in *Orientalism*, operates as a signifier that assigns people to certain cultural identities, marks them with a historical destiny and an origin, and signals essential differences with regard to others (Europe). The question is not "What is Latin America?"—a question typical of the history of ideas. Rather, what interests genealogy is the question, "How does Latin Americanism function as a discourse?" Following Foucault, Rama has shown that discourses of the self are not related to a "subject" understood as the *origin* of these discourses but to a set of relations of forces, discursive orders, and power struggles. Genealogy, Foucault tells us,

> does not pretend to go back in time to restore an unbroken continuity that operates beyond the dispersion of forgotten things. . . . Genealogy does not resemble the evolution of a species and does not map the destiny of a people. On the contrary, to follow the complex course of descent . . . is to identify the accidents, the minute deviations—or conversely, the complete reversals—the errors, the false praises, and the

faulty calculations that gave birth to those things that continue to exist and have value for us.

("NIETZSCHE, GENEALOGY, HISTORY" 146)

That is to say, instead of using narrative to create a series of *continuities* that would make it possible to reconstruct the *evolution* of Latin American thought, such as Zea proposed, genealogy is concerned with locating the ruptures, gaps, fissures, and lines of flight that attempt to deny Latin Americanism. This is not motivated by some malevolent, destructive pleasure, but rather a suspicion that it is precisely here, in the space of the outside, that the *voices* (not the *texts*) that destabilize the norms of writing in the lettered city are articulated.[21] The task of genealogy is to show that behind the masks of the "Latin American subject" (Roig) and the "assumptive project" (Zea) developed by the philosophy of history there are much less heroic and profane concerns, namely those of a multiplicity of subjects who create *oral strategies of resistance* to navigate the contingencies of the present.[22]

However, this first step must be complemented with an analysis that shows us what type of *order of knowledge* Roig and Zea's Latin Americanist discourses are inscribed in. If we look to Foucault's description of the modern episteme in *The Order of Things*, we will realize that the register of the philosophy of history belongs to the system of humanist discourses that managed to prevail in academic circles starting in the middle of the nineteenth century (217ff.). In this system of signs, knowledge could not be developed in the unified and unifying background of the *mathesis universalis*, as was the case in the classical episteme, but necessarily required an *unfounded foundation* that would give coherence and unity to its contents. From Kant onward, this foundation will be sought in the a priori conditions of consciousness established by a subject capable of elaborating objective representations of itself. In this way, the figure of *reflection* appears, which in Hegel becomes the historical return of consciousness to itself so as to seek there the ultimate foundations of its own essence. This return attributes a liberatory role to thought, in the sense of a promise that is slowly being revealed to humans, whose historical crystallization takes place in the sphere of *international politics*. The philosophy of history therefore acts as the representation that a subject—which *exists prior to* power relations and the discourses that constitute them—makes of its becoming in history. This appears as the place where the promise of human liberation is gradually fulfilled through revolutions and counterrevolutions. Thus history is recounted as a dialectical process of the consciousness's self-constitution through critical reflection, which allows the subject to progress toward the configuration of new forms of self-consciousness that bring together and synthesize the elements of the previous era.

Foucault himself pointed out the problems of the modern order of knowledge in general and of the philosophy of history in particular. In an epistemological framework in which the truth of knowledge is maintained by a single subject's representations, it is evident that small histories lack significance. The exigencies of sex, race, age, and social condition or even the simple affective avatars of empirical subjects are integrated into a fully comprehensive transcendental space where one searches for the greater meaning in life. We turn our gaze from what is close to us to where the letrados always wanted to look: toward the purest, most abstract forms, the noblest ideas, the most elevated thoughts. There, far away, one must seek the secret of the connection between words and things. Knowing this will be essential to knowing who we are, discovering our identity, breaking the chains that bind us to the age of minority. *Differences* are subsumed in a discursive order that assigns each of us our role in the staging of history and prescribes goals for us to achieve.

It is precisely to this discursive order that Roig and Zea's Latin Americanist narrative belongs. Their philosophy of history functions by using all the motifs and figures defined by that archeological network of knowledge that Foucault called the *modern episteme*. There exists a logic of history, a transcendental subject, some objectivizations of consciousness, and some critical intellectuals who discover that they themselves are valuable and incidentally reveal the secret of what is ours. For Zea, the logic of history is the juxtaposition of projects through which Latin American consciousness is able to arduously elevate itself until it achieves self-recognition. The wars of independence in the nineteenth century, the Mexican Revolution, the nationalisms and populisms of the twentieth century, the revolutions in Cuba and Nicaragua, all these political events are seen as moments of the "dialectic of the Latin American consciousness" (Zea, *Dialéctica de la conciencia americana*). Latin American history has been a historical learning process of coming to consciousness and of affirming the Same against the outside interference of colonialism, the slow but effective emergence of a universal experience of what it means to be human. However, Zea has little to tell us about the *victims* and the suffering caused by this teleological learning process or about the regimes of truth that have resulted from it. Nor does he explain why certain thinkers or ideological currents are selected for his reconstruction of the history of ideas while others are mysteriously excluded. Unsurprisingly, for the philosophy of history, words always keep their meaning, as do desires their orientation and ideas their logic. In the philosophy of history, there is no room for dissonance, hybridity, and discontinuity.

For his part, Roig presents Latin American history as a project based on regulative anthropological ideas that therefore has a few specific goals: the development of an "America for us," such as it was conceived by Bolívar. The Kantian *ought to be* is combined with the Marxist dialectic to construct a metanarrative in which a Bolivarian utopia is the central axis around which the entire history of Latin American thought is ordered. It tells us nothing about the moral and state-centered authoritarianism that came along with the ideology of Gran Colombia, as is expressed in documents like the *Carta de Jamaica* and the *Discurso de Angostura*. These show us the rationality of a sovereign power whose paradoxical objective is to produce freedom *out of subjugation*.[23] The moral and political unity of Latin America, under the safe guidance of a strong state, appears to be the great humanistic imperative to which all the continent's social forces must submit. The bureaucratized, corrupt, and self-referential world of *international politics* (what else could achieve such goals?) is presented as the place where the "promise of liberation" will be fulfilled. Like Kant and Hegel, Roig seems to be convinced that the fundamental problem of the human race is political freedom at the core of the state, since happiness and perpetual peace depend on it. The slow but sure approach toward a league of nations—in which Latin American unity would be only a preliminary and necessary moment—takes on the characteristics of a moral imperative.

By activating the modern register of the "philosophy of history," Roig and Zea produce a discourse that marks a normative trajectory for life, which, in addition, bestows upon letrados the role of legislators and interpreters of this life. The orality of the real city, where accidents, ruptures, and deviations predominate, is fixed in the discourses of the lettered city, accentuating the unities, continuities, and totalizations. However, is there another way to narrate history? Foucault speaks of an effective history that is counterposed to the philosophy of history. While the former appears as a totality in which society, culture, and the economy are dialectically connected, as if between them existed a kind of preestablished harmony, the latter is presented as the proper sphere of *differences*. Or, as Foucault puts it:

> "Effective" history differs from traditional history in being without constants. Nothing in man—not even his body—is sufficiently stable to serve as the basis for self-recognition or for understanding other men. . . . Knowledge, even under the banner of history, does not depend on "rediscovery," and it emphatically excludes the "rediscovery of ourselves." History becomes "effective" to the degree that it introduces discontinuity into our very being.
>
> ("NIETZSCHE, GENEALOGY, HISTORY" 153–54)

More than seeking the traces of a Latin American identity, genealogy is concerned with showing the emergence of the discourses and relations of power that produced this identity. As in Rama's study of the lettered city, it also shows us that these identity discourses have nothing to do with a nature, culture, or form of being that is designated "Latin American," but are instead related to the ambitions of the letrados and their endemic connections to politics. Therefore, the objective of genealogy is to *undo* the historical continuities to which identity discourses are bound so that in its place the *multiplicity* of lines that run through us can emerge. This is genealogy as the historical outlining of singular practices and apparatuses and not as the search for an origin that functions as some sort of mirror in which we should recognize ourselves.

5

THE AESTHETICS OF THE BEAUTIFUL IN SPANISH AMERICAN MODERNISM

In the recent boom in Latin American literary and cultural studies during the last several years, the work of Puerto Rican theorist and novelist Iris M. Zavala is of particular note, especially her writings on fin de siècle Hispanic modernisms. She is among the first scholars to initiate a productive dialogue between literary criticism and contemporary philosophy that can further the study of Latin American history and culture. Among other thinkers, Roland Barthes, Michel Foucault, Jacques Lacan, Paul de Man, Julia Kristeva, and especially Mikhail Bakhtin are the main influences on Zavala's elaboration of a *cultural critique* aimed at clarifying the social problematics of the Latin American world.

I am interested in examining Zavala's interpretation of the set of narratives, social practices, and discursive formations that are traditionally known by the name of *modernism*. Following Federico de Onís's definition, Zavala understands Latin American modernism as the symptom and result of a profound cultural crisis that began toward the end of the nineteenth century and lasted until 1930. The specificity of this phenomenon is based in the fact that, in contrast to what occurred in Europe, Latin American modernism adopted a markedly antiauthoritarian, anticolonial, and socialist quality. This was how the intellectuals of the era understood it, as Zavala shows, citing articles published by the Venezuelan columnist Pedro Emilio Coll in the newspaper *Mercure de France* in 1897. Here literary modernism is directly associated with the Cuban war for independence, and the poet José Martí is seen as a "living symbol of a new mental state" (Zavala, "On the (Mis-)uses of the Post-modern" 89–90). In this view, modernism was not only a revolt against the nineteenth-century myth of progress, but moreover a *decolonial project* carried out by a broad range of fin de siècle Latin American intellectuals. Martí had been the herald, Rodó the ideologist, and Darío the indisputable leader of this emancipatory project.

Based on Bakhtin's thesis, specifically his description of the "intellectual proletariat," Zavala understands modernism as a collective project propelled by a new class of bohemians, writers, women, anarchists, and dissidents who positioned themselves as alternative *subjects* ("The Social Imaginary" 23). This group of people generated an aesthetic (the "poetics of negation"), which was characterized by emancipatory narratives in which society appears as a *de-alienated community*.[1] These men and women created "social imaginaries" in which they projected fantasies, counterimages, and utopian representations in an effort to delegitimize the ideological codes of a colonial and positivist order that tried to turn them into *objects*. Modernist texts, in contrast, were narratives of collective and personal emancipation from the development of industrial capitalism in Latin America, which was threatening to subsume social heterogeneities in a dynamic of control and dominance.

For Zavala, the literary enunciation of this project corresponds to the project of an *alternate modernity* in Latin America, understood not as modernization, that is, as a faith in the redemptive virtues of industry and technology, but rather as the realization of a *morally emancipated* community. A community that, free from the coercive power of instrumental reason, finally makes full humanization possible (Zavala, *Colonialism and Culture* 129). The tropes, forms, words, and figurative language of modernist texts are integrated into a social project that, according to Zavala, corresponds to what Kant called the "aesthetics of the beautiful:"

> This is the anarchist and socialist poetics of negation, of open-ended discourses and a *philosophy of the beautiful* which provides the referential dimensions of texts in novels, short stories, poetry, theater, and graphical material. . . . It is an appeal to the community made *a priori*, and *the idea of beauty* is situated in freedom and a feeling shared between artist and audience, which echoes Kant's ideas on the beautiful.
>
> (136–37)

As we know, for Kant the beautiful is not a property of objects; it is not something that corresponds to the thing-in-itself; rather, its foundation is the subject's particular aesthetic experience. Someone who has an experience of the beautiful is able to subtract themselves from the world of objects, free themselves of pragmatic restrictions, and assume a disinterested attitude toward the beautiful. What Zavala appears to be saying is that the feeling of the beautiful that is characteristic of Latin American modernism entailed an emancipatory attitude because, in contrast to the dominant positivism of the era, it generated lines of flight with regard to the objective world that prioritizes the natural laws of science. This escape allowed Latin American artists to generate a series of decolonizing "social imaginaries." In Zavala's view, modernism was the attempt to oppose the pragmatic and utilitarian values of industrial capitalism—which was present in Latin America toward the end of the nineteenth century—with other values like communitarianism, viewing existence as ludic, and acquiring a disinterested attitude. This, of course, assumed denouncing the "danger" of the economic and bourgeois sense of life, the idea of material progress, mechanization, and the primacy of utility.

Next, with the help of literary critics like Ángel Rama and Rafael Gutiérrez Girardot, I would like to begin a critical exploration of modernism and attempt to evaluate Zavala's hypothesis by asking 1. whether Latin American modernism was actually an original phenomenon, distinct from aesthetic currents in Europe during the same era; 2. whether it is possible to characterize Latin American modernism as permeated by what Kant called the aesthetic of the beautiful; and 3. whether this aesthetic of the beautiful engenders a decolonizing perspective or, in contrast, a reactivation of old colonial narratives.

1. MODERNITY AND MODERNISM IN LATIN AMERICA

I will begin with the diagnosis Uruguayan critic Ángel Rama offers in his classic work *Rubén Darío y el modernismo* (Rubén Darío and modernism). Like Zavala, Rama is not interested in separating aesthetic phenomena from socioeconomic phenomena but rather in reflecting on their complex articulation and analyzing Latin American modernism in the framework of the imperial expansion of capitalism at the end of the nineteenth century. This development (which in Latin America took the form of the neocolonial order) caused a profound spiritual crisis in the heart of the intellectual milieus in both central and peripheral countries. Modernism was an artistic phenomenon that perfectly reflected the content of this spiritual crisis (Rama, *Rubén Darío y el modernismo* 26). The values that held sway over creativity in the periphery came into conflict with those of the metropolis around the issues of profit, the utility of art, and the market. According to Rama, this explains why Latin American writers distanced themselves from peninsular Spanish literary models, as well as why they began to turn their attention toward France. However, in this apparently sycophantic imitation of French models, Rama observes within Latin American writing a bourgeoning desire for autonomy from the European metropolis as well as a decolonizing perspective, which the Uruguayan critic assesses as an aesthetic prolongation of the nineteenth-century independence movement:

> The goal proposed by Rubén Darío was practically the same as that of the late neoclassicals and early romantics of the independence era: the poetic autonomy of Spanish America as part of the general process of continental freedom, which meant establishing a new cultural sphere that could oppose the Spanish one from which it came, with the tacit acceptance of this new literature in the larger conglomeration of European civilization, which had its roots in the Greco-Roman world.
>
> (*RUBÉN DARÍO Y EL MODERNISMO* 5)

Rama sees the modernists as founders of Latin American aesthetic and cultural independence, in a gesture similar to Arturo Roig's identification of the intellectuals of the generation of 1838 (Alberdi, Sarmiento, Lastarria, and Bilbao) as the origin of Latin American mental emancipation, as we saw in the previous chapter. However, in contrast to Roig, Rama ends up showing to what extent this project was a miserable failure. The expansion of industrial capitalism toward peripheral regions necessarily obliged Latin American writers to adapt themselves to commercial logics that ruptured the old colonial function of the criollo aristocracy. In this kind of society, governed by the economic criteria of production, there is no longer any place for poets, and being one begins to be seen as shameful: "The image constructed of [the poet] in public was of an antisocial vagabond, a man given to drunkenness and orgies, excitable and unbalanced, deceitful, a delicate and incapable aesthete who is, in a word—and this is the worst of all—unproductive" (Rama, *Rubén Darío y el modernismo* 57).

Cornered by an economic logic that excluded them, as well as by the birth of a new social class (the bourgeoisie) that no longer had a place for them, many modernist poets ended up occupying the exact social position that this commercial logic assigned to them: they became decadent, filthy, asocial, and unproductive figures who were trying to recover a certain hierarchy, albeit an inverted one (59). What began as an anticolonial project in the aesthetic realm ended up being a flagrant subjection of writers to the new structures of capitalism. Before aesthetics, what changed at the end of the nineteenth century was the *social function* of letrados in Latin America. Those modernists who did not assume the marginal place assigned to them ended up establishing a commercial relationship with writing and began to work as journalists. They needed to find a respectable place in the world of production, to find new sources of income in an increasingly urbanized world, and journalism seemed to be the right field for that, especially in cities like Mexico City, Santiago, Montevideo, and Buenos Aires. However, the tendency of certain modernists toward the aesthetics of "art for art's sake," which was very much in spite of their declared hostility to the utilitarian values of the bourgeoisie, is seen by Rama as the perfect correlate to the liberal individualism that began to gain prominence in Latin America at the end of the nineteenth century. The effort that caused modernist writers to *adapt themselves* to the demands of the new socioeconomic structure was actually not always conscious. The liberal ideology that favors novelty and originality as the motivating attitudes of free competition between individuals is thus transported to the terrain of art:

> Subjectivization reinforces the criterion of the dissimilarity of men, opens the road toward originality as the beginning—or as the spark—of creation, and aims for this to be protected from all imitation and become unique in the market place, functioning as a true "manufacturing patent." . . . When Darío enters the literary world, liberalism had already prevailed in the Americas, and its operation on the level of literature established a single golden rule: be yourself.
>
> (RAMA, *RUBÉN DARÍO Y EL MODERNISMO* 16–17)

For Rama, modernism must not be seen as *external* to modernization, that is to say, as a kind of writing uncontaminated by the advance of industrial capitalism in Latin America, but rather as a phenomenon made possible by this very logic. In other words, *industrial capitalism is the condition of possibility of modernism:* this is Rama's most thoroughly developed thesis in his famous work *La ciudad letrada* (*The Lettered City*). In this book, he shows how even critical dissent in the world of letters ultimately yielded to the modernized space of the lettered city in three modalities: the figures of the lawyer, the journalist, and the university professor.[2] These professional fields, into which dissident letrados were funneled, gave shape to the new neighborhoods of the lettered city, along with other emerging areas of study like sociology and economics, all within the framework of a nascent middle class. Rama does not interpret the declarations of the University of Córdoba reforms of 1918 as a call for decolonization inspired by the spirit of modernism but rather as the middle class's attempt at upward social mobility (*The Lettered City* 57–58). The modernists were destined to become part of the social dynamics of the rising bourgeois class, whom they nominally abhorred. As Octavio Paz put it, this was the desire of a minority eager to participate in the historical movement of the same modernity that they felt unjustly marginalized them ("El Caracol y la sirena").

In his book *Modernismo: Supuestos históricos y culturales* (Modernism: Historical and cultural assumptions), Rafael Gutiérrez Girardot offers a reading that in some ways parallels Rama's. He begins by criticizing the Third Worldist leftist intellectuals of the 1970s for having made modernism into a *native* phenomenon that is clearly distinct from the late nineteenth-century modern lyricism of Europe. In this sense, he says, they are not very different from right-wing nationalists for whom eliminating all appearances of the foreign from Latin America would suffice for the region to be able to find its true internal essence. Thinking of modernism as something "specifically Latin American" is a mistake due to an inherent nationalist reductionism and an ignorance of the socioeconomic context of global capitalist expansion in which modernism operates. On this point, Gutiérrez Girardot agrees completely with Rama:

> This is to say that the "specificities," which up to now have been considered the only dominant factor, should be placed in the broader

> historical context of the expansion of capitalism and bourgeois society, the complex network of "dependencies" between the metropolitan centers, their provincial regions, and the so-called peripheral countries. The comparison of the literatures of metropolitan and peripheral countries will be advantageous only if one keeps in mind their social contexts.
>
> (*MODERNISMO* 20)

Gutiérrez Girardot proposes considering modernism as a literary phenomenon that, in a contradictory way, *accompanied* the processes of capitalist modernization that unfolded in Europe and Latin America beginning in the eighteenth century. Therefore, there is no externality in the relation between modernism and modernization. The cultural phenomena of modern Europe are not external to those of Latin America, as both the center and the periphery are united in a single global structure: capitalism. The difference, then, is not about essence but rather uniquely about *position.*[3] Center and periphery constitute inherent instances of the same process of capitalist expansion, forming a single, interconnected *world system.* On this point, Gutiérrez Girardot appears to take up the thesis of Brazilian critic Roberto Schwarz, who, based on dependency theory, resists the romantic perspectives that see in literature the possibility of a progressive self-discovery of the "national being." For Schwarz there is no national (or Latin American) literature that *preexists* the forms of Western culture that have expanded along with capitalism since the sixteenth century. Thus European cultural (in this case, literary) phenomena do not constitute an ideological veil that hides our "true Latin American being."

With this path now open, Gutiérrez Girardot is prepared to characterize modernism as an artistic movement that originated in Germany at the end of the eighteenth century with the aesthetics of *Sturm und Drang.* It made art into a new mythology that replaced religion as the latter was swept away by the emerging processes of secularization—a new religion of beauty that begins with a redefinition of urban forms of thinking and feeling after the death of God (66). This gives rise to the idea of an "aesthetic education of humanity" led by poets and writers who are responsible for the redemption of the world of pathologies generated by industrialization. These authors' *romantic* gesture separates art from mundane reality and seeks a new foundation for a world that has lost its center. Urban life, dominated by the worship of money, is rejected in the name of a "return" to imaginary exteriorities:

> This return—to the earth, to the countryside, to the native soil, to the peasant life—had two aspects. The first was a reaction against the "alienations" of modernity, which is the origin of the so-called critique of culture and critique of time, and of which Spengler's *The Decline of the West* and Ortega y Gasset's *The Revolt of the Masses* (among many others) are exemplary. The famous "discovery" of the Castilian landscape of the so-called Generation of '98 and the "discovery" of the indigenous past—that is, Latin American indigenism (and criolloism)—are forms of this kind of critique of modernity.
>
> (*MODERNISMO* 86)

For Gutiérrez Girardot, figures as distinct from one another as Friedrich Schiller, Oscar Wilde, Rodó, Stefan Georg, Darío, Ramón del Valle-Inclán, Nietzsche, Miguel de Unamuno, Antonio Machado, and José Asunción Silva share the same aesthetic sentiment: horror at the emergence of the bourgeois world that makes them feel like pariahs, as if they had been banished from the truth. Art was the only horizon they had that was capable of offering alternatives to the decadence they saw all around. "They met in cafes because there they found what society had denied them: recognition, an audience, contacts, admiration, followers, and because they were fleeing from the solitude of their sorry attic apartments" (Gutiérrez Girardot, *Modernismo* 118).

What is there to say then about writers like José Martí, whom Zavala identifies as an "apostle" of emancipatory movements in the political and cultural realms? From Gutiérrez Girardot's perspective, this is a romantic interpretation that seeks in "Our America" the foundation of a new society free from modern pathologies. This reveals almost all the tropes Martí uses in his famous essay, where he rebukes the immature thinkers who deny the local in the name of the foreign. Martí wants to see in the Indian, the Black, and the peasant some *exteriorities* uncontaminated by modernity, a revolutionary energy that will be able to save "Our America" from imperialist interventions and offer an alternative to the dehumanizing life promoted by capital. We recall that Latin American modernists did not initially rebel against the pathologies of industrial civilization, which in our time are less evident, but rather against the threat that U.S. economic imperialism represented for the spiritual life of the continent. U.S. imperialism was the closest experience the modernist writers had with modernity (Fernández Retamar, *Para el perfil definitivo del hombre* 207–18).

Latin American modernism and European modernism thus have the same essential quality: the rejection of the bourgeois values adopted by elites oriented toward capitalist development. The intention of Latin American modernists is to renounce a vulgar life reduced to the logic of money and power. However, as in Europe, and as we shall see in what follows, our modernists' rejection of industry, science, and imperialism was enacted from the horizon of the aesthetics of the beautiful.

2. THE MYTHOLOGY OF LATIN AMERICAN REASON

Gutiérrez Girardot suggests that the roots of modernism are in the aesthetics of German Romanticism, whose program was first formulated in 1797 in the document "The Oldest Systematic Program of German Idealism."[4] Other notable literary critics, such as Octavio Paz, have also recognized that Latin American modernism was a romantic reaction to the dominance of positivism in the region, characterizing it as a "nostalgia for cosmic unity" ("El Caracol y la sirena" 103), which in Paz's opinion is explained by the special quality that positivism took on in its reception in Latin America. While in Europe, positivism was the ideology of a liberal bourgeoisie interested in industrial progress, in Latin America it became a tool used by the powerful land-owning oligarchy who sought to defend their privileges by systematically dismantling metaphysics and religion. The result was a crisis experienced by intellectuals at the end of the nineteenth century, which was similar to that which tormented the German Romantics a century before: nostalgia for the old religious beliefs and fear of the contingency of life, which in a certain sense demands always recovering the unity that was lost through poetry. Modernism was consequently the response to the spiritual void that positivism created in the traditional elite classes of Latin America. As Paz remarks, it was our true romanticism. Hence the modernists desire to seek reconciliation and harmony, just as the German Romantics had in their day (*Children of the Mire* 81–84).

It is worth investigating the line of thought Paz and Gutiérrez Girardot follow here in order to begin to elucidate what the *aesthetics of the beautiful* means in Latin American modernism, thus relating back to our discussion of Iris Zavala's assessment of modernism. The best way to do this is to briefly examine the contents of "The Oldest Systematic Program of German Idealism." This text, written in Tübingen in a libertarian spirit inspired by the French Revolution, makes a strong criticism of the "mechanical society" in which individualism and the competition for money reign. To this is opposed the "organic society," in which all members teleologically order themselves to serve the interests of the totality, that is to say, they do not interact as individual actors in the market but rather effectuate the idea of freedom in a communitarian way. In the "mechanical society," the state is a farce that is maintained solely by the power of its own *legality*, not by the free consent of the population. Indeed, the document affirms, "We must therefore go beyond the state!" (161).

What, then, is being proposed in "The Oldest Systematic Program of German Idealism?" If it is neither the state nor analytic reason, then what is the normative criterion that can legitimize an organic society? The young German Romantics' answer, like Schiller's during the same era, was an *aestheticization of society* where poetry will occupy a fundamental place: "Poetry thereby obtains a higher dignity; it becomes again in the end what it was in the beginning—*teacher of (history) the human race*" (162). Poetry will replace religion in its role as a social unifier and thus guarantee the formation of a general will. The utopia of the young German Romantics is a world where poetry can close the gap between positive law (of the state or the market) and community in such a way that the former will be the product of the sovereign will of the latter, a society in which people are governed by the autonomous dictates of their own will and not by the coercion of external imperatives. Aesthetic education seeks to make society rational, but by first transforming people's hearts before changing social and economic structures. It is in this sense that the author of "The Oldest Systematic Program of German Idealism" writes of a new "mythology of reason": an organic system of beliefs that are firmly based on the *ethos* of the community and capable of connecting individuals and giving meaning to collective action. The function of this new mythology is *to reconcile, harmonize, and unify* that which was violently separated by the Enlightenment: the objective world and the subjective world, the community and the individual, theory and praxis, morality and ethics, nature and humanity.

Schiller also advocates for this new mythology of reason in addressing the Kantian distinction between the beautiful and the sublime. As we know, Kant said that art allows us to find a balance between the different human faculties, since it is only in aesthetic enjoyment that we are totally disinterested. The beauty of the soul lies in the reconciliation (*Versöhnung*) of theoretical life with moral life through aesthetic experience. Following Kant on this point, Schiller becomes aware of the *fragmentation* of society in his time and turns to the aesthetic life as a form of therapy. In his concept, the modern world only valorizes our rational nature and forgets our sensible nature. The result is a society in which the logic of money and political power is predominant, and science is elevated as the only form of true knowledge.

In the sixth letter of *On the Aesthetic Education of Man*, Schiller compares the moderns and the ancients in order to highlight the pathologies of contemporary society. The Greeks were an organic people who enjoyed a perfect unity between all the components of their social life. The true, the good, and the beautiful existed simultaneously, in a single practical and cognitive act. There was no separation between theory and praxis, between reason and sensibility, or between nature and morality. "Poetry had not yet courted wit, and speculation had not yet prostituted itself by sophistry" (38). Modern man, in contrast, has tragically become fragmented, separated by virtue of the three faculties of the human spirit (understanding, reason, and sensibility), each one of which tends to delimit its own territory to the exclusion of the other two. This makes it so that man cannot develop all his potentialities, but only part of them.[5] That divorce between faculties corresponds to an increasingly greater specialization in the arts and sciences, which leads to the formation of a culture of experts who are increasingly alienated from everyday concerns. In the political sphere, this division (*Entzweiung*) manifests in the formation of nation-states, with some of them usually becoming enemies; on the social level, it is seen in the increasingly rigorous separation between social strata and professions (39). If we look to the legal field, this fragmentation is made clear in the distance between laws and the people and between legality and ethics.

In short, Schiller's diagnosis consists of the following: modern man is a broken man, tragically divided in diverse and conflict-ridden fields of activity. In modern society it is not freedom but political anarchy and moral barbarism that prevail. That is to say, modern society is not an *organism*, as in ancient Greece, but rather a *mechanism* in which man is not seen as an end unto itself but as a means, as the gear in a great clockwork machinery that functions on the basis of externally imposed, intellectualized rules.[6] The German Romantics' program for an aesthetic education of humanity was therefore not about shaping citizens' will but rather *their sensibility*. Aesthetic education is a therapy that a sick modern society needs to overcome its own spiritual fragmentation. In a word, it is the project of *unifying reason* and *reconciling* man with his own essence. The aesthetic culture Schiller would like to see established should take charge of reestablishing the fundamental unity of human nature that has been hidden by modernity: "we must be at liberty to restore by means of a higher Art this wholeness in our nature that Art has destroyed" (44).

We can see what makes up the aesthetic of the beautiful that characterized the Romantic program of the *new mythology of reason* and what, according to Octavio Paz and Rafael Gutiérrez Girardot also permeated the sensibility of Latin American modernism toward the end of the nineteenth century. Next, I would like to review the writings of a selection of modernist thinkers in order to identify the qualities of the aesthetic of the beautiful and to show what kind of images of Latin America it generates. I will focus on some emblematic texts by José Enrique Rodó, Alfonso Reyes, and José Vasconcelos in order to sketch out the emergence of what I would like to call a *mythology of Latin American reason*.

We will begin with José Enrique Rodó, one of the most important Latin American modernist thinkers. In the third part of his famous work *Ariel*, which Arturo Ardao considers one of the most crucial expressions of Latin Americanist militancy (111), Rodó praises what he calls the "Greek miracle." Recounting, point by point, the motifs suggested by the German Romantics,[7] he says that the Greeks' greatness is due to their ability to *unify* all human faculties:

> The incomparable beauty of Athens, the longevity of the model this goddess of a city bequeathed to us, were owing to a concept of life based on the total harmony of all human faculties and the mutual agreement that all energies should be directed toward the glory and power of mankind. Athens knew how to exalt both the ideal and the real, reason and instinct, the forces of the spirit and those of the body. It sculpted all four faculties of the soul.
>
> (*ARIEL* 43 [TRANSLATION MODIFIED])

Greece is presented here as the pinnacle of *humanity* throughout all known history up to the present. It functions as a model in relation to which modernity appears as a necessary decadence, as what predominates in modern civilization is the progressive differentiation of these faculties of the soul. With the dominance of positivism and commercialism, the ancient Greek ideal of *disinterested contemplation* has been lost, only to be replaced by material utility and pragmatism (44). Therefore, Rodó exhorts the youth of Latin America to take care in following the pragmatic ideals of U.S. society and culture, with its legacy of Protestant Puritanism that divorced life from the sense of the beautiful (52). The result was the appearance of an essentially voluntarist culture, which devalued any action that was without immediate utility. In a similar way, the institution of *democracy* is monstrously deformed in comparison to what it once was for the ancient Athenians. In the United States, democracy has been used only as a tool for leveling society, that is to say, for the dominance of vulgarity and mediocrity. It is the hegemony of a wealthy industrial bourgeoisie that now believes itself to be authorized to impose its tasteless vision of the world as the only one valid for the entire planet. Hence life in that country is dominated entirely by the idea of the "self-made man" who is capable of becoming rich through his own effort and will. Nothing like this is visible in the world of ancient Athens, where democracy guaranteed the superiority of those who improved themselves, those who knew how to cultivate the sense of the beautiful (87).[8] Therefore, Rodó believes that, properly understood, democracy should favor a government of the most cultured, instead of privileging the tastes of mediocre men, as happened in the United States.

However, against the utilitarianism that prevailed in the United States, Rodó sees hope for the future of the Latin American continent.

While North America has enriched the world in terms of science and technology (albeit at the cost of an aesthetic and moral impoverishment), Latin America can represent the balance the planet needs. Rodó traces a curious genealogy that connects Latin American nations to the cultural legacy of the Greeks, with all the ideal elements that would entail:

> We Latin Americans have a heritage of race, a great ethnic tradition, to maintain, a sacred place in the pages of history that depends upon us for its continuation. . . . So it was that the most genial and civilizing of cultures turned upon an axis supported by the poles of Athens and Sparta. America must continue to maintain the dualism of its original composition, which re-creates in history the classic myth of the two eagles released simultaneously from the two poles in order that each should reach the limits of its domain at the same moment.
>
> (*ARIEL* 73)

In this disconcerting passage, Rodó sees the American continent as the result of two different Greek legacies: while North America is the cultural heir of Sparta, Latin America is the heir of Athens. The Latinity of the Americas is the rich inheritance that comes from Athens through Imperial Rome, passing later through European Christianity, and hence through Spain's civilizing mission, arriving at our shores and producing the independence movement. The religion, language, and spiritual disposition of these peoples is the patrimony of Roman Catholic humanism, which, in contrast to Nordic-Protestant humanism, consists of the Mediterranean region of Europe (Italy, Spain, and France). Rodó has a deep love for Spain as the foremother of these nations because of that nation's contributions to the humanization of men and its participation in the universalist orientation of humanity. Additionally, France represents for him a constant tendency toward the universal, the beautiful, and the cosmopolitan. However, Rodó dedicates not a single word to the place of Indigenous and Afro-descendant peoples in this "Latin American identity." For him, all that matters is the Greco-Roman legacy, the genius of the Spanish and French, with their inclination toward aesthetic, disinterested ideals. Thus what positivism saw as a defect turns into a virtue: disinterest in technical and economic rationality and the redemptive promises of industrialism. In this view, the identifying traits of Latin America are generosity of sacrifice, a sense of the beautiful, and prioritizing the community over the individual.

As we can see, Rodó's strategy is to create a "we" by comparing two homogeneous identities: Latin Americans and North Americans: two forms of life, two different spirits that generate mutually exclusive values and forms of experience. The North American spirit (symbolized by Caliban) is characterized by the dominance of *technology*—what the "Oldest Systematic Program of German Idealism" calls "mechanical society"—while the Latin American spirit (symbolized by Ariel) is distinguished by the prevalence of *beauty*. Technology predominates in the North; beauty predominates in the South. Rodó believed that, counter to the gloomy diagnoses of Gustave Le Bon and other positivists, Latin America is still young and has something to contribute to the humanization of the world. What he wanted was for Latin America to become conscious of itself, of its own cultural inheritance and historical destiny, in order to thereby ward off the danger of U.S. cultural imperialism:

> And this is why the vision of an America de-Latinized of its own will, without threat of conquest, and reconstituted in the image and likeness of the North, now looms in the nightmares of many who are genuinely concerned about our future. . . . I do not, however, see what is to be gained from denaturalizing the character—the *personality*—of a nation, from imposing an identification with a foreign model, while sacrificing irreplaceable uniqueness. Nor do I see anything to be gained from the ingenuous belief that identity can somehow be achieved through artificial and improvised imitation. Michelet believed that the mindless transferal of what is natural and spontaneous in one society to another where it has neither natural nor historical roots was like attempting to introduce a *dead thing* into a *living organism* by simple implantation.
>
> (RODÓ, *ARIEL* 71–72 [TRANSLATION MODIFIED; MY EMPHASIS])

The Arielist ideals proclaimed by Rodó had a particular effect on the core members of the Ateneo de la Juventud, a Mexico City–based cultural institution that was active between 1906 and 1914 and existed during the fall of Porfirio Díaz and the outbreak of the Mexican Revolution. Among its members were the philosophers Antonio Caso and José Vasconcelos, the literary critic Pedro Henríquez Ureña, and the writer Alfonso Reyes.

The Ateneo was one of the intellectual milieus in which Rodó's Latin Americanist ideas had the strongest repercussions, as its history runs parallel to the history of Arielism (García Morales, *El Ateneo de México* 119–31). Like Rodó, the members of the Ateneo believed that it was necessary to offer a civilizing alternative to the materialist ideals of positivism in Latin America and to recover the aesthetic values of the ancient Greek world. The name they chose for their cultural institution was no coincidence. Faced with the United States' "Carthaginian" commercialism, which threatened the entire continent, it became necessary to take up the humanist values that emerged from ancient Athens as a form of resistance. Therefore, the figure of Rodó functioned for them as a grand beacon that could light the way for this return to the Greeks. So great was their admiration for the Uruguayan critic that the young Alfonso Reyes managed to get his father, General Bernardo Reyes, to fund an edition of *Ariel* that could freely circulate among the youth of Mexico. The prologue to this edition (which saw a print run of five hundred copies) was written by Pedro Henríquez Ureña,[9] who, at one of the conferences hosted by the Ateneo in 1910 to commemorate the independence centennial, referred to Rodó not only as one of the "greatest Latin American teachers," on the same level as figures like Andrés Bello and Faustino Domingo Sarmiento, but also a "classicist," a promoter of classical studies (335).

Greek humanism and philosophical antipositivism were the frameworks that inspired the cultural activities of the Ateneo de la Juventud.[10] They attacked the very heart of the positivist politics imposed in Mexico during Díaz's dictatorship and, in addition, they offered a different interpretation of Latin American history. We will recall that, for positivists like Gabino Barreda and Justo Sierra, the Spanish-Catholic inheritance was one of the causes of Latin American countries' cultural and spiritual backwardness. According to them, through the inspiration of the theological spirit (Barreda) and by being foreign to the virtues of *homo economicus* (Sierra), the culture inherited from Spain should be replaced by the positivist spirit, as was undeniably happening in Mexico. The members of the Ateneo, in contrast, had a very different assessment of the Spanish legacy, especially of its literature. Spain no longer appears as a sign of barbarism that must be buried, but rather as an instrument of civilization, as it is through Spain that we received the influence of the

Mediterranean Latin quality that characterizes our continent. When Spain closes itself off from the influences of the Anglo-Saxon world, it is not turning its back on the future in the name of theology, as positivism attempted to show, but rather it is preserving the best of the values inherited from the Greco-Roman world, values that will form the basis of a civilized future.

Alfonso Reyes takes up all of Rodó's themes and, also like Rodó, progresses further in the construction of a *mythology of Latin American reason*. In the latter's perspective, one of the essential elements for the elaboration of this mythology was the establishment of a direct link between the aesthetics of the beautiful and Latin American cultural identity. Therefore, Reyes particularly values the introduction of classical Greek humanism to Mexican culture and thinks it should serve as the antidote to the predominance of positivism during the regime of Porfirio Díaz. Reyes's Hellenism was actually an educational program (*paideia*) that was meant to run parallel to the political renewal proclaimed by the Mexican Revolution.[11] We will soon see what the characteristics of this humanist project were and how, through this project, Reyes worked to create a Latin American mythology.

We begin by examining a 1941 article by Reyes, "Ciencia social y deber social" ("Social science and social duty"), to identify the form taken by his critique of positivism. In this article, Reyes responds to two complementary questions: How is it possible that Western civilization has come to its current state (just after the outbreak of World War II)? And what is the role of Latin American countries in this situation? In his response to the first question, Reyes holds positivism responsible for the crisis that Western culture was undergoing at the time. Positivism favored separating politics and morality, causing knowledge to remain dissociated from the spiritual needs of man.[12] Reyes is referring in particular to "social science," which Barreda and Sierra had identified as the sole basis for society to achieve knowledge of itself. In Reyes's opinion, positivism reduced the social sciences to pure empirical knowledge and forgot that the human being also possesses an aesthetic and moral dimension ("Ciencia social y deber social" 106).

Note that Reyes's critique is not far from the vision outlined in "The Oldest Systematic Program of German Idealism." Modern European culture fostered a splitting within humanity and generated a violent separation of its cognitive faculties. If we compare modernity with the culture of the Middle Ages, Reyes tells us, "each piece appears to us as crafted much better in itself than the somewhat rough bricks of the previous era. But the pieces no longer easily fit in the puzzle for lack of an overall plan" (107). We live in a culture of experts in which diverse human abilities are separated and lose their *unity*. Positivism destroys the organicity that medieval European society still had and advocates for what the Romantics called a "mechanical society" with neither life nor unity, where it is no longer possible to achieve the Greek ideal of paideia. The tragedy of the Second World War and the advance of fascism are palpable proof that in Europe the humanist ideals of the ancient Greek world have been lost and that it is necessary to look for these ideals elsewhere.

In light of this, and in response to the second question, Reyes argues that, while "Europe vacillated and was the losing party," "our America is the last redoubt of the human" (109–11). This means that in Latin America positivism did not achieve a complete mechanization of society, as it had in Europe, but rather that the organicity of society is still alive. Therefore, Reyes sees Latin America as the place where it will be possible to achieve the humanist ideal of the ancient Greek world that was never realized in Europe: Latin America as the place where true humanization will become reality.[13]

To justify this claim, Reyes presents two arguments, both developed in his 1936 article "Notas sobre la inteligencia americana" ("Notes on the Latin American intellect"). The first refers to the "natural internationalism" of Latin American culture. By this, he means that, unlike what happened in Europe, the "Latin American intellect" (i.e., the intelligentsia, the letrados) possesses a decidedly *cosmopolitan* orientation that gives it a staunch inclination toward peace (87). While European intellectuals have believed in a self-sufficient culture and have therefore not needed to look to other cultures to take the best from them, Latin American intellectuals have always had to pay attention to Europe, starting in primary school. This, Reyes states, is the great advantage of having arrived late to the banquet of modernity. Since Spain did not allow the creation of a vernacular culture, but rather vertically imposed its own, this made it so that Latin American countries had to look toward Europe, even once they had gained their political independence. Accustomed to dealing with foreign ideas as if they were their own, Latin

American intellectuals, like the ancient Greeks, possess a universalist vocation to which mestizaje has undoubtedly contributed. The populations of Latin America have brought together Indigenous elements, the masses of Iberian conquistadors, European immigrants, and African slaves who have learned to live together. In his 1942 talk "Posición de América" ("The position of Latin America"), Reyes says that

> the peoples of Latin America, driven by their similar historical formation, are less foreign to each other than the nations of the old world. There is a community of cultural goods, religion, and language. And due to their ethnic understanding, they are singularly prepared to refrain from exaggerating the exceedingly small value of racial differences. . . . The result of this great homogeneity in the national majorities of Latin America has been that our peoples have, according to Bolívar's dream, been able to develop a certain continuous and harmonious labor of international conversation for more than half a century, much earlier than the European League, and much more effective in the long run.
>
> (265–66)

The formation of Latin American populations themselves has contributed in this region to the elimination of the prejudices of ancestry and race to the point that there the only meaningful category is that of the human—just as the ancient Greeks saw it. For Reyes, Latin America is a group of organic societies that are for that very reason in a position to complete the universal process of synthesis.[14] Reyes compares Latin American cultural synthesis to the organic processes that form water: the formula H_2O is not simply the mechanical combining of dispersed elements but rather the formation of a new element that in itself contains both of the old ones ("Notas sobre la inteligencia americana" 88). However, even though Latin America is *culturally* prepared to undertake on its own soil the great synthesis of humanity as a whole and once again take up the humanist legacy of the Greeks, the question is whether Latin America is *politically* prepared for it. According to Reyes, in difficult moments, Latin America has been called to carry out its mission, and it must do so even though it has not yet been able to configure a *political language* that would allow it to wield its privileged cultural position in the community of nations ("Ciencia social y deber social" 118).

What must be done so that Latin America may find that political language required by the West for surviving barbarism? Like Rodó, Reyes believes it is essential to develop a large-scale educational project (paideia) controlled by a minority of intellectuals and whose philosophical reason is outlined in the "Oldest Systematic Program of German Idealism": priority is given to beauty over science. In Reyes's opinion, Latin American intellectuals have never had a scientific vocation but rather a literary one, a direct inheritance from Spain. The proof is that it was always writers and poets who disseminated knowledge about Latin American reality. Therefore, in Latin America there has never been any disconnect between knowledge and morality or between theory and practice as occurred in Europe. So that Latin America can find its true political language, it should not be the scientists (as positivism declared) but the poets and writers who take on the spiritual leadership of nations.

> It is up to the guiding minorities, the prophets, the teachers, and the writers to direct Latin American will toward taking a position in culture, since they gave birth to the cultural movements. . . . Their action should be practiced on the youth, for whom everything is new, the new and the old, and who with the same proud facility see similarities in one another when it leads to life. Let us dedicate all our effort to the Latin American youth of that near and heroic future. One day, the world will thank them.
>
> (REYES, "POSICIÓN DE AMÉRICA" 269–70)

However, the question remains: What is the proper political language for Latin America? Reyes seems to have no doubt that this language is nothing other than *utopia*. If Latin America wants to fulfill its historical mission, then it should develop a politics that keeps in mind what the continent always was: the place of utopias. This is precisely the source of the fallacy of positivism: the failure to understand that, due to their cultural formation, Latin American societies had difficulties with educational programs based on science rather than paideia. Latin America does not owe its historical vocation to science but to the imagination and to poetry. Before the conquest, the Americas were invented by poets. This is the thesis Reyes develops in his famous essay "Última Tule" ("Ultima Thule").

This thesis is that the ancient Greeks, to whom Schiller attributed the ability to simultaneously experience beauty and truth, were the first to invent the Americas. In his dialogues *Critias* and *Timaeus*, Plato mentions Atlantis, an island society that was culturally superior to even the Athenian polis, favored for its climate and vegetation, where people lived in peace and wisdom. Although Reyes mentions other predecessors of the invention of the Americas, the myth of Atlantis stands out in particular for its influence on Italian Renaissance humanism. The humanists who translated Plato in Italy at that time also began to dream of Atlantis and set in motion the desire of European intellectuals to find this lost island. However, they also influenced the cartographers and sailors "who carried out what others wrote of and thus came to constitute a true, militant humanism" ("Última Tule" 28). Columbus's project was not, as is generally thought, the opening up of a new route to the Orient, but rather the search for the Atlantis imagined by the ancient Greeks:

> Christopher Columbus is not an isolated individual, who provincially fell from the sky with an undiscovered continent in his head. It is true that he spoke of unknown lands that were, in Martín Alonso's quaint phrase, "as if kept in a drawer." However, he was not the first to speak of them; on this and many other topics he did nothing more than pan for gold dust in the river of a secular tradition. Focusing on Columbus, we can contemplate an entire multitude of wise and practical men, some sane, some not, who prepare, assist, and follow him. . . . The dreams of Ophir and Cathay are not foreign to the Discovery. Atlantis, resuscitated by the humanists, stands in for the Americas. Cipango and the Antilles represent here the movement from chimera to reality, from the portent to the fact.
>
> (REYES, "ÚLTIMA TULE" 16–17)

The dream of the ancient poets, now recovered by humanists, became a *vox populi* in the dreams of adventurers. Before becoming a reality, the Americas were already in men's hearts. Therefore, once they were discovered, they were defined to the world as the place where it will be possible to build an egalitarian society, where humanity can be completely free, and where happiness will be fairly distributed (58). None of the great minds of the Renaissance could escape this dream: Desiderius Erasmus,

Sir Thomas More, François Rabelais, Michel de Montaigne, Francis Bacon, Torquato Tasso, Tomasso Campanella. All European reformers tried to manifest the utopia of freedom in the Americas. Not even the violence of Spanish conquest and colonization could snuff the poets' ideal. Socialists, communists, anarchists, and spiritualists all looked toward the Americas as if it were a promised land, a refuge for humanity, a space where political and religious enterprises that no longer fit within the limits of old Europe could be possible (60). Thus Reyes ends his essay with the following words: "The Americas are like the theater for all attempts at human happiness, for all efforts to achieve the good. And today, compared to the disasters of the Old World, the Americas have the value of hope" (61).

This was how the myth of Latin American reason was developed. If history has a meaning, it cannot be anything other than the complete unification and emancipation of the human race. In contrast to Hegel's famous verdict, Reyes argues that Latin America is destined from its very *origins* to be the stage for universal resolution. Latin America was and must continue being a *regulative idea* for politics around the world, like *Ur-Pflanze* discussed by Johann Wolfgang von Goethe, Schiller, and the German Romantics: the place where all opposites are reconciled ("Capricho de América" 78).

However, this Latin Americanist mythology, sketched out by Rodó and Reyes, came to its paroxysmal conclusion with the work of José Vasconcelos, who, like them, also greatly admired the Greeks. He was president of the Ateneo de la Juventud, and as the Mexican secretary of education he promoted the construction of fine arts academies throughout the country as well as the publication of popular editions of books by Homer, Plato, and Plotinus, which were to be distributed for free in all of Mexico's schools. Vasconcelos once famously said to Obregón, "What this country needs is to read the *Iliad*. I'm going to distribute one hundred thousand books by Homer in schools throughout the nation and in the libraries we are going to set up." As we also know, the title of Vasconcelos's only autobiographical book is *El Ulises criollo* (The criollo Ulysses).

However, his ideal was not simply to promote a return to the ancient Greeks and to make paideia into an adequate method for generating national unity, but rather to show that the Greeks' ideals would be carried out by a fifth race that would synthesize the highest achievements of Eastern and Western cultures. This fifth race, according to Vasconcelos's prophecy, is taking shape in Latin America:

> Its predestination obeys the design of constituting the cradle of a fifth race into which all nations will fuse with each other to replace the four races that have been forging History apart from each other. The dispersion will come to an end on American soil; unity will be consummated there by the triumph of fecund love and the improvement of all the human races. . . . The so-called Latin peoples, because they have been more faithful to their divine mission in America, are the ones called upon to consummate this mission. Such fidelity to the occult design is the guarantee of our triumph.
>
> (*THE COSMIC RACE* 18)

Unity is the key word here. Vasconcelos portrays Latin America as the continent where the unity of the entire human race will be consummated and where the aesthetic ideal of the ancient Greeks will finally be realized. Note that in the creation of this mythology Vasconcelos takes elements from both Reyes and Rodó. Reyes's idea of cultural synthesis adds to the conflict Rodó posits between the Latins and the Anglo-Saxons, which for Vasconcelos embodies two forms of completely different knowledge. The Anglo-Saxons, in whom reason predominates over aesthetics, have fulfilled their historical mission and should open the way for the Latin peoples, who embody that mode of aesthetic knowledge announced by the Greeks and who represent the future of humanity.[15] The mission of the Anglo-Saxon race, to demonstrate the importance of scientific-technological rationalism, was fully achieved during the modern era, but the price humanity had to pay for this achievement was high: the *disassociation* of all cognitive faculties. The sacred mission of the fifth, mestizo race, the *cosmic race* that is currently being formed in Latin America, is to recover once again the unity of human faculties. This destiny of the cosmic race is inevitable, as it is already given by the laws of history. Vasconcelos argues that the history of humanity must necessarily go through three phases that, nevertheless, do not correspond to the three stages proposed by Auguste Comte: "The three stages indicated by this law are: The material or warlike, the intellectual or political, and the spiritual or aesthetic. They represent a process that is gradually liberating us from the domination of necessity and, step by step, is submitting all life to the superior norms of feeling and fantasy" (*The Cosmic Race* 28).

Note that the history of humanity oscillates between absolute submission of life to the empire of necessity and the complete liberation from this necessity through aesthetic contemplation. For Vasconcelos, the telos of history is nothing other than the cultural dominance of the Kantian *aesthetic of the beautiful*, which could not be accomplished by the peoples of antiquity, who were still involved in resolving the problems of scarcity and war (the material or warlike stage). However, modern peoples were also unable to accomplish it as they in large part addressed this old problem through the rationalized development of science and technology (the intellectual or political stage). It will be only in a third, future stage, "whose approach is already being announced in a thousand ways," when the aesthetic of the beautiful will finally encounter its moment of glory (Vasconcelos, *The Cosmic Race* 29). This will also be the moment of global hegemony for *the Latins*, whom Rodó already had already characterized as a people for whom an *aesthetic* form of knowledge predominates.[16]

For the moment, I am interested in examining how Vasconcelos visualized this aesthetic future of humanity. First is his reflection on the moment in which Latins will conquer the tropics, which Vasconcelos presents in the second part of *The Cosmic Race*. There he writes that Latin American peoples will attain global political and aesthetic hegemony when they colonize the Amazon region, the most lush and fertile area on the planet. All great civilizations were born in the tropics, thus they also will be in the future, when the moment of Latin hegemony arrives. Instead of trying to use the architectonic models of reason developed in modernity by the Anglo-Saxons and imposing them on tropical nature, Latins will construct fabulous baroque cities in which the proliferation of nature will predominate:

> The conquest of the Tropics will transform all aspects of life. Architecture will abandon the Gothic arch, the vault, and, in general, the roof, which answers to the need for shelter. The pyramid will again develop. Colonnades and perhaps spiral constructions will be raised in useless

> ostentation of beauty, because the new aesthetics will try to adapt itself to the endless curve of the spiral, which represents the freedom of desire and the triumph of Being in the conquest of infinity. The landscape, brimming with colors and rhythms, will communicate its wealth to the emotions. Reality will be like fantasy.
>
> (VASCONCELOS, *THE COSMIC RACE* 24)

The aesthetic of the future Latin American race will not be utilitarian, it will not seek the functionality of spaces; instead it will break entirely with the rationality of forms. It will not promote intervening in nature but rather contemplating it, that is to say, it will favor the integration of human life in a world where fantasy reigns rather than the narrow reality of reason. A world whose capital, "Universopolis," will be constructed in the very heart of the Amazon jungle, from which "the preaching, the squadrons, and the airplanes propagandizing the good news will set forth" (25). As if that were not enough, Vasconcelos affirms without hesitation that during the third stage of human evolution, whose epicenter will be Latin America, the "law of personal taste" will entirely dominate the choice of sexual partners. This means that pure *aesthetic enjoyment* will determine marriages, gradually refining the race, which becomes more beautiful from a physical and moral point of view. In the future world dominated by the mestizo Latin race, *there will be no place for ugly people.*[17] What Vasconcelos says is that the predominance of the "law of the personal taste" will engender a *population-based selection* (no longer natural but aesthetic) in which the ugliest and least talented people would tend to disappear, while the more beautiful would prevail. It is a kind of aesthetic social Darwinism that inexorably condemns "anti-aesthetic" races like Blacks to extinction:

> The awareness of the species itself would gradually develop an astute Mendelianism, as soon as it sees itself free from physical pressure, ignorance and misery. In this way, in a very few generations, monstrosities will disappear. . . . The lower types of the species will be absorbed by the superior type. In this manner, for example, the Black could be redeemed, and step by step, by voluntary extinction, the uglier stocks will give way to the more handsome. . . . In a few decades of *aesthetic eugenics*, the Black may disappear, together with the types that a free instinct of

> beauty may go on signaling as fundamentally recessive and undeserving, for that reason, of perpetuation.
>
> (VASCONCELOS, *THE COSMIC RACE* 32 [EMPHASIS ADDED])

Vasconcelos takes all the consequences of that which in Rodó seems to be merely a call for Latin American dignity against the imperialist pretensions of the United States, and which in Reyes is a cry of hope in response to the catastrophe of the Second World War. The modernists' *Latin Americanism* is an exoticization of Latin America, which functions similarly to Edward Said's notion of Orientalism. Except in the former case it is a matter of the colonialism not of colonizers but of Latin American intellectuals themselves, who see their role as that of announcing to the world Vasconcelos's famous motto: "Through my race the spirit will speak."[18] Many modernists thought that the only way to stop the voracious advance of positivism and U.S. imperialism was to promote Latin American unity as a single cultural or political block that could respond to external forces. The recognition of *Latin American identity* was seen as the only way to overcome the economic and political colonialism of the United states. However, paradoxically, the aestheticist declaration of this cultural identity presupposed the reactivation of old colonial figures. The mythology of Latin American reason and the idea of a mestizo continent where opposites are reconciled continued to function as a *colonial discourse* in which groups of people such as Blacks or Indigenous populations appear as *dysfunctional* in the process of the humanization of humanity.[19]

3. FINAL REFLECTION: LATIN AMERICA AS A METANARRATIVE

It seems clear that, according to the argument presented up to this point, the aesthetics of the beautiful, proclaimed by Latin American modernist intellectuals in the late nineteenth century, is not associated with a program of *cultural decolonization*, as Iris Zavala suggests, but rather assumes the creation of a colonial discourse focused on a specific mythology: *Latin Americanism*. I would like to close with a brief analysis that shows why the aesthetic of the beautiful is so easily connected with totalizing discursive formations like Latin Americanism. For this purpose, I will make use of Jean-François Lyotard's reflections and commentaries on Kant's *Critique of Judgment* in his book *Enthusiasm*.

Like Kant, Lyotard addresses a conflict between the feeling of the beautiful and the sublime, emphasizing the negative quality of the latter. While the beautiful maintains a relationship with understanding, the sublime is connected with reason and therefore does not make use of either forms or imagination. Hence the pleasure generated by the sublime has nothing to do with the future, reconciliation, or harmony, nor with the pleasure of proportion and unity, but rather with the *feeling of ambivalence* (Kant's example is the raging sea), with the pleasure of disassociation and finitude. However, while the Romantics kept to the feeling of beauty in order to find a *bridge* that would help reconcile the faculties of desiring and thinking, Lyotard says that these faculties are radically *heterogeneous*. It is not possible to resolve the differend between the true and the good through the beautiful. To the contrary, the feeling of the sublime helps us recognize that there are no preestablished continuities between truth and morality. They are two completely distinct language games that operate under entirely different rules.

For Lyotard, the idea that beauty serves to reconcile the human being with himself is nothing other than a *metanarrative*, now that we know there is no such thing as a unitary subject that has fundamentally "disassociated" from the processes of modernization, as the Romantics wanted and as Latin Americanist mythology also pretends. Therefore, the aesthetics of the sublime breaks with the ideal of a preestablished harmony that was established by a series of *continuities* between the true, the good, and the beautiful. It is no longer a matter of recuperating the unity of human faculties that have been split apart by modernity, as Schiller and the young Germans of "The Oldest Systematic Program of German Idealism" held. Rather, what is necessary to understand is that each of these faculties carries out functions that are irreducible to the others. This does not mean postulating an incommunicability between different faculties but rather that the communication offered by the sublime is very different from that offered by the beautiful. If, in the aesthetics of the beautiful, social life is represented as a continent where all inhabitants walk on the same ground, the aesthetics of the sublime, in contrast, thinks of it as an *archipelago* where everyone walks on different ground, separate from each other:

> If in turn an object must be presented for the Idea of the faculties' shifting gears if we understand them as capacities for knowledge in the large sense . . . I would propose an archipelago. Each phrase family would be like an island; the faculty of judgment would be, at least in part, like an outfitter or an admiral who launches expeditions from one island to another sent out to present to the one what they have found (invented, in the old sense of the word) in the other, and which might serve to the first one as an "as-if" intuition to validate it.
>
> (LYOTARD, *ENTHUSIASM* 12).

The aesthetic in this case does not lie in eliminating the water that separates the different islands in order to construct highways, but rather in learning to navigate among them. If we follow the matrix of the beautiful, society would have to be thought as an organism whose parts should be coordinated by a central effort charged with the moral education of citizens. However, if we follow the matrix of the sublime, citizens elaborate their own strategies, which allow them to transversally maneuver the sea of heterogeneities. In the latter case, there is absolutely nothing that exists that guarantees an aesthetic judgment can also simultaneously be a moral judgment, much less a political judgment, as Iris Zavala has proposed. There is no transcendental subject (man, culture, identity) that can a priori salvage the division between the aesthetic and the political. The connections between these two spheres should be constructed a posteriori and *immanently*, instead of searching for a Latin Americanist mythology like that imagined by modernist intellectuals.

Our discomfort with *Latin Americanism* is due to the fact that all its motifs (harmony, unity, reconciliation, and consensus) refer to an episteme that postulates the subject as a transcendental unity that helps to invisibilize *differends*. Such narratives opt out of the game of heterogeneities and project an imaginary that largely ends up legitimizing a political praxis that seeks homogenization. Therefore, we think that the modernist sensibility prepared the road for the nationalist and populist regimes that arose in Latin America in the 1930s. It is not difficult to see the relationship of the aesthetics of the beautiful with APRA's attempts to discursively legitimize a continental identity found on an ontology of the telluric (Orrego, Haya de la Torre), or even with the humanist mass education projects of the Mexican state (Vasconcelos). The reduction of all cultural differences to a single principle—a romanticized mestizoism or indigenism—was the way to ensure the emergence of a popular state that would at the same time guarantee national unity.

From this point of view, it is not difficult to understand that the aesthetics of the beautiful, with its tendency to resolve differends in a transcendental positivism, ultimately imposed its law on the social imaginaries of modernists who were born in the home of the modernized city and raised on the homogenizing logic that inspired the emergence of populism as an alternative to the development of economic and political liberalism in the first phase of industrialization in Latin America. Modernist narratives about Latin America, as Ángel Rama has clearly shown, were metanarratives derived from the use of literature.

6

POSTCOLONIAL REASON AND LATIN AMERICAN PHILOSOPHY

1. COLONIAL INHERITANCES AND POSTCOLONIAL THEORIES

When Edward Said published *Orientalism* at the end of the 1970s, few could have imagined that this book would inaugurate a new field of academic research. By taking as his object of study the different discursive forms through which Europe produced and codified a knowledge of the Orient, Said highlights the connections between imperialism and the human sciences, thereby following a route taken some years earlier by Michel Foucault, who studied the rules that configure a discourse's truth, thereby revealing the places where that truth is constructed and how it circulates or is administered by determinate regimes of power. Said broadens this focus and explores how eighteenth- and nineteenth-century European states discursively constructed a truth about peripheral cultures, especially those that are under their control. The power exercised by imperial countries through freely entering other territories and *disposing* of their resources favors the production of a series of historical, archaeological, sociological, and ethnographic studies of the Orient.

The work begun by Said was later continued by Indian theorists like Homi Bhabha and Gayatri Chakravorty Spivak, who focused their attention on how colonial discourse turns the colonized into an object of study. Spivak argues that the history of modern imperialism is marked by an "epistemic violence" in which scientific and humanist discourses on the non-European world constitute a *metaphysics* that subsumes differences and heterogeneities in a homogeneous language. The "other" is represented as a unitary essence, as an entity that is at the disposal of experts and can thus be known, classified, and controlled. In this way, the subaltern is stripped of its place of enunciation and cannot speak. Indeed, the subaltern is "spoken" by European Enlightenment discourse, which, according to Spivak, represents the world through engaging in an act of violence on it. For Enlightenment rationality, knowing is equivalent to suppressing, grasping (*begreifen*), dominating, objectifying, and reducing a multiplicity to a unity. Hence Spivak's assertion that there is no representation of the other without *cathexis*, that is, without a self-projection of the subject who enunciates onto a subject who is spoken. Hence, as well, her thesis that there is no colonized subject who, breaking into imperial structures from outside, can articulate a voice for themselves through the discourses of European human sciences. Indeed, any attempt to represent the subaltern in a discourse articulated around the rules of modern Western knowledge (sociology, ethnography, history, etc.) is an epistemic reinforcement of the mechanisms of colonial domination (Spivak).

For his part, Homi Bhabha uses Freudian and Lacanian psychoanalysis to show that those European discourses in which the "other" appears as an external, unitary essence are actually imperial fantasies, oneiric images projected toward the outside in which Europe represents the object of desire. Both Renaissance utopias and discourses on the "noble savage" are fetishizations of an object that can only be controlled to the extent that it is reduced to a representable unity. Discourses of identity are not independent from a series of colonial institutions that narratively produce the "other" as a homogeneous whole. Therefore, combating colonial practices does not mean appealing to a supposed authenticity of the colonized subject, since this type of narrative suffers from the same logocentric substantialism it is meant to overcome. Bhabha opts instead for a *reconfiguration of the signs* used by colonial discourse (see *The Location of Culture*). This means adopting a discursive strategy that, through hybrid representations of the colonized ("white but not quite"), shows the decenterings, heterogeneities, and contingencies of what colonial discourse has portrayed as a substantial unity. This reevaluation of differences does away with the illusion of a form of control that is rationally programmed from the center.

This work by Said, Bhabha, and Spivak soon sparked a very widespread polemic about so-called postcolonial studies and their relationship to other discourses like cultural studies and gender studies.[1] I will not focus on the postcolonial theory developed by these three thinkers, as I am primarily interested in the reception and modification of the aforementioned debate in the field of Latin American cultural studies, particularly in the United States, and more specifically in how these efforts to advance toward a new understanding of Latin American intellectual traditions *originated in the United States*. In this context, we can say that the "postcolonial question" is connected to Latin American debates on postmodernity, which had already begun in the mid-1980s and whose resonance has not been at all negligible in Europe and the United States.[2] In my view, the reflections initiated by the Latin American Subaltern Studies Group, as it named itself in its "Founding Statement" (1995), can serve as a bridge between the two debates on postmodernity and on postcoloniality, as well as serve as a starting point for the thesis I will present shortly.[3]

This group of academics, the majority of whom are Latin American intellectuals living in the United States, who have learned how to live between both worlds, set out to account for the changes that occurred in Latin America in the last two decades of the twentieth century. The process of democratization in the Southern Cone, the failure of communism and the consequent dismantling of revolutionary projects, the new social dynamic created by the effect of the mass media and the transnational economy, the redefinition of the political and cultural spaces throughout almost the entire subcontinent, and the new leading role of the bourgeoning Hispanic community in the United States are all phenomena that demand a fundamental revision of the epistemologies on which Latin American social sciences operated until the 1970s (Latin American Subaltern Studies Group 135). Above all, and following in the footsteps of the Subaltern Studies Group in India led by Ranajit Guha, the Latin American group is interested in revising a certain type of historiography that primarily functions on binary paradigms of social analysis. Concretely, this refers to dependency theory, which in its radical opposition between the center and the periphery, high culture and popular culture, development and underdevelopment, First and Third Worlds, oppressors and oppressed, ignored the *hybrid and mutant* quality of Latin American subaltern groups. Problems related to sexual, racial, or language discrimination, as well as alternative models of sexuality and different forms of knowledge, were integrated into totalizing categories like "people," "class," and "nation," or synthesized into metanarratives that privileged Eurocentric and androcentric models of subjectivity (Latin American Subaltern Studies Group 143). These paradigms were incapable of comprehending the leading role that a series of social subjects that were unassimilable to the Enlightenment conception of politics began to have in the 1970s. The demands of women, as well as some artistic expressions, such as rock, reggae, and salsa music, constituted forms of *self-representation* that exceeded the hegemonic models of understanding political struggles. They expressed a rejection of the representative role that had been assumed by intellectual and artistic avant-gardes in previous years. Unlike the grand identitarian narratives created by magical realism and liberation theology, small histories began to gain visibility, those of women, homosexuals, political prisoners, people with AIDS, homeless children, prostitutes, street vendors, and the socially marginalized of all kinds, who *orally* constructed their own representations (Latin American Subaltern Studies Group 140).

The Latin American Subaltern Studies Group's "Founding Statement" brings together some of the topics discussed by cultural critics in the 1980s and points to the impossibility of continuing to write the history of our continent through an Enlightenment epistemology. I will not discuss these topics here, as I have already done so in the present book.[4] Instead, I would like to focus on the work of one member of the group, the Argentine sociologist Walter Mignolo, who establishes an important distinction between the place of enunciation of English-language postcolonial theories and those articulated from within Latin America. More precisely, I am interested this concept of *locus enuntiationis*, as it is what Mignolo proposes as a means to conduct a creative rereading of *Latin American philosophy*.

Indeed, in his work as a semiologist and scholar of several Andean texts, Mignolo realizes the need for establishing a difference between "modalities of saying articulated in Renaissance (or Enlightenment) philosophy of language, on the one hand, and modalities of saying articulated in communities outside of the regional history, writing, and thought of Europe" (Mignolo, "Decires fuera de lugar" 9). This is the case, for example, with the place of enunciation constructed by Indigenous chroniclers like Felipe Guamán Poma de Ayala and Santacruz Pachacuti Yamqui. Mignolo's thesis is that this place of enunciation cannot be understood through theories that presuppose a complicity between verbal acts and alphabetical writing,[5] because from the perspective of Western epistemology, knowledge is a subjective operation of abstraction (from myth to logos) that is materialized in *writing*. In particular, from the perspective of modern epistemology, which began to be consolidated precisely through the conquest of the Americas, the truth is not something that is in the cosmos, as Guamán Poma and Santacruz Pachacuti argue, but rather is in the subject's *internal* activity. Hence the history of modern knowledge coincides with the individual biography of the men that produce it. However, Mignolo writes, "in Andean and Mesoamerican cultures, autobiography as such is not conceivable since human life is a calculus that integrates existence into a cosmology, which is articulated in Mesoamerican calendars or in the Andean system of *ceques* [ritual pathways]" ("Decires fuera de lugar" 16).

Mignolo points to the existence of *telling subjects* in the sixteenth century, like Guamán Poma de Ayala and Santacruz Pachacuti, that make use of alphabetical writing in order to construct a place of enunciation that is very different from that which serves as the basis for Western knowledge and thus escapes the analysis of semiological theories of enunciation. Without a doubt, this is a place that adopts European elements into its own practices (alphabetical writing and drawing), but it integrates them into a symbolic order of Andean culture, as is the case with Guamán Poma's "Mapa Mundi del Reino de las Indias" and Santacruz Pachacuti's cosmological ideograms ("Decires fuera de lugar" 12–19). In the first case, even though the mappemonde is a European cartographic genre that was very common during the Renaissance, Guamán Poma "phagocytizes" it from traditional Incan cosmology based in the four *suyus* (regions), whose center is the sacred city of Cuzco.[6] The result, Mignolo writes, is the emergence of a *border epistemology* born from the intersection of the Andean and Spanish cultures, but one in which the latter is repositioned as internal to the former. In short, it is an indigenization of European culture.

Mignolo concludes from all this that the place of enunciation in the center of a colonial situation, like that of the Andean region in the sixteenth century, produces a series of *anticolonial narratives* that are, genealogically speaking, the starting point of postcolonial reason:

> My argument was meant to suggest that Pachacuti, Guamán Poma, Garcilaso, Ixtlilxochitl, Diego Muñoz Camargo, and so many others, now that they are not just names that must be restituted to the history of the Americas, but rather that, fundamentally, are forms of saying that have the same power for the practice of thought in the Americas as Descartes, Freud, Marx, or Nietzsche have had in the history of modern Europe. How can we propose a counterdiscourse to the hegemonic narrative constructed in colonizing languages (Spanish, Portuguese, Italian, French, English, German) that turned the ancient Greek and Roman ruins into legitimate forms of thought? Why should we only think starting from Greek and Roman ruins and not Andean and Mesoamerican ruins?
>
> ("DECIRES FUERA DE LUGAR" 28)

This intriguing passage shows us what the concept of *postcolonial reason* means for Mignolo: it is a form of thought that is articulated from out of the colonial legacy and, more concretely, from out of the *ruins* left by this legacy. It is not a critique of colonialism from the margins of European history, as with Bartolomé de las Casas, for example, but rather one that comes from the ruins left over from the collision of that same European history with those who have been subalternized by the processes of European colonization. Out of this interstice emerged the subjects mentioned above in the passage from Mignolo (Pachacuti, Guamán Poma, Inca Garcilaso de la Vega, Fernando de Alva Cortés Ixtlilxochitl), which, although they mean *nothing* for the history of modern critical thought (in contrast to figures like Freud, Nietzsche, or Marx), are for Mignolo examples of those *anticolonial narratives* that emerge when the subaltern themselves appropriate the language of the colonizer in order to articulate certain "sayings from outside."[7] Postcolonial reason is the kind of historical narrative that, instead of starting from the ruins of thought, seeks to rehabilitate knowledges that have been subjugated by the processes of literacy in Latin America during the sixteenth and seventeenth centuries and later by the modern philosophy and science of the eighteenth and nineteenth centuries.[8]

Now, Mignolo says that one of the stumbling blocks of his proposal is that *Anglophone* postcolonial theories—in particular, those of Said, Bhabha, and Spivak—do not recognize the colonial Iberian legacy. For these theorists, postcolonial critique emerges from the fissure that resulted from the collision between English and French imperialism in the eighteenth and nineteenth centuries and the local histories of the Middle East and India. This is why, according to Mignolo, these hypotheses connect more easily with postmodern reason than with postcolonial reason, and it is why they refer regularly to thinkers like Foucault, Lacan, and Derrida to construct their critical discourses. Actually, postmodern and postcolonial reason are "different sides of the same cube" ("Occidentalización" 29). While postmodernity is a countermodern discourse that was first articulated in settler colonies like the United States and Canada, postcolonialism is an anticolonial discourse that emerged in deep settler colonies, like those of the Spanish and Portuguese. Or, put differently, while the locus enunciationis of postmodern theories is in the colonies that abandoned their peripheral condition in order to become centers (e.g., the United States), that of postcolonial theories is located in colonies that never abandoned their marginal and peripheral condition. In both cases there is a critique of the colonial legacies of modernity, but they are articulated from different places of enunciation.

Thus, by locating itself at the place of enunciation of the British and French legacies, postcolonial studies loses sight of the countermodern narratives that have been produced in Mexico and Peru ever since European colonization began. Therefore, one of Mignolo's central arguments is the attempt to show the importance of the Iberian colonial legacies in order to articulate a postcolonial critique of modernity. This is precisely the purpose of his article "Occidentalización, imperialismo, globalización" ("Occidentalization, imperialism, globalization"), where he polemicizes against Jorge Klor de Alva's thesis that postcolonial theories have been more of a concern for the English and French colonial legacies than for those of the Spanish and Portuguese. Accepting the fact that the majority of anticolonial narratives emerged in regions that experienced the second stage of Westernization, developed fundamentally by English and French expansionism, Mignolo highlights the contributions of the Caribbean region, which experienced the influence of these legacies with more intensity. Writers who have lived with the legacies of European colonization, such as Frantz Fanon, Edouard Glissant, Aimé Césaire, Fernando Ortiz, and Roberto Fernández Retamar, generated a kind of thought that perfectly exemplifies what Mignolo calls *postcolonial reason.* By citing these names, Mignolo is attempting to show that the former Spanish and Portuguese colonies also articulated a counterdiscourse that contests the colonial legacies of modernity. Concepts like Fernando Ortiz's "transculturation" or figures like "Caliban" in Fernández Retamar are *geohistorical categories* that discursively construct a border place of enunciation ("Occidentalización" 27–35). In Mignolo's words:

> By insisting on the connection between the place of theorization (being of, coming from, and being in) and the *locus* of enunciation, I am emphasizing that these *loci* of enunciation are not given but rather are represented; and I am not assuming that only people who come from this or that place can theorize X. I want to insist on the fact that I am not presenting the argument in deterministic terms, but in the open field of logical possibilities, of *historical circumstances*, and of personal sensibility. In other words, I am suggesting that those for whom the colonial legacies are real (e.g., those who are harmed by them) are more (logically, historically, and emotionally) inclined than others to theorize the past in terms of colonial histories.
>
> ("OCCIDENTALIZACIÓN" 33 [EMPHASIS ADDED])

From what has been said up to this point, it is clear that the project of tracing a history of postcolonial reason that takes as its foundation the Iberian colonial legacies should not be conceived of as a simple *derivation* of the postcolonial theories of authors like Said, Bhabha, and Spivak. Nor is it a simplistic gesture that seeks to establish an equivalence between the geographical place where one lives and the kind of thought that is articulated from that place. It is a distinct project that makes use of the creation of a *border thinking* between modernity and coloniality that emerges from the Iberian colonial legacies. Thus there is no need to resort to the critical tradition of European thinkers like Marx, Nietzsche,

Foucault, and Derrida. In their place, Mignolo prefers to turn to a different critical tradition: *Latin American philosophy.* Why? Because it is an intellectual tradition that challenges the very idea that Latin America is not an appropriate place for philosophy but rather for lesser arts like literature and visual art. Latin American philosophy has proven that it is possible to think *from* Latin America, taking up its own cultural traditions and history as the place for philosophy. In this way, Mignolo believes he has found a kind of thought that, analogous to what occurred in the sixteenth century with Guamán Poma and Santacruz Pachacuti, is able to *cannibalize* a central institution of European culture—philosophy—in order to articulate an *anticolonial and antimodern* narrative that is much more radical than that of European philosophy: it is one thing to criticize modernity from the margins of Europe, as Marx, Nietzsche, and Foucault did, and quite another to criticize it from the interstice between modern European history and its colonial legacies in the Americas.

For Mignolo, Latin American philosophy functions as a kind of *postcolonial reason*, and he identifies three figures in this tradition of thought: Leopoldo Zea, Enrique Dussel, and Rodolfo Kusch, whose theoretical concerns are inscribed in a long tradition of seeking to define (or redefine) the place occupied by Latin America within universal history. In his 1958 book *América en la Historia* (The Americas in history), Leopoldo Zea initiates an effort to think critically about Occidentalism, but, in Mignolo's opinion, his adherence to Toynbee's historicism prevents Zea from separating himself from a markedly European place of enunciation, from where the discourse he is trying to surpass is itself articulated. This was only thirty years after the publication of Zea's *Discurso desde la marginación y la barbarie* (Discourse from marginalization and barbarism), in which he takes up the discourse of Prospero and Caliban in order to reinterpret Hegel's *Lectures on the Philosophy of History.* In this book, Zea traces a parallel between Latin America and Russia and describes them as marginal (subaltern) cultures of the West. This hybrid situation of knowing that one simultaneously belongs and does not belong to the West has provoked in these two cultural areas a *cannibalization* of the central European discourse of modernity. This discourse's Eurocentric pretensions are criticized *in a Western language* (philosophy) that profanes it in its originary purity and *relocates* it, that enunciates it from and on the basis of colonial legacies (Mignolo, "Occidentalización" 27–28).

Rodolfo Kusch's project is to recover a style of thinking rooted in the urban and Indigenous subcultures of the Andes, and, according to Mignolo, it aims to create a border place of enunciation. This would be an attempt to revitalize forms of thought traditionally considered to be ethnographic material, but not alternative knowledges to the Eurocentric discourses of modernity. However, what Mignolo emphasizes is that this project is not a search for an authentically Latin American thought, but rather a reflection on what it means to think *in* Latin America, that is to say, from a marginal zone of the West where modernity and coloniality independently intersect. In this sense, the term *phagocytization,* coined by Kusch, is equivalent to Fernando Ortiz's term *transculturation* (Mignolo, "Occidentalización" 32–33). It is an effort to theorize situations and practices characterized by their *simultaneous* belonging to different geocultural spaces. The "phagocytization" of whiteness by indigeneity, or as Kusch puts it, of *ser* by *estar,* acquires for Mignolo the same meaning as Zea's notion of "cannibalization." Neither is operating with binary categories that oppose the European to the non-European, the barbarous to the civilized, rather they construct an intermediary zone, a *third space* where dualisms between the self and the other are no longer possible (see Mignolo, *The Darker Side of the Renaissance* 1–25).

The third Latin American philosopher Mignolo mentions, Enrique Dussel, has a different yet complementary approach to those of Rodolfo Kusch and Leopoldo Zea, as it is a critique of Westernization from the peripheral experience of colonization. Although, at the beginning of the 1970s, Dussel saw the philosophy of liberation as a postmodern position, Mignolo argues that it is closer to the perspective of postcolonial reason. Indeed, Dussel's philosophy constitutes a *geocultural* outlook, as it is fully conscious that the activity of philosophy in New York or Paris is not the same thing as doing philosophy in Mexico City, Havana, or Bogotá. It is thus a valuable attempt to *localize philosophy,* to liberate it from the ontologism of modern thought, in order to construct a history of modernity that no longer begins in Europe but in the asymmetrical interaction between Europe and its colonies:

> Dussel exposes the myth of modernity in order to confront other alternative interpretations. While Horkheimer and Adorno, as well as other postmodernists like Lyotard, Rorty, or Vattimo, propose a critique of reason (a violent, coercive, and genocidal reason), Dussel himself offers a critique of the irrational moment of the Enlightenment as a sacrificial myth. His critique is not a negation of reason but an affirmation of the reason of the other. The intersection between the idea of an egocentric modernity based in its appropriation of the (classical) Greco-Roman legacy and the emergence of the idea of modernity from the margins (that is, a countermodernity), clarifies that history did not begin in Greece, and that the different historical beginnings are simultaneously subject to diverse *loci* of enunciation. I propose instead, that this simple axiom is fundamental for postcolonial reason.
>
> ("OCCIDENTALIZACIÓN" 35)

In this strategic gesture of appropriating such a Western and Eurocentric register as philosophy, Mignolo sees the political creation of a place of enunciation. The philosophy of liberation makes visible what Leopoldo Zea points out: the slave Caliban appropriates the language of his master Prospero and condemns him with it. Dussel says to Europeans in their own language (philosophy): "The ego cogito has totalized us and reduced us to the category of objects." However, in so doing, he breaks with the modern episteme that legitimizes domination and creates a border place where a project of liberation can be articulated.

In Zea, Kusch, and Dussel, Mignolo sees a kind of postcolonial reason to which he himself feels connected, and which is not articulated from within a modern European episteme, but rather a different epistemic place that emerges from the border between the legacies of modern central Europe and colonialist Iberia—a knowledge born in the interstice between two worlds, just like Mignolo himself. In the introduction to his book *The Darker Side of the Renaissance*, Mignolo writes of being the son of Italian immigrants who settled in the peripheral nation of Argentina and later of studying in Europe and finally emigrating to the United States, where he became a citizen and university professor (6). Undoubtedly, this situation of being *crossed* by different cultural traditions has made it possible to interpret the tradition of Latin American philosophy as a *pluritopic hermeneutics*.

2. FROM THE GEOCULTURE OF REASON TO THE ARCHAEOLOGY OF DISCOURSES

I would now like to discuss Mignolo's argument, beginning with what seems to me to be its most problematic element: the relation it establishes between geoculture and the place of enunciation. In his article "Decires fuera de lugar," Mignolo recognizes that Rodolfo Kusch's reading led him to contemplate "the soil where not just saying but also thinking is rooted" (19).[9] In fact, one of Kusch's central theses is that all thought is linked to a habitat, to a specific form of being-in-the-world that maintains a close relationship with the geographical landscape. This is what led to his development of the category of "the geoculture of thought." Let us consider, for example, the following passage:

> The ecology of a place, a habitat, is always covered over by group thought, and the latter is responsible for dressing up the habitat in question in the clothing of a cultural landscape. . . . It is a thought conditioned by place, that is, a thought that refers to a context that is firmly constructed through the intersection of geography and culture. . . . The idea of a thought that results from an intersection between the geographical and the cultural leads to the philosophical problem of the presence of ground in thought and consequently opens up to the question: Does all thought suffer the gravity of the ground, or is it possible to achieve a thought that escapes all gravity?
>
> (KUSCH, *ESBOZO DE UNA ANTROPOLOGÍA FILOSÓFICA AMERICANA* 14–15)

What does Kusch mean by the expression "ground in thought?" We might say before all else that it is not a simplistic (and colonial) thesis according to which geography *determines* thought.[10] What Kusch is trying to say is that the life of any human group is necessarily *established* in a symbolic mold, a kind of cultural morphology (à la Spengler) that serves as a ground (*Grund*). Now, this ground cannot ever be disassociated from the way in which the members of a community experience living-in-this-place, in *this* particular geographical place and not in any other. Why? Because living on a mesa is not the same thing as living on the plains. The *practical* skills that members of a community should develop are completely distinct in each and every case. And given that, for Kusch, thinking means the capacity to resolve practical problems, there would thus exist a "plains thought," and a "mesa thought," and a "highlands thought," etc. The *experience of place* is therefore inextricably linked to thought. It is clear then that the "ground" Kusch writes of is not something *empirical* (rivers, mountains, and valleys), but it does function as a *geographical a priori* that serves as the condition of possibility of thought, so much so that, for him, no thought can ever escape the gravity of the ground.

Returning to Mignolo, we can now understand that when he says, "place of enunciation" (*locus enunciationis*), he is not referring to the linguistic act of producing an utterance (*enunciado*) as it is usually understood in semiotic theories. For Mignolo, enunciation is not in itself a linguistic act but a *geocultural act* with linguistic implications. So the difference between one place of enunciation and another has nothing to do with the different modalities of production of utterances (*enunciados*) but rather with a difference of ground, that is to say, with a different *experience* of place. We have already seen how Mignolo offers us several examples of his thesis: postmodern theories are one thing and postcolonial theories are another. This is because both kinds of thought are rooted in different geocultural grounds. And even staying with the example of postcolonial theories, those that are articulated from Anglophone colonial legacies are one thing and those that are articulated from the Iberian colonial legacies are quite another. Thus, the difference between Homi Bhabha and Enrique Dussel does not originate so much in their argumentative strategies, the different theoretical paradigms they use, their writing, etc., but rather in the fact that they are rooted in different "grounds" and do not share the same postcolonial reason. Hence Mignolo's insistence on distancing his theoretical proposals from those of postcolonial studies and affiliating himself instead with theories that share the same geocultural sensibility, as in the case of Latin American philosophy.

What is the problem with Mignolo's theoretical proposals? I can see at least five theoretical problems. The first of these is the *appeal to the foundation*. Although his thesis can be seen as the attempt to strip modern European scientific reason of its role as the unquestioned tribunal that decides which forms of thought are valid and which are not, his recourse to Kusch's philosophy leads him precisely in the *opposite* direction.

Instead of removing reason from its place as the unfounded foundation in order to leave that place *empty*, what Mignolo does is replace one foundation with another. Now the place of reason is a geocultural concern that appears as a fundamental dimension of human existence, as the ultimate principle that explains both saying and knowing. This means that what is said remains normatively connected to one *previous* moment that completely escapes the act of enunciation itself and therefore can be neither named nor questioned.

This appeal to the ground (*Grund*) leads to another, directly related problem: the *dehistoricization of the enunciative practice*. When geoculture operates as an origin, the act of enunciation that derives from it is immediately dispossessed of its temporal dimension. We should recall that for Kusch, as for Heidegger, language is the house where life roots itself to a human community. Without the shelter and ontological security language offers, human life would not be like this; rather, it would be reduced to simple animal life. Kusch does not think of language in historical but rather in *metaphysical* terms, and his ideal of human life is not one characterized by change, discontinuity, and the emergence of the new, but rather by rootedness to the earth and to the mother tongue, by detachment and accommodation to one's habitat.

There is a third problem related to this: *the attribution of tradition as the true narrative*. The ontological security offered by language and culture, its absolute value of truth, entails the need to submit to the exercise of a power legitimated by tradition, insofar as it appears as the privileged medium for access to the truth. Or, to put it another way, if the value of the truth of discourses lies in belonging to a geoculture, then the ethical and political practices produced by such a geoculture cannot by critically questioned. The value of the truth of a geocultural tradition resides uniquely in its antiquity, in its ancestrality, and in its telluric connection to the mythical origin of the community.

A fourth type of problem is Mignolo's equivocal use of the term *border epistemology*. It seems inconsistent to me to suggest that the place of enunciation is not something given beforehand, but rather produced, and at the same time say that when that locus is created in a colonial situation (the asymmetrical intersection of cultures) the subaltern cultural elements end up "phagocytizing" the dominating elements, as Mignolo argues, following Kusch's thesis (the phagocytization of *ser* by *estar*).[11] If we look to the case of Guamán Poma's chronicle, we will see not only that his Spanish is Quechuacized, but that his Quechua is *also* Hispanicized. This means that the text already assumes a "cut" in relation to the prevailing norms of knowledge on *both sides* of the border. What the place of enunciation does, at least in this case, is precisely to proclaim its *nonbelonging* to either side of the border. In Guamán Poma there is a *discontinuity* regarding the knowledges articulated by European alphabetic writing as well as with those of his own Incan culture. The epistemic Quechuacization of European culture is also an epistemic Hispanicization of Quechua culture. Thus, there is no "phagocytization" of one thing by the other here, but rather an *epistemic break* in response to both and the emergence of something entirely new. However, this is something that Mignolo does not satisfactorily explain.

Finally, I want to discuss one last type of theoretical problem in Mignolo's argument: his use of an *externalist explanation* of the enunciative practice. I am not referring here to the proposal of geoculture as a foundation but rather to the idea that enunciation always has a subject that supports it. In the introduction to *The Darker Side of the Renaissance*, Mignolo criticizes Foucault for not inquiring whether the enunciating subject is a man or a woman, or to what ethnic group or social class the subject belongs (5). This ignores the fact that Foucault does not *need* to ask these questions because his purpose is to explain the functioning of the enunciative practice without using the model that postulates the transcendental activity of a speaking subject who operates from a position outside of enunciation itself. The question we could ask Mignolo is, what would happen if the enunciating subject did not *preexist* the act of enunciation (insofar as the speaking subject belongs to a geoculture) but was instead a *product* of enunciation itself? This is precisely the theoretical problem I want to discuss in order to reconsider Mignolo's thesis.

In fact, the question with which Foucault begins his theory of the act of enunciation in *The Archaeology of Knowledge* is not "who enunciates?" but rather "how does one enunciate?" That is to say, Foucault does not view utterances as the translation of operations that are undertaken from a position that is external to the utterance itself (in the domain of geoculture or the internal processes of consciousness) but rather as a set of relations between signs that are explained through the rules of their own formation. Foucault abandons the question of *foundation* and focuses on the question of *functioning*. It is of no use to recur to notions like tradition, mentality, or culture to explain the functioning of utterances, as such notions are from the very beginning enunciative products. This makes it clear that a theory of the act of enunciation is heading in the wrong direction if its purpose is to determine whether the subject who speaks is Indigenous or European, man or woman, bourgeois or proletarian. What matters in this analysis is the mode of existence of utterances and not the speaking subject. Therefore, we will say that the history of postcolonial reason Mignolo proposes should be replaced by an archaeology of discourses.

Instead of explaining an epistemic break like the one effectuated by Guamán Poma's *Primer nueva corónica y buen gobierno* (*The First New Chronicle and Good Government*) as a search for the sociocultural characteristics of the speaking subject (Guamán Poma de Ayala was a man, a descendent of Indigenous nobility, a Quechua speaker, raised by Spaniards, etc.), or instead of presupposing that Dussel, Kusch, and Zea's discourses generate a rupture with the modern episteme by being articulated from the colonial legacies of Latin America, what we should concentrate on is how utterances function in both Guamán Poma's chronicle and the texts written by the three philosophers just mentioned. In a word, to trace a historical archaeology of the functioning of discourses in order to determine if they produce epistemic breaks. The reflections that follow are dedicated to this topic.

3. THE MODERN EPISTEME AND LATIN AMERICAN PHILOSOPHY

Utterances are historically organized in a series of codifications or rules of the game of enunciative practice, which Foucault called *epistemes*, that is to say, a set of rules and procedures of exclusion that make possible the formation of discourses in a determinate era and govern the relations between different domains of knowledge. It is the geological organization of knowledges on which our experience of the world is ordered in a determinate historical moment. In short, the episteme functions as an a priori that is neither transcendental (Kant) nor anthropological (Roig) but *historical*, which Foucault defines as "the fundamental codes of a culture—those governing its language, its schemas of perception, its exchanges, its techniques, its values, the hierarchy of its practices" (*The Order of Things* xxii). It is clear that he is not referring here to an a priori constructed on top of history and shaped by an eternal structure, but rather to an *empirical order* on the basis of which words are enunciated, gestures are understood, and philosophical and scientific discourses are articulated.

In the seventh chapter of *The Order of Things*, Foucault argues that the modern order of knowledge defines knowledge as a *representation of representation*. If the *classical* episteme has broken with the idea that words reproduce the order of the world and instead postulated that knowledge is a system of signs that represents and orders things, the *modern* episteme goes much further: not only does it grant representation the possibility of representing objects but also the possibility of representing itself in the very act of representation, which is to say, making visible the principles that determine the act of knowledge. In this way, the figure of *reflection* appears, the figure of the return of knowledge of oneself in order to seek there the foundations of the truth about a new object called *man*. However, in Foucault's opinion, the source of the episteme's paradox is that, in order to represent man as a finite being (which can be the object of scientific knowledge), the subject must become both empirical and transcendental at the same time. In other words, the *modern* order of knowledge is a field that is split between objectivity and subjectivity as modes of explaining the conditions of possibility of representation.

In Foucault's analysis, the modern episteme is drawn between two poles. The pole of *objectivity* produces the notion that the study of man should be undertaken exclusively on the basis of empirical data, using so-called scientific disciplines. Objective data are the sole material with which science works; therefore, scientific knowledge cannot include anything that is not part of this material. The pole of *subjectivity*, in contrast, argues that even scientific disciplines function through the formulation of a priori hypotheses that order experience but are not part of it. That is to say, there is an ordering activity of the knowing subject that cannot be *deduced* from but rather transcends empirical data. We see here the division between those knowledges emphasizing *material* conditions of representation and those investigating *spiritual* conditions. This constitutive tension of the modern episteme opens up the question of man from two simultaneously opposed and complementary directions: which elements of man come from the objective world (studied by the physical and chemical sciences) and which come from the subjective world (studied by psychology, phenomenology, and spiritualist metaphysics)? We have on the one hand, *positivism*, and on the other, *humanism*. This is the "empirico-transcendental doublet" Foucault spoke of.

It seems to me that the register of "Latin American philosophy" was born from this internal division of the modern episteme. It is an order that makes possible the distinction between the "natural sciences" and the "spiritual sciences" (*Geisteswissenschaften*), and which tries to isolate a zone of human values that can *escape from* the purely quantitative logic of positive knowledges. This zone also serves as a normative foundation that allows man to be truly human and to live an authentic existence that is free from alienation and external domination. The classic studies of the history of Latin American philosophy, like Francisco Miró Quesada's, for example, show how it emerged out of *Geisteswissenschaften* and in opposition to the positivism that reigned in the large majority of Latin American countries starting in the late nineteenth century. Phenomenology, hermeneutics, and existentialism, tendencies opened up by the modern episteme to serve as a counterweight to the positive sciences, ultimately contributed to the consolidation of the register of "Latin American philosophy" (Francisco Miró Quesada, *Despertar y proyecto del filosofar latinoamericano* 25–74).

In this context we must ask what the epistemological stature of Latin American philosophy is, and with that we can take up Mignolo's reading of Leopoldo Zea, Enrique Dussel, and Rodolfo Kusch once more. What I want to show is that we are not faced with a rupture of the modern episteme, as Mignolo suggests; rather, we stand before a *humanist and anticolonial* narrative made possible by the modern episteme itself. I am interested, above all, in examining those figures that allow these philosophers to enunciate a *Latin American exteriority* with respect to the positivist values of the West. On the one hand, we have the Western world, characterized by the objectifying predominance of technical and instrumental reason, while, on the other hand, we have a human zone that is removed from this world and in which men can truly be free. This is a dualism that, as we will see, operates according to the rules of the modern episteme.

Let us first consider the meaning of the category *phagocytization* introduced by the Argentine philosopher Rodolfo Kusch, which Mignolo identifies as an attempt to theorize the cultural spaces of the border in a postcolonial way. Kusch's central hypothesis is that in Latin America, specifically the Andean region, two antagonistic forms of life exist: one is European and located in large cities, and it is fundamentally oriented toward the domination of nature through science and technology. It is an attitude based in order, morality, and work, which drives humans to want to be-someone [*ser-alguien*] in the world and causes them to project themselves toward the future. Kusch calls this form of life the "culture of *ser*" (*América Profunda* 112). The other, derived from Indigenous cultures and located in the countryside and in the poorer outskirts of large cities, is committed to geographical space and the ground. It is a form of life connected to the cycles of nature. Far from seeking to dominate the latter and promoting projects of individual self-realization, the "culture of *ser*" is oriented toward the here and now; it is deeply communitarian, feminine, resigned to the contingencies of life, and conforms to what exists (Kusch, *América Profunda* 101–6). They are two forms of life whose unresolved tension is present throughout the entirety of the historical development of Latin America.

However, in Kusch the phagocytizing synthesis is not an "assumptive project" in Zea's sense, nor is it an "analectic praxis" as in Dussel, but rather a process of interculturality that is carried out on the threshold of historical consciousness or, as Kusch himself says, "on the margins of what is officially considered culture and civilization" (*América Profunda* 173). Phagocytization is not something conscious but rather a process that operates at the deepest levels of culture, where man experiences his own belonging to the ground, to the land, and to the telluric. This is the *absorption of ser by estar*, the process through which the "culture of *ser*" is Latin Americanized, dissolved in the "primordial ooze of life" of mere *estar* that constitutes the ultimate foundation of human existence. Therefore, phagocytization is not an exclusively Latin American phenomenon, since the telluric dimension is the primary environment for all humans, the originary abode where we find shelter. There have also been frustrated phagocytization processes in Europe, as modernity set in motion a dynamic that ends up destroying tradition, the sense of belonging to the land, the simple life of the countryside, without cities or commodities. In Europe, there are no longer any primary social forms that can dissolve the tension of *ser* and transform it into new modes of life.

Taking up once again some themes from Freud, Heidegger, and Spengler, Kusch argues that European culture is exhausted and neuroticized because it has lost the telluric world that had permitted it to resolve the tension of living permanently on the intellectualist level of *ser* (*América Profunda* 180). In contrast, in regions like Latin America the Indigenous and popular legacy of *estar*, with all its collectivist, religious, and seminal life force, perseveres. The small history of *ser* in Latin America is swallowed up by the large history of *estar*, which explains the failure of all Westernizing and modernizing projects in the region. For Kusch, it will not be the urban intellectuals, technocrats, or politicians who will carry out the processes of phagocytization in Latin America but rather the illiterate masses. As Kusch writes, "In them lies the other part of our continent, that of *mere estar*, with which we can redeem ourselves" (*América Profunda* 185).

Thus it seems clear that Kusch's philosophy operates precisely according to the rules of formation of the discourses opened up by the modern episteme. His categories of *ser* and *estar* function in a dichotomous language that opposes the city and the countryside, Europe and America, reason and emotion, assigning to the latter of each pair the role of serving as spaces for the true humanization of man. There is a zone dominated by instrumental reason, where man is alienated in the midst of a culture of objects and where the value of change is prioritized: this is the "culture of *ser*." However, outside this culture of *ser*, and in a clear antagonistic relationship with it, there is another zone where use value is prioritized and human life is not reduced to the category of object. This is the "culture of *estar*," which Kusch claims to observe in Indigenous populations. The paradox is that a discourse like this, articulated from the modern episteme, poses the existence of other-knowledges that break with Western logocentrism. I am not saying that such knowledges do not exist. What I am pointing out is the massive contradiction that underlies this enunciation in Kusch and Mignolo's discourses. From out of the modern episteme's rules of enunciation emerges a discourse that formulates (*enuncia*) an exteriority to it. This is precisely the contradiction of *anticolonial narratives.*

Foucault explains very well how this kind of paradox functions in *The Order of Things*. Discourses in the history of philosophy that are seen as antithetical to one another, such as those of Francis Bacon and René Descartes (empiricism vs. rationalism), actually belong to the *same* (classical) episteme but are located at different poles of it. It is possible that a discourse might emerge that could combine empiricist and rationalist elements, like, for example, Destutt de Tracy's *Eléments d'idéologie*, but this would not mean that we have arrived at a "border epistemology." At most, we can observe here a *displacement* to the interior of the *same* classical episteme, but at no point does this constitute an epistemic break. However, perhaps the most interesting case of all those Foucault analyzes in *The Order of Things* is that of Karl Marx. While philosophers like Louis Althusser argued that Marx effectuated an epistemic break from the economic science of his time ("Marx's theoretical revolution"), Foucault shows that his discourse actually fits the *same* epistemic rules that marked the discourse of classical economics. That is to say, Marx and David Ricardo are thinkers of the same episteme. The fact that Marx was a Jew or a political revolutionary has absolutely *nothing* to do with the kind of epistemic rules that gave shape to the way his discourse was articulated. Just like Rodolfo Kusch, Marx did not provoke an epistemic break, nor did he generate a "border" episteme.

What of Leopoldo Zea, the second of the Latin American philosophers whom Mignolo considers to have advanced toward a break with the modern episteme? In his book *Filosofía de la historia americana* (Philosophy of Latin American history), Zea says that the history of Latin America is characterized by a "juxtaposition of negations." This means that, instead of taking on and adopting outside influences in a dialectical movement rooted in its own culture, Latin America has preferred to deny itself and turn its historical attention toward a foundation built on foreign experiences. Once independence was achieved in the nineteenth century, criollo elites attempted to expunge the Indigenous and Spanish past in order to mechanically adopt sociopolitical ideas from France, England, and the United States. It tried to cancel the colonial past through its abrupt denial in order to begin everything again from a zero point, assuming as its own the historical experiences of other nations. Like Emma Bovary, Flaubert's famous heroine, Latin American nations historically failed because they saw themselves as different than how they actually were. Instead of taking account of its own cultural reality, Latin America prefers to deny itself in order to adopt as its own a foreign reality (Zea, *Filosofía de la historia americana* 20). The result was naturally dependence on and imitation of the habits, customs, and ways of life of the colonizer. This institutionalized "Bovarism," this "strange and absurd philosophy of history," Zea asserts, "is not practiced only by the peoples of Latin America but also by all peoples across the globe who have suffered the impact of the expansion of the Western world (*Filosofía de la historia americana* 166).

However, Zea is convinced that there are alternatives with which the vicious circle of dependency can be broken. One option is visible in Shakespeare's *The Tempest*, in which the slave Caliban rebels against his master Prospero with the following words: "You taught me language; and my profit on't / Is, I know how to curse. The red plague rid you / For learning me your language!" (19). Zea sees in this scene the key to a new philosophy of history that would be free of Bovarism. For instead of denying in one fell swoop the colonial past of Europe, as all civilizing projects have always tried to do, it becomes necessary to assimilate European modernity so that, *using this same language*, Latin America can become conscious of itself and adopt a critical attitude in response to its colonial legacies. According to Zea, modernity made possible what Hegel called a dialectical experience of history. The past is not denied but rather absorbed, assimilated so that it will not return, and converted into a tool for the construction of the future (*Aufgehoben*) (*Filosofía de la historia americana* 165). Modernity, that is to say, the dialectical assimilation of history, the coming to critical consciousness in response to what one is and what one wants to be, is Europe's greatest contribution to humanity. Thus it is not through the negation of modernity but through the radicalization of its emancipatory potential that colonialism will be overcome.

It is evident that, for Zea, the liberation of Latin America—and of the Third World in general—will only arrive if one takes on the *critical language* of modernity. A language whose model Zea seeks in Hegel's dialectic. Like the latter, Zea wants to articulate a philosophy of history aiming toward a grand project of cultural and political synthesis in Latin America (the "assumptive project") that privileges unity over diversity, harmony over divergence, and the beautiful over the sublime. This synthesis would be not only Latin American but also global: the advent of a new humanity for which neither Prosperos nor Calibans exist, only "men and nothing more."

Nevertheless, Zea's humanist discourse is inscribed in the perimeter demarcated by the modern episteme, as the figure of the "man and nothing more" fulfills the role of the *transcendental subject* that fixes history into a normative course. In other words, by suggesting that it is the origin of meaning, language, and history, the transcendental subject creates the conditions for the empirical subject to be able to liberate itself from all that dehumanizes it. We see here the same paradox that we pointed out before in Kusch's discourse: out of the humanist language engendered by the modern episteme comes a discourse that postulates the end of dehumanization. That is to say, the modern episteme's rules of enunciation favor an *anticolonial narrative* that, in the register of "the philosophy of history," postulates an exteriority in response to that same modern episteme. Therefore it is evident that the epistemic break does not depend on *what one says*—as Mignolo would have it—but rather *how one says it*. It is not enough to condemn Prospero with his own language; rather, it is necessary *to transgress that language*. And it is precisely this that Zea does not do. Although it is articulated from within the colonial legacies of Latin America, his discourse remains loyal to all the humanist registers authorized by the modern order of knowledge and in those in which liberation appears either as the overcoming of false consciousness (Bovarism) or as the cancellation of all alienations that separate us from our true human nature.

Finally, from the same archaeological perspective, we will analyze the discourse of Enrique Dussel, the third of the Latin American philosophers whom Mignolo credits with helping to advance toward a rupture with the modern regime of knowledge. Dussel also declares the need to go beyond the ontological and colonialist thought of modernity, but this enunciation is inevitably articulated from within the rules set out by the modern episteme. In effect, using the language of philosophers such as Martin Heidegger, Paul Ricoeur, and Emmanuel Levinas, Dussel compares the ethical and political world of European modernity, as well as its enthusiasm for objectification and colonization, with the ethical and political world of the *peoples* of the Third World, who are located outside of that modernity. Modern European thought is typified by its permanent self-referentiality, that is to say, by its inability to open itself to the interpellation of other forms of thought and other cultural referents that are external to it (Dussel, *Introducción a la filosofía de la liberación* 114). It is a thought of "sameness" that cannot see the "other" as anything other than an *object* to be subjugated. Dussel argues that the Indian, the Black, the peasant, and the worker—in a word, the people—were ignored in their otherness and subsumed by the sameness of European culture reproduced in Latin America by its criollo proxies. The result of all this was the political, pedagogical, and erotic alienation of Latin American peoples (115). Contrary to this, Dussel proposes a cultural and political dealienation that begins with recognizing the radical exteriority of the "other," which is to say, by understanding that beyond the European ontology of totality, forces of change are emerging in the Latin American, Asian, and African periphery.[12] The task of a philosophy of liberation is to conceptualize and strengthen these forces.

Following the work of Ricoeur, Dussel claims that the exteriority of Third World peoples is expressed in a set of images, myths, and unconscious symbolic structures. The function of philosophy is to discover (to bring to light) the ethical and mythical core around which the life of peoples is unconsciously organized and which is generally seen in the Enlightenment thought of the elites as something that is folkloric and irrational. Its objective is to accept the prephilosophical world of Latin America, the sphere of everyday life, in order to discover what constitutes the ontological horizon of comprehensibility that symbolically structures the life of the people. Here, in the ethos of popular culture, Dussel sees the embodiment of a rationality that is completely different from that of European modernity ("Cultura imperial" 122). It is not a rationality centered on the deification of a monological subject (the Cartesian "I think") that denies the other's humanity, but rather one generated by the face-to-face experience, by solidarity with those who suffer, and by knowing how to listen to the voice of the oppressed other. Popular culture has its own unconscious ways of relating to others, of working, spending free time, loving, speaking, and having fun, that are radically opposed to the promotion of imperial culture in schools and in mass media. However, due to what has traditionally been excluded and denied, Latin American popular culture still does not possess a clear knowledge of its being-other in relation to modernity. The task of Latin American philosophy is precisely to discover what constitutes that alterity and to share this knowledge with the people. To this end, the participation of critical intellectuals is necessary, because the people, who have been colonized and subjugated by the oppressive Totality, cannot critically lead themselves or construct for themselves a project of total liberation. Like a teacher or prophet, the philosopher of liberation must be capable of articulating the voice of those who have no voice, of creating awareness of those popular values that imperial culture has kept in the unconscious, thus fertilizing the seeds that will bring about its definitive liberation (Dussel, *Filosofía ética latinoamericana III*, 180–81). As with Moses and other Old Testament prophets, the profession of the philosopher of liberation sets out from a concrete experience: letting oneself be interpellated by the voice of the oppressed. This philosopher's mission is to free the people from the ideological obstacles that impede critical thought and action. The philosopher of liberation's responsibility is to articulate a philosophy that opposes the errors of the dominant European culture and speaks for the people, for the dispossessed of the world, for all those who cannot through their own means understand the mechanisms of domination used by the oppressor.[13]

The theme of alienation and disalienation assumes that those unconscious forces separating man from his own nature and preventing him from seeing his oppressed condition can nevertheless be observed through critical rationality and brought back to consciousness. However, this figure of argumentation, as Foucault shows, is typical of the modern episteme. It proposes that all our conscious and rational choices are fixed in a preconscious lifeworld (*Lebenswelt*) that functions "behind our backs" but can nonetheless be brought into view through a *second-degree observation*. However, what makes possible this observation that observes what cannot be observed from within everyday life? If we place ourselves in the pure empiricalness of everyday life, our functioning as empirical subjects escapes from our view; but if we reflexively divide ourselves in order to observe that empiricalness, then this functioning will become apparent to us. It is precisely this figure of *division* that Foucault claims is typical of the modern episteme.

Let us recall that, according to Foucault, humanist discourses appeared at the same moment in which *man* is represented as a condition of possibility of his own experience, that is to say, at the point at which life, language, and labor begin to be *represented*. While in the framework of the *classical* episteme these fields of experience were outside representation, the modern episteme generates, in contrast, the possibility of a second-degree observation of them. Man can now divide himself in order to see himself as an empirical subject and observe his own observations. *Only then* is the discourse of human alienation, as well as its counterpart, the discourse of liberation, made possible. The *value* of experience (life, language, and labor as experiences that are oppressed by imperialism) now depends on the representative activity of the subject. This is why Dussel can *say* that the critical intellectual is a guide for the blind, a constructor of identities, and a representative who speaks in place of others and is located in the perspective of the *transcendental subject*. Dussel's philosophy is not to be found in an external relation to modern European thought, as both Mignolo and Dussel himself affirm. To the contrary, all the figures used in his discourse are possible thanks to the same rules that make possible the truth of discourses of modern knowledge. What we have here is in fact a typical *modern humanist discourse*, as the Colombian philosopher Roberto Salazar Ramos points out:

> The project of Latin American philosophy of liberation bears similarities to the project of modernity: the belief in universal history, universal subjectivity, and universal culture; only in the case of Latin American philosophy was this universality seen and perceived from the margins of modernity, yet was also part of it. . . . Latin American philosophy was unintentionally postulated as a philosophy of modernity for Latin America: in order to cease being "colonies" or "peripheral nations," it was necessary to reach modernity. The utopian aspect of Latin American modernity originated not in an imperialist modernity (as in Europe) but in a humanist modernity of autonomous, reconciled, and fully emancipated subjectivity.
>
> ("EL EJERCICIO DE LA FILOSOFÍA COMO ARQUEOLOGÍA" 45)

Thus it seems to me that when Mignolo claims that the thought of Dussel, Kusch, and Zea are examples of a "border epistemology," he is confusing the *place* of enunciation with referents taken from cultural history or sociology, because this place has *nothing* to do with the empirical fact that the speaking subject is European or Indigenous, Jew or Christian,

Black or white. What should be examined are not the empirical characteristics of the speaking subject but the *epistemic rules* that make the subject's enunciations possible. Archaeologically we can even argue that there is no epistemic externality between Dussel and Gadamer, as Mignolo questionably claims in his introduction to *The Darker Side of the Renaissance*. They both, regardless of their empirical situations, speak from the same division generated by the modern episteme's attempt to salvage a section of humanity with respect to the positive sciences and capitalism. Both cases are examples of Western humanism, although they are speaking from different places on the political spectrum.

To conclude: in principle, the archaeology of discourses is not concerned with who the subject of a discourse is, where they live, to what culture they belong, or what their political beliefs are; rather, it is only interested in *discursive practices*, without trying to explain itself by referring to external variables in sociological, anthropological, or geopolitical registers. Of course, this *does not mean* that discursive practices are in any way *disarticulated* from the economic, political, and social realms. They are articulated to these areas, but they are not *reducible* to them. This seems to me to be the problem with Walter Mignolo's thesis, namely that the locus of enunciation is geoculturally determined. This thesis confronts us directly with the typically humanist assumption of the transcendentality of culture in opposition to the rationality of discourses—a basic presupposition of modern *Kulturwissenschaften*. This is a dangerous and incorrect path. It is dangerous because it could lead us to the legitimation of any kind of political or moral authoritarianism, simply *because* it is rooted in non-Western traditions and "other-knowledges." It is incorrect because it leads to the theorization of an *epistemic alterity* that is nonexistent in Latin American discourses, just as in Mignolo's reading of Kusch, Dussel, and Zea. An epistemic break is not produced when the universal pretensions of philosophy are criticized in the philosophical register, in imitation of Caliban's gesture. As long as Caliban continues to speak in the same philosophical register as his modern master, there will be no dissolution, only displacement, and always within the *same* episteme.

7

THE BIRTH OF LATIN AMERICA AS A PHILOSOPHICAL PROBLEM IN MEXICO

1. INTRODUCTION: THE PHILOSOPHICAL FIELD IN LATIN AMERICA

In an article published in the Buenos Aires newspaper *La Nación* on December 29, 1940, the Argentine philosopher Francisco Romero announced the arrival of "philosophical normality" in Latin America ("Sobre la filosofía en Iberoamérica" 68). With this concept, Romero was referring to the professionalization of the practice of philosophy in the continent, that is to say, its consolidation as a legitimately recognized "profession" with its own jurisdiction. This entailed the regular publication of specialized articles and books, the creation of university professors of philosophy, the formation of a specific subjectivity (the professional "philosopher," in contrast to the "man of letters"), the development of a cultural market that could facilitate the circulation of its products, and, ultimately, the differentiation of what Pierre Bourdieu called a "philosophical field" as autonomous in relation to other fields of cultural production. In this sense, philosophical normality was for Romero "the practice of philosophy as an ordinary function of culture, along with the other preoccupations of the intelligentsia" (69).

Although philosophy had been cultivated in Latin America for almost the entire colonial period and a good part of the nineteenth century, it was only around the middle of the twentieth century that it achieved the level of a discipline, that is to say, a set of theoretical and practical institutional propositions capable of creating problems for investigation, of defining a set of canonical authors and texts, as well as of proposing plans for organized study of both this canon and its problems. Prior to this date, there was no properly existing philosophical community in Latin America, only cultured individuals and sporadic afficionados who were recognized in society as essayists and men of letters but not as philosophers.[1]

Pierre Bourdieu showed that the autonomization of the "philosophical field" necessarily entails *atopia*, which is the tendency of the philosopher to think outside the social world in which that thinking takes place. For Bourdieu, participation in any academic field presupposes a tacit complicity with the rules of the game that define who is located in the field and who is located outside it. For what concerns us here, the golden rule that legitimizes belonging to the philosophical field is the following: only the "philosopher" is able to adopt a point of view about which it is not possible to adopt any point of view. This means that what differentiates philosophers from sociologists, anthropologists, or any other social scientists, is their universalist perspective, which can elevate them to a more general point of view than any of the "particular sciences." That is to say, while social scientists see themselves as obligated to turn social space into an object of study in which they immerse themselves, philosophers have the luxury of bracketing off this space and concentrating on thematizing universal problems, as it is only through them that "pure thought" is practiced. Thus, according to Bourdieu, the *illusio* of philosophy is based in the examination of problems, authors, and texts from a determinate historical moment, or theoretical concepts that are always connected to a specific field of struggles, often limited to the borders of one language or nation, and treating them as if they were universal.

However, the way in which Bourdieu describes the autonomization of the philosophical field does not coincide exactly with Romero's concept of "philosophical normalization." Unlike what happened in Europe and the United States, the configuration of a specifically philosophical field in Latin America has not assumed that the social space from which philosophy is practiced can be ignored. The professional practice of philosophy, although it often entails the adoption of a canon and some arbitrarily fixed themes from the philosophical centers of the Western world, has not *necessarily* meant bracketing off the social world in which philosophy takes place. In fact, by proposing this concept of "philosophical normalization," Romero affirmed that a central element of such normalization was to make Latin America a problem worthy of being addressed with the conceptual tools of philosophy:

> The present concern for philosophy in Latin America offers very rich and diverse conditions and aspects that provoke exposition and commentary. However, underneath the visible and obvious facts, the way it has been incubated and continues to grow within the deepest part of this movement, as well as the consequences that should be taken from this new stage in the maturation of knowledge in the region, far exceed the mere register of a bundle of new cultural occupations and the rosy outlooks that can be deduced for the near or distant future of these studies. The facts and what lies beneath them invite reflection on much broader topics: the entire course of culture in these lands, their future role within and outside of Latin America, the types and paths of spirituality in Latin America, and the specificity of the Latin American "event."
>
> (ROMERO, "SOBRE LA FILOSOFÍA EN IBEROAMÉRICA" 72–73)

Romero does not see philosophical reflection on "the entire course of culture in these lands" as a symptom of theoretical immaturity or lack of structural differentiation in relation to the also emerging field of social sciences. It is clear today, as then, that the guardians of philosophical orthodoxy in Latin America continue to deem any attempt to philosophically think problems like cultural identity, the social production of knowledges, or the historical development of Latin American societies as "lacking rigor." These problems, they argue, belong to the field of social sciences (those that are still considered "minor sciences"), not to philosophy, whose object of study is "universality as universal" and not particularity or contingency. However, the history of Latin American philosophy amply demonstrates, despite ferocious orthodox opposition, that what we will call here "philosophical Latin Americanism" has not been completely expelled from the discipline.

The origins of philosophical reflection on Latin American history and culture can be framed by two symbolic dates: 1930 and 1968. In 1930, a global economic crisis was generated by the New York Stock Exchange, and this had important consequences for the economy and the field of cultural production in Latin America. Effectively, it was during the 1930s that the majority of Latin American governments were obliged to adopt a series of protectionist and autarkic measures (import substitutions) as a means to combat the devastating effects of the crisis. Many governments that during the nineteenth century favored the ideology of economic free exchange turned down the path of state intervention, thus opening the doors to nationalism. On the geopolitical level, one of the consequences of the crisis was the United States' replacement of England as the hegemonic power of the world system, which instigated the birth of populist and anti-imperialist ideologies throughout Latin America. These factors, as we shall see, directly affected how Latin American intellectuals of the era positioned themselves in their respective fields of artistic and theoretical production.

For his part, Immanuel Wallerstein posits the year 1968 as the beginning of a global cultural and ideological revolution against liberalism as the dominant geoculture of the capitalist world-system (*Geopolitics and Geoculture* 65–83). This date symbolically marks when Marxist social theory began to acquire power in the Latin American academy, the same year as the Mexican student uprising and its brutal repression at the Plaza de las Tres Culturas in Tlatelolco, as well as the (admittedly timid) emergence of new social movements in the framework of the military dictatorships in Latin America during the 1970s. With regard to what concerns us here, 1968 is also the year Peruvian philosopher Augusto Salazar Bondy's book *¿Existe una filosofía en nuestra América?* (Does a philosophy exist in our America?) was published, a text that marked the beginning of a different way of constructing Latin America as a philosophical problem. I am referring here to the shift from "philosophical Latin Americanism" to the *philosophy of liberation*.

The fact is, between 1930 and 1968, many professional philosophers in Latin America participated in an intellectual polemic that exceeded the bounds of the disciplinary field of philosophy. The need to critically reflect on the space of the social from which one reflected (that is to say, to transgress Bourdieu's golden rule) was in the air they breathed. As Miró Quesada astutely points out, not a single Western intellectual center ever generated a philosophical movement with a continental reach and the purpose of meditating on the essence of one culture in particular, and much less one that investigated the possibility or impossibility of constructing a philosophy specific to one culture ("La filosofía de lo americano" 1027).

The period we have chosen to investigate is particularly fertile in works dedicated to philosophical reflection on "the problem of Latin America." I will mention only some of the most well-known and widely discussed among them. In Argentina: *Filosofía argentina* (Argentine philosophy [1940]) by Alejandro Korn; *¿Hay una filosofía Iberoamericana?* (Is there a Latin American philosophy? [1948]) by Risieri Frondizi; *El mito gaucho* (The gaucho myth [1948]) by Carlos Astrada; *La seducción de la barbarie: Análisis herético de un continente mestizo* (The seduction of barbarism: A heretical analysis of a mestizo continent [1953]) by Rodolfo Kusch; *El pecado original de América* (Latin America's original sin [1954]) by Héctor A. Murena; *América bifronte: Ensayo de ontología y filosofía de la historia* (Two-sided Latin America: An essay on the ontology and philosophy of history [1961]) by Alberto Caturelli; *Filosofía de la cultura y de los valores* (Philosophy of culture and values [1962]) by Octavio Derisi; *América profunda* (Deep Latin America [1962]) by Rodolfo Kusch; and *Indios, porteños y dioses* (Indians, Buenos Aireans, and gods [1966]), also by Kusch. In Peru: *Pueblo continente* (People of the continent [1937]) by Antenor Orrego; *Espacio-Tiempo-Histórico* (Historical-Space-Time [1948]) by Víctor Raúl Haya de la Torre; and *La filosofía en Iberoamérica* (Philosophy in Latin America [1949]) by Alberto Wagner de Reyna. In Bolivia: *Sentido y proyección del Kollasuyo* (Meaning and projection of Kollasuyo [1939]) by Roberto Prudencio; and *Pachamama: Diálogo sobre el porvenir de la cultura en Bolivia* (Pachamama: Dialogue on the future of culture in Bolivia [1942]) by Guillermo Francovich. In Venezuela: *El problema de América* (The problem of Latin America [1959]) by Ernesto Mayz Valenilla. And in Chile: *El sentimiento de lo humano en América: Antropología de la convivencia* (The Meaning of the human in Latin America: An anthropology of coexistence [1953]) by Féliz Schwartzmann.

This philosophical phenomenon was so obvious that its first monographic studies were also written in the same period: *Contemporary Latin American Philosophy* (1954) by Aníbal Sánchez Reulet; *La filosofía en el Uruguay en el siglo XX* (Philosophy in Uruguay in the twentieth century [1956]) by Arturo Ardao; *¿Cuáles son los grandes temas de la filosofía latinoamericana?* (What are the main themes of Latin American philosophy? [1958]) by Victoria de Caturla Brú; *Historia de la filosofía en Latinoamérica* (History of philosophy in Latin America [1958]) by Mafredo Kempff Mercado; *Filosofía de lo mexicano* (Philosophy of Mexicanness [1960]) by Abelardo Villegas; *El desarrollo de las ideas en la sociedad argentina del siglo XX* (The development of ideas in twentieth-century Argentine society [1965]) by Francisco Romero; *Problemas de la historia de las ideas filosóficas en Argentina* (Problems of the history of philosophical ideas in Argentina [1966]) by Coriolano Alberini; *Major Trends in Mexican Philosophy* (1966) by Mariano de la Cueva; *Filosofía española en América* (Spanish Philosophy in Latin America [1967]) by José Luis Abellán; *Historia de las ideas en el Perú contemporaneo* (The history of ideas in contemporary Peru [1967]) by Augusto Salazar Bondy; and *La filosofía iberoamericana* (Latin American philosophy [1968]) by Francisco Larroyo.

This impressive panorama cannot be sufficiently covered in the present work, so I have decided to focus on a single country, Mexico. My choice is based on two fundamental reasons: the first is that, in Mexico, state nationalism emerged with greater force than in other Latin American countries because of the triumph of the Revolution of 1910. In Octavio Paz's opinion, the strictly *revolutionary* quality of the popular uprising consisted in having founded Mexico not on a general notion of "Man," as liberals had wanted during the nineteenth century, but rather on the actual situation of the inhabitants of Mexican territory (*The Labyrinth of Solitude* 141). In this way, the grand dream of the liberal reformists to construct a nation destined to develop according to a set of universal and abstract principles was reduced to a utopian ideal. The Mexican Revolution was not motivated by any universal ideology, as it was in the cases of the French and Russian Revolutions, but rather its ability to weave together a web of *symbols*—and not ideological discourses—which profoundly marked the sensibility and imagination of all Mexicans (137). If, as Paz says, the Mexican Revolution brought to light "deep Mexico," that which had been repressed and hidden behind the liberal projects and dictatorships of the nineteenth century, then it is clear why it was precisely in this country where a philosophical movement developed to uncover the invisible or "subterranean history" of

Mexican culture and, by extension, of Latin American culture as a whole. The Mexican Revolution, with its nationalist, anti-imperialist, and anti-oligarchic tendencies, instigated a philosophical reflection on "Mexican being" and "Latin American being."

The second reason for my choice is that, more than any other Latin American country—with the possible exception of Argentina—in Mexico, philosophy transformed more rapidly into an autonomous institutionalized field. This is, to an extent, the result of the great emphasis the Partido Revolucionario Institucional (PRI) placed on higher education policies and consequently the proliferation of prestigious academic centers like the Universidad Nacional Autónoma Metropolitana (UNAM) and the Colegio de México (COLMEX), which very quickly became institutional beacons for the entire continent. These two institutions played an important socializing role for Mexican intellectual elites in the twentieth century, and the majority of the philosophers that we will consider in this chapter passed through them at some point (see Camp, *Intellectuals and the State in Twentieth-Century Mexico* 199–236).

2. JOSÉ VASCONCELOS: THE PROJECT OF A PHILOSOPHY FOR THE "COSMIC RACE"

The controversial figure of José Vasconcelos occupies a primary position in Latin American philosophy, as he was one of the first Mexican men of letters at the beginning of the twentieth century to call himself a "philosopher" and, in any case, the first to boast of having constructed his own philosophical system. Vasconcelos took on the task of orienting the activity of an entire race of men, the "cosmic race," that, according to him, was taking shape in Latin America. He fervently opposed the claim some intellectuals made that the Indian was the "foundation of nationality" and instead defended mestizaje as the symbol of national identity. As the secretary of public education (1921–1924) and rector of UNAM, he carried out a pedagogical project intended to shape the new Latin American man according to the humanist ideals of a mestizo race that would govern the entire world. Thus he developed a massive public literacy campaign and enthusiastically supported the work of the great Mexican muralists Diego Rivera, José Clemente Orozco, and David Alfaro

Siquieros, who depicted the pride of the "fifth race" on buildings, schools, and libraries in Mexico.

Vasconcelos was a Hispanic Catholic with a prophetic vocation, which he felt called him to develop a "system of beliefs" (as Ortega y Gasset called it) that would be valid for all Latin America. His Latin Americanist ideals are influenced by the Uruguayan José Enrique Rodó, whose essay *Ariel* sounded an alarm against the tendency of many politicians and intellectuals to "de-Latinize" Latin American culture, offering as a substitute the scientistic and individualistic culture of the United States. According to Rodó, imitating the Anglo-Saxon model entailed the grave danger of forgetting the great humanistic values of Mediterranean culture, of which Latin America was the legitimate heir via Spain. Like Rodó, Vasconcelos was convinced of the natural superiority of Latin, Catholic, and mestizo culture over Anglo-Saxon, Protestant, and white culture. All his political and pedagogical work was directed at combating the *nordomanía* ("mania for the North") Rodó spoke of, with the goal of cultivating the superior values that Latin America had received as part of its Spanish cultural legacy.

Participating in the "anti-imperialism of rights" that was so dear to the elite Hispanophiles and letrados of the early twentieth century (with their dread of bourgeois culture, the technologization of everyday life, and the "Protestant work ethic"), Vasconcelos argues that Latin America must defend itself from U.S. cultural expansion to the South, which necessitates developing an ideology that will mark out the paths for its future evolution:

> All people who aspire to leave a mark on history, all nations that initiate their own era, are for that reason (as well as due to the demands of their own development) obligated to undertake a reevaluation of all values and to implement a provisional or perennial construction of concepts. None of the important races escapes the duty of judging for itself all the precepts it has inherited or imported and then adapted into its own cultural plans, or to formulate them again if that is what is dictated by the sovereignty that beats in the heart of the life it brings about. We cannot then exempt ourselves from defining a philosophy—that is, a renewed and sincere way of contemplating the universe.
>
> ("EL PENSAMIENTO IBEROAMERICANO" 49–50).

Convinced that his personal mission was the elaboration of this philosophy, Vasconcelos embarked on a project to reconstruct the evolution of mestizo culture in Latin America as well as to show, prophetically, what his mission within universal history consisted of. This intellectual project is expressed in two books written in the middle of the 1920s, but it did not reach a continental level of dissemination until the 1930s: *La raza cósmica: Misión de la raza Iberoamericana* (1925) (*The Cosmic Race* [1997]) and *Indología: Una interpretación de la cultura iberoamericana* (Indology: An interpretation of Latin American culture [1926]). We will focus our attention on the ideas developed in these two books.

Vasconcelos starts from the assumption that Latin America constitutes an ethnic and cultural unity that was slowly formed during the three centuries of Spanish colonization, but systematically ignored by the liberal elites during the nineteenth century, once the wars of independence had begun.[2] Such cultural unity, the result of the biological union of the Indian, the Black, and the European, was conceived under the aegis of the Spanish Crown in the territory it named the "West Indies." This is why—and not because the privileged object of investigation was the Indian—Vasconcelos called his philosophical project *Indology* ("Los motivos del escudo 122).

Influenced by Bergson's ideas, Vasconcelos attempts to show that the ascendant movement of life has certainly arrived, along with humanity, at an exceptional point, but it is not stopping yet. The evolution of different human cultures is driven by the struggle between life and matter, or, more precisely, it represents the purpose of life as the defeat of the resistance of matter and the achievement of self-knowledge through intuition. This effort is "objectivized" in the constitution of different races. In this philosophical context, Vasconcelos wonders: What is the role of the Latin American mestizo race in the process of universal evolution? He hopes to show that this race, more than any other, manifests the evolutionary climax of the *elan vital* announced by Bergson. In order to respond to this question, he initially makes use of studies by geologists like Alfred Wegener (with his theory of continental drift) to show that the Maya civilization is earlier than the oldest civilizations of the East and of Europe and a direct descendant of the inhabitants of ancient Atlantis. These "red men," endowed with an extraordinary wisdom, later transmitted to Egypt, were actually the fathers of human civilization. The Latin American race is then very old, geologically speaking, even older than Europe itself (Vasconcelos, *The Cosmic Race* 7–8) From this point of view, the positivist and liberal nineteenth-century idea that national identity should be modeled on European and Anglo-Saxon traditions was completely aberrant. Our roots are not European, since even Western (Greco-Roman) civilization itself is rooted in the wisdom of the Atlanteans.

Based on these ideas, Vasconcelos wants to show that the Atlanteans established the foundations of civilization and disappeared after having completed this mission. After its decline, Hellenic culture was formed and began the development of white civilization, whose destiny was to expand over the face of the earth and return once again to Latin America "to consummate the task of recivilization and repopulation" (Vasconcelos, *The Cosmic Race* 9). Civilization left the Americas then returned to them again, strengthened by the material and scientific contributions of Western man. In other words, it returned enriched with the development of intellectual knowledge, impelled by the white race. The moment has come in which Latin America will lay the foundations for a new civilizing stage of humanity: the configuration of the "cosmic race."

Like Rodó, Vasconcelos works with the cultural conflict and struggle between the Latins and the Anglo-Saxons, key concepts for the configuration of his philosophical mythology. The cultural struggle between the Latins and the Anglo-Saxons is the expression of what is taking place on the metaphysical level: the elan vital, which is made objective in the white race through the fabulous unfolding of intellectual knowledge, begins to exhaust itself and head toward its own disappearance. This leaves open a path for the emergence of races for which the objectivization of this vital force has been predominantly instinctive, but which have not had political prominence since the evolution of humanity was still conditioned by the material domination of the forces of nature. Once this domination was fully consolidated, the vital impulse advanced toward a new stage of development. For Vasconcelos, the Latins and the Anglo-Saxons embody two distinct forms of knowledge. The Anglo-Saxons, in whom intelligence predominates over instinct, have fulfilled their historical mission and should yield to the Latins, who give form to a vitally ascendant mode of knowledge: intuition. The decline of some and the emergence of others is the product of an *evolutionary struggle* that Vasconcelos, like Bergson, wishes to reconstitute both metaphysically and historically.

Those involved in the discovery and conquest of the Americas were the two most vigorous branches of the white race: the Anglo-Saxons and the Latins. The first group (Protestant immigrants) took control of the North and protected the purity of their bloodlines, while the second group (Catholic immigrants) controlled the South and mixed with the Indigenous populations and, later, with Africans. From this intersection was born a new race that combines the legacy of the Atlanteans with the legacy of the Latins. The Anglo-Saxons, based in science and technology, were able to impose their ideals on the Latins. The wars for independence, the construction of Latin American nationalities in the nineteenth century, the institutionalization of positivism—in Vasconcelos's opinion, all these processes represented the cultural defeat of the Latins by their Anglo-Saxon "enemies," and this was because of the dearth of political vision among the men who led the rebellion against Spain (*The Cosmic Race* 11, 34). What could have been the beginning of a "great Latin confederation," such as that dreamed of by Bolívar, ended up being a great betrayal of the ideals of race:

> The greatest battle was lost on the day that each one of the Iberian republics went forth alone, to live her own life apart from her sisters, concerting treaties and receiving false benefits, without tending to the common interests of the race. The founders of our new nationalism were, without knowing it, the best allies of the Anglo-Saxons, our rivals in the possession of the continent. . . . We Spaniards by blood or by culture, began by denying our traditions at the moment of our emancipation. We broke off from the past, and some even denied their blood, saying it would have been better if the conquest of our regions had been accomplished by the English. . . . At any rate, the anti-Hispanic preaching and the corresponding anglicizing, skillfully spread by the English themselves, perverted our judgment from the beginning.
>
> (10–11, 14)

Thus, while the Anglo-Saxons were united, the Latins were divided. For Vasconcelos, this means that the philosophy of the mestizo race cannot be based in the battles for independence or in the heroes that fought against the colonialist legacy, as the liberal positivist ideology of the nineteenth century had proclaimed. These liberal myths are in Vasconcelos's opinion permeated by a cultural Anglo-Saxonism that is foreign to Latin America's specificities. Therefore, while liberalism and positivism considered the Indo-Iberian legacy to be the source of barbarism (Sarmiento), Vasconcelos simply inverts the terms. Now the mestizo legacy is purified and washed clean in order to make it the foundation of Latin American freedom and solidarity. According to the Mexican philosopher, the cultural and metaphysical bases for the emergence of a great future civilization was created by the mixing of the Spaniard and the Indian. In this way, Vasconcelos was thus opposed to the outright indigenism that other university and political colleagues in Mexico supported at the time. With mestizaje, the Spanish "Latinized" the Indigenous peoples and transmitted the humanistic and aesthetic ideals of the race to them: "Even the pure Indians are Hispanized, they are Latinized, just as the environment itself is Latinized. . . . The Indian has no other door to the future but the door of modern culture, nor any other road but the road already cleared by Latin civilization" (16). Vasconcelos's tone is optimistic with respect to the potential of the Latin race. Its destiny obeys the plan to constitute the birthplace of a "fifth race" in which all peoples will merge in order to replace the four previous races that, in isolation from each other, forged the history of humanity. In the Americas, this dispersion will end, and the definitive unity of the human race will begin. This is how the third, definitive, and final period of the history of humanity will begin, the "aesthetic stage" that will replace the material and intellectual stages:

> In the third period, whose approach is already announced in a thousand ways, the orientation of conduct will not be sought in pitiful reason that explains but does not discover. It will rather be sought in creative feeling and convincing beauty. Norms will be given by fantasy, the supreme faculty. . . . Instead of rules, constant inspiration. . . . The ethical imperative itself will be surpassed. Beyond good and evil, in a world of aesthetic *pathos*, the only thing that will matter will be that the act, being beautiful, shall produce joy. To do our whim, not our duty; to follow the path of taste, not of appetite or syllogism; to live joy grounded in love—such is the third stage.
>
> (29)

Note the way Vasconcelos transfers the metaphysical categories Bergson uses in his description of instinct to the sphere of culture. Unlike intelligence, which always uses the mediation of the concept, instinct is fundamentally a matter of *sympathy*, that is to say, an immediate union with the indivisible foundations of life. Intuitive knowledge is immediate because it is verifiable without needing to refer to concepts, symbols, judgments, reasoning, or what Bergson called the *cinematographic apparatus* of intelligence. Intuition reaches the absolute because it places us directly in the world of the spirit and knows inner reality but not outer reality, whereas intelligence only encompasses the surface of things. All this means that a society in which instinct predominates will necessarily develop a *superior morality* to those societies where intelligence is dominant. Bergson develops this idea in his final book, *The Two Sources of Morality and Religion*, where he compares the two moralities that are born from the dominance of either instinct or intelligence. The morality of the "open society," founded on instinct and embodied in personalities like Jesus Christ and other saintly humans, is based on emotion, charity, and love of one's neighbor. It was not born from either the doctrines or the positivity of laws, but rather grows out of love for humanity and is expressed in relations of mutual sympathy. It is, in the end, the morality of the Gospel, of the Christian ethic.

However, Bergson did not believe that at some point a "mystical society" would manage to constitute itself and encompass all of humanity, but rather that mystical individuals would continue to draw humanity further down the road of true morality. In contrast, Vasconcelos thinks that an entire race, embodying the "open society" Bergson spoke of, is now taking shape. Nature does not only produce privileged souls, but entire peoples that embody the civilizing drive of the elan vital. However, this era will not be inaugurated by Europe or the United States—because the white race already fulfilled its commitment and is frankly in decline—but rather by Latin America: "Only the Iberian part of the continent possesses the spiritual factors, the race, and the territory necessary for the great enterprise of initiating the new universal era of Humanity" (*The Cosmic Race* 38–39).

The "cosmic race" must be Catholic and conscious of having a universally redemptive mission. The spiritual regeneration of humanity will begin in Mexico, spread through all the countries of Latin America, and expand from there to every nation on earth. Vasconcelos had been developing this "providential plan" since the 1920s, when he attempted to make it reality as secretary of education and rector of UNAM. When he was asked to explain the meaning of the motto "Through my race the spirit will speak," which he ordered to be part of the UNAM coat of arms, he said that the eagle represents Mexico, while the condor symbolizes "the collective saga of the brother peoples of the continent." The two joined around the map of Latin America symbolizes "the unity of our race," whose universal mission is declared in this motto. And the "spirit" in question is the Holy Spirit, which symbolizes the highest moral ideals of humanity proclaimed by the Catholic religion (Vasconcelos, "Los motivos del escudo" 74–79).

Latin America will disseminate Christ's message everywhere and will create an original philosophy that is authentically Latin American, but universally valid because it will be based on intellectual knowledge, which is a faculty available to all men. Latin Americans will formulate the principles of a new interpretation of the world according to the fundamentally emotive specificity of their race.

3. SAMUEL RAMOS: PSYCHOANALYST OF MEXICAN CULTURE

Vasconcelos declared Latin America's entrance into cultural adulthood and the consequent advent of the "cosmic race." However, not all Mexican intellectuals shared his opinion. Behind the nationalist exaltation there was a hidden desire on the part of a certain segment of the political right to put a mask over Mexico's history. This suspicion inspired Samuel Ramos's critique of Vasconcelos's philosophical ideals. If, for the latter, history had situated Mexico in the enviable position of being able to embody superior forms of the human spirit, for Ramos this opinion was symptomatic of a *self-deception* that was developing in Mexican culture. What Ramos sought to do was sketch out the origins of this artifice and investigate *México profundo* in order to use criticism to shed light on what caused the Mexican people to fail, incapable of taking advantage of their historical opportunities. If Mexicans have failed in their attempts to achieve modernity, it is not the fault of "Anglo-Saxon imperialism," as Vasconcelos's nationalist rhetoric proclaimed, but rather due to the inherent vices of their own colonial legacy. Ramos argues that Mexico must become conscious of these vices, thus tearing off a nationalist disguise that has hidden the truth.

Ramos came from a liberal, middle-class family in Michoacán, and his philosophical education was primarily autodidactic. However, in 1945, he was named director of the Department of Philosophy and Literature at UNAM, as well as coordinator of the Humanities program until his death in 1959. Even since he was quite young, he repudiated Bergsonian vitalism—so dear to Vasconcelos—and was opposed to the Arielism personified by the intellectuals of the already legendary Ateneo de la Juventud. In an essay titled "El ocaso de Ariel" ("The twilight of Ariel" [1925]), Ramos rejected Rodó's romantic and sickly sweet tone and argued that his message of Latin American redemption had been thwarted. He also rejected the conventional, academic style of Antonio Caso and openly challenged his status as Mexico's philosopher king, which no one had questioned until that point (Miller, *In the Shadow of the State* 144–45). This harsh critique of the generation of the Ateneo intellectuals has a simple explanation: Ramos, like many other young intellectuals at the beginning of the 1930s, saw them as the symbol of an alliance between the idea of the philosopher as architect of "national identity," and the identification between the state and the nation, which had been declared by Mexican governments the previous decade. It was not until the events of 1928 and 1929 (the assassination of President-elect Obregón, the presidential election fraud, and the creation of the PRI) that some intellectuals began to identify a separation between the state and the nation. In his book *El perfil del hombre y la cultura en México*, published in 1934, Ramos outlines a forceful critique of the nationalist discourse of Mexicanness (*mexicanidad*), which was very fashionable at the time.

The central thesis of the book comes from the framework of Adlerian psychoanalysis: the "Mexican character" has functioned in accordance with a psychological mechanism that was primarily formed during the nation's cultural childhood. At the same time, Ramos tries to remind us that, for psychoanalysis, man is not an entity that exists independently in time, but rather is rooted in the past and determined by it. The way in which the past acts and determines present conduct depends on what this past's characteristics are, and studying this is precisely the object of psychoanalysis. Therefore we must pay attention to the fundamental experiences of childhood. As the patient that Ramos is examining is not an individual person but an entire culture, we will need to go back to this culture's historical childhood: "It seems to me that we should look for the historical origins of our race's feelings of inferiority in the Conquest and colonization" (*El perfil del hombre y la cultura en México* 100). Thus, it is a matter of discovering what this childhood fixation consists of, this fixation that conditions Mexican cultural life and prevents it from achieving the psychological maturity it needs to attain modernity.

Ramos begins his analysis noting that Mexican culture can be characterized from its very origins as a *derivative* culture: the Spanish conquistadors destroyed Indigenous cultures and transplanted their own to the Americas. This means that Mexican culture did not have a natural birth. It did not develop as the fruit of something rooted in its own soil, but rather was constituted by the insertion of foreign elements from a foreign culture. This transplanting was carried out by two powerful vehicles, language and religion, maintained by an institution that fought to pull the Spanish colonies out of modernity: the Catholic Church (103). The children of Spaniards and Indians, the mestizos, began to be educated on a foundation that included an absolute reverence for foreign culture, which was considered superior. Their own culture was seen as inferior and in need of "redemption." This is how the mestizo psychological profile is generated: the tendency toward mimesis.

> Mexicans have imitated for a long time, but without knowing what they are imitating. In good faith, they believed they were civilizing the country. Mimesis has been an unconscious phenomenon that reveals a peculiar feature of mestizo psychology. This is not the vanity of pretending to be a culture that has decided on imitation. Rather, this unconscious tendency hides the lack of culture not only from external view but also from Mexicans themselves. In order for something to be imitated, one must believe it is worth imitating. Thus, our mimeticism could not be explained if there were no clear understanding of the value of culture. However, as soon as this value is revealed to the Mexican consciousness, in comparison, our own reality is disdained, and the individual feels inferior. Therefore, imitation appears as a psychological defense mechanism that, by creating an appearance of culture, liberates us from that depressing feeling.
>
> (98)

Thinking of oneself as "different" produced feelings of fear and anxiety in the mestizo because this difference had been categorized as a mark of inferiority by the conquistadors. This is why the painful feeling of difference had to be eliminated by mimesis, by the steadfast imitation of the cultural models established by the conquistadors themselves, as well as by *burying one's head in the sand*: denying the unpleasant but actual reality in order to fit into comforting but false transplants. The feeling of inferiority, as Adler noted, appears in the child when he realizes how much less power he has in comparison to his parents.

To all this we can add the psychological character of the two races that gave rise to the mestizo: the Spanish and the Indigenous. The Spaniard, originally a passionate, individualist, and enterprising man, began to transform his psychology when he was confronted with a world that frightened and overwhelmed him (106). The only way he could find to protect himself from feeling inferior in the face of the virgin nature of the Americas was to take refuge in bureaucracy. Because of this, the criollos, direct descendants of the Spanish, became a lazy class resigned to inactivity. They did not consider work to be a virtue but rather a disgrace, an activity suitable only for slaves (107). The Indigenous populations, for their part, were inherently psychologically disposed toward passivity, resistant to any kind of change or renovation. Their lack of creativity can be seen in their artistic forms, which constantly repeat themselves. For Ramos, Indigenous architectonic style is revealed to be a "cheap fantasy," since it is dominated by religious ritualism. Ramos calls this basic feature of the Indigenous personality "Egyptianism."[3] Opposed to change and dynamism, the Spanish and the Indigenous peoples appeared as races that were not psychologically fit for the transformations demanded by the modern world. This explains why the changes that have taken place in Mexican history are more apparent than real, as they are disguises (fashions) that hide one and the same spiritual background: resistance to change. In Ramos's opinion, the history of Mexico is actually the unconscious repetition of a childhood neurosis (108).

Adler describes neurotic behavior as the tendency to set unrealistic goals for oneself, with the singular purpose of demonstrating one's superiority, which compensates for the anxiety generated by an unconscious conception of oneself as inferior. According to this definition, Ramos argues that the criollos who took charge of the destiny of young, postindependence nations in Latin America set a goal for themselves that was completely impossible: achieving modernity. This objective was unachievable because it was not supported by the real conditions of Mexican culture but rather an unconscious desire to identify with Europe. Before recognizing their own inability to be modern, nineteenth-century Mexican criollos preferred to take refuge in the realm of fiction, as this satisfied the compensatory impulse toward superiority (110). In the case of the criollos, this fiction of superiority became visible in the repulsion they felt toward all other Mexicans—Indians and peasants—that, according to them, lived "outside of civilization."

However, the criollos' imitation did not only consist in wanting to adopt foreign elements because they thought they were better than their own, but rather, unfortunately, they also thought that the reality they wanted this adoption to take place in was prepared for it. Mexican leaders imitated European leaders because they assumed that their nation was on par with modern nations, thus hiding the actual circumstances of Mexico and its own failure to be inventive and creative in proposing solutions. Ramos argues that, in addition to a defective ability to appreciate things, Mexicans suffer from pathological laziness and inertia. Mexican society lacks discipline and organization, and individuals drift like scattered atoms without any collective plan, similar to "a primitive horde in which men competed for things like hungry beasts" (123). Therefore, the Mexican is a being who lacks an internal equilibrium. He is continually tormented by the knowledge that he is inferior to people in modern countries, which causes him to have a foul disposition and be aggressive, touchy, and nervous. To compensate for this angst, he wants to be a man who dominates over all others due to his bravery and masculinity (124).

Ramos illustrates his thesis through an ingenious analysis of the Mexican *pelado*, the urban, lower-class, mestizo man who lives on the outer edges of the capital and who, in order to hide his social and economic weakness, has developed a fictitious personality that is diametrically opposed to reality. He operates on the basis of the masculine-feminine opposition, taken from Adler. This transfer of values is an attempt to alleviate the feelings of anxiety that are produced when one becomes conscious of one's own misery. The pelado seeks out conflict in order to bolster his own self-esteem, to find a point of support that allows him to recover faith in himself. All human power resides in the male sexual organs (*los huevos*—"balls"). The phallus suggests to him the idea of a power he actually does not have, but one that he wants to have (120). He uses foul and aggressive language, has an explosive temperament, and is to be approached with caution, and these ideas of masculinity are for him connected with nationality. As the pelado sees it, his race is characterized by machismo and bravery; even though Europeans and North Americans may be more educated and technologically developed, Mexicans feel superior to them because they are "braver and more manly":

> Even when the Mexican "*pelado*" is completely disgraced, he consoles himself by shouting to all the world that he has "big balls" [*muchos huevos*]. What is important is to declare that what resides in these organs is not only a kind of sexual power, but all kinds of human power. For the "*pelado*," when a man triumphs in any activity anywhere, it is because "he has big balls." . . . When he compares himself to civilized foreigners and his incompetence is laid bare, he consoles himself by saying: "A European has science, art, technology, et cetera, et cetera; we don't have any of that here, but . . . we are very masculine." Masculine in the zoological sense of the word, which is to say, a male who partakes of all his animal powers.
>
> (120)

Ramos concludes by saying, "As self-deception consists in believing that one already is what one wants to be, as soon as the Mexican is satisfied with his image, he abandons the effort to effectively improve himself" (126). Thus the Mexican avoids having to demonstrate to the world the bravery he brags about so much. Instead of achieving modernity through work (a sign of masculine activity) he prefers to spend years without undergoing any change (a sign of feminine passivity). While the modern world is transformed and new forms of life, art, and thought emerge, he continues "the same as one hundred years ago," and his life transpires in an Egyptian immutability. However, if someone dares to criticize him, he becomes aggressive and nationalistic. He needs to be convinced that others are inferior to him. As neurotic as it may be, "he lives enclosed within himself, like a crustacean in its shell, mistrustful of others, dripping with malice, so that no one will get close to him" (127).

Ramos's assessment of mestizaje, Hispanicness, and Catholicism is diametrically opposed to Vasconcelos's. Like the latter, he rejects indigenism, but he repudiates Vasconcelos's nationalist vision of a "cosmic race." Mestizaje has not helped to elevate but rather to debase the moral character of Mexican culture. Nor does Ramos share the vision of Anglo-Saxon culture as "spiritually inferior" to Latin culture, since he considers the belief that Latin American countries are superior to modern nations to be a defense mechanism justifying the cultural inability of Latin Americans to achieve modernity.

4. JOSÉ GAOS AND EDUARDO NICOL: THE POSSIBILITY OF A HISPANIC PHILOSOPHY

With the administration of President Lázaro Cárdenas, Mexican politics acquired a more nationalist and statist dimension. In spite of the reservations expressed by Arielist intellectuals, industrialization of the country was an inevitable process. Like almost all other Latin American countries, Mexico had to cope with the global economic crisis through import substitutions. Industrialization required significant investment in infrastructure, communication technology, energy production, and the construction of new factories, which implied a larger state intervention on behalf of the industrial sector. However, these measures had to be accompanied by improvements in the Mexican educational system. Therefore, Cárdenas created the Instituto Politécnico Nacional (National Polytechnical Institute) and supported the creation of other institutions like the Casa de España (which in 1940 changed its name to El Colegio de México), and the publishing house Fondo de Cultura Económica, initially conceived of as a way to educate Mexican technical workers in economics.

José Gaos left Spain in 1939, fleeing Francoism and the impending world war, just as his teacher José Ortega y Gasset had done the same year. However, while Ortega went to Argentina, Gaos headed to Mexico, as he had been invited by the first director of the recently founded Casa de España, the historian Daniel Cosío Villegas.[4] Gaos came to be rector of the University of Madrid in the middle of the Spanish Civil War, and at that point he was considered Ortega's favorite student. Other renowned Spanish philosophers arrived in Mexico both before and after Gaos did: Joaquín Xirau, José María Gallegos Rocafull, Luis Recasens Siches,

Eugenio Imaz, Eduardo Nicol, Adolfo Sánchez Vázquez, Ramón Xirau, María Zambrano, and Juan David García Bacca, all of whom unquestionably contributed to the formation of a "philosophical field" in Mexico (Medin, *Ortega y Gasset en la cultura hispanoamericana* 137–38).

It is more than just a commonplace to claim that Ortega y Gasset's philosophy found its fullest expression in Latin America in Gaos's work. In fact, Ortega's philosophy could not have found a more appropriate place to be accepted than Mexico in its nationalist, postrevolutionary period. Furthermore, there is no individual more appropriate for this dissemination than his favorite disciple, as there were few who experienced the same level of affinity with his teacher's thought as Gaos, who combined two of Ortega's theories and creatively developed them during his time in Mexico: the critique of rationalism and the idea of a Hispanic philosophy.

According to the rationalist presuppositions established in Plato's day and recuperated by European Enlightenment thinkers, philosophy is concerned with the "universal and necessary," with that which transcends spatiotemporal determinations and remains invariable. To ask about a concrete object of knowledge—like, for example, Spanish culture—is a matter for the empirical sciences, not philosophy. Based on these presuppositions, a "Mexican philosophy" or a "Spanish philosophy" is little more than an absurdity, a contradiction in terms. For this reason, what was attractive about Ortega y Gasset in Mexico and other Latin American countries was that he showed philosophy to be only truly philosophy as such when it reflects on the concrete *circumstances* in which it unfolds. In this regard, Ortega is similar to other philosophical currents of the time, such as phenomenology and existentialism, but with a significant difference: he does not limit himself to focusing on general problems of everyday life (as Heidegger did), rather, he aims to reflect on the *specific* qualities of his own Spanish culture in a European context. Like Heidegger, he argues that knowledge of reality always comes out of a concrete horizon, from the lived experience of the person who gains this knowledge (*Dasein*). However, Ortega goes beyond Heidegger to show that an essential part of that horizon is made up of problems related to one's mother tongue, national history, inherited cultural values, and the "racial" stability of the questioning subject. In his *Meditations on Quixote*, he writes: "The individual cannot get his bearings in the universe except through his race, because he is immersed in it like the drop of water in the passing cloud" (103).[5]

The thesis that allows Ortega y Gasset to take this turn toward a philosophical focus on national culture is formulated in the following terms: "I am myself plus my circumstance, and if I do not save it, I cannot save myself" (*Meditations on Quixote* 45). The basic idea is that philosophy begins with meditating on the things that are closest to us, that affect us most intensely. From a rationalist position, this thesis would imply a renunciation of grasping the truth, which is not given in the most immediate (multiple, empirical) things, but rather in those that are farthest away, in the ultimate principles of reality that are grasped by pure thought, abstracting from empirical circumstances. The result is a theory that is consistent with itself from a logical perspective but foreign to the reality of things and the enemy of life. Ortega, in contrast, establishes the need to do philosophy from within the circumstances in which we are immersed, because it is through those circumstances that the world is opened up to us: "My natural exit toward the universe is through the mountain passes of the Guadarrama or the plain of Ontígola. This sector of circumstantial reality forms the other half of my person; only through it can I integrate myself and be fully myself" (45).

In his 1945 book *Pensamiento de lengua española*, Gaos returns to the central motifs of Ortega's thought and argues, in light of the current crisis in Europe (the rise of fascism and the Second World War), that rationalist philosophy, with all its scientific and technological power, can no longer "save" Western culture because it has been one of the fundamental causes of the crisis. However, this failure of rationalism can and should be productive. Gaos refers to the fact that World War II generated in Europe the sensation of living in a world where principles have stopped being eternal in order to turn into organs of struggle, belligerent weapons (33). For the first time, and instigated by death and suffering, Europe became conscious of living in a world without principles. The fundamental lesson that Europe learned from the crisis is the radical historicity of all humanity and, therefore, the collapse of metaphysics.

The "salvation" of Western culture will need to be expressed through a historicist, asystematic, and literary form of thought that is capable of avoiding the traps of rationalism. Gaos opines that this thought will not come from Europe but rather from Hispanic countries, where rationalism never set down deep roots.[6] In contrast, what did put down roots in Latin America was an *immanentist* thought that, even if it did come from eighteenth-century Enlightenment Europe, took on, in this region of the world, different material and formal qualities than it had in Europe. Gaos's central thesis is that Latin America has known how to express, better than any other region of the West, the *radically antimetaphysical* spirit of the modern era. This is a proposition that directly contradicts Vasconcelos's opinion that Latin America embodies a mystical, Christian thought; it also clashes with Ramos's view that Spain and its colonies remained on the margins of Western cultural development.

Gaos shows that the Enlightenment broke with the metaphysical concern for the "beyond" and defined the task of thought as a preoccupation with the "things of life" and the problems of "this world." Human life is no longer oriented toward the "salvation of the soul" or the contemplation of nature and divine revelation, but rather toward the "business of being human." The Enlightenment defines human life as radical reality and displays a kind of asystematic thought (closely linked to the literary) that makes this reality its sole object of interest. Think, for example, of the thought of the French *philosophes* of the eighteenth century, closely resembling the literature of ideas and always applied to ethical, aesthetic, and political problems:

> It is possible that any undertaking of this nature must be, by this very nature itself and by its object and purpose, the work of [a] thought that is "applied"—in the senses of direction and of firmness and intensity—to "this world," "this life," "whatever is closest," with the correlative disregard—or feigned disregard—of any "other world," "other life," or "beyond;" the work of an ametaphysical, if not antimetaphysical, thought that is irreligious in the sense that it is indifferent to religion if not antireligious; the work of a thought that is simply inattentive to the "transcendental" that is hidden behind politics, ethics, aesthetics, and pedagogy—in sum, an *immanentism*.
>
> (GAOS, *PENSAMIENTO DE LENGUA ESPAÑOLA* 88)

Gaos's idea is that modern life came to Latin American countries under the influence of Enlightenment thought. The eighteenth century is not only the century of the French Revolution but also the century in which the spiritual preparation of Latin American revolutions took place. We are referring here not only to the wars of independence against Spanish colonialism but also to the process of spiritual and political reform that occurred both in Latin America and Spain during the eighteenth century known as the *Bourbon Reforms* (90). This is the same liberal, modern, and proto-republican movement that in the Americas brought about the process of independence and in Spain initiated the rupture with its traditional and imperialist self-image (38). But while this process achieved its objective in Latin America, in Spain it seems to have been interrupted, even thwarted, as shown by the triumph of Francoism and regression into what Ortega y Gasset called the "sanctimony" of traditionalist Spanish culture. On this topic, he argued that "Spain is its own last colony, it remains its own colony, the only Latin American nation that, from the common imperial past, is still not independent, not only spiritually but also politically" (40).

Gaos argues that modern life began in Latin America in the eighteenth century with Enlightenment, rather than rationalist, thought.[7] Thus on both sides of the continent there was a kind of asystematic and antimetaphysical thought that, beginning in the late eighteenth century generated the question of Latin America and, a century later, of Spain (53–54). Under the presuppositions of rationalism, this kind of questioning of national identity and culture would have been impossible. Thus Gaos fully identifies with his teacher Ortega y Gasset's basic thesis: if we want to save the West from the current crisis, we need a "vital reason" that can recognize the *radical historicity* of the human being. However, this reason is not expressed through hermeneutics, phenomenology, or existentialism, which continue to circle around the idea of a "philosophical system" and, for that matter, continue to be tied to some form of rationalism. In addition, he asserts that only in Latin America has philosophy become *thought* and abandoned the idea of a system in order to take essayistic, literary, political, aesthetic, and pedagogical forms. It is in "Latin American thought" that the Enlightenment project of the radical historicity of existence takes shape in the most sublime way.

However, not all Spanish philosophers who emigrated to Mexico shared Gaos's views. Greater or lesser sympathy with republican and/or nationalist ideas of the time, the position of power one occupied in Mexican academia, as well as the philosophical and political training one received in pre-Franco Europe overdetermined the way that each of these immigrants approached the topic of Latin American philosophy. Nevertheless, not many wrote about it. One who did was Eduardo Nicol, who arrived in Mexico in 1939—the same year as Gaos—and was immediately hired as a professor at UNAM, where he founded the Instituto de Investigaciones Filosóficas (Institute for Philosophical Research). In 1961, he published *El problema de la filosofía hispánica* [The problem of Hispanic philosophy), in which he responded to the arguments of Gaos and all supporters of a philosophical nationalism in Mexico.

Unlike Gaos, Nicol greatly valued the systematic, even scientific character of philosophy. Faithful to the classical tradition, he considered philosophy to be the only real and possible "science of sciences." All others are "particular sciences," specific manifestations of "that unique and radical desire for truth which was given the name of philosophy" (*El problema de la filosofía hispánica* 37). Therefore, like Ramos, he rejected any kind of "irrationalist" thought as well as any sign of cultural relativism in the field of science. If philosophy is a science, then it possesses a universal language that has no cultural particularities. "In its highest form of practice, philosophy lacks any *couleur locale*" (79). Just as it is impossible to speak of a Spanish physics or mathematics, it is also impossible to speak of a Spanish philosophy—at most, one can say there is a Spanish contribution to the common and universal heritage that is "philosophy" (34–35). Nicol's position is at first glance opposed to Gaos's. Hence his equally different evaluation of Ortega's thought and influence. Although he does not question the importance of Ortega's work, he does lament the "essayistic" quality of his thought. Ortega tried to be a philosopher in the strict sense of the word, but he did not fulfill his promise, since his thought lacked the great inspiration that only comes to great philosophers through methodical and systematic investigation (250–52).

Although Nicol takes up the challenge of reflecting at length on the "problem of Hispanic philosophy," he takes care to explain that these analyses do not have philosophical qualities and therefore are not the work of "professional" philosophers but rather "intellectuals" who participate in public debate:

> I do not know if I need to remind you, before entering into the material in depth, that these reflections on Hispanic philosophy are nothing

> other than "ideology." This is not science. I reiterate my clarification of this point, not to justify myself, but rather to inform you that you should not grant my opinions the same authority that is always possessed by scientific theories. These opinions revolve around the small history of our philosophy. It is normal, or better stated, it is common to explain with greater emphasis and to defend more vigorously opinions rather than scientific ideas. This is explained by the fact that, the more valid these ideas are for all, the more easily those who thought of them let go of them. While we, as always, remain very attached to our personal opinions, to the extent that we identify with them and consider any discrepancy that arises to be an affront.
>
> (45)

Nicol situates his reflections on Hispanic philosophy in the field of *doxa* and not in the field of *episteme*, since the question of the possibility or necessity of such a philosophy is necessarily *prescientific*, that is to say, it is located in the realm of personal opinion. This is precisely the great problem philosophical activity has had in Latin America: it seems that philosophy cannot be practiced here without previously debating the nature and style of what one wants to do. While the French, English, or Germans do what they do without talking so much about it, without wondering if what they are doing is original or not, Latin Americans want to extensively discuss what they *should* do before they do it (21). Given these conditions, Nicol wants to participate in the debate, certain that it is an "ideological" discussion that has nothing to do with the practice of philosophy *sensu stricto*. And he wants to do it not so much because the topics up for debate are interesting in and of themselves but rather because they have to do with understanding Latin American culture, which Nicol, even though he is a philosopher, feels part of as an individual.

According to Nicol, with the exception of activity within colonial universities in the seventeenth and eighteenth centuries, one could say that philosophy has never existed in Latin America, only *philosophical ideologies*. For this reason, the history of philosophy in Latin America ("the small history of our philosophy") has to be divided into two stages: the first is the prephilosophical (doxic, strictly speaking) era in which philosophical theses were still to be found mixed with political ideologies; the second is characterized by the shift from doxa to episteme, that is to say, by the slow professionalization of the practice of philosophy, which Francisco Romero called the "normalization" of philosophy (46). The first stage began in the nineteenth century and extended into the twentieth, while the second stage is still beginning to take shape, and it is not yet possible to discuss it with sufficient distance. Nicol therefore focuses on the history of the prephilosophical era, which he divides into two further stages corresponding to two kinds of ideologies: the ideology of independence and the ideology of revolution.

When the leaders of Latin American revolution against Spain completed their task, they found themselves before an even greater challenge: it was becoming necessary to construct new Latin American nationalities through the elaboration of an ideology that would account for "national being" and contribute to the creation of an autonomous, distinctive, and culturally appropriate ethos. A series of *thinkers* emerged that put themselves to the task of reflecting on the problem of "national identity" (Bello, Montalvo, Sarmiento, Lastarria, Varona, Martí, Rodó, and others), using certain concepts taken from philosophy. Nicol insists that this was a political and not a theoretical matter, which for philosophy as it is practiced would have to be a genre of ideology, but not scientific or speculative (52). These thinkers' originality lay not in the contributions some of them made to the universal tradition of philosophy but in the *passion* with which they used philosophical ideas in their capacity as politicians and educators. None of them contributed, for example, to the formation of a new philosophical concept of "Man," but simply adopted the idea of man formed by the European Enlightenment. For this reason—much to their chagrin—their ideas did not have any significant impact on the population, only on the lettered minority. Society did not undergo any transformation in either its structure or in its habits and customs. The ideology of independence never became a revolutionary ideology (57).

Another very distinct thing happened toward the end of the twentieth century in Mexico, where there was a political rebellion without any precedent in Latin America. Nicol argues that this case is "exemplary" because the uprising generated a nationalist ideology that sought to resolve the question of "national being" (59). Only now the philosophical tools that were used didn't come from either eighteenth-century

Enlightenment thought or from positivism, but rather from vitalism and historicism. Without mentioning names, Nicol appears to be referring to the thinkers affiliated with the Ateneo de la Juventud. The tone of this new ideology is optimistic, as it corresponds to all thought that is based on a revolutionary process (72). Revolutionary ideologues express their confidence in Mexico's and Latin America's promising future. They know that, unlike what occurred in Europe, the peoples of Latin America are more open and willing to change. However, Nicol argues that in this case the same thing happened as with the ideology of independence in the previous century: what they produced was not philosophy but political ideology in "philosophical packaging."

It is precisely this nonrigorous, prescientific perspective that explains why some revolutionary ideologies, in spite of their optimistic tone, have made use of philosophies that are asynchronic with their own local character. This is the case with Ortega y Gasset's circumstantialism and Sartre's existentialism, philosophies that came from within a Europe that was in significant decline (74–75). Ortega's thought has negative and irrationalist overtones, which can be explained by its origins in a situation of despair: assessing Spain's peripheral situation with regard to the countries of central Europe; Sartre's existentialism was also born out of the despair, if not desperation, that was produced by the crisis of the European bourgeoisie after the war. The extemporaneous adaptation of this philosophical pessimism to a situation of optimism and cultural rebirth, such as Latin America was experiencing in the middle of the twentieth century, can only be explained by the ideological way in which Ortega and Sartre were received there.

However, in the 1970s, Nicol asserted that the moment when Latin American philosophy would finally overcome the prescientific baggage that had held it down until then had finally arrived: "At this point in time, Latin American philosophy already has the necessary technical resources to pose the problem of man in the universal terms of episteme, of philosophy as a rigorous science" (72). This means that economic, political, and social crises should not be considered from the point of view of man as man. After the last world war, the world certainly experienced a cultural shift that must be taken up as a philosophical problem and not remain only of concern to the economics or politics of this or that country, but rather, fundamentally, to the ethos of man (77). The problem is essentially ethical, and now Latin American philosophers must address it without having to be preoccupied by feeling different from their colleagues in other parts of the world. The Latin American philosopher will overcome his condition of being "Latin American" to the extent that he converts what can happen to him as an *individual* into material for reflection on what can happen to *man* (66).

5. LEOPOLDO ZEA: THE PHILOSOPHY OF LATIN AMERICAN HISTORY

When José Gaos took on the position of instructor at the Colegio de México, he was assigned to teach a collective seminar on Latin America that, besides reading selected "classics" of Latin American thought, also included discussion of contemporary topics in economics, politics, and society (Gómez-Martínez, *Pensamiento de la liberación* 117). Some of the most important Latin American philosophers of the following decades participated in this seminar, including: Edmundo O'Gorman, Augusto Salazar Bondy, Fernando Salmerón, Antonio Gómez Robledo, Luis Villoro, Francisco Miró Quesada, Emilio Uranga, and a young student who had to work nights as a postal employee in order to finance his education named Leopoldo Zea. From very early on, Gaos recognized Zea's philosophical potential and encouraged him to write *El positivismo en México* (*Positivism in Mexico*), earning him a scholarship to complete his studies in the United States. In fact, Zea quickly became Gaos's most fervent successor and the Latin American herald of his basic idea: the formulation and valorization of a "Latin American" philosophy.

Leopoldo Zea was interested from a very young age in Ortega's thesis of the "salvation of circumstances" (see Medin, *Ortega y Gasset en la cultura hispanoamericana* 7–36). He knew, as did his teacher Gaos, that the authenticity of philosophical discourses does not depend on the logical relations these ideas maintain with themselves, but rather on the way in which they are used to resolve important problems. Out of this perspective, Zea formulated the following question: What kind of discourses have been articulated in Latin America in response to the region's historical needs? Has it simply been a matter of the ideological reception of European philosophy, as Nicol argues, or is it about truly creative and original responses? Zea devoted his doctoral thesis, published as *Positivism in Mexico*, to responding to these questions and to studying the impact of positivist ideas in Mexican politics toward the end of the nineteenth century.

As Zea writes, this study "deals with a problem that concerns all philosophies. It is the problem of the relationship between philosophy and history, that is, the relationship between ideas and their reality" (*Positivism in Mexico* 3). What Zea wants to investigate is not positivism as a set of abstract theories that are disconnected from social reality, as appears to be the case, for example, in the "histories of philosophy" that are commonly studied in universities. If the most important thing were to investigate only the internal and universal development of positivist ideas, then only a few names would be relevant (Auguste Comte, John Stuart Mill, Herbert Spencer, Ernst Haeckel), without taking into account either their biography or their cultural background (4). What *Mexican* positivists might have said or thought is completely uninteresting, as they would have contributed nothing to the universal heritage of positivist philosophy (recall Nicol's thesis). Furthermore, we can confirm that all these Mexican thinkers did was repeat the ideas of European positivists, and, even worse, they were "poor imitations," lacking in the least scientific rigor (5). However, if what one wants to investigate is not positivism as a philosophical doctrine but rather its significant relations with a specific historical circumstance (in this case, the Mexican circumstance), then the hermeneutic perspective radically changes:

> Ortega said that "an idea is an act that man performs in view of predetermined circumstances and a definite end. . . . Every philosophy possesses truth proportionate to reality, provided this reality is historical rather than permanent. It is impossible to jump the fence of history. When history changes, philosophy, too, has to change, since it is a philosophy of reality, which is historical. . . . Instead of dealing with abstractions, one connects these ideas with the culture in which they appear. . . . Positivism may be a doctrine with universal appeal, but the form in which it was interpreted and applied by the Mexicans is Mexican. To understand the Mexican interpretation of positivism, it is necessary to examine Mexican history, that is, the history of those who

> used positivism to justify their interests, which were not the same as the interests of the founders of positivism.
>
> (7, 9–10, 12)

The originality of positivism in Mexico originates in how this doctrine was used by certain individuals to resolve a series of social, political, and educational problems. Therefore, if what is addressed here are the historical circumstances in which these ideas have taken shape, and not thought itself as a system that is disembodied from ideas, then we can see what is completely invisible to Nicol: the originality of Latin American philosophy. Here we can clearly see Zea's desire to affirm his own Mexican reality and to discover everything that could be authentic about it in relation to European culture, which entailed a critique of Nicol's argument that before the twentieth century there was no properly philosophical consciousness in Latin America.

Nevertheless, Zea agrees with Nicol on one point: one can only think philosophically if one addresses man as man, and not the situation of this or that man in particular. Thus, if Zea claims to consider philosophical ideas in their historical circumstantiality, it is because he is convinced it is the only possible way to access knowledge of the Latin American man as a member of the human community. In his opinion, it is not through a "scientific," universal theory that one gains knowledge of the human, but rather through the knowledge of how specific men take charge of their own historical circumstances:

> Philosophy is a way to interpret man. Man is a being with many activities, including philosophy. Thus, to understand man, that is, to understand what kind of being he is, it is necessary to interpret his different activities. . . . Philosophical concepts in themselves are not important; what is important is the "why" of philosophical concepts. This "why" is found in history. It is necessary to look for the philosophical "why" of certain men in the history of their civilization and in their own biographies.
>
> (10)

Studying positivism in Mexico revealed to Zea how a group of individuals sought to understand the problems of the Mexican circumstance at the end of the nineteenth century, using European conceptual tools to gain awareness of the Mexican world and transform it according to specific interests. For Zea, it is through this "coming to consciousness" that the Latin American man has begun to humanize and value himself as a member of the human community. The *history of ideas* thus becomes the means to achieve a philosophical knowledge of how the Latin American man has conceived of himself as valuable. The philosopher's task is therefore to reconstruct and interpret this history of ideas, demonstrating how it reveals what it means to be "Man" in this part of the planet.

In his 1952 essay "La filosofía como compromiso" ("Philosophy as commitment"), Zea returns to the question of the relationship between history and philosophy, supported by Jean-Paul Sartre's existentialist thesis.[8] Ortega's idea of the "salvation of circumstances," which was at the center of Zea's investigation of positivism in Mexico, is now seen from the Sartrean perspective of *commitment* (*engagement*) that the philosopher enjoys with his own world. In the case of the Latin American thinker, this responsibility should be expressed in the development of a historical theory that can show the "place" to which Latin American peoples belong in the scope of world history:

> But what should we, the Americans, or more specifically, we, the Latin Americans, take on? For what situation must we be responsible? What comments must our philosophy responsibly make? After all, if we are to be faithful to what we have laid out here, we have to affirm that our *situation* is not that of Jean-Paul Sartre. Our *situation* is not that of the European bourgeoisie. Our philosophy, if it is to be responsible, does not have to make the same commitments that contemporary European philosophy does. . . . It is also for this reason that we want a philosophy that makes itself aware of the *position* that falls to Latin American peoples within this community, to take responsibility for it. . . . The not wanting to become aware of our *situation* explains in part why we have been unable to have our own philosophy, as other great peoples of the world have. What would our philosophy attend to? What kind of person or what kind of culture would it *rescue*? In the face of what situation would philosophy develop? About what would our philosophers philosophize?
>
> (ZEA, "PHILOSOPHY AS COMMITMENT" 137–38)

Zea's philosophical project, as he saw it in 1952, was the construction of a *philosophy of history* that would bring Latin American peoples to consciousness regarding their place in universal history and ultimately allow them to take responsibility for it. It would have to begin by showing how Latin Americans have used the conceptual tools of European philosophy to take control of their own problems. Zea sees positivism, romanticism, the Enlightenment, and historicism as "currents of thought" that were not brought to Latin America in order to be theoretically discussed in the ivory towers of academe but rather to be applied to reality and to resolve practical problems. The task of a Latin American philosophy would be to disentangle the internal logic of this appropriation of ideas and thereby to access this sense of its history. Zea sees this philosophical coming-to-consciousness as an indispensable requirement for Latin America to shape a society based on its own interests and whose inhabitants are fully developed people responsible for themselves and humanity as a whole.

Understood by Zea as the ability to creatively resolve problems of circumstance, "thought" is the means through which men become humanized and recognize themselves as such. In this process, *intellectual elites* play a fundamental role (as Ortega had already seen), because they direct and articulate thought according to the needs of the present. In Zea's view, it is through his thinkers and letrados that the "Latin American man" acquired knowledge of what he has been, is, and could be in history. It is from this perspective that the task of a "philosophy of Latin American history" would set about analyzing the underlying logic of these intellectual elites' adaptation of European philosophical models.

In his book *Filosofía de la historia americana* (1978), Zea describes the internal logic of these adaptations as a result of the efforts of Latin Americans to do away with their own past. Letrados see Latin American reality itself as something strange and imperfect that must be abruptly denied, so as to construct over its ruins a completely different reality that is influenced by philosophical models from Europe and the United States (17). This means that the adoption of foreign ideas was motivated by the desire to be free of a past seen as the root of all the continent's evil. The meaning of Latin American history resides in the continued juxtaposition of what Zea calls "historical projects." Thus, for example, the *Hispanic project* of colonization in the sixteenth century wanted to completely deny the history of the Indigenous, pre-Colombian past and adopt the humanist ideals of the European Renaissance. The *project of liberty* of the eighteenth-century criollos attempted to deny their Spanish past through the adoption of Enlightenment ideas. The *civilizing project* of the emergent bourgeoisie in the nineteenth century sought to deny the racial mestizaje of the previous four centuries by embracing positivism, etc. In all these examples, Latin American elites help themselves to European philosophical currents so as to construct a society that might realize the humanist ideal of freedom, which Zea, like Hegel, considers the ultimate goal of universal history. It is just that in Latin America the path to achieving it took a different direction, opposed to what Hegel attributes to Europe in his philosophy of history:

> The philosophy of [European] history, exemplarily expressed in Hegel, will therefore be the antipode of the philosophy of history expressed in our America. The philosophy of European or Western history is characterized by Hegelian *Aufhebung*, which Gaos discusses. It is a dialectical philosophy that makes the past a tool of the present and the future through an effort to absorb or assimilate. . . . In this sense, our philosophy of history is its antipode, stubborn as it has been in closing its eyes to reality itself, including its past, attempting to ignore it by regarding it as improper and foreign. . . . Thus, on the one hand, European or Western history as a history of absorption or assimilation, and on the other, Latin American history, built of juxtapositions.
>
> (119)

While Europe historically achieved freedom for men through a *dialectical* process in which the past is assimilated and integrated into a future-oriented project, in Latin America the opposite occurred: the road to freedom was not dialectical but rather took place in fits and starts; the past was not assimilated to the present and projected to the future (as in *Aufhebung*), rather it was categorically denied, juxtaposing foreign models over it. Instead of constructing on top of the foundations that had been built in the past, as had been the case in Europe, Latin Americans chose to destroy those foundations and then rebuild them time and time again. While Europe developed its own tools for building the future, Latin America denied its own abilities and took what others had already done, believing it to be superior. Borrowing an expression from Antonio Caso, Zea writes that *Bovarism* is the logic that runs throughout all of Latin American history, from the sixteenth century to the beginning of the twentieth. Like Flaubert's heroine, Madame Bovary, Latin America organized its own economic, political, and social life on top of the denial of its own reality and the consequent adoption of a foreign reality (20), always denying what has been, so as to project over the void that which it wants to be.

However, Zea points out that this "logic of Bovarism," which is in line with Samuel Ramos's pessimistic diagnosis, is evidence that the path taken by European knowledge is not the only one that leads to the ultimate goal of universal history. Like Hegel, Zea is convinced that history is the path that humanity as a whole follows toward a definite goal at which all the peoples of the earth will have to arrive, sooner or later. For Zea, universal history has *one* direction and *one* finality of its own—the full humanization of man—in which Latin American history in particular necessarily participates. Through their moral life, art, political institutions, and, above all, philosophy, each of the historical peoples represents a link in the universal process of the knowledge of himself that man continues to gain. The end is certainly the same for everyone, but the paths each of us takes is different. Although the dialectic was perhaps the most appropriate historical trajectory for Europe, what is certain is that Latin America also managed to arrive at the same destination, just by other routes.

To demonstrate this thesis, Zea begins with the Hegelian prophecy according to which the struggle over the unfolding of human possibilities could one day be transferred to Latin America, taking the form of a dialectical confrontation between North America and South America. Dead in 1831, Hegel was unable to witness the impressive and meteoric rise of the United States as a military and technological power in the twentieth century, nor did he witness the constant struggle in Latin America for economic, political, and social liberation. Thus Zea proposes to take up Hegel's narrative once again and reconstruct, from the perspective of the late twentieth century, a process that was for Hegel still a distant prediction. In the introduction to his book *Dialéctica de la conciencia americana* (Dialectic of Latin American consciousness [1976]), Zea writes:

> In this book, we will talk about the ups and downs, the victories and defeats of this struggle through which the spirit, and the humanity embodied by the peoples that make up America in its double expression in an attempt to continue the narrative of the history of the spirit that in Hegel had reached the extraordinary stage represented by the French Revolution of 1789 and its American predecessor, the revolution of 1776. In this revolution, Hegel could see the specificity of a future of which he did not want to speak, refusing to make predictions. We are attempting a philosophy of history in our America, as a concrete expression of the history of humanity striving to achieve the idea of liberty for all, to achieve its maximum expression.
>
> (21)

Closely following Hegel's prediction, Zea contemplates the history of the Latin American continent as the result of a confrontation between "Anglo-Saxon consciousness," which is heir of the libertarian ideals of European modernity, and the "Latin consciousness," which claims its own part of this inheritance. Here he adopts and modifies one of the central themes of the Arielist thought of Rodó and Vasconcelos: approaching with caution the technological and political imperialism of the United States. While Hegel thought North America would play a civilizing role in this process, Zea wants to show that the German philosopher's intuition was based on a half-truth, as, although the United States certainly took over from Europe and embodied Western ideals of freedom in extraordinary fashion, it was a freedom reserved exclusively for themselves and systematically denied to other men. The United States, the first country in history to announce the right of all men to be free, resisted recognizing this same right for Latin American peoples throughout the entire twentieth century. Even worse, in the name of freedom, equality, and brotherhood, the United States used Latin America as a tool in the service of its own economic and political interests and generated anti-U.S. sentiment and struggles for cultural autonomy.

What Zea attempts to show is that the struggle against U.S. imperial aggression unleashed the *assumptive project*, the moment when Latin America returns to itself and definitively assumes its past.[9] As a result of the United States' repeated interventions in the Caribbean in the late nineteenth century, the new urban bourgeoisie and intellectuals began to realize the need to politically challenge the economic and military expansion of the large nation to the North. Thus a nationalist, Latin Americanist spirit began to develop, first appearing in the Mexican Revolution of 1910. Demand for national sovereignty, the socialization of private property, centralization of political power, the protective leadership of the state, import substitutions, the cult of heroes and caudillos were all policies adopted for the first time in Mexico and then later adopted by other Latin American countries during the first half of the twentieth century: from the APRA in Peru and the Batllist Revolution in Uruguay, to Getulio Vargas's Estado Novo in Brazil and Peronism in Argentina, finally culminating in the Cuban Revolution of 1959.

With these political movements (and taking advantage of the conjuncture of the economic crisis generated by two world wars in Europe), Latin America was able to successfully confront U.S. imperialist expansionism and to become aware of their own strengths and abilities. The "libertarian wave" of Latin American populism, led in the twentieth century by nationalist intellectuals and the bourgeoisie, demanded Latin America's right to participate in the same benefits that modernity had brought to European nations: economic prosperity, democracy, political freedoms, cultural autonomy, and social justice. For the first time, a region of the Third World demanded the same rights the colonizing powers had declared all over the world but had refused to recognize in other nations. The significance of this fact is, in Zea's view, universal, as it opened up the path toward a true humanization for *all* humanity:

> It would be from America and in America that the spirit, conscious of a larger freedom, would confront itself in order to give birth to a new humanity. It will be this struggle that gives meaning to the history of [Latin] America in the twentieth century. A history that will transcend its natural borders as part of a larger history in which the final destiny of humanity will be judged. In the demands for freedom born

in [Latin] America, many other peoples will find the meaning of their own demands.

(22–23)

In his philosophy of history, and revisiting a central motif of Gaos's thought, Leopoldo Zea presents twentieth-century Latin America as the leader of a new consciousness of humanity that will replace an exhausted Europe, completing the mission begun by the United States in the nineteenth century. It was in Latin America that the processes of decolonization began, many years later taken up by other regions of the world, like Africa, Asia, and Oceania. The flags raised in the 1960s by Third World leaders like Nasser, Ho Chi Minh, and Yasser Arafat, were those raised *previously* in Latin America by figures such as Emiliano Zapata, Lázaro Cárdenas, Getulio Vargas, Juan Domingo Perón, Víctor Manuel Haya de la Torre, and other politicians of the time. All of them realized that nationalism was the only way Latin America could return to itself and resist the imperialist voraciousness of its powerful neighbor. As Zea explains, "A nationalism that was neither xenophobic nor chauvinistic, but rather a recovery of the habits, customs, and institutions of the triple Amerindian, African, and Spanish legacy, that is, of all those elements that constitute Latin American identity" (144). Through its autarkic policies, the national-populist state opened up a path that would later be shown to be viable for all oppressed Third World nations. Starting with the consciousness Latin America acquired of its own cultural identity, the human being began a new stage in the universal process of humanization.

6. EMILIO URANGA AND EDMUNDO O'GORMAN: THE ONTOLOGY OF LATIN AMERICA

In 1948, a handful of young Mexican philosophers decided to found a working group called Hiperión. The group consisted of Ricard Guerra, Joaquín Sánchez Macgrégor, Jorge Portilla, Salvador Reyes Nevares, Emilio Uranga, Fausto Vega, and Luis Villoro—all students of José Gaos,[10] who was very proud of his young "Hyperions" because he saw in them the culmination of his efforts as a professor, to the extent that he eventually claimed this philosophical movement was, in the history of Mexican ideas, comparable to the distinguished group of thinkers affiliated with the Ateneo de la Juventud (Díaz Ruanova, *Los existencialistas mexicanos* 201). Villoro, a founding member, expressed the group's intentions as follows:

> The Hiperión Group encourages a conscious project of [Mexican] *self knowledge* that provides us with the basis for a subsequent transformation. It is no longer strictly a question of what the circumstance is like but rather of the principles that condition and account for it. From historical and psychological investigation, there is a shift to *ontological inquiry*, which accounts for the elements of our history and psychology, bringing these elements back to the *ontic qualities* on which they are based. And the philosophy that justifies this new project will no longer be historicism. Rather, existential philosophy, which addresses being and not just mere occurrence, will provide the appropriate tools to justify the task.
>
> ("EMILIO URANGA" 105–6)

The characteristic theme of the Hiperión Group is the *ontological* nature of Mexican being. Even though philosophers such as Vasconcelos, Caso, Ramos, and even Gaos himself had already taken on the concern of moving toward a Mexican *self-gnosis*, none of them had done it using the concepts of existentialist philosophy. All used privileged historical, political, or psychological elements in their analysis, forgetting that an investigation of "Mexican being" must be carried out in terms of a *fundamental ontology*, such as was formulated by Heidegger, and not in historicist terms, as Ortega y Gasset did. Therefore, in contrast to Eduardo Nicol, for whom the adoption of existentialism as a method to think the problem of Mexicanness was a symptom of philosophical atavism and immaturity, the members of the Hiperión Group believed that philosophical knowledge par excellence is constituted by fundamental ontology. If what one wants is to arrive at a *philosophical* knowledge of what it means to be Mexican or Latin American, it is necessary to abandon the humanist and historicist categories that have set the frame of the problem up until now.

Emilio Uranga, recognized by Villoro as the "elder brother" of the group, the *primus inter pares*, devoted himself perhaps most intensely to the development of an "ontology of the Mexican" program. This program was established with his polemical book, *Análisis del ser mexicano* (Analysis of Mexican being), published in 1952 and dedicated to his friend, the poet and essayist Octavio Paz.[11] His criticism addressed all thinkers who studied Mexican culture in anthropological terms. Uranga cites the famous paragraph 10 from *Being and Time*, where Heidegger affirms that the question of Dasein must precede the question of man, and therefore any analysis of culture that privileges aspects of the biological, historical, or psychological order is condemned to fail. Actually, Heidegger argues, one can only respond to the question of man from an existential analytic, because humanity is not something that man "has," but rather something that "happens" to him. This is an *ontological* rather than ontic problem. Thus, knowledge of man as Dasein is not a problem that must be solved by the sciences of biology, history, psychology, or anthropology, but rather is a task for philosophical ontology.

Based on these premises, Uranga argues that the ontology of the Mexican should methodically precede all other investigations of the Mexican man. The question of the Mexican cannot be adequately addressed in terms of race (Vasconcelos), circumstance (Gaos, Zea), his humanity (Nicol), or his psychology (Ramos) if the ontological foundations of Mexicanness are not dealt with first. "More radical than speaking of the Mexican as a man is speaking of the Mexican as a being" (Uranga, *Análisis del ser mexicano* 61). It is a matter of showing that the Mexican's Mexicanness is a point of reference that is *ontologically prior* to his humanity. The question then becomes, what are the ontological qualities that characterize the Mexican and make him the being that he is and not another?

Uranga again bases his argument on Heidegger's critique of Western metaphysics and claims that the philosophical tradition conceives of man's being as "substance" and not as "accident," in such a way that substance appears as what is genuine while accident is barely a "shadow" of being, an "imperfect" being with no foundation (57). This was the metaphysical conception of being that the Spanish conquistadors brought to the Americas. The famous sixteenth-century polemic over the "humanity of the Indian" centered on a *question of foundation*: does the Indian have a soul—that is to say, substance—or not? The ontological model used as the criterion to measure a man's substantiality was medieval

European Scholasticism. Thus, some philosophers of the time believed that the Indian was without substance and was merely an accident, which one could and must enslave. Uranga suggests that the metaphysical conception of being has formed the basis of all Western colonialist projects: "In ontological terminology: all interpretation of man as a substantial creature strikes us as inhuman. At the origins of our history, we were devalued for not being like European "man." With the same spiritual slant, today we return to that qualification and do not recognize as "human" anything constructed in Europe that is based on the substantiality of human "dignity" (62). Always based on Heidegger, Uranga attempts to subvert this colonial vision of being and think Mexicanness from a *postmetaphysical* point of view. This means that instead of privileging substance as what is "truly human," it becomes necessary to show that man is constitutionally accidental and, as such, can only be humanized to the extent that he lives in close proximity to death. Man, as Heidegger would say, is a "being-toward-death." Any attempt at substantialization implies a "forgetting of Being" and is for that very reason a step toward "inauthentic existence" (62).

It is now clear what Uranga's philosophical project consists of: the positive evaluation of all the qualities of the Mexican that Ramos identified as an "inferiority complex." The mistrust with which the Mexican approaches everything, the melancholia and reluctance of his character, the cult of death he professes—these are not deviations from some Eurocentric and substantialist model of humanity, but rather they show his proximity to the accidental and thus constitute a proof of his authenticity. The Mexican *is* accidental, and thus he is an authentic "man." For him, life does not possess the "sporting," comforting, and harmonious quality that it does for the European (in his blind will to substantialization), but rather is controlled by a "vague and obscure suffering" (64). As accident, the Mexican is constantly threatened by displacement, with nothing to hold on to, always out in the cold. However, it is precisely in this ontological precariousness that his authenticity and advantage over nihilistic tendencies originates.

Criticizing the humanist ideals of the Ateneo de la Juventud from Heidegger's fundamental ontology can also generate a reading that is very different from Uranga's. The "forgetting of Being" (*Seinsvergessenheit*) that Heidegger discusses could be directed against the historical optimism espoused by Zea, Gaos, and their disciples in the Hiperión Group. The thesis that Latin America—with Mexico at its head—will, at some point, finally take on the role of providing spiritual leadership to the postwar Western world could be revealed as a symptom of the inauthentic way in which Latin American man has always experienced his own temporality. This is the suspicion that inspired philosopher and historian Edmundo O'Gorman to compose his book *La invención de América* (*The Invention of America*), published in 1958.

O'Gorman is interested in the particular way that Latin American historiography has functioned and therefore turns to chapter 5 of division 1 of *Being and Time*, where Heidegger develops his ideas about history as a science and criticizes the vulgar idea according to which the past is something that has "already happened" and that has nothing to do with the present. For Heidegger, this is an "inauthentic" understanding of temporality held by people who are incapable of approaching life as a freely chosen project. The vulgar person who does not assume his life as his own represents the past as a kind of tomb for inert moments that have already ceased to be. In contrast, the "authentic" person freely assumes their temporality and represents the past as an integral part of the present. To take on life as a *project* means being able to choose for oneself the possibilities that are opened between birth and death, that is, to take advantage of one's own temporal legacy in order to integrate it in a creative project ("handing oneself down").

All of this shows that the understanding of what history is does not depend on how scientific historiography is, but rather on a "*factical existential choice*" of what elements "deserve" to be objects of study for historical science (Heidegger, *Being and Time* 447). For Heidegger, the question of the "Being of history" is only possible from a preunderstanding of temporality that is rooted in everyday life (*Lebenswelt*). The *meaning* that historiography gives to history depends on the form (authentic or inauthentic) in which people live their own temporality *here and now* (444). What people understand by "history," as an object of historical science, ultimately depends on a prescientific choice.

When O'Gorman then asks about how historiography functions in Latin America, what he wants to know is the way that Latin Americans have "lived" their own temporality. He is encouraged by the suspicion that the "mythology of Latin America" constructed by Reyes, Vasconcelos, Diego Rivera, and other Mexican intellectuals in previous decades is a *symptom* of the "inauthentic" way that Latin Americans have always lived their own lives.[12] From this point of view, O'Gorman's arguments are different from those of Uranga and closer, in fact, to those of Samuel Ramos: Latin America has always lived in a fiction, believing in the possibility of actualizing a modern way of life for which it was not *ontologically* prepared.

O'Gorman proposes to refute the ontic vision of Latin American history held by the intellectuals of the Ateneo de la Juventud: Latin America as a "thing in itself." For him, this vision "springs from a previous assumption in their way of thinking, which, as an a priori principle, conditions all of their reasoning and which, at least since the time of the Greeks, has been one of the foundations of Western philosophical thought. We allude to the ancient and venerable idea that things are something in themselves, *per se*" (O'Gorman, *The Invention of America* 40–41). We should recall that, for Heidegger, Western metaphysics from Plato to Nietzsche has inquired about beings (*Seiende*) but not about the Being of beings, which has led to a "forgetting" or hiding of Being (*Sein*). Therefore, metaphysics must be destroyed in order to open up the path to ontology. And it is precisely this that O'Gorman attempts: a *destruction of Latin American metaphysics.*

According to O'Gorman's reconstruction, the idea of Latin America as a "thing in itself" appears with the Renaissance representation of the "discovery of the Americas." The ontic meaning of Columbus's voyage has its roots in the metaphysical conceptions of the world that predominated in the fifteenth century. O'Gorman refers specifically to the medieval idea of the *orbis terrarum*: the earth is a giant island divided into three parts, Europe, Asia, and Africa, which God has granted to humanity to inhabit. Columbus believed that the lands at which he had arrived were one part of this giant island, specifically Asia. To his knowledge, he had not discovered a "New World," but rather had arrived in an unprecedented way to the same world that had always been known, the only world *thinkable* in that era (116). Thus the idea that Columbus "discovered America" had nothing to do with Columbus himself, but rather only began to take hold with Amerigo Vespucci, who declared that the lands Columbus had reached were a *different* part of the *orbis terrarum*: neither Europe nor Asia nor Africa (114). Vespucci—not Columbus—conceived of the hypothesis of a "New World," even if he did nothing to attribute a "Being" to this new entity. This only occurred with the map drawn by Martin Waldseemüller in 1507, in which these new lands were presented as a single geographical entity that was independent of the *orbis terrarum* and, furthermore, given a name: "America" (124).

Now, what is the structure of this "object" called "America," invented by Western historiography? O'Gorman devotes the fourth and final section of his book to resolving this question. His primary thesis is that the "Being of America" directly depends on the significance that European consciousness gives to it, once it is clear that it is a "fourth part of the world" in addition to Europe, Asia, and Africa. In the background, as we have pointed out, is the Heideggerian thesis that facts in and of themselves have no significance but rather depend on how humans assume their own project. The "meaning" Europeans gave (prescientifically) to America was, from the beginning, that possibility of becoming another Europe, which is why it was called the New World.

But, according to O'Gorman, this ontological program assigned to Latin America confronted the following dilemma: either this new Europe would adapt new circumstances to the European model, or it would take this model as a *starting point* for creatively transforming it (135). These two alternatives, imitation and originality, correspond with the way of life in the two Americas, the Latin and the Anglo-Saxon, which in turn correspond to the two ways of existing pointed out by Heidegger: the inauthentic and the authentic. Thus O'Gorman takes up once again the famous Arielist motif, but gives it a value that is inverse to that bestowed upon it by the modernists Rodó and Vasconcelos. The Spaniard wanted to actualize "American being" by transplanting the Spanish model to new lands, which would result in a society where creativity had no place. Later, once the criollos had achieved independence, they did the same thing: they attempted to reproduce French and English models in Latin America instead of creating their own models. The history of Latin America in general, and of Mexico in particular, is a clear example of "inauthentic existence." Instead of "handing oneself down," as Heidegger would say, Latin Americans have always attempted to reproduce falsely the lives of other men. This explains the ontological imbalance and unease that people in this part of the world experience (137). Latin America never creatively transformed its legacy and traditions, but always looked outside itself at what others were doing instead.

These arguments contradict the Latin Americanist optimism of the Ateneo de la Juventud. In fact, O'Gorman, like Ramos, was convinced

Vasconcelos's thesis that Latin America would take Europe's place as the spiritual leader of the world implied a "concealment" of Latin American Being; a false image that proves the thesis that collective life in this part of the world is inauthentic:

> We must add, however, that the historical life of Latin America at a later period no longer merits this description, for underlying the wars for independence and the many violent upheavals which are so typical of that history there is a design and an attempt to live a form of life that may truly be considered its own. The desire for historical autonomy found its chief inspiration in the history of the other America, where the European model had been actualized through the other channel, and where new forms of historical life had been produced by and for a peculiar new type of man who, certainly not by chance, has been universally granted the name of American.
>
> (143)

Latin America has never stopped being a colony, as decoloniality strictly requires the attainment of "ontological independence," which we are still far from achieving. In turn, the United States chose the creative path in the face of the European model. Instead of seeing the New World as a place to obtain privileges (as occurred in Latin America), the U.S. elevated personal freedom, creativity, and work as supreme values. Thus the program of fully realizing a "second Europe" with which America was born into the European consciousness: not as a replica but as creation and as historical authenticity. The United States assumed its European inheritance (its past) and took its fate into its own hands and created an ontologically modern (autonomous) country, which is the condition of possibility for economic and technological development (144). The failure to recognize this, as can be seen with the Arielists of the past and contemporary Latin Americanists intellectuals, is the product of the resentment that characterizes those who live an inauthentic existence.

EPILOGUE

The global economic crisis of the 1930s generated a series of nationalist and populist movements throughout Latin America that revived the question of national and continental identity. This debate, in which the majority of Latin American intellectuals participated, coincided with the gradual autonomization of the philosophical field in the region. In spite of the fact, pointed out by Bourdieu, that the rules of the philosophical field prohibit the thematization of the empirical circumstances within which they are thought, these nascent philosophers could not resist the need to make Latin America an object of philosophical meditation. Thus a continental movement emerged that took on the question of the subcontinent's cultural identity. And it was in Mexico that "philosophical Latin Americanism" found one of its most original expressions.

Why did a philosophical debate around such an orthodox problem as national or regional identity emerge in Latin America? We submit that what was at stake was the *meaning* that should be given to the processes of Westernization and modernization in the region during the mid-twentieth century. Among some sectors of the intelligentsia, the idea circulated that it was precisely these processes that had instigated the two world wars that completely destroyed Europe, and that, fortunately, Latin America remained outside these events. It was the moment of questioning the "Being of America" with the goal of outlining a sui generis modernity, different from Europe's, that might also avoid the latter's disgraces. However, other intellectuals had a completely different evaluation. The world wars were not the consequence of modernization but rather its lack (fascism and nationalism as premodern phenomena), and it was precisely this lack that was revealed as a historical mark of Latin American culture. In sum, what was at stake in "philosophical Latin Americanism" was the *question of modernity*—a question that, as we have seen, was a central concern for intellectuals in a country like Mexico in the mid-twentieth century.

APPENDIX 1

FROM THE HISTORY OF IDEAS TO THE LOCALIZED GENEALOGY OF PRACTICES

AN INTERVIEW WITH SANTIAGO CASTRO-GÓMEZ

Santiago, thank you for allowing us this opportunity to interview you. Let's talk about your trajectory. In 1984, you came to the Department of Philosophy at Universidad Santo Tomás. Why did you choose this university, and what was the department like in those years?

Thank you for the interview. When I enrolled at Universidad Santo Tomás, the Department of Philosophy was dominated by the Latin Americanist discourse of the Bogotá Group. I remember that, at first, I was very struck by the strong populist rhetoric that ran throughout this discourse. For example, it was very common to encounter axioms like: the people is the true subject of philosophy and is endowed with a special "knowledge" thanks to its "external" condition with respect to the dominant rationality, according to which the philosopher's moral responsibility is to articulate the voice of the oppressed, etc. In general, there was a rather messianic sentiment in the air regarding the immediate future of Latin America. There was a certain hope in the coming of a Christianity-friendly socialism (like in Nicaragua), and some even thought that philosophy would play a very important role in this process. Looking back on things from a distance, I would say that this amounted to a Latin Americanist metaphysics without any empirical referents that obstructed any *political* analysis of what was really happening in Colombia. Thinking about it today, I see it as a sadly curious situation: while in 1985 the country was on the verge of a historic catastrophe that was vociferously declared by innumerable empirical signs (the growing threat of drug trafficking, the siege of the Palace of Justice, etc.), the philosophers of liberation who criticized the "abstract universalism" of their colleagues only saw the signs of a Christian socialism. The "diagnosis of our time" initiated by the Bogotá Group turned out to be merely an illusion.

However, in spite of all the predictions that never came true, I remember the exciting atmosphere of the department, particularly how passionate it all was. This group believed in something, wagered on something, took a position in favor of something, wanted to think *from* Colombia, and that was a good thing, especially if we keep in mind the excessive emphasis on "pure theory" that reigned in almost all academic philosophy departments at the time.

Could you please define for us, in concrete terms, what the Bogotá Group was and how it influenced your intellectual project?

The Bogotá Group was a group of professors from Universidad Santo Tomás in the mid-1970s who took up the question of "Latin American philosophy," in the form of the "history of ideas" (Gaos, Zea, Roig, Ardao, and Miró Quesada) and as the "philosophy of liberation" (Salazar Bondy, Dussel, and Scannone et al.). Its members included Germán Marquínez Argote, Jaime Rubio Angulo, Francisco Beltrán Peña, Joaquín Zabalza Iriarte, Luis José González, Eudoro Rodríguez, Teresa Houghton, Saúl Barato, Gloria Isabel Reyes, Juan José Sanz, Daniel Herrera Restrepo, and Roberto Salazar Ramos, among others. The group did a remarkable job of discussing and disseminating these problems in Colombia, a country that had never exhibited any Latin Americanist tendencies. It created institutions [at Universidad Santo Tomás] that exist to this day, like the journal *Cuadernos de Filosofía Latinoamericano*, the Centro de Enseñanza Desescolarizada (CED), the Biblioteca de Autores Colombianos (BAC), the graduate program in Latin American philosophy, and several international Latin American philosophy conferences, which, at the time, caused bewilderment and outrage within the local philosophical community. I would say that it was authentic and that, in time, it will receive the appreciation it is due from historians of Colombian philosophy. Unfortunately, nowadays, no one seems to remember—or no one wants to remember.

What kind of influence did the Bogotá Group have on my intellectual project? A significant influence, in the sense that it showed me both a path for my work and the wrong way to go down that path. I already mentioned some of the common axioms in the Department of Philosophy that made me personally feel alienated, but I must distinguish between the populist rhetoric of the philosophy of liberation and the methodological reflections on the history of ideas. It is my impression that, at that time, the Bogotá Group tended to confuse the two, or at least they did not clearly establish the differences between them. I viscerally rejected the philosophy of liberation, but I was very interested in the history of ideas. I was fascinated by the project of tracing a history of our intellectual traditions, and I closely read Leopoldo Zea's early works (*El positivismo en México, El pensamiento latinoamericano*), as well as the methodological studies of Arturo Roig and Horacio Cerutti. I thought it was important to think the history of Colombia from a philosophical perspective and to investigate why we have ended up where we are. However, in time, I realized that the history of ideas was not the best way for me to successfully complete this project.

Tell us about your relationship with Roberto Salazar Ramos. We know that he directed your graduate thesis on John Locke, and we are curious to know why you wrote your thesis on British empiricism when the language spoken at Universidad de Santo Tomás was Latin American philosophy.

First of all, Roberto Salazar was the professor for my contemporary philosophy course, and I remember that the first reading he assigned us was Nietzsche's *On the Genealogy of Morals*. To approach twentieth-century philosophy through a retrospective reading of Nietzsche was something very new to me at the time. But what was most striking to me about Roberto was how he *used* Michel Foucault's thought. At the Fourth Latin American Philosophy Conference in 1986, he had already begun what we could call an "internal archaeology" of the Bogotá Group revealing the limits of Latin Americanist discourse. Roberto's "critical use" of Foucault has been one of the most enduring influences on my work up to the present day. If one can still speak in these terms, Roberto was a true "master" in my eyes.

As for British empiricism, I was primarily interested in its method, its modus operandi. Studying the "birth" of these ideas, their immanent genesis, the central role that sensation has for the whole process, the body, as well as the entirely pragmatic dimension of language and discourses, was undoubtedly an important methodological exercise that brought me to a much better understanding of what Nietzsche and Foucault meant by "genealogy." Although Roberto initially suggested that I do my thesis on the thought of Julio Enrique Blanco, he finally understood why I didn't want to do a thesis on the history of ideas, but rather one that would give me the methodological tools to think. I believe it was an excellent decision.

In 1988, you graduated from Universidad Santo Tomás and then immediately afterward traveled to Germany. Why Germany? What was your experience with philosophy like there?

Why Germany? Well, the truth is that I left Colombia because I wanted to make a change in my life, I wanted to experience something else, another language, another way of seeing life. I never thought that one day I would obtain a doctorate or that I was beginning an "academic career." At that time there were no scholarships of any kind, nor was there the enormous pressure people today feel to go abroad to get doctorate degrees. Of course, Germany caught my attention because of its important philosophical tradition, and, starting in 1986, I had begun to take German classes at the Instituto Goethe, but I didn't really know if I wanted to study abroad or not, let alone when. I finally contacted a German institute in Stuttgart by mail, sold the four things I owned, bought a plane ticket, and left without thinking too much about it. I initially went to Stuttgart to study German at the university, because what I'd learned at the Goethe was barely enough to say "Ich spreche kein Deutsch" (I don't speak German). After two years, I took the German university entrance exam and applied to a master's degree program in philosophy at the University of Tübingen, where I was admitted and began my studies in 1990.

Life in Stuttgart was hard, but when I got to Tübingen things completely changed. I got a much better job (weekends only) that left me with sufficient time for my studies. My professors included Rüdigner Bubner, Manfred Frank, Günter Figal, Otried Höffe, and Helmut Fahrenbach. I took seminars on the Frankfurt School with Fahrenbach, on Nietzsche and Heidegger with Figal, on French poststructuralism with Frank (who preferred to call it "neostructuralism"), on Hegel with Bubner, and on Rawls and Kant with Höffe. I received an excellent education and, above all, I acquired a certain philosophical dexterity in dealing with authors like Nietzsche and Foucault, who would be important for my work later on. Tübingen was a kind of golden age in my personal and intellectual life. It was like being in a waking dream.

In 1996, you published* Critique of Latin American Reason. *We know that this book closely follows the approach and methods of Michel Foucault, but we are interested to know whether this prompted you to rethink the questions you encountered at Universidad Santo Tomás. How did the idea for the book come to you? What is a "critique of Latin American reason?"

Actually, I still hadn't finished my master's degree when I wrote *Critique of Latin American Reason*. But there was some precedent for the writing of this book, which I can talk about briefly. In Tübingen I encountered a world of enormous intellectual wealth. I'm not only referring here to the Department of Philosophy but even more particularly outside it. There were several Latin American scholars at the university, primarily from Mexico and the Southern Cone. I got together with some of them to establish a study group called Latin American Thought, and we met every Friday to read and discuss texts about the intellectual history of Latin America. Along with Erna von der Walde, I founded the journal *Disens*, but we only had enough fuel (and money) for three issues. The journal sought to publish contributions to what was seen at the time as a new, Latin American "cultural theory," later known by the name *cultural studies*. In Germany (at least in some circles) there was a lot of enthusiasm for this kind of work. In Berlin, Monika Walter and Hermann Herlinghaus had edited the collection *Posmodernidad en la periferia: Enfoques latinoamericanos de la nueva teoría cultural* (1994), and, in the same year, Birgit Scharlau—a professor in Frankfurt and the future director of my doctoral thesis—edited the volume *Lateinamerika Denken: Kulturtheoretische Grenzgänge zwischen Moderne und Postmoderne*. Both books were definitive for me, as they showed me a very different path for thinking modernity in Latin America. A path that was *opposite* to what I had learned with the Bogotá Group at Universidad Santo Tomás.

What I am trying to say is that, when I began to write *Critique of Latin American Reason* (in the summer of 1995), I already had within my power all the necessary elements for constructing a critique of the project of Latin American philosophy. These elements were: 1. a more or less thorough knowledge of authors like Nietzsche and Foucault, which I acquired in the philosophy seminars I took in Tübingen; 2. a knowledge of the history of ideas, which I had gained as a philosophy student at Universidad Santo Tomás; 3. a knowledge of the debates on both postmodernity in Latin America and postcolonial studies, thanks to my intellectual collaboration with Erna and to the texts I mentioned. The result was a book that I see today as a kind of shedding of old skin. I had to get rid of what I had learned in order to think for myself. I had to kill the father, and that father bore the stepmother's name: "Latin American philosophy." The truth is that writing *Critique of Latin American Reason* left me transformed, both intellectually and vitally.

As you put it so well, the presence of Foucault in the book is obvious. But it is a use of Foucault that I learned by reading two authors completely foreign to the philosophical tradition: Ángel Rama and Edward Said. In fact, the book was an attempt at a kind of archaeology of Latin Americanism inspired by Said's famous work *Orientalism*. Just as, for Said, Orientalism is a discursive formation rooted in power relations that engender a certain identitarian representation of the "Orient" and the "Oriental," it also seemed to me that Latin Americanism had these same qualities. It is a family of discourses that creates an object of knowledge called Latin America and endows it with an identity, ontological qualities, a teleology, etc.; Latin America not as an entity that preexists its discursive formation—not as a "thing-in-itself" with an identity prior to the historical power relations in which they are inscribed as a discourse. The practice the book proposes is identifying what kind of power relations generate this discursive formation that I call Latin Americanism, demonstrating that Latin American philosophy clearly belongs to that same family of discourses.

My central argument was therefore that Latin Americanism is the group of discourses that produces an entity endowed with its own ethos and cultural identities, which it claims are "external" to the processes of modernization. But the "new cultural critique" I was talking about before helped me to understand that this Latin American exteriority to modernity is the nostalgic, populist, and humanist perspective of a segment of the criollo intelligentsia that has an interest in maintaining the privileges writing and literacy give them over the rest of the population. Latin Americanism appears as a colonial legacy that seeks to defend the ancestral rights of the "lettered city" (as Ángel Rama called it) in Latin America.

The book enthusiastically embraces postmodern philosophy, which it uses to criticize the ideals of Latin Americanism. What is the source of this enthusiasm? Why so much emphasis on the problem of postmodernity in Latin America?

I would say that the "enthusiasm" you're talking about was not so much for postmodern *philosophy* but for the kind of historical events that, at that time, were revealing the postmodern *condition*. When I was in Germany, I had the opportunity to witness the fall of the Berlin Wall in 1989, not just on television but also in speaking with Germans who came from the East and told me what their lives were like there. To see all these people going from one side of a border to the other through a broken wall was like seeing a dam burst when water that has long been held back violently rushes through to the other side and no one can do anything to stop it. With time, we have just begun to understand that the fall of the Wall was the symbol of the end of the Cold War as well as the beginning of the total *inundation* of the world by capitalism. The ideological and political dams that contained it finally broke, and its waters invaded the entire planet. Of course, this process, which today we call "globalization," had begun much earlier, but a palpable symbol of its existence was necessary for us to really believe it, and the fall of the Berlin Wall served as exactly that.

What I mean is that 1989 *symbolized* the end of one era and the beginning of another. The era of national and regional capitalism, of struggles to control the state as a way to bring about socialist revolution, of the dichotomies between an "inside" and an "outside" of the system, of the postulation of a "Third World" as a moral and political alternative to imperialism, etc. That is, not only did the twentieth century come to an end in November 1989, but that date also marks the demise of the symbolic world that defined modern politics for more than one hundred fifty years. This is what in the book I call postmodernity. I am not using this concept to refer to a historical era that comes *after* modernity but rather to the *consummation* of modernity by global capitalism. My argument is that postmodernity is not the "overcoming" but rather the *globalization* of modernity in terms of the commodification of everyday life. This is what begins to seem obvious, starting with the fall of the Berlin Wall. With the dam definitively broken, nothing can prevent *life itself* (and not just certain aspects of it) from becoming "liquid," as Bauman says.

You can understand then why the debate on postmodernity in Latin America was so important at the time. It was not just another debate on the level of, say, what happened in 1992, when there was discussion about whether or not the quincentennial of the discovery or conquest of the Americas should be celebrated. This was a different kind of debate. What was under discussion was whether or not the theoretical and political tools used at that time for critiques of capitalism in Latin America were adequate for a historical moment in which global capitalism was shaping up to be the "condition of possibility" of life itself on this continent. That was the point. In *Critique of Latin American Reason* I took a very clear position in this regard, in line with what other authors, like García Canclini, Martín-Barbero, Yúdice, Richard, and Hopenhayn et al. were doing at the same time. In my opinion, Latin Americanism had functioned quite well as a tool for struggle when it was still possible to think in terms of regional and cultural spheres of "exteriority" that were capable of interpellating capitalism. But given the Berlin Wall event, it seemed clear that things were different.

The book also exhibits a permanent dialogue with cultural studies, with which you became familiar in Germany. Being that you are a philosopher, what did you find so interesting about cultural studies?

What I became familiar with in Germany was a *style of thinking* about Latin America that helped me disentangle myself from Latin American philosophy. It taught me to use other categories of analysis and allowed me to build a bridge between philosophy and the social sciences. Remember that both Jesús Martín-Barbero and Néstor García Canclini are philosophers by training. Martín-Barbero did his doctorate in Leuven with a thesis directed by Jean Ladrière, and García Canclini did his in France, writing his thesis on Merleau-Ponty under the direction of Paul Ricoeur. So, I realized that in order to critique Latin American philosophy, I didn't need to become the extreme opposite, a universalist philosopher who clings to the exegesis of European texts and disregards any type of reflection on Latin America because he considers it a low-status activity more appropriate to the social sciences. Rather, it is possible to continue to think Latin America from a practice that combines philosophical reflection with the empirical work of the social sciences. This was precisely what scholars like Martín-Barbero and García Canclini were doing. To stop being ashamed to speak philosophically about Colombia and Latin America without falling into either the Latin Americanism or universalism of these philosophers: this, I believe, was the greatest lesson I learned from "cultural studies."

What sort of reception did* Critique of Latin American Reason *have? What is the significance of this book for your intellectual trajectory?

To my surprise, it had an excellent reception. In fact, I never expected any reception at all. I wrote the book to get rid of some old baggage, as I said, but I also was taking advantage of the opportunity Editorial Puvill in Barcelona offered in the competition they held for new writers. I entered the competition and won. I never imagined that I would publish a book before finishing my studies, and much less that it would be published in Europe. But this fact was very helpful for reasons of visibility (Puvill is a Spanish publisher that is distributed to all the libraries in Europe and the United States), and it wasn't long before I began to hear about the first reactions to the book. I received letters from Leopoldo Zea, Enrique Dussel, and Arturo Roig, as well as invitations from Horacio Cerutti to visit Mexico and from Pablo Guadarrama to travel to Cuba. And, most significantly with regard to my future, I was offered the position of full professor in the Department of Philosophy at Universidad Javeriana. It is incredible that a book can change one's life, but that's what happened. Beyond all the conceptual problems it may have, what is certain is that the text managed to touch some nerves and revitalize a debate that was almost dead. A testament to this are the numerous reviews the book received in a little less than three years. In sum, I can say that *Critique of Latin American Reason* is the most important book I have written up to this point, not only due to its personal significance but also because it was there that I began to delineate a research program that would later manifest in *La hybris del punto cero* (2005; *Zero-Point Hubris*) and *Tejidos Oníricos* (2009; Oneiric constitutions). It is a kind of programmatic work.

Even up to the present day, many criticize the book for being too postmodern. They say that it proposes nothing, that it is only destructive. What do you think of these critiques?

It is logical that the practitioners of Latin American philosophy think the book seems "too postmodern." In fact, the bulk of critical reviews were echoing criticisms that the Marxist and humanist left at the time were making of Foucault, Derrida, Vattimo, and Lyotard. However, I should recognize that, in appropriating an avant-garde gesture (which I now distance myself from), the book intentionally sought to provoke the outrage of certain readers, primarily in the first chapter, which is titled "Postmodernity's Challenges to Latin American Philosophy," where I survey the arguments of some postmodern philosophers to articulate a critique of the discourses of Latin American philosophy, which at that time were proudly regarded as "progressive." The text therefore was meant to provoke a certain "philosophical left" that I did not in any way see as progressive but rather as conservative and nostalgic. Many of the critiques leveled at it missed the mark by not realizing that it was precisely that very nostalgic gesture that prevented them from seeing that the Latin American masses had already been interpellated by the signs of modernity through the market and the culture industries. To continue insisting on the old theme of Latin American "exteriority" was like trying to block out the sun with your hand.

It isn't surprising that the book provoked the irritation of many Latin Americanist philosophers, since almost all of them were wagering on a humanist project of *reappropriation* in which Latin America appears as an "exteriority" in relation to the modern world, and in which the task of the intellectual is to help recuperate some kind of identity that was either lost or whisked away by the modernizing elites. *Critique of Latin American Reason*, in contrast, argues that the suggestion that Latin America is a world external to modernity is a Macondoist and romantic gesture that reveals the Marxist left's nostalgia for a world in which they could still aspire to call themselves "organic intellectuals." But the intensification of modernity by mass media corporations and cultural consumption across broad sectors of society (what I call "postmodernity") caused that world to disappear and undermined the messianic pretensions of the Marxist left with which many Latin Americanist philosophers were affiliated. Think, for example, of liberation theology and the philosophy of liberation, which dreamed of a people that was not corrupted by the pathologies of modernity, insofar as this latter was seen as a "European" phenomenon that only affects elites who are alienated from their own Latin American reality. But when what today we call cultural studies demonstrated that the people are not uncorrupted but rather are able to develop strategies to "enter and exit modernity" without relying on the support of Enlightenment intellectuals, then the humanist project of reappropriation is left without any empirical basis. I think I say at one point that the philosophy of liberation is a romanticization of the poor that converts them into a kind of transcendental subject, under the "safe guidance" of nostalgic intellectuals.

It is true that the book is . . . did you say "destructive?" Well, it's not so much destructive as it is *deconstructive*. During the writing process, I felt like I was getting something off my back. It was not the time to propose new things, but rather to shake off all the old things. To be sure, if I had to write the book again today, I certainly would not make use of the same avant-garde gesture of "total rupture."

What I mean by "destructive" is that this "postmodern turn" you discern in Latin American philosophy comes before the political project that characterized it.

Let's be clear. The book *is not* a crusade against the legitimate aspirations to decolonization and the overcoming of cultural and economic dependency in our countries. Not in any way. What it is fighting against is rather the *language* in which such aspirations were formulated by Latin American philosophy—a language marked by the utopia of reappropriation, which understood political struggles as a romantic attempt to overcome social antagonisms. In contrast, to think a politics without resorting to the *foundation* (which is what I propose in the book) presupposes both integrating conflict as part of politics itself and understanding that these struggles do not aim at the elimination of opacity and power but rather at their agonal management without any guarantee of what the result of that management may be. The book resonates with the kind of politics that some Southern Cone cultural theorists (Martin Hopenhayn, Beatriz Sarlo, Carlos Altamirano, Nelly Richard et al.) defended in the 1990s, just when those countries were coming out of military dictatorships and transitioning to democracy.

Do you have any of your own criticisms of the book after fifteen years?

Yes, of course. Perhaps the main one is, as I said before, the iconoclastic and avant-garde language that runs throughout the text. In those days, I was very excited by my readings of Foucault, Deleuze, and Lyotard, and in a philosophically conservative environment like the departments at Tübingen and Frankfurt, where the most "advanced" work was the ethics of discourse defended by Jürgen Habermas and Karl-Otto Apel, which sought to complete what they called the "inclusive project of modernity." The three French philosophers I just mentioned, on the other hand, argued that we had entered a kind of "new era" of discourse, an episteme or "image of thought" that posited *definitive* ruptures to the mode of being of modern discourses. These French philosophers resonated with me almost instinctively, so I took their side in the debate without thinking about it too much. That led me to overestimate their diagnoses and to assume overly sharp ruptures between the "old" and the "new," thus reproducing the same modernist gesture that I was criticizing so vociferously. And, clearly, by critically evaluating Latin Americanist philosophy through that avant-garde lens, the result could not but have been a caricature of some of its arguments. This was accurately pointed out by some of the reviews of the book. On the other hand, in my defense, I must say that if I had to write the book again after fifteen years, I would surely try to be more cautious with the language I used, but I would basically maintain the same critiques I made at the time.

Let's return to your trajectory. In view of the success of* Critique of Latin American Reason, *you received an invitation to return to Colombia in 1998 and become part of the Department of Philosophy at Unversidad Javeriana and then at the Instituto Pensar. Can you tell us about your experience as a philosopher at the Instituto?

I finished my master's at Tübingen by the end of 1996 and I enrolled in a doctoral program at the University of Frankfurt to work with Professor Scharlau. But before obtaining my doctorate in Frankfurt I decided to accept the offer to come to Colombia. Manuel Domínguez, who at that time was the chair of the Department of Philosophy at Javeriana, invited me to be part of a team that would supposedly initiate a research program in Latin American philosophy within the department, but that project never came to pass. What did "come together," however, was something much more interesting: the creation of Instituto Pensar. Only a few months after arriving in Colombia, the rector of Javeriana invited me to join the initial team that would help shape the Instituto.

Twelve years of experience at Instituto Pensar allowed me to realize the importance of *transdisciplinarity*. To me, the Instituto represented the loss of my identity as a philosopher, as I realized that when working in emerging areas like cultural, postcolonial, gender, and environmental studies, insisting on calling oneself a "philosopher," "anthropologist," "historian," or "sociologist" didn't make much sense. What was important for a research team like the one at Instituto Pensar was the kind of *questions* we posed for ourselves and not the "discipline" from which those questions derived. In fact, as I said earlier, I was interested in situating myself on the *border* between the social sciences and philosophy, and, so as not to get lost along the way, I used a methodological tool that I still recur to today: genealogy. Thus I do not consider myself so much a philosopher as a genealogist. My books *La hybris del punto cero* and *Tejidos Oníricos* are not "about philosophy" in the strict sense, but they are genealogies.

During these years at Instituto Pensar, you began to conceive of the ideas that would take shape in* La hybris del punto cero *and* Tejidos Oníricos. *Do these books attempt to open up a new space for "Latin American philosophy," or do they convey a completely different thought that can no longer be pigeonholed in this way?

I have no intention of continuing the project of Latin American philosophy by other means. As I explained, that project remained definitively buried with the *Critique of Latin American Reason*. However, I also cannot say that there is a complete lack of continuity with some of the themes I studied at Universidad Santo Tomás. Seeing these things again from a distance, today I understand that both *La hybris* and *Tejidos* are methodological attempts to move from the "history of ideas" to a "localized genealogy of practices." Even though it is a complex topic that is still developing, I will try to explain it briefly.

The initial project of Latin American philosophy, as it was formulated in Mexico in the 1940s by José Gaos and Leopoldo Zea, attempted to resume Ortega y Gasset's historicism in the form of the history of ideas. However, it seems to me that this was where the difficulties began: let us recall that Ortega himself denied that the study of "ideas" could account for the historical circumstances in which human life takes place. For Ortega, what was important was to examine the *function* of ideas, their *pragmatics*, as this is the only possible way to understand how humans "live" a concrete circumstance. Ortega was interested in what we would call an effective history of ideas, that is, in the way that ideas become *everyday experience* and turn into "beliefs," as he himself says in several texts. In contrast, Gaos and Zea developed a completely different project: outlining a history of those ideas and ideological currents (the Enlightenment, romanticism, positivism, etc.) through which Latin American intellectual elites thought their own historical circumstances. Look at the difference: in one case, we have a project that seeks to examine the radical historicity of humans through the study of their *modes of experience* in a concrete circumstance. In the other, we have a project that no longer examines historical experience through the analysis of *practices*, but rather through something that, because it does not refer to concrete practices, goes beyond all experience: something called Latin American thought. We arrive at the following paradox, which Ortega had already noted: the history of ideas is the history of something that *has no history.*

What Gaos and Zea were hoping was that, after outlining the history of how the elites of each Latin American country have thought their own circumstances, one can then move on to a second moment when an "authentically Latin American" philosophy can be formulated on that basis. The history of ideas functioned as a prior moment, as a condition of possibility for the formulation of a philosophy of Latin American circumstances. If you think about it, this is a complete abandonment of Ortega's philosophical project. Instead of philosophically reflecting on the *problem of life*, as Ortega proposes, what Gaos and Zea do is concentrate their efforts on a prephilosophical task like the history of ideas. The truly philosophical task—to give an account of the problem of the historicity of human life in a concrete circumstance—was distorted and postponed. And what finally happened was that the practitioners of the history of ideas ended up believing that it was a properly philosophical task. They ended up believing that doing Latin American philosophy amounted to tracing the history of the ideas formulated by criollo elites (Bello, Alberdi, Sarmiento, Bilbao, Rodó, Vasconcelos et al.). The preparatory labor of constructing the Latin Americanist archive became an end in itself. To summarize, I would say that the project of Latin American philosophy as the history of ideas was stillborn because, instead of continuing the interesting line of philosophical investigation opened up by Ortega, Leopoldo Zea got lost in the labyrinths of intellectual nationalism and the temptations of a Latin Americanist mythology that reigned throughout the continent for a good part of the twentieth century. This is precisely one of the central themes I cover in *Critique of Latin American Reason.*

Now, let's say that this "dead end" of Latin American philosophy is the very point where my work begins. Without trying to invoke a "specter," as Derrida would say, I wanted to resume Ortega's historicist project, this time not as phenomenology or hermeneutics but rather as *genealogy.* I can't go into detail on this point right now, but in general it is a matter of progressing toward an analysis of practices that generate a particular experience of the world, using Colombian history as a laboratory. That is to say, instead of a "history of ideas," I would like to work on a "localized genealogy of practices." The idea is to resume Ortega's historicist project as read through the lens of Nietzsche and Foucault, but not to move closer to a "Latin American philosophy." Rather, the idea is to move toward a genealogy of the techniques of government that have made life in Colombia into an object of politics. As you can see, this is Ortega's problem of life in circumstance, only now thought in biopolitical terms.

Then you definitively believe that it no longer makes sense to keep asking whether or not a Latin American philosophy is possible? What is that project about?

Yes, definitively. It seems to me that the question of the existence of a Latin American philosophy is a *fallacy* in the technical sense of the term, that is to say, it presumes exactly what it should try to demonstrate. Why? Because it starts from the assumption that the signifier *Latin America* refers to a thing-in-itself. That is, what should be the philosophical question—namely how is the signifier *Latin America* produced and what truth-effects does it have—is left to the side, and instead *it is assumed* that Latin America existed prior to its discursive signification and that, because we were born in this "place," we are Latin Americans. I don't know if you're following me here. What I want to say is that the question of Latin American philosophy assumes precisely that which should be the *result* of a philosophical investigation. The result of a historical process of *production*, namely Latin America, is taken as if it were something that had already been constituted. This explains why people who are interested in this topic are bogged down by *existential* dilemmas like: "How can one be both Latin American and a philosopher at the same time?" or "What philosophy makes sense *in* and *from* Latin America?" Or they get tangled up in *political* and *moral* statements like: "Latin American philosophy should distinguish itself from European philosophy by exhibiting anticolonial and emancipatory qualities." Things like that. What is the problem with these kinds of questions and statements? All of them start from the assumption that Latin America is a "place," a "culture," or even a moral imperative, and that everyone who is born in that place and shares that culture are "Latin Americans," or "Latin Americanists" if they share the same moral imperative but were not born there. Therefore, I say that all Latin Americanist philosophers always *assume* the existence of a "Latin American identity," or because they need it to affirm themselves as philosophers with the same rights as German and French philosophers, or because they want to assert or recover it in order to restore dignity to their poor, tormented nations.

I think that *Critique of Latin American Reason* offers enough arguments to show that Latin America is not a "place of enunciation" and much less a "culture," but rather a *signifier* that operates in one form or another according to the historical *dispositifs* of power in which it is inscribed. Furthermore, I would say that in "Latin American philosophy," in particular, "Latin America" occupies the position of the *master signifier*. Therefore, the book is not actually about Latin America but rather Latin Americanism as that family of discursive practices and relations of power that generate that *truth-effect* called "Latin American identity." Note the difference here: I am not assuming that identity, but rather genealogically examining its processes of production, circulation, and consumption. I am not talking about Latin America as if it were a thing-in-itself, but rather about the processes of Latin Americanization. Nor am I assuming that something called "Colombia" or "Colombian identity" exists, rather I am trying to discover the technologies that produce them and how they function historically.

So, no thought can call itself "Colombian" or "Latin American?"

No. Nor is there any European, Arab, Chinese, Indigenous, or French, etc., thought. And I don't say this because I am thinking of the well-worn universality-particularity binarism, in whose claws the debate over whether or not Latin American philosophy exists remains trapped. I am not saying that philosophy and science are "universal" knowledges that are valid for everyone, regardless of individual nationality, and that therefore to talk of a Latin American philosophy is as absurd as talking about a Latin American mathematics or physics. That is not the point. What I am saying is that "thinking" is the use of a set of *sign ordering technologies* through which we "problematize" the world. Technologies that have historically emerged in different locations on the planet (only some of them came from Greece) but which operate with complete independence from the *function* they had in the "place" of their emergence.

Just because today we use a kind of logic of argumentation whose origins can be traced to ancient Greece does not mean that our thought is "Greek." Or just because in our daily lives we use information management technologies that historically originated in modern Europe does not mean that we think as "Europeans." In this regard, sign ordering technologies are not much different than any other technology, and here I refer particularly to Gilbert Simondon's reflections on the topic. But let me return to the argument: thinking is not a "spiritual" activity, it is not something that comes from the "soul" of an individual, a culture, or a nation. Just because Lao-Tse was born in China does not mean that the technologies he used to problematize his world were "Chinese." Or, just because Saint Augustine was a Christian does not mean that his philosophy is "Christian." These taxonomies are perhaps very useful for the history of ideas, or for the publishing industry, or the curricula of university programs, but are of little help in tracing the localized genealogies of philosophical practices. I say "thinking" is not an activity that can be understood through someone's ideas, culture, or biography, but that they must be examined from the point of view of their *modes of problematization*. What do they *do* with language? How does a concept *function*? What kind of *technologies* produce it? How are these sign-ordering technologies connected to behavior management technologies? These are the kinds of questions that *genealogies of Colombianness* investigate. Their objective is not "Colombian thought" or "Colombian identity," but rather the historical articulation between different discursive and governmental regimes.

Please explain to us the "genealogies of Colombianness" you have been working on recently at Instituto Pensar. What do these genealogies have to do with the techniques of government you just mentioned? What is the truly creative part of this project?

Let's begin at the beginning. Genealogy is a method of historical and philosophical analysis created by Nietzsche and later continued by Foucault, and, in our own era, Peter Sloterdijk and Giorgio Agamben, whose purpose is to trace the emergence in the past of certain forms of *experience* that continue to influence the present and constitute us as the subjects we are today. The basic assumption of genealogy is that people are entirely the products of their historical practices, and that the latter are necessarily multiple, contingent, and antagonistic. Practices, on the other hand, unlike ideas, are *behaviors that are subject to rules*. Their place of inscription is not so much the mind as the body. A practice can be learned and carried out innumerable times, insofar as the *technologies* that govern it have been incorporated and have become *habitus*. They are endowed with a *rationality* that does not depend on the subjects who carry them out, but one that instead constitutes the historical becoming of those subjects. Through these technologies, people become what they are and gain the ability to "deal with the world" in multiple ways. They are forms of *experience*, and genealogy is the study of their historical emergence in a concrete circumstance, with *circumstance* understood here not in an idealist way (as Ortega did) but rather as a set of *localized power relations*.

Now, the concept of practice refers to what people actually do when they speak or act. We are not talking here about what people "think" they do or what they "want" to do but rather what they *effectively* do. And, from this point of view, what is interesting to genealogy as *effective history* are the practices themselves and not the practitioners. The story this tells is not that of subjects and their "ideas," but rather the story of practices. I understand genealogy as a deanthropologized history, because practices are not *derived* from an operator outside the regime of practices itself, as, for example the notions of "subject," "mentality," "culture," "modernity," "Latin America," "Colombia," etc. Instead, they should be analyzed according to the rationality that unfolds in those dispositifs.

The "genealogies of Colombianness" I'm working on are not concerned with investigating a Colombian "mentality" or a "Colombian culture" or the "subjects" that have contributed to the definition of a "national identity," but rather seek to trace historically the discursive and nondiscursive practices, particularly the *techniques of government*, through which a set of *forms of experience* has emerged that characterizes us as who we are today. The "creative" aspect of it, as you put it, is that, unlike the history of ideas, genealogy is not interested in the way that mentalities or ideas are historically transformed, but rather in how practices emerge and operate in a space-time that is determined by these practices, that is to say, in a *circumstance*. The "history" traced by genealogy is that of the circumstantiality of practices and not of their *correlates*. For example, this means that instead of doing a history of "women" in Colombia, one does a genealogy of the historical practices of "feminization"; instead of a history of the Colombian state, it would be a genealogy of the historical practices of nationalization; instead of a history of races or classes in Colombia, a genealogy of the historical practices of racialization and classification, etc. I don't know if I am clearly explaining myself. Practices are one thing, and their correlates are something altogether different. The key is not to confuse the two. "Woman," "race," "state," and "class," but also "Colombia" and "Latin America," are not objects that *preexist* the set of discursive and nondiscursive practices they produce. These objects do not have a history *in itself* that can be reconstructed through, for example, what intellectuals have thought or written about them, as the history of ideas attempts to do. Or to be more precise: the history of these objects is the history of their *production*.

It is clear from what you have just said that, unlike the history of ideas, genealogy does not examine what certain intellectuals have said about Colombia or Latin America but rather the way they have said it, their discursive practices. But how should we view these practices? What must a scholar do to study practices, especially those of the past? And if the historical practices that coexist in a historical moment are innumerable, then wouldn't genealogy be a methodologically impossible task?

These are very difficult questions to respond to in a couple words! You're right, there are multiple historical practices, but genealogy does not seek to trace the history of each individual practice, as that would be a never-ending task. What genealogy seeks to do is to write the history of the "regimes of practices" (as Foucault puts it), that is, the set of practices that resonate together in a dispositif. Genealogy is an analytic of dispositifs. And although several dispositifs can certainly coexist in one historical moment, what genealogy seeks is not just to observe the functioning of each particular dispositif but rather to produce a cartography of the *relations* between dispositifs, showing how they confront, fight, or articulate with one another as well as observing the power relations between dispositifs and the *hegemonies* that are established between these struggles. The emphasis is not on the subjects who struggle or on their intentions, but on the dispositifs that empirically articulate the *modes of struggle*. That is the point.

To give you an example, in *La hybris del punto cero* I draw a map of confrontations between two dispositifs that entered into conflict beginning in the second half of the eighteenth century in New Granada: the "dispositif of whiteness" and the "biopolitical dispositif." So then: the task is not to trace the genealogy of the *singular* practices articulated in each of these dispositifs, nor is it to identify the empirical subjects that develop in them. What is important is to see the rationality of each dispositif, how and through what technologies it functions. There would be no point, for me, in concentrating, for example, only on the Bourbons' inoculation campaigns in the second half of the eighteenth century or on the hygienic measures implemented in Bogotá as a response to the smallpox epidemics, etc. This is the kind of work a historian should do. A genealogist, in contrast, tries to establish a complex relation between these particular kinds of medicalization practices and other governmental practices implemented by the Bourbons, like the practices of nationalization, mobilization, and scientization of the territory, etc., attempting to see how the rationality of the so-called biopolitical dispositif functions *as a whole*.

Exactly the same thing occurs in *Tejidos Oníricos* when I examine the dispositif of "mobility" in Bogotá toward the end of the twentieth century. The emphasis is not on the *singular* practices (paving of streets, public lighting, construction of working-class neighborhoods, etc.) but on how the dispositif as a whole functions. Here the question is not about the emergence of capitalism in Colombia as an "empirical datum," but rather about the emergence of certain techniques of government that create "conditions of existence" for the subjects who identify with a lifestyle centered on permanent mobility. Thus what is important for the genealogist is not so much singular practices but the functioning of a *network of practices* that is, although from a particular point of view, empirical and heterogeneous, articulated and functioning together according to a kind of rationality. And here comes the methodological problem that might really irritate historians and social scientists: the *rationality* of a set of practices is never reducible to the empiricalness of singular practices; rather, it grows through a set of relations that are, let us say, transcendental to the empiricism of *each one* of them. The dispositifs I examine in my books (whiteness, biopolitics, and mobility) are not empirical, but rather operate as *conditions of possibility* of the empirical functioning of practices. These are never articulated in a "natural" form, there is no "isomorphy" of practices (as is assumed in analyses that focus on the *correlates* of practices like class, race, gender, etc.). In this sense, I insist, the history of practices is not the history of their singularity but of their "grammar," of what articulates them a priori. It is a history of the rationality of dispositifs.

The other part of your question has to do with the kind of research one ought to do in order to study practices. Well, this is also an interesting topic. We philosophers have been trained to see texts, books, documents as endowed with an "aura" that distinguishes them from other kinds of documents that are considered "less dignified," like magazines, manuals, and newspapers, etc. Philosophy is thus inscribed in an old, humanist tradition that makes "high culture" the only paradigm of civilization. Well, genealogy directly breaks with this kind of humanism. Its object of analysis, as we have already said, is not "ideas" but historical practices, and to arrive at these one must build an *archive*. It is not a simple matter of the "source" that historians are so concerned with, but rather the discursive register of practices. The work of all genealogy has two moments: the first is building an archive that allows the genealogist to see *what is being done and what is being said* at a determinate historical moment. But this requires "getting one's hands dirty" and doing the work that the historians of ideas could never do: examining the regulation of schools and factories, hygiene manuals, civic education primers, school textbooks, architectural designs, legal and medical files, police case files, newspaper and magazine editorials, photographic and other audiovisual material, etc. It requires reading "minor" documents (as Deleuze would say) instead of focusing on the great authors and intellectuals, on eminent men. Building an archive that gives us access to the *materiality* of practices would bring us to the second methodological moment I mentioned earlier: disentangling the *mode of articulation* of practices from their functioning. As you will see, the genealogist must do something that the historians of ideas never wanted to or could do, since almost all of them were trained in the discipline of philosophy: begin building the archive in order to write history *themselves*.

Now let's talk about your most well-known book,* La hybris del punto cero, *published in 2005 by Universidad Javeriana. It has been widely commented on in various academic circles in Colombia; it has gone through three editions and has even won some scholarly prizes. To what do you attribute the interest sparked by this book in the Colombian academic community? Can you tell us what conclusions the research brought you to?

Well, I must first say that *La hybris* is my doctoral thesis, which I defended at the University of Frankfurt in 2003, and it was originally written in German under the title *Aufklärung als kolonialer Diskurs* but later revised for its publication in Colombia. I would say that the academic circumstances favored the circulation of a book such as this one. Remember that between 1997 and 1999 three cultural studies events took place in Colombia that were organized by the recently founded Ministry of Culture and the Universidad Nacional. Immediately afterward came the meteoric spread of so-called area studies (cultural, postcolonial, literary, environmental, science and technology, etc.), which in a matter of a few years managed to become programs in Colombian universities—at least in Bogotá. *La hybris del punto cero*, along with other books, like Zandra Pedraza's *En cuerpo y alma* and Mauricio Nieto's *Remedios para el Imperio*, began to be seen as paradigmatic examples of the new "area studies" that no one actually knew anything about but which were gaining a lot of attention among students. I am sure that if you asked Zandra if her book is about "cultural studies" or Mauricio if his book is "social science studies," both would probably say no. I would say the same with respect to *La hybris*, because it does not belong to any field of "postcolonial studies" (despite the fact that the publisher presented it as such), but rather is an investigation focused on the *border space* between philosophy, sociology, and history, without concretely belonging to any of these three disciplines. It is what we might call a *transdisciplinary* text. And even though it is still considered "offensive" in certain parts of Colombian academia, in other (admittedly minority, but growing) sectors, a great need exists for building bridges and traveling between disciplines. This explains to me, at least in part, the book's broad reception.

As for the research itself, I already mentioned that *La hybris* tries to construct a cartography of the powers that were operating in Nueva Granada during the second half of the eighteenth century, right on the precipice of the wars for independence. First of all, the book discusses the emergence of the "dispositif of whiteness" at the beginning of the seventeenth century and describes its functioning through what I call a *logic of filiation and alliance*. This is a power reproduced through relational strategies among the criollo elites that seeks to focus on the close circle of kinship networks that are ultimately defined in relation to the degree of "purity of [their] blood"; it is a power linked to blood and soil that generates a habitus of inherited privileges and which is exercised *against* other social groups in Nueva Granada, like Blacks, Indians, and mestizos—the so-called *castas*. The book shows some of the technologies of reproduction and staging of this kind of power, which I call the *coloniality of power*, following the Peruvian sociologist Aníbal Quijano.

Then, in a second moment, the book documents the emergence of a dispositif of power that is completely different from what I call the "biopolitical dispositif," whose emergence is a result of the reforms that the Bourbon dynasty implemented throughout the Spanish colonies during the second half of the eighteenth century. Unlike the first, this second dispositif does not seek to concentrate power in criollo kinship networks but rather in the *state*, which I assume is necessarily a declaration of war against the purity of blood that assured criollo hegemony over social space. The Bourbons wanted to make the state the only principle of intelligibility for all social relations. And this basically means that both the Church and the supposed criollo nobility would have to unconditionally submit to the hegemony of the state. In order to achieve this, a series of mechanisms were developed to remove criollos from the councils, to expropriate from the Church its monopoly over education and health, to nationalize the economy, and—something that enraged the criollos—to support mestizo social mobility.

To summarize, the book describes a war between two completely different dispositifs of power. To put it very roughly, the conclusion I reached is the following: the dispositif of whiteness ultimately managed to subjugate and claim hegemony over the biopolitical dispositif. That is to say, this tendency of the dispositif of whiteness to "expel the state" ended up consolidating with the social space of Nueva Granada, with the long-term consequences of regional and patrimonial interests being imposed on the state and converting it into an instrument of their power. In turn, this entailed a perpetuation of the habitus that makes the [social] capital of whiteness into a privileged vehicle for social elevation and prestige. The patrimonial appropriation of state power in place of the nationalization of patrimonial powers: that was the outcome of the struggle.

Is what you call the "coloniality of power" related to Foucault's notion of sovereign power?

No, not in any way. The sovereign power Foucault discusses is related to the ancient royal right to "take life or let live." Invested with a God-given power, the king has the right to dispose entirely of the life of his subjects, subtracting their life power and employing it as it pleases him: in battle, in agricultural work, as tribute, etc. The coloniality of power, in contrast, has nothing to do with the power of the Spanish king but rather with how the power of the criollo elites is reproduced in the local environment of the Spanish colonies. It is a power that, in a certain sense, is *opposed* to sovereign power insofar as the criollo elites of the seventeenth century managed to impose their own particular interests over the interests of the Crown. Hence the famous *dictum*, "Obey but don't follow." Moreover, it is a power that operates with very different technologies. The coloniality of power functions through the codification of associative memory: what someone "is" depends on their ancestors. *Birth* already marks people with their potential for mobility. I don't mean by this that "purity of blood" was not a factor that was also at work in the maintenance of sovereign power, but I would say that the latter is defined by other technologies, like, for example, the conquest and annexation of territories. The technologies of the coloniality of power, in contrast, center on the perpetuation of the privileges inherited by criollos through the racialization of alliances with the goal of preventing "intruders" (Blacks, Indians, and mestizos) from accessing kinship networks. These were technologies of defense. Reactive strategies.

It is necessary to distinguish the coloniality of power from other kinds of power that operated in the social space of Nueva Granada during the sixteenth through eighteenth centuries. Not everything was the coloniality of power! Sovereign and pastoral power were also present there. And all of them pointed in different directions and operated with different technologies. Pastoral power, for example, sought to subjugate the will of some to others, ensuring obedience and resignation through technologies like confession, penitence, and moral exhortation. Therefore, roughly speaking, pastoral power is directed toward the control of subjectivity, sovereign power toward the control of territory, and the coloniality of power toward the control of the purity of blood. Three different powers that use different technologies. This does not in any way exclude the *strategic articulation of powers*, as in fact occurred between pastoral and sovereign powers (for example, in the case of Indigenous reservations), or also between sovereign power and the coloniality of power (in the case of the defeat of the Comunero uprising).[1] But it would be a distortion to believe that sovereignty, pastoralism, and coloniality were *the same thing*, a unified machinery of colonial domination—as many still believe.

Foucault talks about genealogy as an "ontology of the present." Do you also see it this way? What does the eighteenth century have to do with our present? The Colombia of today with the Nueva Granada of the past?

Well, that is precisely the point. Nueva Granada in the eighteenth century is not "in the past," but rather is a part of present-day Colombia. In a certain sense, we still are in Nueva Granada. What a genealogy does is map out the forces that constitute us as who we are, but, in order to achieve this, it first looks to see at what point in the past these forces emerged so that we can still recognize them today and uncover what historical constellations of power engendered them. The objective of this exercise is the *denaturalization* of these forces. In general, we do not know what constitutes us. It is permanently "behind us" as an a priori that weighs heavily over all that we do and desire in the present. Only insofar as we understand "what we are made of" are we capable of transforming ourselves. This, precisely, is the function of genealogy. It maps the present through a cartography of the past with the goal of transforming the present. However, it does not seek to "say the truth" about the present and the past, but rather to get us accustomed to participating in the struggle over their *meaning*. Genealogy attempts to offer a knowledge of our historical a prioris. Therefore, it is a "critical" activity in the best sense of the word.

In my case in particular, I have been interested in those periods of Colombian history in which forces have emerged that are still possible to clearly recognize today. This is the case with the years from 1750 to 1816 in *La hybris del punto cero* and the years from 1910 to 1930 in *Tejidos Oníricos*. Now I am working on a third book that will focus on the 1970s. I do not refer to these dates from the perspective of a historian, but rather that of a genealogist, looking for clues with which to understand the present. To respond to your question, I will refer only to the first case. The cartography of powers mapped in *La hybris* addresses our present in at least two ways. First, it tells us that the tendency to patrimonially appropriate power is a colonial legacy that weighs heavily over political activity in present-day Colombia. We often wonder why political capital usually concentrates in the hands of a few families or regional groups in the face of which state sovereignty is left impotent. What we see today is how the state has been turned into the spoils of war for these local elites. How state resources, which supposedly belong to everyone, are *pillaged* by a few landowning families that seek to consolidate their private power at the expense of the public good. Well, *La hybris del punto cero* shows that this predominance of local powers over the centralized power of the state has its roots in the way that the dispositif of whiteness managed to "capture" and neutralize the technologies of state reason. The *naturalized* tendency of political elites in this country is to rob the state, to take advantage of the public good and use it for the reproduction of a *parastate* power based on land ownership. The creation of multiple states within the state—in other words, the *expulsion of the state* by patrimonial powers—is a long-standing historical tendency in Colombia. It is a colonial legacy.

But *La hybris del punto cero* is about our present in another sense as well: the indifference and disinterest of the great majority of Colombians toward the public sphere, which is today occupied almost entirely by private media organizations. We have just recently seen how in the Arab world the multitudes rose up to demand change, to demonstrate their outrage with corrupt and autocratic governments. In 1989 we saw how the multitudes of Eastern Europe rose up against actually existing socialism. This even happened in some Latin American countries as well, including the Brazilian uprising to remove Fernando Collor de Melo from office and the presidents overthrown by popular unrest in Ecuador. But nothing like this ever happened in Colombia. There are no signs of such "civil courage" here, where people are capable of putting up with *any* kind of abuse of the public sphere, which never incites political rage in the multitudes, who prefer to stay at home and watch the news instead of taking to the streets to express their indignation. It doesn't matter whether it's the parapolitics scandal, illegal wiretapping, the "false-positive" murders, the theft of royalties—nothing can incite mass outrage among Colombians. We go from one media scandal to another and we just watch like passive spectators. Why? I think this is also a question of a colonial legacy, namely that the dispositif of whiteness assumes the *constant humiliation* of anyone whose blood is not "pure." The "pathos of distance" that the white criollo elite established forced everyone else to bow their heads in recognition of their own misery, so as to see themselves as covered by the "stain of the earth" of which they were meant to feel ashamed. The belief in the lack of one's own value, the feeling of impotence regarding what "happens," the conviction that "nothing can be done," seems to be a naturalized attitude for many Colombians. If you add to this the fear that has spread through the population as the result of continuous civil wars for over two hundred years, summary executions, kidnappings, forced disappearances, and massacres, then it becomes pretty clear.

In the eighteenth century, however, there was a moment in which the "thymotic energies" (as Sloterdijk calls them) of the common people woke up and unleashed a massive uprising known as the Comuneros movement. For the first time, people believed that *they themselves* were capable of generating change. With its triumph, this movement has been a tremendous source of pride (*Stolz*) for the population, a proof that "blood purity" meant absolutely nothing, the most important aspect of which was that it was something that everyone could construct together with their own power. But unfortunately things didn't turn out that way. The Comuneros movement was betrayed by several factions of the criollo elite of the region who preferred to align themselves with the Spanish authorities before putting their own patrimonial interests at risk. The Comunero leaders were hunted down and murdered. The pride that brought people out of their villages to unite together against the Bourbon state was stomped out. With their self-confidence affected, the feeling of permanent self-humiliation returned. It seemed that Colombians' affective world was inscribed with the tendency to believe that rebellion was not worth the trouble, nor was risking one's own skin, since in any case everything will return to the same as it was before. The best we can do is "go fishing in the river of revolt" and accept before anything else that things have always been this way and that they will continue to be like this. As Fernando González astutely put it, "we bear colonialism within ourselves."

However, and this is important, I'm not talking about the Colombian "mentality" here, nor about behavioral tendencies rooted in the "collective unconscious." I'm not interested in a "characterology" of Colombians, nor of the phenomena of consciousness or unconsciousness, but rather the way in which the world of *affects* is historically marked by power relations. Both in *La hybris* and *Tejidos* I focus on showing that dispositifs are anchored in molecular and not just molar ways. A dispositif of power will be more effective if it can increase its ability to mobilize *molecular* dimensions of subjectivity like attention, will, affect, and desire. It is precisely here where the greatest power of the colonial legacies reside, not only in external phenomena like economic imperialism.

You just mentioned the legacies of colonialism and their importance for understanding the present. In the first chapter of* La hybris del punto cero, *you use the work of the modernidad/colonialidad group as a theoretical framework to think this problem, and your name is frequently associated with this collective of Latin American intellectuals. Can you tell us what your interest in this group is?

Before responding to your question, let me clarify that the first chapter of *La hybris* is not a "theoretical framework" but rather an attempt at an archaeology of the classical sciences that serves as a preamble to the genealogy of powers that unfolds in the following chapters. What I am trying to show is that the experience of colonialism operates as a condition of possibility in the eighteenth century for the birth of different knowledges of human life that exhibit pretensions of *epistemic purity*, that is to say, that attempt to situate themselves at a perspectival "zero point" so as to represent without being represented. This classical space of knowledge, I argue, was possible thanks not only to the objectivization of the experience of madness, as Foucault shows, but *also* due to the objectivization of the experience of barbarism that was brought about by European colonialism in the preceding centuries, as Aníbal Quijano, Walter Mignolo, and Enrique Dussel show. In the eighteenth century, a regime of truth was established in which reason remains pure of all barbarism, given that the latter is displaced to humanity's distant past, that is to say, to a time when reason itself had not yet come to light. The ego cogito, on the basis of which the classical order of representation is organized, can no longer be madness or barbarism. It must be completely "pure" of these determinations.

Starting in the eighteenth century, with the construction of the classical order, reason has come to see that barbarism is no longer a threat but an object of knowledge that confirms the epistemic supremacy of that order over all other knowledges. It has been able to make it part of its own domain, where it represents barbarism as its own other, its remote past. Hence, from an Enlightenment perspective, the Indian has ceased to be a troubling figure (as had been the case for the conquistadors and missionaries of the sixteenth century) and now appears as an inoffensive "inhabitant of the past." Thus my reference to the work of authors like Mignolo, Quijano, and Dussel is not merely descriptive or simply for "theoretical references"; rather, I am *using* this work to advance toward an archaeological practice that I am certain none of them would approve of.

Now, going back to your question, I don't think that modernidad/colonialidad is a group, much less a collective, but rather a heterogeneous network of scholars. A "collective" is a group of people who come together *because* they share a similar way of thinking, while a "network" never assumes such a thing. In a network, some things connect and others do not. Connections are made where they can be, and the rest does not matter. You can't put Enrique Dussel, Aníbal Quijano, Walter Mignolo, and Arturo Escobar together and expect that they will form a "collective." Each one of them has a consolidated trajectory, has developed their own ideas and analytical categories such that they can connect on some points, but there will always be many others to which no connection is possible. There are many differences of opinions among the scholars who participate in the modernidad/colonialidad network, and this is not only with regard to theoretical topics. But it is normal that this would occur in a "network." In my case, in particular, the relationship I have had with modernidad/colonialidad is a typical network relation that combines resonance and dissonance.

The resonances are primarily related to the distinction the network makes between the notions of colonialism and coloniality. While the former refers to the military subjugation, territorial occupation, and legal administration of a people by a foreign imperial power, the latter refers to the *legacies* that colonialism leaves in the symbolic, affective, and cognitive orders of that people, even after the territorial occupation and legal administration has ended. Therefore, we say that even though colonialism ended in Latin America in the nineteenth century with the wars for independence, coloniality still continues to the present day. And I would add that while colonialism, but also neocolonialism and imperialism, are phenomena that almost exclusively refer to the *molar* order, coloniality *also* refers to experiences of the *molecular* order. Of course one cannot separate the two things, the molar and the molecular, but it's a question of *accents*. Thus, in talking about the colonial legacies in Colombia, I am referring not so much to a macrophysics of global powers but primarily to a *microphysics of power* that resides in our historical experience. The accent is on the molecular, not the molar.

The dissonances have to do with this question of accents and take place primarily on the level of methodology. Some participants in the network focus their analysis on imperialism or racism, or on questions of ideology and global migration, hence their preference for a historical macrosociology in the style of Immanuel Wallerstein: the analysis of the world system. Without disregarding the valuable contributions that this general view of things can give us, I prefer to emphasize the molecular dimension of the colonial legacies, hence my preference for an analytical method like genealogy. I'm not saying that world-systems analysis and genealogy are like two faces of the same coin. To the complete contrary, they are very different methodologies, and, in some instances, they are diametrically opposed, which generates a number of important methodological frictions between my work and that of others like Quijano and Mignolo, for example. But I think that reflecting on this point now would take us too far afield. I have commented broadly on this topic in an article titled "Michel Foucault y la colonialidad del poder."

Let's move on to discussing your third book,* Tejidos Oníricos, *which was published in 2009 but has not been as successful as* Critique of Latin American Reason *and* La hybris del punto cero. *What do you think is the reason for this? Let's talk about this work a bit.

Well, I don't know. I don't write books so that they will be "successful." Once books are published, they no longer belong to their authors and take on lives of their own. But regardless of public reactions (if there are any), I must admit that *Tejidos Oníricos* is like a "slow child" that one learns to love more than the others. For me, it is a special book, both for the style in which it was written as for the conceptual wagers at stake in it. In this book in particular, I am seeking to broaden the kind of molecular analytic of power I began in *La hybris*, because I am convinced that any social order whatsoever can only occur insofar as it is "anchored" in the world of affects, habits, and desires. People don't follow a social order out of obligation or because they support it ideologically, or because they are participating in some kind of "rational consensus" à la Habermas. One cannot create or destroy a social order with just revolutionary slogans, nor can you do so simply at gunpoint. Something must happen on the *molecular level* for a social order to appear or disappear. So my question then is: How is capitalism constructed in Colombia? How is it that capitalism is beginning to acquire hegemony in a social space marked by colonial legacies? Capitalism is not explained simply by the existence of machinery, businesses, flows of capital, banks, and imperial wars. You have to explain why people behave "capitalistically." That is to say, you have to show how peoples' *lives* are moved by the *desire* to "progress." We don't gain much by talking about "foreign ideologies of progress," like Marxism and the history of ideas. We must instead talk about the *immanent experience* of progress, that is, the "desire to progress" inscribed in the body.

To address this topic in the book, I concentrate on the emergence in the 1910s and 1920s in Bogotá of what I call the "dispositif of mobility." This analysis allows me to understand the emergence of a kind of subjectivity that can appropriate for itself the vital horizon of capitalist production in Colombia. The dispositif of mobility is the set of technologies that make possible the kineticization of existence, the acceleration of life, and the mobilization of desires. My thesis is that, without the kineticization of life, without the subjection of life to permanent mobilization, the existence of a capitalist market economy is not possible. This is why in *Tejidos Oníricos* the metaphor of the locomotive is central, because it tries to explain how the discourses of progress functioned in Colombia at the beginning of the twentieth century. The locomotive was a symbol of the progress about which many Colombians had begun to *dream* in that era. One had to "get on the train" of modernity, and this seemed like an urgent and, in any case, unavoidable need. But getting on this train necessarily meant learning how to *move*. The book therefore analyzes topics like the construction of railways, waterworks, and sewers, lights for public streets, the construction of working-class neighborhoods, the implementation of rapid transit, and the centrality of the automobile. The creation of an urban infrastructure of permanent mobility has one specific purpose: to generate an *experience* centered on the generalized deciphering of flows. A society in which people, ideas, bodies, and especially work are "fixed" to specific places cannot be a capitalist society. What the dispositif of mobility does is combat the territorial fixing of desires, knowledges, and the labor force, as "territoriality" is the primary obstacle for the flow of commodities. The "progress" of a country, person, or business depends on its capacity for flow and its ability to decipher itself.

In many parts of* Tejidos Oníricos *you no longer refer much to the Foucault of* The Order of Things *or* The History of Sexuality, vol. 1: The Will to Knowledge, *as you did in* La hybris del punto cero, *but rather to Foucault's lectures in* Security, Territory, Population. *Why is that?

It's true. In *Security, Territory, Population* Foucault reflects on the emergence of certain techniques of government that no longer result from state intervention into life itself, which I discussed in *La hybris*, but rather produce "areas of existence" in which the free will of individuals would themselves generate the necessary dynamic for the mobility of commodities. Foucault calls these *liberal techniques of government* that function in a very different way from the techniques of state reason. Here Foucault sees liberalism not as an "ideology" but as a form of behavior management, as a technique of government. Foucault's thesis, which I use in the book, is that these techniques function through the creation of an "environment," a milieu. They do not *directly* intervene on bodies, like disciplines, neither are they limited to managing a series of general biological variables like birth, mortality, and morbidity. Governments create certain *conditions of existence* within which their subjects freely move. That is to say: they create certain "conditions of freedom" for those subjects that assume as their "own" the call to permanent mobilization and essentially "identify" with progress. Hence my emphasis in the book on studying topics like urbanism, neighborhood planning and design, transportation, and the placement of factories. Why? Because liberal techniques of government create an artificial environment that can *mobilize the molecular world of affect and desire*. They are techniques that *interpellate* subjects who function through *interpellation*.

As we know, "interpellation" is a category used by Louis Althusser, and my book takes up this category, although I read it in a Foucauldian way. That is, instead of talking about "ideological state apparatuses," I prefer to talk about techniques of government that operate through interpellation, which, I insist, are not *of* the state but that can be implemented *through* the state. They are techniques that serve to govern behavior through symbolic persuasion, the call to "be somebody in the world," the appeal to be modern subjects, *seduction*. Therefore, the book opens with a chapter dedicated entirely to the Centennial Exhibition celebrated in Bogotá in 1910, and it closes with another dedicated to an analysis of fashion, sports, and entertainment, as these areas staged for the first time in Colombia an "artificial" environment (milieu) where people felt called, summoned, and interpellated to become modern subjects. And what does it mean to be "modern?" That these subjects, urged on like this, see themselves as capable of "progressing," of defeating suffering and eliminating the *tragic* factors of existence. It is the adoption of a habitus, a particular disposition of conquest and exteriority, of always moving "beyond" the limits drawn by the traditional spheres of the family, religion, language, and culture. "Modernity," and in particular its most representative institution, capitalism, thus appears like a machine designed to destroy such spheres.

By mentioning "spheres," you necessarily evoke the figure of German philosopher Peter Sloterdijk, and in your introduction to the book you explicitly recognize his influence. Can you expand on this point?

Yes. I would say that Sloterdijk's influence can be felt in two ways in the book. One is *explicit* and has to do with the question of space. For Sloterdijk, the central issue is not who we are but rather *where we are*, what kind of spaces we inhabit. This is also evident in Foucault. Therefore, the book focuses on the urbanization of Bogotá, on the creation of technologically produced spaces where people exist in permanent movement, always abandoning their primary spheres of socialization. But the other element present in the book is not explicit but rather *implicit* and has to do with Sloterdijk's critique of humanism. In "Rules for the Human Zoo" he says that humanism, as a discourse that postulates the human capacity for living life according to the dictates of reason and morality, has completely failed. In support of this thesis, he turns to Heidegger's "Letter on Humanism," which argues that after Auschwitz and Hiroshima it is impossible to restore the humanist myth and believe that man will gradually become humanized.

I think that the same thing happens when one thinks in a country like Colombia, where violence is intrinsic to the processes of modernization, which innumerable studies have shown. Violence exists not because of the *lack* of modernization in contexts marked by colonial legacies. We should recall that coloniality is the filter through which we experience modernity. It is not surprising that both *La hybris del punto cero* and *Tejidos Oníricos* are not based in a perspective that either celebrates or laments Colombia's "entrance" to modernity, but rather in one that shows how life is trapped in a (mutually dependent) crossfire between modernity and coloniality. In both books, modernity is seen not as an "unfinished project" or as something that has been "delayed" in Colombia but rather as an experience that frequently oscillates between biopolitics and thanatopolitics. It "lets" one segment of the population live, but often *at the cost* of the death of another. Some should die so that others may live. It is a *tragic* history.

But aren't you saying then that the humanist tradition has been proven wrong by the tragedy of Colombian history and that therefore one cannot use it to think that history?

Exactly. Our intellectuals still think Colombia from a humanist perspective that identifies universal "modernity" as the panacea through which the country will be able to "exit" underdevelopment, violence, feudalism, authoritarianism, etc. They think of the "evils" of the country as a simple matter of the *absence or lack of modernity*. What I say is that the history of the processes of modernization itself, not only in Colombia but around the entire world (including the so-called First World), has proven completely false this humanist vision according to which people will one day "grow up" and govern ourselves according to moral and rational imperatives. In fact, what has happened is the exact opposite. We have not become freer, nor more autonomous, nor more prosperous in Colombia, but rather further subjected to violence and corruption, increased inequality, the reign of public indifference, etc.

And these phenomena can no longer be attributed to "external" factors, as Marxism tended to argue in the 1960s and 1970s. Genealogy, as I said before, focuses on local practices. It does not "deduce" these practices from constellations that come from "outside," like colonialism or imperialism, but rather it seeks to analyze them on the basis of their own historical rationality.

If I have chosen genealogy as a tool for thinking Colombian history, it has not been on a whim, nor because it is a "fashionable theory," nor due to any Eurocentric atavism. It is because genealogy is a method of analysis that allows me to avoid the traps of humanism. It shows us that today we are the product of what we have been, and that what we have been is not a "deviation" from some previously established model (modernity) or caused by some "fatal mistake" committed by the ruling elites. What we are *today* in Colombia is precisely an effect of that which we have *become*, and this is not because of some kind of "cunning of reason" but because we are a product of the historical road we have traveled. And genealogy seeks to trace precisely the form in which that road was so haphazardly built. But the humanist vision that predominates in academia refuses to recognize this. They continue to talk of "historical errors," of the "imperfect" way we are connected to modernity, and of "external powers" that have prevented us from being what we should be, etc. They obliterate coloniality in the name of a pure modernity that is offered as the universal destiny of the human race.

It sounds as if we are determined by our colonial past. Isn't that a rather despairing view?

We are not "determined," because history is an *open* process. But this opening is in no way absolute or automatic. To examine its "limits" is precisely what the practice of genealogical criticism does—to understand that "another world is possible," but not *which* other world, since we always have to account for our past whether we want to or not. We cannot make a tabula rasa of our own modern/colonial history and pretend that if "we correct some mistakes" we will some day be able to join the club of First World countries. That is pure populism. We cannot "socially engineer" a past that *we still are*. This is precisely what differentiates genealogy from those "humanist" forms of narrating Colombian history. We must understand that the political future of this country is not just based on what we "want to do," as Marxism proposes, nor on what it would be "desirable to do," as liberalism proposes, but rather on *what has effectively already happened.* Given that the only reality is that which one makes and has made, given that we are entirely the product of our own historical practices, then what *we can* do in the present will always have to begin with what we have done in the past. What I am trying to say here is that genealogy allows us to understand that only by recognizing our own radical historicity does the world of politics open up to us. That is to say, that political action must account for the games of truth and the spaces of power that have constituted us in history as moral subjects, always with the goal of transforming us. Ortega already told us that history is the only resource we have for launching ourselves into the future. There is nothing else. Therefore, unlike humanism, genealogy is not concerned with utopias, because the "forgetting" of our historical games of truth, marked by modernity/coloniality, necessarily entails political excess and its most immediate consequences: terror and cruelty—which we already know quite a bit about in Colombia.

I don't know if I understood you correctly, but it seems that you are saying that the political value of genealogy originates in its critique of utopias.

Correct, because utopias by definition deny space and, consequently, make a tabula rasa of power. They are a manifestation of political voluntarism. Foucault and Sloterdijk have already shown how power is always spatialized and how these spaces of power change over time. As long as we do not develop a critique of those modern/colonial games of truth with which we have been constituted as subjects in historically defined *spaces of power,* we will continue to believe that the construction of alternate political futures in this country is a matter of pure will or of directing the attack against external enemies. I therefore prefer not to talk about utopias but rather about *heterotopias,* of the construction of "other spaces" that we can use to constitute ourselves as moral and political subjects, to transform ourselves into ourselves *through and against* the spaces of power that have shaped our history (counterspaces), instead of hoping for voluntarist solutions that will resolve our problems.

Finally, Santiago, tell us what you're currently working on.

Right now I'm working on two projects. On the one hand, I am building an archive of the years 1958–1969 in three cities, Bogotá, Medellín, and Calí, with the purpose of examining the establishment at that time of what we could call a "plane of immanence." I am referring here to a certain core attitude that contemplates the possibility of *revolutionizing the world* through one's own moral powers, without needing to recur to a previously "given" meaning of existence. It is a moment in which one could begin to *believe* that the total emancipation of the imagination and of life itself is possible in a country like Colombia. I think that this is the attitude one begins to observe in people like the Nadaists, hippies, rockers, communists, performers, the *cocacolos*, intellectuals, artists, and even priests.[2] The idea would be to examine the ways in which these people constituted themselves as moral subjects of their own actions, that is to say, to look at how they subjectivized themselves through a certain *parrhesia*, a "courage of truth" that caused them to risk their lives in everything they did and said. I am still not very sure where this project is going, as I will have to see what the archive tell me. But I hope that it will constitute the final book of my trilogy on Colombian history, the series on the genealogies of Colombianness.

The other project, which is more long-term, has to do with philosophy in Colombia. This is concretely related to some of the topics we've discussed in this interview, with the shift from a traditional "history of philosophy in Colombia," centered on the university and on the works of professional philosophers toward a *genealogy of the philosophical practices* that are not restricted to either the university or the activity of philosophers, and in any case begins much earlier than when the majority of historians of ideas usually date the "beginning" of modern philosophy in Colombia: the foundation of the Institute of Philosophy at the Universidad Nacional in 1946. It is not clear yet where this project will go either, but for the time being I have created a research group made up of professors and students from various universities, and we want to move outside of the annoying scholarly networks established by Colciencias.[3] Thus it will be some time before I can tell you what kind of results these projects have achieved. We'll have to wait and see.

APPENDIX 2

SANTIAGO CASTRO-GÓMEZ'S *CRITIQUE OF LATIN AMERICAN REASON*: CONTEMPORARY PROVOCATIONS

CHAPTER 1: POSTMODERNISM'S CHALLENGES TO LATIN AMERICAN PHILOSOPHY

Don Deere—Fordham University

Chapter 1 of *Critique of Latin American Reason* leads us to ask, in relation to the ontology of Latin American reality in the present: what is critique? Castro-Gómez considers whether the postmodern crisis of the Enlightenment subject must be seen as neutralizing the possibilities of critical reason. Does the decentering of the subject and of heroic narratives of progress undermine the critique of colonial modernity in Latin America? Castro-Gómez firmly answers "no," disagreeing with criticisms voiced against postmodernity at the time in Latin America. Rather than seeing postmodernity as an elitist, imported, Eurocentric discourse, he sees it as defining the ontology of the present in Latin America. It is not reducible to neoliberalism, to the late stages of capitalist production, the "withdrawal of the state and the expansion of the market" (16). Also not reducible to false consciousness, postmodern disenchantment is a tool for radical critique that unbinds false unities.

My first question is whether he sees this fragmentary ontological reality of postmodernity in Latin America as an emancipatory phenomenon in itself, or as bearing an overlooked emancipatory potential. In light of

Castro-Gómez's hesitations in the prologue about postmodern discourse, and his later shift to a discourse of transmodern politics in recent work, it is worth asking which resources he draws from the postmodern turn, and where he sees its potential limitations.

He emphasizes the critical dimensions of *dissensus*, *perspectivism*, and an overall *agonistic* view of politics. Avoiding a foundational Cartesian subject or Marx's collective subject, and against a harmonizing consensus of reason or politics, he advocates an unbinding dissensus as the resource for democratic pluralism. He recognizes that Dussel's philosophy of liberation offers its own critique of the subject, when Dussel demonstrates that the modern rational ego cogito is identical with the dominating colonizing *ego conquiro*. This reverses, but does not displace, the modern episteme's binary logic, homogenizing the other as a unified, unequivocal source of justice and the good. Where Dussel conceives the "other" of modernity as an "exteriority," Castro-Gómez turns toward an "outside." Here I wonder what this shift to the outside means for Castro-Gómez, and for the other critical terms of this chapter: dissensus, agonism, and perspectivism. Instead of the utopia of perfect harmony, does Castro-Gómez's outside name the heterotopia of another possibility, the possibility of the event?

CHAPTER 2: MODERNITY, RATIONALIZATION, AND CULTURAL IDENTITY IN LATIN AMERICA

Rocío Zambrana—Emory University

Chapter 2 of *Crítica* is key to discussions about and beyond this remarkable book. Assessing the social sciences and cultural studies in Latin America, Santiago launches a critique of discourses about an authentic Latin American rationality. The chapter is an important reflection on the critique of modernity in the context of "globalization" and neoliberalism. Moreover, the chapter exposes the inaccuracy and danger of identity-based claims about the "radical alterity" of a Latin American rationality (3). The full force of this argument culminates in chapter 6, where Santiago shows that processes of subalternization, where the "other" "appears as an external, unitary essence," in fact express "imperial fantasies" that establish the other as that which is to "be known, classified, controlled" (137). Notions of alterity, exteriority, authenticity, and identity reproduce rather than resist the colonial gesture.

The chapter engages the work of Cristián Parker and Pedro Morandé, for whom a genuine Latin American rationality is exterior to processes of modernization. Intuitions of pre-Columbian cultures that have survived in spite of the cultural synthesis of Hispanic, African, and Indigenous traditions establish the radical alterity of Latin American rationality (3). Santiago sees in these efforts to distill a Latin American ethos opposed to the pathos of Western modernity a misunderstanding of critiques of instrumental rationality as totalizing. Processes of rationalization are contingent and yield a multiplicity of rationalities that respond to the project of modernization in specific spaces-times.

Santiago then explores the hybridization of modernity and tradition in the work of Jesús Martín-Barbero, Néstor García Canclini, and José Joaquín Brunner. Because of symbolic, technological, and financial mediation, Latin American rationality is not strictly opposed to but is rather traversed by modernity (33). On the one hand, models that subsume modernity under objectifying rationalization cannot "explain the multitemporal and radically heterogeneous experience of living in Latin America during the second half of the twentieth century" (47). Processes of modernization operate in light of the particular history—of political, economic, and cultural specificities—that captures. On the other hand, positing a Latin American rationality that remains radically other to such processes amounts to a false exit from history.

Question 1: Calling into question the idea of radical alterity is crucial. Santiago shows how it implies a monolithic, totalizing view of modernity/rationality, which obscures that modernization is effective precisely *by* producing, organizing, or maintaining heterogeneous, discontinuous, conflicting rationalities, temporalities, modes of knowing, sensing, being, relating. Alterity and authenticity indexes a colonial fantasy that delivers the "other" to dispossession and control.

But how would Santiago pursue these arguments today? Still in light of "hybridity?" Aníbal Quijano's notion of coloniality of power offers a productive contrast. It emphasizes the historical-structural heterogeneity of the global matrix of colonial power of which rationality/modernity is the epistemic center. If one grants that this is not a totalizing or monolithic account of power, can we think of Latin American rationality/rationalities beyond absolute subsumption *or* radical alterity?[1] As a product of the coloniality of power? As a feature of the ongoing productivity of the coloniality of power?

Question 2: I am interested in Santiago's discussion of Morandé's distinction between *lo criollo* and *lo mestizo*. While lo criollo indexes racial hierarchy through proximity to whiteness, lo mestizo represents a cultural synthesis in "ritual praxis." What is the role of race, as the central technology of capitalist modernity, in the account of hybridity and nonpurity that sets the coordinates for the discussion in *Crítica*?

In the book's concluding interview, Santiago clarifies the difference between Foucault's analysis of sovereign power and the coloniality of power. The latter concerns the power of criollo elites in the context of the Spanish colonies. This form of power continues the racial hierarchy installed in the conquest and colonial period by "the perpetuation of the privileges inherited by criollos through the racialization of alliances with the goal of preventing 'intruders' (Blacks, Indians, and mestizos) from accessing kinship networks. These were technologies of defense . . . reactive strategies" (232). This racial order is rearticulated in the twentieth and twenty-first centuries through the project of modernization, indeed "development." Could Santiago say more about how he sees race and the racial order that organizes Latin American reason in and beyond the book?

Question 3: What are the further implications of the critique of radical alterity? While I agree about its pitfalls and dangers, especially at the hands of criollo elites, in academia and various political spaces, it is crucial to acknowledge the presence of communities, ancestral knowledges, and other modes of being and relating in resistance to or fugitivity from ongoing colonial dispossession. Black, Indigenous, and Afro-Indigenous communities, as Yuderkys Espinosa Miñoso has shown, build from countermemory despite centuries of dispossession, seeking autonomy from the state/capital. I suspect that how we understand alterity and exteriority here is key. How should we understand the critique of Latin American reason in the face of forms of resistance and fugitivity that have been operative since the conquest, slave trade, colonial period, postcolonial period, and present?

CHAPTER 3: POPULISM AND PHILOSOPHY

Barnor Hesse—Northwestern University

What are the political ethnographies and historiographies that inform ontological claims inscribed in the concept of Latin America? In addition, how do political ethnographies and historiographies that do not inform these ontological claims make possible what does inform them? In chapter 3 of *Critique of Latin American Reason*, Santiago Castro-Gómez argues that the emergence of Latin American philosophy and critical thought cannot be understood outside its engagements with and inscriptions in the development of populism in Latin America. In that landscape and lineage, populism meant something very distinctive. It was a defining epistemological condition of possibility for the idea of Latin America and, at the same time, a defining political discourse of Latin American modernity that originated nowhere else. Populism was a significant alternative or supplement to liberalism and democracy because it was uniquely inscribed in and emergent from the construction and mobilization of a seductively affective idea of "the people." During the 1930s, populism in Latin America was radicalized in economic crises, sometimes antiliberal, sometimes antidemocratic, sometimes both, as a statist, top-down, construction of "the people" who were commandeered to political and economic tasks and projects in the light of regimes unable to absorb or unwilling to countenance democratic demands.

Although, Castro-Gómez does not put matters in these terms, arguably given the colonial-racial-settler-slavery foundations of Latin America and its enduring mimetic responses to European modernity and Western civilization, the task of reimagining the people for Latin American intellectuals was as *racially compelling as it was racially precarious*. This is the background that ontologically haunts Castro-Gómez's identification of the three main strategies undertaken by writers in conceptualizing the Latin American people. He describes these as "in search of deep America," "mestizaje," and the "idealization of Latin American ethics." Each of these resulted in different ways of trying to think through in populist terms the *unifying cultural demography of Indigenous Latin American and European modernity Latin America*. If this is indeed an orthodox genealogy of the predicaments if not undecidabilities of the ontological commitments of Latin American political philosophy, I wonder what an *alternative critical genealogy* might contribute to this representation. There are two questions I have that concern the colonial-racial logic of what might be described as the *populist unthought* in Castro-Gomez's thinking, which can be revealed in the strategic role he assigns to populism in the meanings of Latin America that he excavates. First, in relation to the time period in which the thinking under discussion emerges, it is worth asking, again, who are "the people" in the populist construction of "the people"? While Castro-Gómez is keen to emphasize that Latin American thought did not attend to the question of difference, it is ironic that he ignores what has long been described as the policies of whitening Latin America, which began in the 1920s–1930s. This involved the circulation of scientific racism as common sense among white elites, the redesign of cities in European styles, the catalyzing of white European immigration, and the repression of Black cultural and political forms and visible/audible Black communities throughout the various nationalist landscapes of Latin America.[2] It is the erasure of any recognition of these colonial-racialized processes in the work of the thinkers under Castro-Gómez's consideration, and in Castro-Gómez's consideration of these thinkers, that leaves radically under-interrogated the political basis for conceptualizing a *white populist appeal* to the people in these thinkers.

My second question follows directly from the first. Over a decade ago, Walter Mignolo questioned of an "excess of confidence regarding the ontology of continental divides." In particular, he asked how the idea of Latin America came about and he stressed the importance of uncoupling its name from its prevailing "cartographic image." In short, Mignolo argued we need to "unravel the geo-politics of knowledge from the perspective of coloniality."[3] What is striking about all the thinkers Castro-Gómez considers, and indeed his own critique of them, is the extent to which the signifier *Latin America* appears to be fixed rather than floating, insofar as, in each instance of its citation, the colonial-racial-settler-slavery structure of Latin America as a contemporary political formation is absent and the presence of Afro-Latin America as the constituent outside a white or mestizaje Latin America is routinely silenced and rendered invisible. We should recall that by the first half of the nineteenth century, after the Latin American wars of independence, in response to the involvement of Black soldiers in that phase of nation-building, many white Latin American governing elites were concerned with preserving "racial harmony," at the expense of forestalling Black citizens making demands about racial equality, thereby avoiding what they described and feared as "race-wars."[4] Socially and discursively, this was the inception of erasing the influences of the *Black Radical Tradition* in Latin America that began with antislavery resistances and the formation of runaway slave maroon or palenque communities in sixteenth-century Mexico.[5] Here we can trace an obscuring of the role of the early nineteenth-century antislavery Black Republic of Haiti in sponsoring and resourcing Simón Bolívar's mobilization of independence movements across Latin America; and also expose the occulting of the demographic, cultural, and political meaning of legacies of racial slavery and the African Diaspora in animating the popular cultures of Latin America while being assailed by racism and anti-Blackness. With this positioning of Blackness as the constitutive outside of Latin America, we need to pause for further thought and ask how and why does the idea of Latin America reproduced by these writers repress this history and contemporaneity. In short, what sustains this deracialized signification of Latin America, both in the writers Santiago-Gómez analyzes as well as in his own commentary? There is much more to the cultural and political meaning of Latin America than white populism.

CHAPTER 4: LATIN AMERICA BEYOND PHILOSOPHY OF HISTORY

Cintia Martínez Velasco—Universidad Nacional Autónoma de México

Critique of Latin American Reason is a book that shifted the paradigms of philosophy in Latin America. It urges us to contemplate *parrhesia*, which Foucault understood as the act of saying the truth, in which "a speaker says something dangerous—different from what the majority believes,"[6] and which corresponds to the rule that "the truth is never the same."[7] This allows us to think about the scope of the book, which has proven to transcend the historical context in which it was written. When

Castro-Gómez says, "Let's be clear. The book *is not* a crusade against the legitimate aspirations to decolonization and the overcoming of cultural and economic dependency in our countries. . . . What it is fighting against is rather the *language* in which such aspirations were formulated by Latin American philosophy" (219), he is expressing a nonantagonistic interest in the decolonial turn. (I mention this in order to defend the book from the mistaken view that it distances itself entirely from the aims of the decolonial project. In one of his classes, Castro-Gómez once said, "One only criticizes what one considers important"). This entails struggling against the language of Latin American philosophy. What would it mean to change this language? What are the political implications of such a change?

For many readers, the discomforting moments of the book (and also of his most recent book *El tonto y los canallas* [The fool and the knaves]) include its characterization of populism as "mass democracy," while at the same time it was revealed that Latin American politics had erased citizens, and that the category of "the people" was obscuring the concrete possibility of disagreement. The parrhesiastic truth calling out to us in the book reveals that the underlying metaphysics of Latin Americanism is related to projects that negate political diversity. This gesture should be tirelessly replicated. I think of it today as a feminist in Mexico, where I can see how the category "the people" does not support women or the plight of feminicide. It is important to return to *Critique of Latin American Reason* because democracy is difficult in the midst of Manichaean auras and caudillos.

In the previous appendix, Castro-Gómez mentions a criticism he himself has made, over the years, about his own book—that it repeats the modernist gesture of distinguishing between the old and the new. In my view, the book also repeats a (perhaps modern?) division between the body and discourse. It annuls the possibility of a nonessentialist understanding of a speaker's sex, gender, and geopolitical conditions. The locus enunciationis is central to decolonial thought as well as to gender studies. Philosophy's task is to find an alternative approach to this problem. Affirming that the subject does not preexist the act of enunciation, and that the subject is the product of enunciation itself, does not obviate the need to problematize the body as a historical and political entity. In my view, the body/discourse divide inhibits adequate consideration of how language is spoken by different bodies that are open to the world. This is also to disagree with the distance taken from the historical at certain moments in chapter 4. I do agree, strongly, with the critical distance Castro- Gómez takes from the simple association between geoculture and thought (Kusch). It was important to debate the episteme of Latin American thought in the second half of the twentieth century. But isn't the Foucauldian view of the subject as the product of enunciation insufficient, if confined to the extensively discussed problem of the subject-subjected? The question of who speaks (and is able to speak) about racism or feminism continues to be difficult to answer, but political organizing obliges us to return to it. Most important, it has left us in a place of truth that, to use Foucault's words, "is never the same."

The change in strategy engendered by Latin American thought's turn towards genealogy represented an abandonment of the usual heroicness adopted by intellectual projects in Latin America. It displaced the embrace of humanist discourse by "enlightened elites" by rejecting historical continuities and by turning to multiplicity as a philosophical concept. This change in approach represented a rejection of any teleological philosophy of history or any project centered on a subject that would preexist the power relations constituting the possibilities for its discursive construction.

Genealogy means, among other things, "to excavate the ground of the Latin Americanist discourses that have pretended to speak in the name of the people, as well as to reveal the heterogeneous strata on which they are constructed" (280, note 21). In this new approach, there were inevitably actors who did not participate in the history of ideas or in those moments in the philosophy of history described by Zea and Roig. I am referring here to all the raced and gendered social subjects that did not belong to the upper classes. One success of the methodological change inspired by Castro-Gómez was the search for those interstices that cracked open both the History and the Grand Politics elaborated by heteronormative criollo elites (and later by the bourgeoisie).

From a distance, after having witnessed the profound influence this book has had on race and gender studies, I would mention at least one valuable aspect of the generation Zea calls "presumptuous." I am referring to the simple epistemological pretension shared by that generation in which figures like Dussel, Freire, Salazar Bondy, Vasconcelos et al. attempted to reach some kind of universal truth based in Latin America. This problem is dealt with very quickly in Castro-Gómez's book. I am suggesting here a shift in focus, for the truth that is sought need not necessarily be framed as univocal, ahistorical, or absolute and might be something that should still be pursued.

Why talk about truths after having read *Critique of Latin American Reason*? I want to cite a few words from Donna Haraway's *Staying with the Trouble: Making Kin in the Chthulucene.* When she writes, "Nothing is connected to everything; everything is connected to something,"[8] the former affirmation maintains that, in spite of everything, it is still possible to think. Her profound reflections on situated knowledge arose from her marginal position as a woman in science and therefore from not being able not to have a body. Haraway shows that knowledge only ever exists as situated knowledge without concluding (and this has left a powerful mark on me) that knowledge needs to be renounced. As she shows in "Situated Knowledges," to not see this would be to perpetuate the dichotomy between universality and particularity. For Haraway, no knowledge emerges from the eyes of God; to the contrary, everything, especially that which is said to be objective, comes from the eyes of situated bodies.

My interest here is to place Castro-Gómez in dialogue with Haraway and to reflect on the renunciation of philosophical, scientific, and abstract or universal knowledges in favor of smaller, local knowledges as unique alternatives to a unitary knowledge. Castro-Gómez suggests that nothing is said except from a position in relation to power. This does not mean, however, that it is impossible to say the truth, to speak of cells, or in political terms, to seek the common good. For Haraway, enunciating the position from which we speak retains these possibilities. Many bridges could be built between feminist epistemology and the critical turns of decolonial discourse. There have been interesting attempts to undertake this within the history of Latin American ideas and question hegemonic discourse's seeming lack of sex and race. Constructing a bridge between these approaches offers an opportunity to recognize that, as Haraway says, we cannot not have a body.

Translated by Andrew Ascherl

CHAPTER 5: THE AESTHETICS OF THE BEAUTIFUL IN SPANISH AMERICAN MODERNISM

Jesús Luzardo—Loyola University Chicago

In the fifth chapter of *Critique of Latin American Reason*, Castro-Gómez evaluates Iris M. Zavala's conception of Latin American modernism as a literary and intellectual tradition. Characterized or "permeated" by a Kantian aesthetics of the beautiful, it was distinct from European modernism and from the positivism and modernization exemplified by the United States. Furthermore, it offered an emancipatory and decolonial perspective. Ultimately, Castro-Gómez rejects Zavala's hypothesis, showing that Latin American modernism, and the "aesthetics of the beautiful" to which it appeals, gained its meaning from *and* engendered a colonial and mythological *Latin Americanism*; that is, a conception of a transcendental, harmonious, and exceptional Latin American reason and identity, which represented the natural and preordained endpoint and the recovery of a tradition—a way of being in the world—that had its origins in ancient Greece.

Following Rafael Gutiérrez Girardot and Octavio Paz, Castro-Gómez traces the roots of Latin American modernism to German Romanticism, to the post-Kantian aesthetics of Schiller and of the "Oldest Systematic Program for German Idealism." Here Romanticism is figured primarily as a reaction to the rationalization and mechanization of society, to the separation between morality and beauty, the mechanical and the organic, the individual and the community. Schiller, Hegel, and Schelling thus offer poetry and art—the "aesthetic education of man" in Schiller's words—as the primary grounds for synthesizing and harmonizing all such oppositions into a unified whole.

He then traces the influence of these romantic currents on the work of three Latin American modernists: José Enrique Rodó, Alfonso Reyes, and José Vasconcelos, each of whom advanced and deepened the project of a "*mythology of Latin American reason.*" These thinkers were united by their belief in and development of a Latin American identity that could resist and overcome the utilitarianism, mechanization, and positivism that characterized Anglo-Saxon thought in Europe and the United States.

This mythological conception of Latin Americanism culminates in the work of Vasconcelos, for whom Latin America and its "cosmic race" is the site "where the unity of the entire human race will be consummated and where the aesthetic ideal of the ancient Greeks will finally be realized."[9] Yet Vasconcelos's utopic vision made only more apparent what was already present in Rodó's *Ariel*, and what is actually constitutive of Latin American modernism and its corresponding mythology of a Latin American reason, namely a white-supremacist and eugenic vision of the continent and the race that conceived of the conquest of America as a civilizing mission and that rendered Blackness and indigeneity dysfunctional and subject to erasure for the improvement of the race.[10]

My "provocations" concern, first, the possibility and potential of romantic aesthetics for liberatory and decolonial purposes. Here my question is whether romantic aesthetics can be disentangled from its nostalgic desire for return, its "hearkening back" to an assumed point of origin. I am thinking here, for example, of María del Rosario Acosta López's work on Schiller's aesthetics as creating a space for critique and for a reconception of freedom.[11]

Second, what, in the view of Castro-Gómez, is entailed for the position of indigeneity and Blackness vis-á-vis Latin American identity, or "Latinidad" by this critique of Latin American reason? His critique of Latin American modernism largely presents this relationship negatively, in terms of Latin American modernism's exclusion of and desire for the erasure of indigeneity and Blackness in the construction of mestizo identity. But here I want to go further and think about the more active (though no less violent) and positive (in Foucault's sense) role that indigeneity and Blackness played, and continues to play, in the constitution of a Latin American identity through enslavement, subjection, domination, capture, and/or assimilation. Finally, given Castro-Gomez's critique of Latin American identity in this chapter and throughout the book, I am curious about the (im)possibility, the (in)stability, and the (mis)uses of formulations such as "Afro-Latinidad." These have become a new site for tension and antagonism, and perhaps for realignment and solidarity, within popular discourses on Latinidad in the Unites States, while remaining undertheorized in corresponding philosophical discourses and debates.

CHAPTER 6: POSTCOLONIAL REASON AND LATIN AMERICAN PHILOSOPHY

Yuderkys Espinosa Miñoso—Grupo Latinoamericano de Estudio, Formación y Acción Feminista (GLEFAS)/FLACSO

In chapter 6, Santiago Castro-Gómez begins his reflections with a brief overview of the impact of postcolonial studies associated with authors such as Said, Spivak, and Bhabha, interrogating their reception within Latin American cultural studies, particularly in the readings that have come from the United States in recent years. In the case of Latin America, debate about postcolonialism was, the author points out, an addition to the debate about postmodernity. Citing the foundational manifesto of the Latin American Subaltern Studies Group, he specifically reads and offers a detailed analysis of early work by one of its members, Walter Mignolo.

As Castro-Gómez recalls, in its manifesto the group declares its interest in revising a kind of Latin American historiography that is primarily based, as is dependency theory, on binary paradigms of social analysis" (138): center-periphery, development-underdevelopment, First World–Third World, etc. To go beyond this kind of analysis, they propose making visible the "hybrid and mutant character of subaltern groups" in the subcontinent.

However, in his extensive and detailed review of some of Mignolo's works, Santiago will conclude that Mignolo ultimately remains trapped in what he is trying to break away from. For Castro-Gómez, Latin American philosophy does not accomplish a rupture with the modern episteme. Rather, it perpetuates the humanist and anticolonial narrative already developed by that same episteme. As he claims, he is interested in examining what makes it possible to articulate a Latin American exteriority in relation to modern positivism.

Castro-Gómez argues that Latin American philosophy seems to emerge out of the division identified by Foucault between the objective world and the subjective world. A tension exists in the modern episteme out of which the interrogation of the human being splits into two directions, both opposed and complementary: the study of the world of the spirit and the study of the material, physical world—in other words, positivism and humanism. According to Castro-Gómez, Latin American philosophy furthers the humanist tendencies opened up within the field of modern philosophy. From there, the author undertakes a new approach to the work of Rodolfo Kusch, Leopoldo Zea, and Enrique Dussel that differs from Mignolo's earlier efforts.

For Castro-Gómez, Kusch's reading of the two antagonistic forms of life described in his thesis on Latin America only demonstrates that his philosophy "operates precisely according to the rules of formation of the discourses opened up by the modern episteme" (155). For Castro-Gómez, this is ultimately a humanism. He then speaks to the paradox of talking about "other-knowledges" (*cononocimientos-otros*) from within a discourse that ultimately does not abandon the modern episteme. As he asserts, this is the contradiction of anticolonial narratives.

He then turns to Leopoldo Zea, who, as the author recalls, found in the figure of Caliban a means of exiting the negation that Latin America has made of itself. This would mean being able to overcome colonialism not through negation but rather through the radicalization of modernity's emancipatory potential. Once again, Castro-Gómez finds a further example of a Latin American philosopher who adopts the "critical language of modernity" rather than establishing an exteriority to the modern episteme. Zea's notion of "man and nothing more" is, he finds, continuous with the transcendental subject of modern philosophy. Similarly, he concludes of Kusch that an anticolonial narrative is made possible by the "modern episteme's rules of enunciation." Therefore, he argues, it is not only a matter of what one says nor of how one says it. It is not enough to condemn Prospero—his language must be transgressed.

Finally, Castro-Gómez examines Dussel's work to show once more how, there being no exteriority in his thought, it is impossible to maintain Mignolo's idea of a "border episteme," at least insofar as these authors could be described. Citing Salazar Ramos, Castro-Gómez concludes that Dussel's project of a philosophy of liberation is rooted in a belief in a universal history, culture, and subject. At most, this would be a Latin American philosophy aspiring to a humanist rather than an imperialist European modernity.

Mignolo's inclusion of these authors within the category of "border epistemology" is problematic, Castro-Gómez concludes, because it requires assuming that the place of enunciation is defined by the speaker's place of origin. The place of enunciation would have nothing to do with whether the subject is "European or Indigenous, Jew or Christian, Black or white" (161–62). What is important here is not how the speaking subject can be empirically described but rather the "epistemic rules" within which their speech occurs.

In *Crítica*, Santiago seems to be alerting us to, and adopting a position about, a very real problem in contemporary social movements, in feminist and antiracist politics, and in certain theoretical analyses associated with these movements: the limits of identity politics. By taking up a Foucauldian archaeological method, the author invites us to consider that what is of concern is neither the subject of enunciation nor its characteristics, but rather its discursive practices. To be sure, these can be articulated, but not entirely so. The danger, as Castro-Gómez himself warns, lies in legitimating authoritarian and unjust practices through the deceptive pretension to epistemic alterity.

What political implications would result from this argument that an alternative epistemology does not ultimately concern the empirical place of enunciation from which the subject speaks, but rather the presumed epistemic rules of the analysis or of the interpretation of the world? At a time when racism and the familiar faces of predatory capitalism are on the rise, how can we take account of this warning without falling back on the universal subject that appears not to be historically determined because its origin and physical characteristics are so familiar. Similarly, I am thinking of Castro-Gómez's claim that, in the end, alterity lies more in how one speaks than in the content of speech itself. It seems to me that this claim is articulated from an epistemological theoretical framework with which it is very much in line: poststructuralism. Today, several decades after the peak of poststructuralism and what we have come to know as its limits, is it still possible to defend this statement or should it be reconsidered and revised? Effectively, and as the author argues, while Caliban continues to speak the language of Prospero, "there will be no dissolution, only displacement" within the same episteme. Yet the episteme is not only a rule of enunciation. The rule entails the world and produces it, while at the same time being produced by the world. Caliban's problem is ultimately that, by learning the master's language he runs the risk of seeing and acting in the world like the master. However, domination is not a totality; there is always mockery, there is always resistance.

Translated by Andrew Ascherl

CHAPTER 6: POSTCOLONIAL REASON AND LATIN AMERICAN PHILOSOPHY

Jimmy Casas Klausen—IRI, PUC-Rio

In chapter 6 of *Critique of Latin American Reason*, Santiago Castro-Gómez undertakes a critical analysis of Walter Mignolo's contribution to the demarcation of a postcolonial Latin American philosophy. Drawing mainly on "early" Foucault, Castro-Gómez concludes that, in Mignolo's presentations of Latin American philosophers, "we are not faced with a rupture of the modern episteme, as Mignolo suggests; rather, we stand before a humanist and anticolonial narrative made possible by the modern episteme itself" (153). Castro-Gómez's critique of the implications of Mignolo's deployment of postcolonial reason seems fully convincing to me. I wish only to ask what we might learn by extending it further, by explicitly weaving an analytic of power into the chapter? What are the implications for the study of colonial and postcolonial power relations of Castro-Gómez's critique of Mignolo? What are the power effects and consequences for an analytic of power of Castro-Gómez's and Mignolo's arguments?

Castro-Gómez's chapter opens with a nod to Edward Said and South Asian postcolonial theory and notes especially the influence of Ranajit Guha's work on the formation of the Latin American Subaltern Studies Group. In *Elementary Aspects of Peasant Insurgency in Colonial India*, Guha famously suggested that, since South Asian insurgency is recorded only in the archives of counterinsurgency—that is, from elite and/or colonial perspectives—subaltern resistance appears as though "in a distorting mirror"; nevertheless, "the distortion has a logic to it."[12] To decode the logic of distortion is to develop an analytics of power and to reconstruct elementary aspects of resistance (not to reveal resistance in some unmediated fashion).

Even though Mignolo had participated in the Latin American Subaltern Studies Group, he distances himself from Guha and his model of power differs substantially.[13] Mignolo's border epistemology and pluritopic theory of enunciation posit access to a persistent/resistant locus of enunciation somehow quasi-exterior to colonial domination, thus also to the modern episteme (148–49)—ultimately a contradictory position, as Castro-Gómez argues (155). That is, Mignolo presumes it is possible to precipitate from the ruins of Andean and Mesoamerican civilizations a rival—hybrid—center of power that he later identifies with decoloniality.[14] At the same time, viewing European colonial power as sovereigntist, Mignolo constructs a monotopic power bloc that implements, banishes, erases, obstructs—what Foucault called a repressive model of power. In short, there is domination in European colonization and Indigenous resistance—two opposed though asymmetrical centers of power.

Why does this matter? Decolonial theory is often deployed, even among critical theorists based in South America, monolithically. In fact, though, and as Castro-Gómez insists, "modernidad/colonialidad" is neither a group nor a collective "but rather a heterogeneous network of scholars" (237). As such, it will prove unhelpful for most purposes to treat them uniformly as a school with a shared diagnosis of power relations. If Castro-Gómez can be said to join a Foucauldian analytics of power with analyses of *modernidad/colonialidad*, then how does *Critique of Latin American Reason* construct power relations? More specifically, how does chapter 6 implicitly model power relations—or point to a model of power relations—in colonial and postcolonial South America? Presumably, in light of its critique of Mignolo, it would demand fine-grained analysis rather than metalevel, continental/hemispheric diagnostics, but what would its "elementary aspects" be?

CHAPTER 7: THE BIRTH OF LATIN AMERICA AS A PHILOSOPHICAL PROBLEM IN MEXICO

Rafael Vizcaíno—DePaul University

In his "The Birth of Latin America as a Philosophical Problem in Mexico," Santiago Castro-Gómez offers a succinct account of how twentieth-century philosophy in Mexico developed a specifically philosophical meditation on the meaning of Latin America. For Castro-Gómez, such entire dialogue, and the distinct positions taken by individual figures such as José Vasconcelos, Samuel Ramos, José Gaos, Leopoldo Zea, Emilio Uranga, and Edmundo O'Gorman, can be conceived as taking a stance on the "question of modernity." Such a move is a paradigmatically *decolonial* analysis insofar as the question of modernity is not conceived from the "rhetoric" (Mignolo) that links modernity to specifically intra-European circumstances cut off from what is taken to be beyond the context of Europe, that is, Renaissance, Reform, and Enlightenment. Instead, the question of modernity is here coupled to that forgotten elsewhere, or, to use a provocative term in the history of Latin American philosophy, to that forgotten *exteriority* without which modernity would not have materialized. This *decolonial* way of framing the field of Latin American philosophy circumvents the usual obstacles that one tends to encounter when working on this field in the "Westernized" university (Ramón Grosfoguel): one is no longer seeking to validate the field's relevance and originality vis-à-vis European philosophy; instead, the field's questions and contributions are already on par with those of European philosophy without making the latter the standard of philosophical excellence.

CHAPTER 7: THE BIRTH OF LATIN AMERICA AS A PHILOSOPHICAL PROBLEM IN MEXICO

Nadia Yala Kisukidi—Université Paris VIII

Chapter 7, "The Birth of Latin America as a Philosophical Problem in Mexico," is striking for many reasons. It presents a series of philosophical problems through the portraits of Latin American philosophers. Mexico is the scene (both geographical and conceptual) of this intellectual history of philosophy. It is traversed by one major question: How did "Latin America" become a problem in the discipline of philosophy?" Moreover, how did it become a "concept"—that is to say, a totalizing idea that subsumes the contradictions of the reality confronting us? But this question hides another, the core of this chapter: "How did "philosophy" itself also become a problem in Latin America?"

Castro-Gómez explains the history of the institutionalization of philosophy and its disciplinarization in Mexico through political events—the Revolution of 1910 and the rise of nationalism. The question of national identity becomes one of the main problems of the intellectual Mexican scene at the beginning of the twentieth century, challenging the universalist claim of (Western) philosophy. Two paths can be followed for understanding the difficulties that arise from the dialectical tension between the idea of philosophy and the idea of "Latin America." The first is a deviation, the second an exit:

1. To understand the stakes, we can try a comparison with the intellectual history of Africa in the twentieth century, especially in the so-called francophone part of the continent. The ontological question "Is there an African philosophy?" became (and still is) an important one in the nineteen-fifties when the ideologies of anticolonialism and languages of liberation rooted in new nationalisms developed in the African continent. Philosophy was embedded in the wider context of the history of decolonization shaking African intellectuals. Through this general ontological question, two problems were underlined:

- Why is Africa a problem for philosophical reason?
- Why is "philosophy" a problem for Africa?

Those interrogations are not rhetorical games: they indicate how the history of "philosophy" was written in the Western world and taught in some African institutions (schools, universities, religious missions) built during the colonization. We can map this history, because the history of philosophy, as it is told in the Western canon, is intertwined with a topology. Reason was born in Greece. Europe is the soil for the development of the Enlightenment. Other areas of the world had religions, wisdoms, but could not create a "civilization" as such. And Africa (the "Black" Africa), in these geographies of philosophical reason, has no spiritual existence at all. We all recognize the well-known Hegelian mapping of reason—but I don't want to focus on this philosophy of history. What is interesting is what African intellectuals have made of the fact of their exclusion from the history of philosophy, from the canon. And, more specifically, what it says about philosophy as a discipline.

Understood through the Western idealization of the life of Reason, the idea of Africa and the idea of philosophy appear as an "oxymoron" (to quote Souleymane Bachir Diagne).[15] The question whether an African philosophy exists took the form of a debate opposing the supporters of ethnophilosophy (the idea that there is an African philosophy, rooted in African cultures, owing nothing to Western intellectual traditions) and their critics. By examining the universality of philosophy, this debate shows how the noun *philosophy* in itself becomes a problem when it travels outside the Western world.

We all know that the Western canon was built and rebuilt from the Middle Ages to the twenty-first century through gestures of exclusion: exclusion of Arabic intellectual traditions, then Indian and Chinese traditions, and so on, from the philosophical library. In addition to these gestures of exclusion, intellectuals tried to retake possession of the noun *philosophy.* Not only did they rewrite another history of philosophy but they did so by showing that philosophy has a value beyond the discipline in itself.

The African debate "Is, or isn't, there an African philosophy?" questions the normativity of a discipline. But it also shows that "philosophy" is an object of "desire." What gives value to philosophy is not only its aim (*philo*) to reach a kind of "universal truth," but also the type of social representations that it causes and creates: to be part of civilization and humanity.

In the Latin American debate that is underscored in this chapter, can these kinds of analyses also be developed? Can we say that philosophy was grasped by Latin American intellectuals as an object of desire, a display of humanity and civilization? In this case, may we conclude that the practice of philosophy in non-Western worlds cannot escape from the framework of "mimesis?"

2. Finally, and as Castro-Gómez shows, through the different portraits of Mexican philosophers (such as Vasconcelos, Ramos), the tension between the universalist dimension of philosophy and the manner of using the discipline to understand the multiple realities (ontological, historical, clinical) of Latin America questions the *being* of philosophy in itself.

Can we say that this tension underlines a new way to exit from "philosophy"? And to create new disciplines? A kind of gesture that would allow us to reconnect with the decolonial turn described by the intellectual moments in this chapter?

APPENDIX: FROM THE HISTORY OF IDEAS TO THE LOCALIZED GENEALOGY OF PRACTICES

María del Rosario Acosta López—University of California, Riverside

Hernán Alejandro Cortés has done a wonderful job guiding the conversation in such a way that the interview provides both an overview of Castro-Gómez's path as a philosopher and critical thinker and a very helpful retrospective reflection on the value of Castro-Gómez's work starting with *Crítica*. *Crítica*, according to Castro-Gómez's own words (and honoring Kant's first critique whose title it suggestively echoes), would have been a means to clear the way for Castro-Gómez's real interest and future projects, namely a *philosophical critique* of Latin America (where the very concept of philosophy and its disciplinary boundaries needs also to be interrogated if the object of study is to be taken seriously) via a genealogical work in which Colombia and "Colombianness" are the primary objects of inquiry.

This "clearing the way" has, on the one hand, a "destructive," or, as Castro-Gómez clarifies in the interview, a "deconstructive" side: there is no future for Latin American philosophy, Castro-Gómez argues, not only because its time has passed but also because as a project it already began as a fallacy in that it presupposes what it actually needs to produce, namely Latin America as an object of study (cf. 227). Faithful to this second side of the question, that is, the historical production of Latin America as "Latin Americanism," *Crítica* posits and creates the conditions of possibility for a more positive side of the project, namely a philosophical critique of Latin America that takes thorough account of the reasons why its point of departure needs to be the destructuring of the very idea of a Latin American philosophy. Such a philosophical critique needs to start by answering the question, as Castro-Gómez puts it, of "*why* we have ended up *where* we are" (211).

Leaving aside for the moment the genealogical inflection, addressed in my second group of questions, I am very interested in this particular formulation. First, because there is the presupposition of a "we." Not only in this specific formulation but, I would venture, behind the project per se. I understand it is a "we" that needs to be interrogated and that has constantly been taken apart historically and archeologically by Castro-Gómez's work, but Castro-Gómez could be pressed further on this aspect of his work—given his strong critique of Latin American philosophy. What differentiates this "we" from the object Latin American philosophy assumes instead of interrogating? How can one answer this question philosophically (why we have ended up where we are) without falling into either a kind of "Latin Americanism" or into the "universalisms" (as Castro-Gómez sometimes calls them) of a philosophy pretending to be "done from nowhere?"

In terms of what these questions entail, I am asking what needs to *happen to philosophy* so as to develop adequate tools for answering this question in the era, as Castro-Gómez describes it, of "global capitalism" (cf. 215)? Further, how would Castro-Gómez actualize this task *today*—must his critique of Latin-American reason also undergo this kind of critique? Is it still an adequate tool for a critique of capitalism and its most extreme current version in the Americas, namely (to use Rocío Zambrana's work) *neoliberal coloniality*?

My second set of questions concerns the political side of the project Castro-Gómez describes as "the legitimate aspirations to decolonization and the overcoming of cultural and economic dependency in our countries" (219). Here I want to pose this question in connection with "genealogy," which Castro-Gómez, working beyond disciplinary boundaries, describes as his methodology. Genealogy, Castro-Gómez says, "maps the present through a cartography of the past, with the goal of *transforming the present*" (233).

The question of genealogical work as differentiated from the history of ideas is key here and seems to be a real entry into the kind of work Castro-Gómez has always pursued. There are at least two components of this work, as he explains when he is pushed (thanks to Cortés) to speak so clearly and self-reflectively about his own methodology. First, genealogy is not history of ideas; neither is it really a history of practice. It is a history of the *grammars* that govern these practices and articulate them a priori, that is, a history of the conditions of possibility or the rationality of *dispositifs* (cf. 229). Second, this means that whoever wants to do genealogical work needs to produce an archive that grants access to the materiality of practices as well, so as then to be able disentangle their mode of articulation from their functioning (cf. 229). Without going further into the connections and the problems that may result from them—between the production of the archive and the uncovering of these grammars, I am interested in paying attention to the way Castro-Gómez describes genealogical work as ultimately opening up a path or clearing the way for politics and political action (cf. 244). Genealogical work, Castro-Gómez says, complicates the connection between past and present. It reminds us that past *is* present, that the forces configured historically in a certain past are still the grammars that structurally give shape to the political forces in the present. In order to *deactivate* them (my word, not Castro-Gómez's), we first need to *denaturalize* them (cf. 233). This is the critical element here: the way in which genealogical work enters into the struggle for meaning by offering a "knowledge of our historical a prioris" (233).

Thinking about how very political the question around memory—and the production and recognition of the ongoing action of the past in the present—has become in Colombia specifically, I wonder how Castro-Gómez would connect this genealogical task to today's most pressing issues in Colombia. *Crítica*, *La Hybris del punto zero,* and *Tejidos Oníricos* all show us how powerful genealogy can be as a mode of critique. How would he describe the political potency lying today in the kind of critique produced in these works (his genealogical works, as he has sometimes put it, on "Colombianness")? What are the political stakes behind doing this kind of work? And would he say that this kind of work also requires a revision in terms of what its operation presupposes? What it presupposes, in my opinion, comes to light clearly today in Colombia's extreme, violent situation: that the contest for memory and history in Colombia not only needs to come to terms with the history of the production of the structures that sustain it today but also, perhaps speaking here from a decolonial perspective, with the question of what notion of history and what criteria for intelligibility have determined what counts and is indexed as historical.

NOTES

PROLOGUE TO THE SECOND EDITION

1. I am referring here to the group of professors at the Universidad Santo Tomás who took up the problem of "Latin American philosophy" in the mid-1970s, which included Jaime Rubio Angulo, Germán Marquínez, Luis José González, Roberto Salazar Ramos, Eudoro Rodríguez, Gloria Reyes, Joaquín Zabalza, Saúl Barato, Teresa Houghton, Juan José Sanz, Carlos Flórez, and Cayetano Páez.

INTRODUCTION

1. "Is the Post- in Postmodernism the Post- in Postcolonial?," *Critical Inquiry* 17, no. 2 (Winter 1991): 336–57, https://doi.org/10.1086/448586.

1. POSTMODERNITY'S CHALLENGES TO LATIN AMERICAN PHILOSOPHY

1. In fact, the thesis of a "Farewell to Dependency Theory" had already been presented in 1974 on the occasion of the Second Latin American Congress of Sociology. José Luis de Imaz, "¿Adiós a la teoría de la dependencia? Una perspectiva desde la Argentina," *Estudios Internacionales* 28 (1974): 49–75. Among the reasons Imaz finds to explain this departure is dependency theory's lofty ambitions to offer a comprehensive explanation of underdevelopment, thereby surpassing the possibilities of empirical verification, as well as the tendency to an "externalism" that would make it difficult to take proper responsibility for the problems in our society.

2. By "disenchantment of the world," I mean the situation that Max Weber described as the "loss of meaning" that results from the processes of rationalization, not an abundance of life or some type of existential nihilism. The thesis I will defend in this chapter is that what we call postmodernity is nothing other than the effect of the irreversible generalization of modernity in Latin America. The processes of modern rationalization, which do not require any transcendental legitimation, have become hegemonic in Latin America not only in the realms of politics and economics but also and particularly in the sphere of *everyday life*. Postmodernity, therefore, is the extension of modernity to the "lifeworld." It is not only a phenomenon that affects intellectuals: it is *a mass experience*.
3. The "modern image of thought," as has been shown by Foucault and Deleuze, is the mode of existence of discourses that emerged between the end of the eighteenth century and the middle of the twentieth century. This refers to the a priori dispositions that make it possible for certain concepts and objects of investigation, for certain problems and modes of enunciation, to be expressed in a specific historical era.
4. Sánchez Vázquez reproduces here, point by point, the arguments of the Greek Marxist political thinker, Alex Callinicos (1992).
5. This unfortunate error in judgment that identifies postmodernity with a "false consciousness" (in the Marxist sense) that legitimizes all kinds of violence against the poor and dispossessed, seems to have become a commonplace for many Latin American intellectuals. The Mexican philosopher Mario Magallón writes, for example, "Neoliberalism and postmodernity are a new ideological, economic, political, social, and cultural form that is characterized by the neoconservatism of the powerful elite." In almost millenarian terms, he adds that postmodernity "constitutes the *final battle* for the definitive overthrow of rationalism. . . . It will overthrow everything: the dialectic, the state, human rights." Mario Magallón, *Filosofía política de la educación en América Latina* (Mexico City: UNAM, 1993), 158. Similar reflections can be found in an article by Cubans Manuel Pi Esquijarosa and Gilberto Valdés Gutiérrez, "El pensamiento latinoamericano ante la putrefacción de la historia," *Casa de las Américas* 196 (1994): 99–111. As we will see later, the basis of this interpretation is its emphasis on the analysis of phenomena of the "consciousness" and not of practical phenomena.
6. To still believe that capitalism today is only relevant to elites alienated from their own reality while the majority of Latin Americans still live in the idyllic world of "use value," is equivalent to ignoring the libidinal effects that capitalism has had on *all* segments of society. That capitalist modes of life are *desired* by the great majority of Latin Americans is not something that can be explained by simply resorting to the trite theme of "false consciousness."
7. On "cultural studies" in Latin America, see Carlos Rincón, "Die neue Kulturtheorien: Vor-Geschichten und Bestandsaufnahme," in Birgit Scharlau, ed., *Lateinamerika denken. Kulturtheoretische Grenzgänge zwischen Moderne und Postmoderne* (Tübingen: Gunter Narr, 1994); and William Rowe and Vivian Schelling, *Memory and Modernity: Popular Culture in Latin America* (London: Verso, 1991).

8. Puerto Rican theorist Iris M. Zavala synthesizes this argument very well by directly associating postmodernity with the hypertechnologized and consumerist world of "postindustrial societies," referring to the analysis of Daniel Bell. Iris M. Zavala, "On the (Mis-)uses of the Post-modern: Hispanic Modernism Revisited," in T. D'Haen and H. Bertend, eds., *Postmodern Fiction in Europe and the Americas* (Amsterdam: Rodopi, 1988). Starting from these premises, Zavala concludes that the concept of postmodernity is not transferable to the Latin American cultural context, where capitalism still finds itself in a "lower stage of development." For Zavala, as for Habermas, modernity continues to be an "unfinished" or "unsuccessful" (as Guadarrama puts it) project in Latin America.
9. In this sense, and in contrast to Guadarrama's opinion, Colombian cultural critic Carlos Rincón has shown that modernity has existed in Latin America as a *simultaneous interaction of the nonsimultaneous* and not as the gradual experience of socioeconomic development. Carlos Rincón, *La no simultaneidad de lo simultáneo: Posmodernidad, globalización y culturas en América Latina* (Bogotá: EUN, 1995). For a commentary on Rincón's book, see Erna Von der Walde, "La alegría de leer: Ficciones latinoamericanas y el debate posmoderno," *Dissens: Revista Internacional de Pensamiento latinoamericano* 2 (1995): 103–10.
10. What is being described here is nothing other than the increasingly significant impact of the *market* on people's daily lives. To the extent that lifestyles cease to be inherited from tradition and begin to be seen as the effect of personal decisions, the "holistic culture" García Delgado discusses begins to erode. Identities and lifestyles now depend on belonging to a "world" symbolically defined by advertising and marketing.
11. See also Beatriz Sarlo, *Escenas de la vida posmoderna: Intelectuales, arte y videocultura en Argentina* (Buenos Aires: Ariel, 1994), 89–93.
12. When I say "clichés," I am not referring to simple misunderstandings. Nor am I saying that Latin Americanist philosophers have "poorly interpreted" postmodern propositions, as such interpretation only occurs when the concepts share the same image of thought. However, when it comes to concepts that inhabit another form of being for discourses, or concepts that come from *outside*, then the response is not interpretation but rather caricature. The concepts that philosophers such as Deleuze, Foucault, Derrida, Lyotard, Vattimo et al. work with emerge as the result of a rupture with the modern order of knowledge and therefore cannot but appear as something "unthought" by those philosophers who still move within that order. The cliché, then, is the form of Latin Americanism's response to that which has exceeded the limits marked out by the episteme of modernity.
13. I am referring here to the attempt to explain the totality of the real on the basis of the Cartesian cogito, which was the image of thought on which the humanist project of modernity was founded.
14. On this point, see Eduardo Subirats, "Transformaciones de la cultura moderna," in J. Tono Martínez, ed., *La polémica de la posmodernidad* (Madrid: Libertarias, 1986).
15. See chapter 5, this volume.

16. "Thus, in place of the continuous chronology of reason, which was invariably traced back to some inaccessible origin, there have appeared scales that are sometimes very brief, distinct from one another, irreducible to a single law, scales that bear a type of history peculiar to each one, and which cannot be reduced to the general model of a consciousness that acquires, progresses, and remembers." Michel Foucault, *The Archaeology of Knowledge and the Discourse on Language,* trans. Alan Sheridan-Smith (New York: Pantheon, 1972), 8.
17. I distance myself from those readings according to which the philosophy and theology of liberation are authentically Latin American expressions of postmodernity. See Neil Larsen, "Posmodernismo e imperialismo: Teoría y política en América Latina," *Nuevo Texto Crítico* 6 (1990): 77–94; and José Luis Gómez Martínez, "Posmodernidad, discurso antrópico y ensayística latinoamericana," *Dissens: Revista internacional de pensamiento latinoamericano* 2 (1996): 45–49.
18. In the 1970s, Dussel wrote of his thought: "Philosophy of liberation is postmodern, popular (of the people, with the people), pro-feminine philosophy. It is philosophy expressed by ('pressed out from') the youth of the world, the oppressed of the earth, the condemned of world history." Enrique Dussel, *Philosophy of Liberation,* trans. Aquilina Martínez and Christine Morkovsky (Maryknoll, NY: Orbis, 1985), viii. See also Dussel's books *Para una de-strucción de la historia de la ética* (Mendoza: Universidad Nacional de Cuyo, 1971); and *Filosofía ética latinoamericana: La política latinoamericana (Antropológica III)* (Bogotá: Universidad Santo Tomás, 1979).
19. Here we should recall the distinction Beatriz Sarlo draws between active consumers and imaginary consumers (*Escenas de la vida posmoderna,* 42). "Popular culture" in Latin America is increasingly *pop culture.* This has resulted in the elevation and maintenance of "authenticity" as the goal of "emancipatory" politics. The popular cannot be defined either ethically or metaphysically, but rather according to its position in the social space of the production and consumption of signs.
20. Jesús Martín-Barbero writes: "To think the crisis from here has as its first condition basing ourselves in that logic according to which our societies are irremediably external to the process of modernity and that our modernity can only be a deformation and degradation of the true modernity. . . . Thinking the crisis thus translates for us the task of accounting for our own particular *discontent in and with modernity.*" Jesús Martín-Barbero, "Modernidad y posmodernidad en la periferia," *Politeia* 11 (1992): 281–88, 282.
21. The expression *democratic struggles* comes from Ernesto Laclau and Chantal Mouffe. It refers to democracy as an institution that prevents power from being *incorporated* in one person or one group of people. The "price" of these struggles is a society without clearly defined foundations and a social structure that cannot be described solely from one point of view. Ernesto Laclau and Chantal Mouffe, *Hegemony and Socialist Strategy: Towards a Radical Democratic Politics* (London: Verso, 1985), 30.
22. On this point, Lyotard writes: "What is needed if we are to understand social relations in this manner, on whatever scale we choose, is not only a theory of communication, but a theory of games which accepts agonistics as a founding principle." Jean-François

Lyotard, *The Postmodern Condition: A Report on Knowledge,* trans. Geoff Bennington and Brian Massumi (Minneapolis: University of Minnesota Press, 1984), 16.

23. "A recognition of the heteromorphous nature of language . . . obviously implies a renunciation of terror, which assumes that they are isomorphic and tries to make them so" (66).
24. See H. C. F. Mansilla, *La cultura del autoritarismo ante los desafíos del presente: Ensayos sobre una teoría crítica de la modernización* (La Paz: CEBEM, 1991), 59–67.
25. It is time we understand that, in the framework of a democratic society, "fundamental" questions cannot be *resolved* but only provisionally *managed,* since in a democracy the place of "unique power" necessarily remains *empty.* The price we have to pay for trying to resolve these fundamental questions is nothing other than the occupation of this unique place in order *to impose* solutions on all parties involved in the conflict.
26. *Ayacucho* is a Quechua word that means "place of the dead." The Peruvian theologian Gustavo Gutiérrez uses it to refer symbolically to the poverty suffered by millions all over the world each year. I am grateful to Nancy Bedford for bringing this point to my attention.
27. I explore this topic more broadly in chapter 3.

2. MODERNITY, RATIONALIZATION, AND CULTURAL IDENTITY IN LATIN AMERICA

1. It is worth pointing out that this project of a hermeneutics of Latin American culture manifested in other, different ways outside of Argentina, as can be seen for example in the work of the Colombian philosopher Jaime Rubio Angulo, one of the founders of the Bogotá Group. See Jaime Rubio Angulo, *Introducción al filosofar* (Bogotá: Universidad Santo Tomás/Centro de Enseñanza Desescolarizada, 1977).
2. Here we can see the influence of Argentine philosopher Rodolfo Kusch's thesis on popular culture, which he maintains is founded on a powerful telluric feeling of rootedness to the land (a culture of *estar* ["being in place"]), that can "phagocytoze" the weak and uprooted rationality of modernity (the culture of *ser* ["being in general"]). I will explore this in greater depth in chapter 6.
3. Cristián Parker attempts to support his thesis by referring to "new discoveries in neurobiology:" the right hemisphere of the brain controls analytic thought, while the left hemisphere controls the artistic, symbolic, and emotive aspects of the brain. On one side, linearity and succession; on the other side, simultaneity and synthesis. Parker's argument is that Westernized countries have made significant use of the right hemisphere, while countries that have resisted Westernization (such as those in Latin America) have predominantly favored the left hemisphere. Therefore, according to Parker, the only alternative to Western civilization, with all the *irrationality* it entails, is to strengthen subaltern cultures that prioritize "other logics": emotivity, symbolic thought, face-to-face encounters, etc.

4. This reading also permeates the discourse of the philosophy of liberation in the 1970s, especially in Enrique Dussel's version, in which modernity is a faceless, "totalizing ontology" that destroys everything in its path and systematically negates the "face-to-face" that is prevalent in the popular cultures of the periphery. Enrique Dussel, *Filosofía ética latinoamericana: La política latinoamericana (Antropológica III)* (Bogotá: Universidad Santo Tomás, 1979).
5. Of course, Habermas does not fare much better in this regard than his predecessors in the Frankfurt School. He correctly criticizes the fatalistic vision of rationalization, but he ends up maintaining the (non-Weberian) thesis that this entails a universal logic of development. The rationalization of Western societies would thus be merely one chapter in the history of "Reason." Jürgen Habermas, *Theory of Communicative Action*, vol. 1: *Reason and the Rationalization of Society*, trans. Thomas A. McCarthy (Boston: Beacon, 1984).
6. In this regard, see Yolana Ruano de la Fuente's excellent study, *Racionalidad y conciencia trágica: La modernidad según Max Weber* (Madrid: Trotta, 1995). See also Australian sociologist Mitchel Dean's *Critical and Effective Histories: Foucault's Methods and Historical Sociology* (New York: Routledge, 1994), whose reading of the topic of rationalization combines Nietzsche, Weber, and Foucault.
7. That the *subjectivity* of people who were converted by these religious orders is permanently untouched by this same evangelization is something that makes sense only to Morandé and other philosophers of liberation.
8. Reductions (*reducciones*) were settlements Jesuits and other Spanish colonizers established for Indigenous populations in order to instill Christian and European values in them. The *Ratio Studiorum* (1598–99) is a text in which the Jesuit plan for education was standardized. The *Ratio* was highly influential on subsequent humanist approaches to education.—TRANS.
9. Morandé sees cinema, for example, as one of modern society's mechanisms of domestication. The images projected onto the screen replace the "hearing" of ritualistic socialization with the "seeing" of linguistic socialization. In this way, viewers internalize the behavioral norms the "system" defines for them.
10. Think, for example, of Dussel's diatribes against the "imperial culture" of mass media. Like Adorno, Dussel thinks that all films say the same thing because they only transmit the ideological message of the "totality." For him, mass culture is a "manipulation of the consciousness" that reduces everything to kitsch. See Dussel, *Filosofía ética latinoamericana III* (172).
11. It is not surprising that televisions occupy a central place in Latin American homes, nor is it surprising that the number of people who watch telenovelas is ten times greater than the number of people who have read one of Gabriel García Márquez's books.
12. Martín-Barbero thus does not endorse the simplistic interpretation of globalization as the result of the "ideological imposition" of mass culture from the United States. For him, rock music—to name only one example—is not a foreign phenomenon that alienates young people in Latin America from their cultural roots, but rather implies a positive reconfiguration of the lifeworld of Latin American youth. We see here the

irruption of new forms of being together, the birth of practices that seek to creatively appropriate time and space. Like Brazilian anthropologist and sociologist Renato Ortiz, Martín-Barbero argues that globalization produces a "new territory" in which novel forms of being-in-the-world can flourish. Globalization is not only an economic and technological phenomenon but is rather, above all, an ontological and cultural phenomenon.

13. García Canclini argues at length that a nation's cultural identity is a "theatrical operation" that has its "ceremonial headquarters" in the museum. Based on a study of the Museo Tamayo in Oaxaca and the Museo Nacional de Antropología in Mexico City, he shows which "strategies of patrimonialization" the Mexican state has made use of. On one hand, the object is inscribed in its separation from the world of social relations. The "Indigenous world" is staged through archaic objects that are carefully kept from all contamination by the "real" Indigenous peoples (who do business in the street, use contemporary electronic devices, wear Western clothing, etc.). On the other hand, these real Indigenous people do not have any say in the museum's choices, combinations, or construction, which is left instead to "experts" (anthropologists, archaeologists, sociologists, etc.). "Mexicanness" is presented only in the form of its pre-Columbian "Indigenous roots" and excludes hybridizations with Blacks, Asians, Spaniards, Jews, etc.

14. Why aristocratic? Because the intellectual elites of Latin America have always wanted to see the popular as something "distinct" from themselves, thus establishing a "pathos of distance" that allows them to preserve their hegemony in the cultural field. This is exactly what happened with Pedro Morandé's "baroque ethos" and Enrique Dussel's philosophy of liberation. The thought of these two Catholic intellectuals resonates with the Church's attempt to undertake an "evangelization of culture" that would make it possible to recover their cultural hegemony over the masses in Latin America. And there was nothing more appropriate for this task than to portray the poor and the oppressed as inhabitants of an "other-culture" whose identity is fixed in orality, ritual, popular religion—that is, practices considered to be outside the "totalizing ethos" of modernity. This folklorization of the popular, this melancholic attempt to convert popular culture into a kind of living zoo (that is to be preserved as "cultural patrimony"), is nothing other than a *colonial gesture*, as we will see in chapter 6.

15. *Tamara* is the name Italo Calvino uses to refer to the symbolic hyperreality of urban life. See Italo Calvino, *Invisible Cities*, trans. William Weaver (New York: Harcourt, 1974).

16. This is what has happened with actually existing neoliberal policies in the majority of Latin American countries. By encouraging the concentration of capital in fewer hands and blocking any policy of social redistribution by the state, neoliberalism promotes a *restricted globalization*, of which only some privileged groups in society can take advantage, instead of moving toward a *democratic globalization*, in which the state adopts cultural policies intended to make it easier for citizens to access international communications networks. If it is true that, as Habermas has shown, the formation of a "postnational identity" is connected with the existence of opportunities for political

participation, it is also true that this would be unthinkable without the ludic exchange of information made possible by new electronic technologies. In a word, without access to media, it is impossible to form *transterritorial identities* capable of confronting the great political challenge of the twenty-first century: learning to live peacefully with heterogeneity and difference.

3. POPULISM AND PHILOSOPHY

1. In the nineteenth century, the theme of how nationalities are constituted became an essential element around which practically all intellectual polemics in Latin America revolved. This situation blurred the dividing line between politics and literature. See Ángel Rama, *The Lettered City*, ed. and trans. John Charles Chasteen (Durham: Duke University Press, 1996); and Roderic A. Camp, *Intellectuals and the State in Twentieth-Century Mexico* (Austin: University of Texas Press, 1985).
2. For a general overview of the influence of populism on cultural life in Latin America, see William Rowe and Vivian Schelling, *Memory and Modernity: Popular Culture in Latin America* (London: Verso, 1991), 181–228.
3. Of course, not everything is "the people" for populism. It is composed only of the humble masses, those who have been traditionally excluded, the majority of them poor. In reality, populist democracy entails a division of society into two equally homogeneous sides: the "oligarchy" and the "people." The former is the rich minority that has traditionally exploited the poor majority. The populist leader portrays himself as the leader of the majority and the adversary of the minority. Populist democracy seeks to impose the will of the majority onto political minorities, who no longer have rights. Thus it is an attempt to politically and culturally homogenize society.
4. Literally translated as "the shirtless ones," this term refers to the impoverished and underprivileged workers who formed the core of Perón's base of support.—TRANS.
5. Here I follow Ernesto Laclau's reading of Latin American socialism as the reduction of Marxism to an essentially populist language.
6. On the originality of Latin American philosophy, see Francisco Miró Quesada's comments in his article "La filosofía de lo americano: Treinta años después," in *Ideas en torno de Latinoamérica* (Mexico City: UNAM, 1986), 2:1024–34.
7. The classic study of philosophy of liberation, which clearly shows the links between this current of thought and Argentine populism, continues to be Horacio Cerutti Goldberg's book *Filosofía de la liberación latinoamericana* (Mexico City: Fondo de Cultura Económica, 1983).
8. Regarding the debate on the category of the "people" in the philosophy of liberation, see Silvio López Velasco's *Reflexões sobre a Filosofia da Libertacão* (Campo Grande: CEFIL, 1991), 474–76.
9. For a critique of the ontologization of the periphery in Dussel's philosophical discourse, see Gustavo Leyva, "Modernidad y Exterioridad en Latinoamérica: La propuesta de la filosofía de la liberación," *Dissens: Revista internacional de pensamiento latinoamericano* 1 (1995): 11–32.

10. Martínez Estrada specifically mentions Domingo Faustino Sarmiento, whom he calls "the most harmful of those dreamers and constructors of images."
11. Kusch's arguments were later taken up by postcolonial writers like Walter Mignolo, as we will see in chapter 6.
12. For this overview of Ferreira da Silva's philosophy, I have relied on the Czech-Brazilian philosopher Vilém Flusser's work, *Brasilien oder die Suche nach dem neuen Menschen: Für eine Phänomenologie der Unterentwicklung* (Mannheim: Bollman, 1994), 232–33, 254–56.
13. "Bolívar is the man of accomplishment. In him, promises and hopes have become the living flesh of history. The great hero has returned after two hundred years of being essentially digested by the continent . . . The most prominent vital energies of all cultures, which in the mestizo withdraw and are paralyzed to a certain degree, become in Bolívar more active, positive, and prolific; they emerge as powerful forms of coordination and harmony; they are transformed into creative impulses and generative, driving forces." Antenor Orrego, *Hacia un humanismo Americano* (Lima: Juan Mejía Baca, 1966), 58–59.
14. For this reason, according to these authors, both democracy and socialism or Marxism should be inculturated in Latin America and not just mechanically transposed from Europe to be applied here. This theme of "inculturation" will be central to liberation theology, as well as for certain philosophers connected to that current, like Argentine Juan Carlos Scannone and Cuban Raúl Fornet-Betancourt.
15. Ramos writes: "Adler states that the inferiority complex appears in a child as soon as he recognizes the insignificance of his own strength compared to the strength of his parents. Mexico at first found itself in relation to the civilized world as that of the child to his parents. This disadvantageous circumstance induced the sense of inferiority that was aggravated by conquest, racial commingling, and even the disproportionate magnitude of nature." Samuel Ramos, "El perfil del hombre y la cultura en México," in *Obras Completas* (Mexico City: UNAM, 1990), 180.
16. For Mansilla's critique of discourses of identity, see H. C. F. Mansilla, "La ensayística latinoamericana y la cuestión de la identidad colectiva," *Dissens: Revista internacional de pensamiento latinoamericano* 2 (1996): 1–16.
17. Mansilla maintains the opposite of the position argued by Pedro Morandé, Cristián Parker, and Juan Carlos Scannone, for whom these paradigms of development have never been able to get to the "ethico-mythical core" of Latin American culture.
18. See Colombian philosopher Roberto Salazar Ramos's reflections on this in *Posmodernidad y verdad: Algunos metarrelatos en la constitución del saber* (Bogotá: USTA, 1994), 181–91.
19. Perhaps it is worth remarking that right behind the idea of an origin lay the thesis that an authentically Latin American philosophy is possible.

4. LATIN AMERICA BEYOND THE PHILOSOPHY OF HISTORY

1. Ortega y Gasset's later text "History as a System" contains his study of circumstantialism, and it also serves as a magnificent synthesis of the entirety of his philosophical

work. José Ortega y Gasset, "History as a System," *Toward a Philosophy of History* (New York: Norton, 1941).

2. In *The Modern Theme*, Ortega writes: "Pure reason cannot supplant life: the culture of abstract intelligence is not, when compared with spontaneity, a further type of life which is self-supporting and can dispense with the first. It is only a tiny island afloat on the sea of primeval vitality. Far from being able to take the place of the latter, it must depend upon and be maintained by it, just as each one of the members of an organism derives its life from the entire structure." José Ortega y Gasset, *The Modern Theme* (New York: Harper and Row, 1961 [1931]), 57.
3. "It is man's beliefs that truly constitute his state. I have spoken of them as a repertory to indicate that the plurality of beliefs on which an individual, a people, or an age is grounded never possesses a completely logical articulation. . . . A belief is not merely an idea that is thought, it is an idea in which one also believes. And believing is not an operation of the intellectual mechanism, but a function of guiding his conduct, his performance of his task" (Ortega y Gasset, "History as a System," 167–68).
4. "The generation is a dynamic compromise between mass and individual and is the most important conception in history. It is, so to speak, the pivot responsible for the movements of historical evolution" (Ortega y Gasset, *The Modern Theme,* 15).
5. On the cultural sphere in Mexico during Gaos's tenure, see José Luis Gómez-Martínez, *Pensamiento de la liberación: Proyección de Ortega y Gasset en Iberoamérica* (Madrid: EGE, 1995), 66–100; and Abelardo Villegas, *El pensamiento mexicano en el siglo XX* (Mexico City: Fondo de Cultura Económica, 1993), 145.
6. We must note that Gaos does not refer to "Latin American" but rather "Spanish American" thought, as he believed that the Spanish experience and the American experience were historically one and the same.
7. Gaos's argument is that there will be no Spanish American thought unless there is a history of Spanish American philosophy. This is a typically historicist argument, in the style of Ortega y Gasset at his best. Given that the past is what there is only because of the history we trace from it in the present, Spanish American philosophy can only exist if a history that values it as such exists. See José Gaos, "En torno a la filosofía mexicana," in Jorge Gracia and Iván Jaksic, eds., *Filosofía e identidad cultural en América Latina* (Caracas: Monte Ávila, 1988).
8. In an essay titled "El pensamiento hispanoamericano" (Hispanic American thought), Gaos writes (in his overlapping style): "'Thought' is that thought which is based not on the systematic and transcendent objects of philosophy but on immanent, human objects that, by the very nature of things, are historical. They are not the potential eternal themes of a system but rather problems of circumstance, that is to say, of the most immediate time and place, and therefore as problems that urgently need resolution, yet use as forms the methods and style of philosophy or science. Or they don't have those objects or use those methods or style but instead think and express themselves in oral and written literary forms and in genres and styles that are not used, at least not to the same extent, by philosophy and science." José Gaos, "El pensamiento hispanoamericano," *Filosofía de la filosofía* (Barcelona: Crítica, 1989 [1944]), 94.

9. "The program of salvation of the Spanish circumstance was an original, indefinitely fertile program of Spanish philosophy—potentially or virtually Spanish American in general, the philosophy of the Spaniard, the philosophy of the Spanish American, Spanish American philosophy. It is about sensing what Ortega himself never saw, which is ultimately that the unity of the Spanish American circumstance existed from the very beginning, but with Spanish America as only one circumstance within the universal whole." José Gaos, *Pensamiento de lengua española,* in *Obras Completas* (Mexico City: UNAM, 1990 [1945]), 6:31–247, 76.
10. José Luís Gómez-Martínez describes this idea as the "fundamental project" of Latin American philosophy (*Pensamiento de la liberación,* 107–201).
11. "The civilizing project will thus be characterized by its preoccupation with achieving the following goals: a change of blood, a change in mindset, and also a change with regard to dependence. . . . One race will replace another; man, up until yesterday educated in abstractions, will be instructed in the use of technologies that are not dependent on the nation, which will be submitted to those who make it possible since they know how to exploit it. Other blood, other masters, and other lords will replace the blood, masters, and lords inherited from colonialism. The blood of the surplus population of civilized Europe; the masters of the utilitarianism and positivism in which the men of Europe and the United States were trained will replace the already anachronistic master formed by colonialism; the industrious creators of the Western *haute bourgeoisie* will replace the likewise already anachronistic nobles and aristocrats left over from the Conquest and colonization" (Zea, *Filosofía de la historia americana,* 257–58).
12. On the motif of the crisis of European culture in Zea's thought, see Gómez-Martínez, *Pensamiento de la liberación,* 158.
13. This problem can be seen clearly in the concept of the history of ideas used by Zea, for whom scholasticism, the Enlightenment, romanticism, and positivism are taken as original models and seen as unitary wholes without any fissures and completely separated from their conditions of production.
14. "The history of ideas could not turn a blind eye to problematics such as those that came out of 'dependency theory,' which definitively imposed the abandonment of all 'phenomenologies,' which as a whole came to an end by showing their ideological face, which is to say, their obscuring or elicitive role." Arturo Andrés Roig, "¿Cómo leer un texto?," in *Historia de las ideas, Teoría del discurso y Pensamiento latinoamericano* (Bogotá: USTA, 1993), 135.
15. "The problematic of discourse analysis has renewed the history of ideas, a renewal that began in the 1940s. The use of these methods has produced a path that we might call radical. It is no longer a matter of looking for the implicit or explicit 'philosophemes' in these thinkers' writings, but rather of understanding the insertion of these 'philosophemes' into the framework of the heterogeneous and unstable reality that is all social reality, beyond the unity that it offers from the concept of the 'discursive universe.' What was once a 'descriptive' history of ideas has now become an 'explicative' or, if one prefers, genetic historiography" (Roig, "¿Cómo leer un texto?" 135).

16. Roig refers to Juan Bautista Alberdi's famous *Fragmento preliminar al estudio del derecho* (1838) (Preliminary fragment for the study of law), where the need for a Latin American philosophy was first articulated, which would be taken up again by Alberdi in his *Curso de filosofía contemporánea* (1840) (Course on contemporary philosophy).
17. Roig refers to Alberdi's polemic with Salvador Ruano, a professor and student of the ideology of Destutt de Tracy, for whom the task of philosophy was to serve as an analytic investigation of ideas that has no relation to historical forms. In contrast, Alberdi defends the possibility and necessity of a Latin American philosophy and denies that Destutt de Tracy's ideology was philosophy, since it lacked any commitment to the social reality in which philosophy takes place. Arturo Andrés Roig, *Teoría y crítica del pensamiento latinoamericano* (Mexico City: Fondo de Cultura Económica, 1981), 289.
18. A study of the influence of Kant on thinkers like Roig and Hinkelammert is a chapter that, sadly, remains to be written in the historiography of Latin American philosophy.
19. "Latin American philosophy . . . is not resolved into a 'philosophy of culture,' but rather, more appropriately said, it is a 'philosophy of the forms of objectification' related to concrete societies, in particular, logically, those that make up our Latin American world. It is not reduced to philosophizing about cultures, a line that has led to external characterizations. Above all, it points to the norms of objectification on the basis of which the objective cultural world has materialized. Indeed, the inquisition into that normative regime must be based on the fundamental question, that of the mode of being—namely, the historical being—of the man behind that constitutive normativity." Arturo Andrés Roig, "La historia de las ideas y la filosofía latinoamericana," in *Historia de las ideas, Teoría del discurso y Pensamiento latinoamericano* (Bogotá: USTA, 1993), 187.
20. The case of Colombia is exemplary. As historian Malcolm Deas has shown, the nineteenth century was the golden age of the country's grammarians, philologists, lexicographers, and Latinists. Early in their careers, several presidents of the era were grammarians and members of the Colombian Academy of Language. Malcolm Deas, "Miguel Antonio Caro y amigos: Gramática y poder en Colombia," *Del poder y la gramática, y otros ensayos sobre historia, política y literatura colombianas* (Bogotá: Tercer Mundo, 1993).
21. Genealogy does not at any point attempt to "represent" these voices. Quite to the contrary, it seeks to excavate the ground of the Latin Americanist discourses that have pretended to speak in the name of the people, as well as to reveal the heterogeneous strata on which they are constructed.
22. On this problem, see Roberto Salazar Ramos, "Los grandes metarrelatos en la interpretación de la historia latinoamericana," in *Reflexión histórica en América Latina: Ponencias VII Congreso Internacional de Filosofía Latinoamericana* (Bogotá: Universidad Santo Tomás, 1993).
23. In effect, the model drawn in these two texts is that of a "gendarme state" charged with correcting the natural inequalities of humans through the law and disciplinary education. In order to be free, Latin American peoples must learn to obey, first the law, then the moral leaders of the people. The people must be educated so that they will exit

from colonial slavery, but this must be done by means of a sovereign power controlled by an executive and an intellectual elite. Codes and statutes are not sufficient; scholars, intellectuals, and leaders are also required. How else can we read Bolívar's proposals for a hereditary senate and a fourth moral power? In this model of the state, the population is considered to be lacking and in need of the paternalistic assistance and mentoring of the state, which is in turn seen as the only option for the construction of the nation.

5. THE AESTHETICS OF THE BEAUTIFUL IN SPANISH AMERICAN MODERNISM

1. Zavala bases this on the thesis of the utopian-social character of the libido, borrowing from the theories of Bakhtin and Lacan. The new social imaginary would from this perspective be the "intellectual proletariat's" sublimated projection of its own frustrations. Iris M. Zavala, "The Social Imaginary: The Cultural Sign of Hispanic Modernism," *Critical Studies* 1 (1989): 125–40, 28.
2. By that time, the processes of modernization had already transformed the lifestyles of elites and some sections of the middle class, although the vast majority of the population continued being subjected to traditional forms of socialization. This was during the time when Latin America had consolidated as an attractive market in order to satisfy the expansionist demands of United States capital, which favored the growth of cities as key centers for trade, the construction of civil works, the export of raw materials, and the import of consumer goods.
3. The consolidation of a society dominated by money caused art and artists to lose their previous role of glorifying aristocratic values. If, in other times, writers acted as chroniclers or singers of the exploits of the dominant class, now, expelled from that world, they were forced to rebel against a society that marginalized them, tending to address their work toward a broader public and in more unfavorable working conditions. Unlike in Europe, where the existence of a market allowed for the promotion of art in specialized institutions (theaters, publishing houses, art galleries, salons, etc.), which made it possible for artists to emancipate themselves from the patronage system maintained by the Church and the aristocracy, the kind of economic infrastructure that allows for the existence of an autonomous literary market did not exist in Latin America (at least until after World War II).
4. Anonymous, although many scholars have attributed its authorship variously to Hegel, Friedrich Schelling, or Friedrich Hölderlin.—TRANS.
5. The problem becomes worse to the extent that society values only those potentialities that are useful for the continued operation of the social machinery, that is to say, the discipline of work. Friedrich Schiller, *On the Aesthetic Education of Man*, trans. Reginald Snell (Mineola, NY: Dover, 2004), 38.
6. Schiller refers to the "predominance of the analytical faculty," which has encroached on all of society's public institutions. The state, the economy, and the law have been

separated from sensibility and morality and have become the pure product of understanding. Thus man is governed by a set of impersonal rules (Schiller, 42).

7. Rodó expressly cites Schiller's *On the Aesthetic Education of Man*. See José Enrique Rodó, *Ariel*, trans. Margaret Sayers Peden (Austin: University of Texas Press, 1988), 49.
8. "Of all the desirable elements of a rational existence, the sense of the beautiful, the clear vision of the beauty of things, is the sense most quickly withered by the sterile and repetitious daily round, making of it an attribute to be preserved by a minority in that society as an abandoned treasure" (Rodó, 49).
9. In this prologue, Henríquez Ureña writes: "By making *Ariel* known in Mexico, which up until now has only felt echoes of its influence, we believe we are providing a service to the Mexican youth. We do not attempt to argue that Rodó offers the only or the most perfectly appropriate teaching for the youth . . . but no one can deny the essential virtue of his doctrines, their fundamental adherence to the highest spirit of humanity, the energetic virtue of their stimulating and persuasive proclamations, or, in short, that *Ariel* is the most powerful inspiration for ideal and action addressed to the youth of our America in the present." Quoted by Alfonso García Morales, *El Ateneo de México 1906–1914: Orígenes de la cultura mexicana contemporánea* (Seville: Escuela de Estudios Hispano-americanos, 1992), 124.
10. The fact that neither Rodó nor any of the members of the Ateneo could read Greek is not an insignificant detail.
11. We should not forget that Alfonso Reyes was a close friend of the German classicist Werner Jäger, about whose famous book, *Paideia*, Reyes wrote an extensive review, titled "De cómo Grecia construyó al hombre" (How Greece constructed man), in *Última Tule y otros ensayos* (Caracas: Biblioteca Ayacucho, 1992). It is also worth mentioning his book *La crítica en la edad ateniense* (Criticism in the Athenian age), in *Obras Completas* (Mexico City: Fondo de Cultura Económica, 1997), vol. 13.
12. "And today, what is this crisis that we are suffering but some nonsense about the specialization in ethics that the North has lost? It is in vain that the Swedish inventor tries to show us that dynamite was conceived to serve industry and the well-being of humans. . . . The worldless specialist uses dynamite to kill people. What a sad destiny for our contemporary discoverers!" Alfonso Reyes, "Ciencia social y deber social," in *Obras Completas* (Mexico City: Fondo de Cultura Económica, 1982), 11:106–25, 106–7.
13. This idea will be taken up again by Leopoldo Zea in his philosophy of history, as we saw in chapter 4.
14. Gutiérrez Girardot correctly notes that this function of synthesis Reyes mentions will not be completed by the people but rather by Latin American intellectuals. Rafael Gutiérrez Girardot, *La imagen de América en Alfonso Reyes* (Madrid: Instituto Iberoamericano de Gotemburgo, 1955), 42.
15. I focus on this and other aspects of Vasconcelos's Latin American mythology in chapter 7.
16. We should recall how in chapter 4 we saw that the Spanish philosopher José Gaos described Spanish American culture as predominantly aesthetic. This shows us how,

from its very beginning, the project of a Latin American philosophy drew deeply from the Latin Americanist mythology created by late nineteenth-century modernists.

17. "The very ugly will not procreate, they will have no desire to procreate. What does it matter, then, that all the races mix with each other if ugliness will find no cradle? Poverty, defective education, the scarcity of beautiful types, the misery that makes people ugly, all those calamities will disappear from the future social stage. . . . Unions will be effected according to the singular law of the third period, the law of sympathy, refined by the sense of beauty; a true sympathy and not the false one that, today, necessity and ignorance impose upon us. Sincerely passionate unions, easily undone in case of error, will produce bright and handsome offspring. The entire species will change its physical makeup and temperament. Superior instincts will prevail and, in a happy synthesis, the elements of beauty apportioned today among different races will endure." José Vasconcelos, *The Cosmic Race: A Bilingual Edition,* trans. Didier. T. Jaén (Baltimore: Johns Hopkins University Press, 1997), 30–31.
18. As secretary of education in Mexico (1921–1924), Vasconcelos made this his project and brought together avant-garde artists—painters like Diego Rivera and David Alfaro Siquieros and musicians like Carlos Cháves and Silvestre Revueltas—to educate the masses in the Latin Americanist ideals of the cosmic race. Color, proportion, tonality, everything should reflect a collective feeling in which differences appear as harmoniously reconciled in a national or continental spirit.
19. Regarding Indigenous peoples, Vasconcelos remarks: "Say what one may, the red men, the illustrious Atlanteans from whom Indians derive, went to sleep millions of years ago, never to awaken. There is no going back in History, for it is all transformation and novelty. No race returns. Each one states its mission, accomplishes it, and passes away. . . . The Indian has no other door to the future but the door of modern culture, nor any other road but the road already cleared by Latin civilization" (Vasconcelos, 16).

6. POSTCOLONIAL REASON AND LATIN AMERICAN PHILOSOPHY

This is the original title of the present chapter, which was initially presented at the Fifth International Symposium on Latin American philosophy held in Santa Clara (Cuba) in January 1995 and later published by the Cuban journal *Islas.*

1. For a study of the different positions in this debate, see Robert Young's *White Mythologies: Writing History and the West* (London: Routledge, 1990).
2. This is demonstrated by the anthologies and studies published in the United States, England, and Germany. See John Beverley, José Oviedo, and Michael Aronna, eds., *The Postmodernism Debate in Latin America* (Durham: Duke University Press, 1995); Birgit Scharlau, ed., *Lateinamerika denken: Kulturtheoretische Grenzgänge zwischen Moderne und Postmoderne* (Tübingen: Gunter Narr, 1994). Hermann Herlinghaus and Monika Walter, eds., *Posmodernidad en la periferia: Enfoques latinoamericanos de la nueva*

teoría cultural (Berlin: Langer, 1994); Alfonso de Toro and Fernando de Toro, eds., *Borders and Margins: Post-Colonialism and Post-Modernism* (Frankfurt/Madrid: Vervuert/ Iberoamericana,1995); George Yúdice, Jean Franco, and Juan Flórez, eds., *On Edge: The Crisis of Contemporary Latin American Culture* (Minneapolis: University of Minnesota Press, 1992); and Pedro Lange-Churión and Eduardo Mendieta, eds., *Latin America and Postmodernity: A Contemporary Reader* (Amherst, NY: Humanity, 1996).

3. This group included Walter Mignolo, Julio Ramos, Patricia Seed, Norma Alarcón, María Milagros López, Ileana Rodríguez, and John Beverley.
4. See chapters 1 and 2.
5. This explains why Guamán Poma's chronicle was initially rejected by scholars in the 1940s and 1950s who considered it to be full of historical and grammatical errors. The work of Rolena Adorno in the 1980s rewrites Guamán Poma's text and shows that what appears as grammatical error in the use of Spanish actually follows the norms of the language spoken by the Incas. The chronicle eventually came to be regarded as a border text between Andean oral culture and European written culture. According to Adorno, it is an oral text.
6. See Rolena Adorno's magisterial analysis of Guamán Poma's "Mapa Mundi" and other drawings in her 1979 article, "Paradigms Lost: A Peruvian Indian Surveys Spanish Colonial Society."
7. On this point Mignolo is in complete disagreement with Spivak, for whom the subaltern "cannot speak" using the epistemic categories of Western rationality. Mignolo believes it is possible to "cannibalize" the colonizer's alphabetical writing in order to turn it against him. This is the critical model of Caliban, according to Roberto Fernández Retamar's formulation.
8. However, for Mignolo, rehabilitating subjugated knowledges does not mean speaking in the name of the subaltern. "I must insist, in order to avoid misunderstandings that result from false hopes, that my intention here is not to "represent" or "describe" a piece of the past, but rather to "think" from the ruins of ancient civilizations the past of the Andes and of the Americas, as well as of the marginal fragments of Western civilization transported across the Atlantic. My intention is to take up again the intellectual force that such ruins and fragments possess, while avoiding transforming them into objects of contemplation, into relics that should be restored, or into a reconstruction of the past that has more than ethical or political justification for the researcher, which is the living force of thought and of culture as a praxis of creativity and survival." Walter Mignolo, "Decires fuera de lugar: Sujetos dicientes, roles sociales y formas de inscripción," *Revista de Crítica Literaria Latinoamericana* 21, no. 41 (1995): 9–31, 10.
9. In the introduction to *The Darker Side of the Renaissance*, Mignolo says that Kusch is the pioneer of "pluritopic hermeneutics:" "Kusch´s analysis, moving from one tradition of thought to the other, was not just an exercise in pluritopic hermeneutics but, I will venture to say, the minimal step to be taken for the constitution of different loci of enunciation and the establishment of a politic of intellectual inquiry that will go beyond cultural relativism." Walter Mignolo, "Introduction: Describing Ourselves Describing Ourselves: Comparatism, Differences, and Pluritopic Hermeneutics," in

The Darker Side of the Renaissance: Literacy, Territoriality, and Colonization (Michigan: University of Michigan Press, 1995), 13.

10. We should recall here the Enlightenment arguments (like the case of Buffon) that established a correlation between geography and intelligence on the basis of which the inferiority of certain populations was proclaimed. See Antonello Gerbi, *La disputa del Nuevo Mundo: Historia de una polémica 1750–1900* [The Dispute of the New World: History of a Polemic, 1750–1900] (Mexico City: Fondo de Cultura Económica, 1993), 7–46. Domingo Sarmiento's thesis advances in a similar direction in the first chapter of *Facundo* (*Life in the Argentine Republic in the Days of the Tyrants; Or, Civilization and Barbarism*), which is titled "Aspecto físico de la República Argentina y caracteres, hábitos e ideas que engendra" ["Physical Aspect of the Argentine Republic and the Forms of Character, Habits, and Ideas Induced by It"].
11. I have already covered this in chapter 3, but I will return to it later.
12. "The Other is metaphysically defined as the poor. . . . It is a metaphysical issue precisely because I designate as 'poor' that which is 'outside' of the project of Totality and therefore all of its values and mediations. The future of the poor is not the project of Totality but another project; however, this project does not currently exist." Enrique Dussel, *Introducción a la filosofía de la liberación* (Bogotá: Nueva América, 1995), 129.
13. For a critique of Dussel's messianism, see Gustavo Leyva, "Modernidad y Exterioridad en Latinoamérica. La propuesta de la filosofía de la liberación," *Dissens: Revista internacional de pensamiento latinoamericano* 1 (1995): 11–32.

7. THE BIRTH OF LATIN AMERICA AS A PHILOSOPHICAL PROBLEM IN MEXICO

This text was originally written in 1999 for Routledge's ultimately never completed History of Latin American Philosophy project. After several years of sitting in a drawer, it was finally published in Mexico in the edited volume *América Latina: giro optico: nuevas visions desde los estudios literarios y culturales*, ed. Ignacio Sánchez Prado (Puebla: Universidad de las Américas, 2006). It is reproduced here with the editor's permission.

1. Some historians of ideas in Latin America argue, however, that around 1900 a generation of philosophers began to take shape, consisting of those known as "founders" or "patriarchs," including Antonio Caso and Vasconcelos in Mexico, Alejandro Korn and Carlos Vaz Ferreira from the Río de la Plata region, Alejandro Deustua in Peru, Raimundo de Farias Brito in Brazil, and Molina Garmendia in Chile; see Germán Marquínez Argote, "Presentación," in *¿Qué es eso de filosofía latinoamericana?* (Bogotá: El Búho, 1981), 5–15. Nonetheless, what best describes this generation of thinkers are its humanist, autodidactic, and extra-academic qualities. Still, one cannot call it a philosophical field, properly speaking, in these conditions.

2. "The consciousness of our unity should be the first factor of our action: we are a separate people." José Vasconcelos, "Los motivos del escudo," in *Obra Selecta* (Caracas: Biblioteca Ayacucho, 1992), 123.
3. "Since before the Conquest, the Indigenous peoples were resistant to all change, all renovation. They lived bound to their traditions, they were habitual and conservative. The will to immutability was ingrained in the style of their culture. For example, their art clearly evinces a propensity to repeat the same forms. . . . Today, popular Indigenous art is inevitably the reproduction of the same model, which is passed on from generation to generation." Samuel Ramos, "El perfil del hombre y la cultura en México," in *Obras Completas* (Mexico City: UNAM, 1990), 1:89–180, 107–8.
4. Unlike Ortega y Gasset, who always felt like an "exile" in Argentina, Gaos saw himself as a "transplant" in Mexico, that is to say, as someone who lived in a foreign country as if he had simply been moved from one part of his place of birth to another. This vital integration with the Mexican cultural and intellectual milieu allowed him to feel like part of a "Hispanic" cultural community, which included Spain and all other Spanish-speaking countries. José Luis Gómez Martínez, *Pensamiento de la liberación: Proyección de Ortega y Gasset en Iberoamérica* (Madrid: EGE, 1995), 118–21.
5. For Ortega, the word *race* has a cultural rather than biological connotation. Thus he speaks of Spaniards as belonging to a "Mediterranean race."
6. Gaos argues that the outcome of the war will entail a "displacement of the center of gravity" of Western culture toward the new continent, which can have significant consequences for Latin America. The reconstitution of power relations in the postwar period will open up a readjustment of historical corpuses, with their cultures, economies, and political forms. Latin American countries should ultimately be prepared to occupy a decisive place in the new global order that will emerge from the ruins of Europe. José Gaos, *Pensamiento de lengua española*, in *Obras Completas* (Mexico City: UNAM, 1990 [1945]), 6:31–247, 36.
7. Recently, Stephen Toulmin developed an idea that is very similar to Gaos's in arguing that modernity followed two different and contradictory lines of thought: at the end of the eighteenth century, rationalism, which ended up imposing itself with the triumph of Newtonianism, and Enlightenment humanism in the sixteenth and seventeenth centuries. See Stephen Toulmin, *Cosmopolis: The Hidden Agenda of Modernity* (Chicago: University of Chicago Press, 1990).
8. On Zea's response to existentialism, see Francisco Miró Quesada, "La filosofía de lo americano: Treinta años después," in *Ideas en torno de Latinoamérica* (Mexico City: UNAM, 1986), 2:1024–34; and Abelardo Villegas, *El pensamiento mexicano en el siglo XX* (Mexico City: Fondo de Cultura Económica, 1993), 145–63.
9. According to Zea, this political moment of "Latin American self-consciousness" was faithfully reflected by thought. Intellectuals like Rodó, Vasconcelos, Ugarte, García Calderón, and many others fought against positivism in the name of the "Latin spirit" proper to Latin American nations. Leopoldo Zea, *El pensamiento latinoamericano* (Barcelona: Ariel, 1976), 424–30.

10. Curiously, while Gaos referred to Leopoldo Zea as "the accepted leader" of the Hiperión Group, neither Luis Villoro nor Emilio Uranga recognized Zea as a member of the group. Oswaldo Díaz Ruanova wrote, "What Zea did was open up doors for us to launch ourselves toward fame." See José Gaos, "México, tema y responsabilidad," in Leopoldo Zea, ed., *Filosofar a la altura del hombre: Discrepar para comprender* (Mexico City: UNAM, 1993), 113–28, 119; Luis Villoro, "Emilio Uranga: La accidentalidad como fundamento de la cultura mexicana," in Emilio Uranga, ed., *Análisis del ser mexicano* (Guanajuato: Gobierno del Estado de Guanajuato, 1990), 9–23, 10; Oswaldo Díaz Ruanova, *Los existencialistas mexicanos* (Mexico City: Rafael Giménez Siles, 1982), 203.
11. Díaz Ruanova writes that "the members of the Hiperión Group had a lot of enemies. Pistol-packing neo-Kantians could not resist the brilliance of these disciples of Gaos. The remaining Thomists hated them. The Marxists distrusted them. This is why Uranga's book was scarcely mentioned by critics" (Díaz Ruanova, 188).
12. See chapter 6, this volume.

APPENDIX 1

This is an edited version of an interview conducted by Hernán Alejandro Cortés, a philosophy student at the Universidad Santo Tomás.

1. The Comunero uprising occurred in 1781 in the Viceroyalty of New Granada in response to increased taxation and costs of tobacco and brandy that issued from the Bourbon reforms.—TRANS.
2. *Nadaismo*—Nadaism, or "Nothing-ism" was a countercultural movement in philosophy and the arts in Colombia during the late 1950s and early 1960s that was influenced by nihilism and existentialism. *Cocacolos* was the name given to a Colombian youth movement of the same era consisting primarily of children of the middle and upper classes.—TRANS.
3. Colciencias is the Columbian Administrative Department of Science, Technology and Innovation.—TRANS.

APPENDIX 2

First presented at a prepublication forum for the Columbia University Press translation of *Critique of Latin American Reason*, Critical Theory in Critical Times Workshop Northwestern University, October 2020, generously supported by a grant from the Andrew W. Mellon Foundation to the International Consortium of Critical Theory Programs.

1. Cf. Santiago Castro-Gómez, "Foucault y la colonialidad del poder," *Tablua Rasa* 6 (2007): 153–72.

2. See George Reid Andrews, *Afro-Latin America, 1800–2000* (New York: Oxford University Press, 2004).
3. Walter Mignolo, *The Idea of Latin America* (New York: Wiley, 2005), xi–xii.
4. See Marixa Lasso, *Myths of Harmony: Race and Republicanism During the Age of Revolution, Colombia, 1795–1831* (Pittsburgh: University of Pittsburgh Press, 2007).
5. See Cedric Robinson, *Black Marxism: The Making of the Black Radical Tradition* (Chapel Hill: University of North Carolina Press, 2000 [1983]).
6. Michel Foucault, "Discourse and Truth: the Problematization of Parrhesia," https://foucault.info/parrhesia//.
7. Michel Foucault, *The Courage of the Truth (The Government of Self and Others II): Lectures at the Collège de France, 1983–1984*, ed. Frédéric Gros, trans. Graham Burchell (New York: Picador, 2011), 340.
8. Donna Haraway, *Staying with the Trouble: Making Kin in the Chthulucene* (Durham: Duke University Press, 2016), 31. See also Donna Haraway, "Situated Knowledges: The Science Question in Feminism and the Privilege of Partial Perspective," *Feminist Studies* 14, no. 3 (1988): 575–99.
9. Santiago Castro-Gómez, *Critique of Latin American Reason*, 129 (this volume). The corresponding page in the Spanish second edition is 143.
10. Castro-Gómez, 114; 147 in the Spanish.
11. See María Del Rosario Acosta López, "The Resistance of Beauty: On Schiller's *Kallias Briefe* in Response to Kant's Aesthetics," *Epoché* 2, no. 1 (2016): 235–49.
12. Ranajit Guha, *Elementary Aspects of Peasant Insurgency in Colonial India* (Durham: Duke University Press, 1999), 333.
13. Walter D. Mignolo, *The Darker Side of the Renaissance: Literacy, Territoriality, and Colonization*, 2d ed. (Ann Arbor: University of Michigan Press, 2003), 127.
14. Mignolo does not use "modernity/coloniality" in *Darker*, noting in the afterword and in *On Decoloniality* that he only discovered it later. It is also important to raise the question of how representing "Latin American" Indigenous resistance/reexistence as the (hybrid) product of civilizational, literate highland cultures "corrects" for European colonial dominance while simultaneously reproducing *other occlusions or subordinations* with a long history (in South America, those between highland and lowland, sedentary and nomadic or seminomadic peoples, those using sign/record systems with material substrates (writing, *quipu*, etc.) and those not).
15. Souleymane Bachir Diagne, "Individual, Community, and Human Rights: A Lesson from Kwasi Wiredu's Philosophy of Personhood," *Transition* 101 (2009): 8–15.

BIBLIOGRAPHY

Adorno, Rolena. "Paradigms Lost: A Peruvian Indian Surveys Spanish Colonial Society." *Studies in Visual Communication* 5, no. 2 (Spring 1979): 78–96.

Aínsa, Fernando. *De la Edad de Oro a El Dorado: Génesis del discurso utópico americano.* Mexico City: Fondo de Cultura Económica, 1992.

Anonymous. "The Oldest Systematic Program of German Idealism." Trans. Diana I. Behler. In Ernst Behler, ed., *Philosophy of German Idealism: Fichte, Jacobi, and Schelling*, 161–63. New York: Continuum, 1987.

Ardao, Arturo. "El americanismo de Rodó." In: *Estudios Latinoamericanos: Historia de las ideas.* Caracas: Monte Ávila, 1978.

Bauman, Zygmunt. *Intimations of Postmodernity.* London: Routledge, 1992.

——. *Modernity and Ambivalence.* London: Polity, 1991.

Bergson, Henri. *The Two Sources of Morality and Religion.* Trans. R. Ashley Audra and Cloudesly Brereton. Notre Dame, IN: Notre Dame University Press, 1977.

Beverley, John, José Oviedo, and Michael Aronna, eds. *The Postmodernism Debate in Latin America.* Durham: Duke University Press, 1995.

Bhabha, Homi. *The Location of Culture.* London: Routledge, 1994.

Biagini, Hugo. *Filosofía americana e identidad: El conflictivo caso argentino.* Buenos Aires: EUDEBA, 1989.

Brunner, José Joaquín. *América Latina: Cultura y modernidad.* Mexico City: Grijalbo, 1992.

Calderón, Fernando. "Latin American Identity and Mixed Temporalities: Or, How to Be Postmodern and Indian at the Same Time." In John Beverly, José Oviedo, and Michael Aronna, eds., *The Postmodernism Debate in Latin America*, 55–64. Durham: Duke University Press, 1995.

Callinicos, Alex. *Against Postmodernism: A Marxist Critique.* Cambridge: Polity Press, 1993.

Calvino, Italo. *Invisible Cities.* Trans. William Weaver. New York: Harcourt, 1974.

Camp, Roderic A. *Intellectuals and the State in Twentieth-Century Mexico.* Austin: University of Texas Press, 1985.

Castro-Gómez, Santiago. *Crítica de la razón latinoamericana*, 2nd ed. Bogotá: Universidad Javeriana, 2011.

——. *Critique of Latin American Reason.* Trans. Andrew Ascherl. New York: Columbia University Press, 2021.

——. *La hybris del punto cero: Ciencia, raza e ilustración en la Nueva Granada, 1750–1816.* Bogotá: Universidad Javeriana, 2005.

——. *Tejidos oneiricos: Movilidad, capitalismo y biopolítica en Bogotá, 1910–1930.* Bogotá: Universidad Javeriana 2009.

——. *Zero-Point Hubris: Science, Race, and Enlightenment in New Granada (1750–1816).* Trans. Don Deere and George Ciccariello-Maher. Lanham, MD: Rowman & Littlefield (forthcoming).

Cerutti Guldberg, Horacio. *Filosofía de la liberación latinoamericana.* Mexico City: Fondo de Cultura Económica, 1983.

——. "Posibilidades y límites de una filosofía latinoamericana 'después' de la 'filosofía de la liberación.'" *La filosofía en América: Trabajos presentados en el IX Congreso Interamericano de Filosofía*, vol. 1. Caracas: Sociedad Venezolana de Filosofía, 1979.

Cullen, Carlos. *Fenomenología de la crisis moral: Sabiduría de la experiencia de los pueblos.* Buenos Aires: Castañeda, 1978.

Dean, Mitchell. *Critical and Effective Histories: Foucault's Methods and Historical Sociology.* New York: Routledge, 1994.

Deas, Malcolm. "Miguel Antonio Caro y amigos: Gramática y poder en Colombia." *Del poder y la gramática, y otros ensayos sobre historia, política y literatura colombianas.* Bogotá: Tercer Mundo, 1993.

De Toro, Alfonso, and Fernando de Toro, eds. *Borders and Margins: Post-Colonialism and Post-Modernism.* Frankfurt/Madrid: Vervuert/Iberoamericana, 1995.

Díaz Ruanova, Oswaldo. *Los existencialistas mexicanos.* Mexico City: Rafael Giménez Siles, 1982.

Dussel, Enrique. "Cultura imperial, cultura ilustrada y liberación de la cultura popular." *Stromata* 1–2 (1974): 93–122.

——. *Filosofía de la liberación.* Bogotá: Nueva América, 1977.

——. *Filosofía ética latinoamericana: La política latinoamericana (Antropológica III).* Bogotá: Universidad Santo Tomás, 1979.

——. *Filosofía ética latinoamericana III: De la erótica a la pedagógica de la liberación.* Mexico City: Edicol, 1977.

——. *Introducción a la filosofía de la liberación.* Bogotá: Nueva América, 1995.

——. *Para una de-strucción de la historia de la ética.* Mendoza: Universidad Nacional de Cuyo, 1971.

——. *Philosophy of Liberation.* Trans. Aquilina Martínez and Christine Morkovsky. Maryknoll, NY: Orbis, 1985.

Fernández Retamar, Roberto. *Para el perfil definitivo del hombre.* Havana: Letras Cubanas, 1981.

Flusser, Vilém. *Brasilien oder die Suche nach dem neuen Menschen: Für eine Phänomenologie der Unterentwicklung.* Mannheim: Bollman, 1994.

Follari, Roberto. *Modernidad y posmodernidad: Una óptica desde América Latina.* Buenos Aires: Rei, 1991.

Foucault, Michel. *The Archaeology of Knowledge and the Discourse on Language.* Trans. Alan Sheridan-Smith. New York: Pantheon, 1972.

——. "Foucault Responds to Sartre." Trans. John Johnston. In Sylvère Lotringer, ed., *Foucault Live: Interviews (1961–1984)*, 35–43. New York: Semiotext(e), 1989.

——. "Nietzsche, Genealogy, History." Trans. Sherry Simon and Donald F. Bouchard. In *Language, Counter-Memory, Practice: Selected Essays and Interviews*, Donald F. Bouchard, ed. Ithaca, NY: Cornell University Press, 1977.

——. *The Order of Things: An Archaeology of the Human Sciences.* Trans. Alan Sheridan-Smith. New York: Random House, 1970.

——. "What Is Enlightenment?" Trans. Catherine Porter. In Paul Rabinow, ed., *The Foucault Reader.* New York: Pantheon, 1984.

Fukuyama, Francis. *The End of History and the Last Man.* New York: Free Press, 1992.

Gaos, José. "En torno a la filosofía mexicana." In *Filosofía e identidad cultural en América Latina*, Jorge Gracia and Iván Jaksic, eds., Caracas: Monte Ávila, 1988.

——. "México, tema y responsabilidad." In Leopoldo Zea, ed., *Filosofar a la altura del hombre: Discrepar para comprender*, 113–28. Mexico City: UNAM, 1993.

——. *Pensamiento de lengua española.* In *Obras Completas*, 6:31–247. Mexico City: UNAM, 1990 [1945].

——. "El pensamiento hispanoamericano." *Filosofía de la filosofía.* Barcelona: Crítica, 1989 [1944].

García Canclini, Néstor. *Consumers and Citizens: Globalization and Multicultural Conflicts.* Trans. George Yúdice. Minneapolis: University of Minnesota Press, 2001.

——. *Hybrid Cultures: Strategies for Entering and Leaving Modernity.* Trans. Christopher L. Chiappari and Silvia L. López. Minneapolis: University of Minnesota Press, 1995 [1989].

——. "Memory and Innovation in the Theory of Art." *South Atlantic Quarterly* 92 (1993): 423–33.

García Delgado, Daniel. "Modernidad y posmodernidad en América Latina: Una perspectiva desde la ciencia política." In D. J. Michelini, J. San Martín, and F. Lagrave, eds., *Modernidad y posmodernidad en América Latina.* Río Cuarto: ICALA, 1991.

García Morales, Alfonso. *El Ateneo de México 1906–1914: Orígenes de la cultura mexicana contemporánea.* Seville: Escuela de Estudios Hispano-americanos, 1992.

Gehlen, Arnold. "Ende der Geschichte?" In Christoph Conrad and Martina Kessel, eds., *Geschichte schreiben in der Postmoderne.* Stuttgart: Reclam, 1994.

Gerbi, Antonello. *La disputa del Nuevo Mundo: Historia de una polémica 1750–1900.* Mexico City: Fondo de Cultura Económica, 1993.

Germani, Gino. *Política y sociedad en una época de transición.* Buenos Aires: Paidós, 1979.

Gómez-Martínez, José Luis. "Una influencia decisiva: El legado de José Gaos al pensamiento iberoamericano." *Cuadernos Americanos* 25 (1991): 49–86.

——. *Pensamiento de la liberación: Proyección de Ortega y Gasset en Iberoamérica.* Madrid: EGE, 1995.

——. "Posmodernidad, discurso antrópico y ensayística latinoamericana." *Dissens: Revista internacional de pensamiento latinoamericano* 2 (1996): 45–49.

Gracia, Jorge, and Iván Jaksic, eds. *Filosofía e identidad cultural en América Latina.* Caracas: Monte Ávila, 1983.

Guadarrama González, Pablo. "La malograda modernidad latinoamericana." *Postmodernismo y crisis del marxismo.* Mexico City: UAEM, 1994.

Guamán Poma de Ayala, Felipe. *The First New Chronicle and Good Government: On the History of the World and the Incas up to 1615.* Ed. and trans. Roland Hamilton. Austin: University of Texas Press, 2009.

Gutiérrez Girardot, Rafael. *La imagen de América en Alfonso Reyes.* Madrid: Instituto Iberoamericano de Gotemburgo, 1955.

——. *Modernismo: Supuestos históricos y culturales.* Mexico City: Fondo de Cultura Económica, 1987.

Habermas, Jürgen. "Foucault: Desenmascaramiento de las ciencias humanas en términos de crítica a la razón." In *El discurso filosófico de la modernidad.* Madrid: Taurus, 1989.

——. "Die Moderne: ein unvollendetes Projekt." Philosophisch-politische Aufsätze 1977–1990. Leipzig: Reclam, 1990.

——. *Theory of Communicative Action*, vol. 1: *Reason and the Rationalization of Society.* Trans. Thomas A. McCarthy. Boston: Beacon, 1984.

Haya de la Torre, Víctor Raúl. *Espacio-Tiempo-Histórico: Cinco ensayos y tres diálogos.* Lima: 1948.

Heidegger, Martin. *Being and Time.* Trans. John Macquarrie and Edward Robinson. New York: Harper and Row, 1962.

Henríquez Ureña, Pedro. "La obra de José Enrique Rodó." *La utopía de América.* Caracas: Biblioteca Ayacucho, 1978.

Herlinghaus, Hermann, and Monika Walter, eds. *Posmodernidad en la periferia: Enfoques latinoamericanos de la nueva teoría cultural.* Berlin: Langer, 1994.

Herrera, Daniel. "El futuro de la filosofía en Colombia." In Germán Marquínez Argote, ed., *La filosofía en Colombia: Historia de las ideas.* Bogotá: El Búho, 1992.

Hinkelammert, Franz. "Frente a la cultura de la postmodernidad: Proyecto político y utopía." In *El capitalismo al desnudo.* Bogotá: El Búho, 1991.

Hopenhayn, Martin. "Postmodernism and Neoliberalism in Latin America." In John Beverly, José Oviedo, and Michael Aronna, eds., *The Postmodernism Debate in Latin America.* Durham: Duke University Press, 1994.

Horkheimer, Max, and Theodor W. Adorno. *Dialectic of Enlightenment: Philosophical Fragments.* Ed. Gunzelin Schmid Noerr. Trans. Edmund Jephcott. Stanford: Stanford University Press, 2002.

Imaz, José Luis de. "¿Adiós a la teoría de la dependencia? Una perspectiva desde la Argentina." *Estudios Internacionales* 28 (1974): 49–75.

Kusch, Rodolfo. *América Profunda,* 2d ed. Buenos Aires: Bonum, 1975.

——. *Esbozo de una antropología filosófica americana.* Buenos Aires: Castañeda, 1978.

Laclau, Ernesto. "Towards a Theory of Populism." In *Politics and Ideology in Marxist Theory: Capitalism, Fascism, Populism.* London: NLB, 1977.

Laclau, Ernesto, and Chantal Mouffe. *Hegemony and Socialist Strategy: Towards a Radical Democratic Politics.* London: Verso, 1985.

Lange-Churión, Pedro, and Eduardo Mendieta, eds. *Latin America and Postmodernity: A Contemporary Reader.* Amherst, NY: Humanity, 1996.

Larsen, Neil. "Posmodernismo e imperialismo: Teoría y política en América Latina." *Nuevo Texto Crítico* 6 (1990): 77–94.

Latin American Subaltern Studies Group. "Founding Statement." In John Beverly, José Oviedo, and Michael Aronna, eds., *The Postmodernism Debate in Latin America.* Durham: Duke University Press, 1995.

Lechner, Norbert. "La democratización en el contexto de una cultura posmoderna." In *Los patios interiores de la democracia.* Santiago: Fondo de Cultura Económica, 1990.

Leyva, Gustavo. "Modernidad y Exterioridad en Latinoamérica: La propuesta de la filosofía de la liberación." *Dissens: Revista internacional de pensamiento latinoamericano* 1 (1995): 11–32.

López Velasco, Silvio. *Reflexões sobre a Filosofia da Libertacão.* Campo Grande: CEFIL, 1991.

Lyotard, Jean-François. *Enthusiasm: The Kantian Critique of History.* Trans. Georges Van Den Abbeele. Stanford: Stanford University Press, 2009.

——. *The Postmodern Condition: A Report on Knowledge.* Trans. Geoff Bennington and Brian Massumi. Minneapolis: University of Minnesota Press, 1984.

Magallón, Mario. *Filosofía política de la educación en América Latina.* Mexico City: UNAM, 1993.

Mansilla, H. C. F. *La cultura del autoritarismo ante los desafíos del presente: Ensayos sobre una teoría crítica de la modernización.* La Paz: CEBEM, 1991.

——. "La ensayística latinoamericana y la cuestión de la identidad colectiva." *Dissens: Revista internacional de pensamiento latinoamericano* 2 (1996): 1–16.

Mariátegui, José Carlos. "El problema de las razas en América Latina." In Aníbal Quijano, ed., *Textos básicos.* Mexico City: Fondo de Cultura Económica, 1991 [1929].

Marquínez Argote, Germán. "Presentación." *¿Qué es eso de filosofía latinoamericana?* Bogotá: El Búho, 1981.

Martín-Barbero, Jesús. *Communication, Culture and Hegemony: From the Media to Mediations.* Trans. Elizabeth Fox and Robert A. White. London: SAGE, 1993.

——. *De los medios a las mediaciones: Comunicación, cultura y hegemonía.* Barcelona: G. Gili, 1991.

——. "Modernidad y posmodernidad en la periferia." *Politeia* 11 (1992): 281–88.

Martínez Estrada, Ezequiel. *Radiografía de la pampa.* Buenos Aires: Pampa, 1933.

——. *X-Ray of the Pampa.* Trans. Alain Swietlicki. Austin: University of Texas Press, 1971.

Medin, Tzvi. *Ortega y Gasset en la cultura hispanoamericana.* Mexico City: Fondo de Cultura Económica, 1994.

Mignolo, Walter. *The Darker Side of the Renaissance: Literacy, Territoriality, and Colonization.* Michigan: University of Michigan Press, 1995.

——. "Decires fuera de lugar: Sujetos dicientes, roles sociales y formas de inscripción." *Revista de Crítica Literaria Latinoamericana* 21, no. 41 (1995): 9–31.

——. "Occidentalización, imperialismo, globalización: Herencias coloniales y teorías poscoloniales." *Revista Iberoamericana* 170–71 (1995): 27–50.

Miller, Nicola. *In the Shadow of the State: Intellectuals and the Quest for National Identity in Twentieth-Century Spanish America.* London: Verso, 1999.

Miró Quesada, Francisco. *Despertar y proyecto del filosofar latinoamericano.* Mexico City: Fondo de Cultura Económica, 1974.

——. "La filosofía de lo americano: Treinta años después." In *Ideas en torno de Latinoamérica,* vol. 2. Mexico City: UNAM, 1986.

Morandé, Pedro. *Cultura y modernización en América Latina: Ensayo sociológico acerca de la crisis del desarrollismo y de su superación.* Santiago: Pontificia Universidad Católica de Chile, 1984.

——. "Grupos sociales y en conflicto." In Peter Hünermann, ed., *Enseñanza Social de la Iglesia en América Latina.* Frankfurt: Vervuert, 1991.

——. "La síntesis cultural hispánica-indígena." *Teología y Vida* 23 (1991): 43–59.

Mouffe, Chantal. *The Return of the Political.* London: Verso, 1993.

Nicol, Eduardo. *El problema de la filosofía hispánica.* Mexico City: Fondo de Cultura Económica, 1998.

O'Donnel, Guillermo. *El Estado burocrático-autoritario.* Buenos Aires: Belgrano, 1982.

O'Gorman, Edmundo. *The Invention of America: An Inquiry Into the Historical Nature of the New World and the Meaning of Its History.* Bloomington: Indiana University Press, 1961.

Orrego, Antenor. "La configuración histórica de la circunstancia americana." In *Ideas en torno de Latinoamérica,* 2:1380–407. Mexico City: UNAM, 1966.

——. *Hacia un humanismo Americano.* Lima: Juan Mejía Baca, 1966.

Ortega y Gasset, José. *España invertebrada.* Madrid: Calpe, 1921.

——. "The Historical Significance of the Theory of Einstein." In *The Modern Theme,* 135–52. New York: Harper and Row, 1961 [1931].

——. "History as a System." In *Toward a Philosophy of History.* New York: Norton, 1941.

——. "Ideas para una historia de la filosofía." In *Historia como sistema y otros ensayos filosóficos.* Madrid: Sarpe, 1984.

——. *Invertebrate Spain.* Trans. Mildred Adams. New York: Norton, 1937.

——. *Meditations on Quixote.* Trans. Evelyn Rugg and Diego Marín. New York: Norton, 1961.

——. *The Modern Theme.* Trans. James Cleugh New York: Harper and Row, 1961 [1931].

París Pombo, María Dolores. *Crisis e identidades colectivas en América Latina.* Mexico City: Plaza y Valdés, 1990.

Parker, Cristián. *Otra lógica en América Latina: Religion popular y modernización capitalista.* Santiago: Fondo de Cultura Económica, 1993.

Paz, Octavio. "El Caracol y la sirena." In *Cuadrivio.* Mexico City: Joaquín Mortiz, 1965.

——. *Children of the Mire: Modern Poetry from Romanticism to the Avant-Garde.* Trans. Rachel Phillips. Cambridge, MA: Harvard University Press, 1991.

——. *The Labyrinth of Solitude and Other Writings.* Trans. Lysander Kemp, Yara Milos, and Rachel Phillips Belash. New York: Grove, 1985.

Pi Esquijarosa, Manuel, and Gilberto Valdés Gutiérrez. "El pensamiento latinoamericano ante la putrefacción de la historia." *Casa de las Américas* 196 (1994): 99–111.

Rama, Ángel. *The Lettered City.* Ed. and trans. John Charles Chasteen. Durham: Duke University Press, 1996.

——. *Rubén Darío y el modernismo: Circunstancia socioeconómica de un arte americano.* Caracas: Universidad Central de Venezuela, 1970.

Ramos, Samuel. "El perfil del hombre y la cultura en México." In *Obras Completas,* 1:89–180. Mexico City: UNAM, 1990.

Reyes, Alfonso. "Capricho de América." In *Obras Completas,* 11:75–78. Mexico City: Fondo de Cultura Económica, 1982.

——. "Ciencia social y deber social." In *Obras Completas,* 11:106–25. Mexico City: Fondo de Cultura Económica, 1982.

——. "La crítica en la edad ateniense." In *Obras Completas,* 13:13–347. Mexico City: Fondo de Cultura Económica, 1997.

——. "De cómo Grecia construyó al hombre." In *Última Tule y otros ensayos.* Caracas: Biblioteca Ayacucho, 1992.

——. "Notas sobre la inteligencia americana." In *Obras Completas,* 11:82–94. Mexico City: Fondo de Cultura Económica, 1982.

——. "Posición de América." In *Obras Completas,* 11:254–70. Mexico City: Fondo de Cultura Económica, 1982.

——. "Última Tule." In *Obras Completas,* 11:11–62. Mexico City: Fondo de Cultura Económica, 1982.

Richard, Nelly. "Latinoamérica y la postmodernidad." In Hermann Herlinghaus and Monika Walter, eds., *Postmodernidad en la periferia: Enfoques latinoamericanos de la nueva teoría cultural,* 210–20. Berlin: Langer, 1994.

Rincón, Carlos. "Die neue Kulturtheorien: Vor-Geschichten und Bestandsaufnahme." In Birgit Scharlau, ed., *Lateinamerika denken. Kulturtheoretische Grenzgänge zwischen Moderne und Postmoderne.* Tübingen: Gunter Narr, 1994.

——. *La no simultaneidad de lo simultáneo: Posmodernidad, globalización y culturas en América Latina.* Bogotá: EUN, 1995.

Rodó, José Enrique. *Ariel.* Trans. Margaret Sayers Peden. Austin: University of Texas Press, 1988.

Roig, Arturo Andrés. "¿Cómo leer un texto?" In *Historia de las ideas, Teoría del discurso y Pensamiento latinoamericano.* Bogotá: USTA, 1993 [1982].

——. *Historia de las ideas, Teoría del discurso y Pensamiento latinoamericano.* Bogotá: USTA, 1993 [1984].

——. "La historia de las ideas cinco lustros después." In *Historia de las ideas, Teoría del discurso y Pensamiento latinoamericano.* Bogotá: USTA, 1993 [1984].

——. "La historia de las ideas y la filosofía latinoamericana." In *Historia de las ideas, Teoría del discurso y Pensamiento latinoamericano.* Bogotá: USTA, 1993 [1984].

——. "La historia de las ideas y la historia de nuestra cultura." In *Historia de las ideas, Teoría del discurso y Pensamiento latinoamericano.* Bogotá: USTA, 1993 [1989].

——. "¿Qué hacer con los relatos, la mañana, la sospecha y la historia? Respuestas a los postmodernos." *Rostro y filosofía de América Latina.* Mendoza: EDIUNC, 1993.

——. "La radical historicidad de todo discurso." In *Historia de las ideas, Teoría del discurso y Pensamiento latinoamericano.* Bogotá: USTA, 1993 [1985].

——. "El siglo XIX latinoamericano y las nuevas formas discursivas." In *Historia de las ideas, Teoría del discurso y Pensamiento latinoamericano.* Bogotá: USTA, 1993.

——. *Teoría y crítica del pensamiento latinoamericano.* Mexico City: Fondo de Cultura Económica, 1981.

Rojas, Rafael. "La otra moral de la teleología cubana." *Casa de las Américas* 194 (1994): 85–96.

Romero, Francisco. "Sobre la filosofía en Iberoamérica." In Germán Marquínez Argote, ed., *¿Qué es eso de filosofía latinoamericana?*, 66–74. Bogotá: El Búho, 1981.

Rowe, William, and Vivian Schelling. *Memory and Modernity: Popular Culture in Latin America.* London: Verso, 1991.

Ruano de la Fuente, Yolanda. *Racionalidad y conciencia trágica: La modernidad según Max Weber.* Madrid: Trotta, 1995.

Rubio Angulo, Jaime. *Introducción al filosofar.* Bogotá: Universidad Santo Tomás/Centro de Enseñanza Desescolarizada, 1977.

Said, Edward. *Orientalism: Western Conceptions of the Orient.* London: Routledge and Kegan Paul, 1978.

Salazar Bondy, Augusto. *¿Existe una filosofía de nuestra América?* Mexico City: Siglo XXI, 1988 [1968].

Salazar Ramos, Roberto. "El ejercicio de la filosofía como arqueología." *Dissens: Revista Internacional de Pensamiento latinoamericano* 1 (1995): 43–50.

——. "Los grandes metarrelatos en la interpretación de la historia latinoamericana." In *Reflexión histórica en América Latina: Ponencias VII Congreso Internacional de Filosofía Latinoamericana.* Bogotá: Universidad Santo Tomás, 1993.

——. *Posmodernidad y verdad: Algunos metarrelatos en la constitución del saber.* Bogotá: USTA, 1994.

Sánchez Vázquez, Adolfo. "Posmodernidad, posmodernismo y socialismo." *Casa de las Américas* 175 (1989): 137–45.

Sarlo, Beatriz. "Basuras culturales, simulacros políticos." In Hermann Herlinghaus and Monika Walter, eds., *Postmodernidad en la periferia: Enfoques latinoamericanos de la nueva teoría cultural.* Berlin: Langer, 1994.

——. *Escenas de la vida posmoderna: Intelectuales, arte y videocultura en Argentina.* Buenos Aires: Ariel, 1994.

Sarmiento, Domingo Faustino. *Life in the Argentine Republic in the Days of the Tyrants; Or, Civilization and Barbarism.* New York: Hafner, 1974.

Scannone, Juan Carlos, ed. *Nuevo punto de partida de la filosofía latinoamericana.* Buenos Aires: Guadalupe, 1990.

——. *Sabiduría popular, símbolo y filosofía: Diálogo internacional en torno de una interpretación latinoamericana.* Buenos Aires: Guadalupe, 1985.

Scharlau, Birgit, ed. *Lateinamerika denken: Kulturtheoretische Grenzgänge zwischen Moderne und Postmoderne.* Tübingen: Gunter Narr, 1994.

Schiller, Friedrich. *On the Aesthetic Education of Man*. Trans. Reginald Snell. Mineola, NY: Dover, 2004.

Schwarz, Roberto. *Misplaced Ideas: Essays on Brazilian Culture*. London: Verso, 1992.

Shakespeare, William. *The Tempest*. Cambridge: Cambridge University Press, 1969.

Spivak, Gayatri Chakravorty. "Can the Subaltern Speak?" In Cary Nelson and Lawrence Grossberg, eds., *Marxism and the Interpretation of Culture*, 271–313. Champaign-Urbana: University of Illinois Press, 1988.

Subirats, Eduardo. "Transformaciones de la cultura moderna." In J. Tono Martínez, ed., *La polémica de la posmodernidad*. Madrid: Libertarias, 1986.

Toulmin, Stephen. *Cosmopolis: The Hidden Agenda of Modernity*. Chicago: University of Chicago Press, 1990.

Uranga, Emilio. *Análisis del ser mexicano*. Guanajuato: Gobierno del Estado de Guanajuato, 1990.

Vargas Lozano, Gabriel. "Reflexiones críticas sobre modernidad y postmodernidad." In *¿Qué hacer con la filosofía en América Latina?* Mexico City: UAM/UAT, 1991.

Vasconcelos, José. *The Cosmic Race: A Bilingual Edition*. Trans. Didier. T. Jaén. Baltimore: Johns Hopkins University Press, 1997.

——. "Los motivos del escudo." *Obra Selecta*. Caracas: Biblioteca Ayacucho, 1992.

——. "El pensamiento iberoamericano." In Germán Marquínez Argote, ed., *¿Qué es eso de filosofía latinoamericana?* Bogotá: El Búho, 1981.

Vattimo, Gianni. *Ética de la interpretación*. Barcelona: Paidós, 1993.

——. *The End of Modernity: Nihilism and Hermeneutics in Postmodern Culture*. Trans. Jon R. Snyder. Baltimore: Johns Hopkins University Press, 1991.

Villegas, Abelardo. *El pensamiento mexicano en el siglo XX*. Mexico City: Fondo de Cultura Económica, 1993.

Villoro, Luis. "Emilio Uranga: La accidentalidad como fundamento de la cultura mexicana." In Emilio Uranga, ed., *Análisis del ser mexicano*, 9–23. Guanajuato: Gobierno del Estado de Guanajuato, 1990.

Vitier, Cintio. *Ese sol del mundo moral: Para una historia de la eticidad cubana*. Havana: Unión, 1995.

Von der Walde, Erna. "La alegría de leer: Ficciones latinoamericanas y el debate posmoderno." *Dissens: Revista Internacional de Pensamiento latinoamericano* 2 (1995): 103–10.

Wallerstein, Immanuel. *Geopolitics and Geoculture: Essays on the Changing World-System*. Cambridge: Cambridge University Press, 1994.

Weber, Max. *The Protestant Ethic and the Spirit of Capitalism*. Trans. Talcott Parsons. London: Routledge, 1992.

Welsch, Wolfgang. "Adornos Ästhetik: Eine implizite Ästhetik des Erhabenen." In *Ästhetisches Denken*. Stuttgart: Reclam, 1993.

——. *Unsere postmoderne Moderne*. Weinheim: VCH Acta Humaniora, 1991.

——. *Vernunft: Die zeitgenössische Vernunftkritik und das Konzept der transversalen Vernunft*. Frankfurt: Suhrkamp, 1995.

Young, Robert. *White Mythologies: Writing History and the West*. London: Routledge, 1990.

Yúdice, George, Jean Franco, and Juan Flórez, eds. *On Edge: The Crisis of Contemporary Latin American Culture*. Minneapolis: University of Minnesota Press, 1992.

Zavala, Iris M. *Colonialism and Culture: Hispanic Modernisms and the Social Imaginary*. Indianapolis: Indiana University Press, 1992.

——. "On the (Mis-)uses of the Post-modern: Hispanic Modernism Revisited." In T. D'Haen and H. Bertend, eds., *Postmodern Fiction in Europe and the Americas*. Amsterdam: Rodopi, 1988.

——. "The Social Imaginary: The Cultural Sign of Hispanic Modernism." *Critical Studies* 1 (1989): 125–40.

Zea, Leopoldo. *Dialéctica de la conciencia americana*. Mexico City: Alianza, 1976.

——. *Filosofía de la historia americana*. Mexico City: Fondo de Cultura Económica, 1978.

——. *El pensamiento latinoamericano*. Barcelona: Ariel, 1976.

——. "Philosophy as Commitment." Trans. Amy A. Oliver. In Carlos Alberto Sánchez and Robert Eli Sanchez Jr., eds., *Mexican Philosophy in the Twentieth Century: Essential Readings*, 125–40. Oxford: Oxford University Press, 2017.

——. *El positivismo en México: Nacimiento, apogeo y decadencia*. Mexico City: Fondo de Cultura Económica, 1968.

——. *Positivism in Mexico*. Trans. Josephine H. Schulte. Austin: University of Texas Press, 1974.

INDEX

CPSIA information can be obtained
at www.ICGtesting.com
Printed in the USA
LVHW011355140122
708606LV00006B/418

9 780231 200073